INNOVATIONS IN EDUCATION

INNOVATIONS IN EDUCATION
REFORMERS AND THEIR CRITICS
Sixth Edition

JOHN MARTIN RICH
The University of Texas at Austin

ALLYN AND BACON
Boston   London   Toronto   Sydney   Tokyo   Singapore

Series Editor: Sean W. Wakely
Series Editorial Assistant: Carol L. Chernaik
Production Coordinator: Marjorie Payne
Editorial-Production Service: Chestnut Hill Enterprises, Inc.
Cover Administrator: Linda Dickinson
Cover Designer: Suzanne Harbison
Manufacturing Buyer: Louise Richardson

Copyright © 1992, 1988, 1985, 1981, 1978, 1975 by Allyn and Bacon
A Division of Simon & Schuster, Inc.
160 Gould Street
Needham Heights, MA 02194

All rights reserved. No part of the material protected by this
copyright notice may be reproduced or utilized in any form or by
any means, electronic or mechanical, including photocopying,
recording, or by any information storage and retrieval system,
without the written permission of the copyright owner.

Library of Congress Cataloging-in-Publication Data

Innovations in education : reformers and their critics / [compiled by]
   John Martin Rich. — 6th ed.
      p.   cm.
   Includes bibliographical references and index.
   ISBN 0‑205‑13299‑5
   1. Educational innovations—United States.   2. Education—United
States—Philosophy.   I. Rich, John Martin.
   LB1027.3.I55   1992
   370.1—dc20   91‑15695
                                   CIP

Printed in the United States of America
10 9 8 7 6 5 4 3 2 1   97 96 95 94 93 92

CONTENTS

Preface   *ix*

PART A   EDUCATIONAL REFORMERS AND THEIR CRITICS   1

CHAPTER 1   GOALS AND CURRICULAR CONNECTIONS   12

Clarifying the Mission of the American High School   *Ernest L.
    Boyer*   13
Educational Goals and Curricular Decisions in the New Carnegie
    Report   *John Martin Rich*   18
Discussion Questions and Activities   23
Suggested Readings   23

CHAPTER 2   RESTRUCTURING SECONDARY SCHOOLS   26

Essential Schools: A First Look   *Theodore R. Sizer*   27
Teaching and Learning: The Dilemma of the American High
    School   *Chester E. Finn, Jr.*   32
Discussion Questions and Activities   35
Suggested Readings   36

CHAPTER 3   THE PAIDEIA PROPOSAL   37

The Paideia Proposal: Rediscovering the Essence of
    Education   *Mortimer Adler*   39
The Paideia Proposal: Noble Ambitions, False Leads, and Symbolic
    Politics   *Willis D. Hawley*   46
Discussion Questions and Activities   50
Suggested Readings   50

CHAPTER 4   CULTURAL LITERACY   52

Cultural Literacy: Let's Get Specific   *E. D. Hirsch, Jr.*   53
Cultural Literacy: What Every Educator Needs to Know   *Thomas
    H. Estes, Carol J. Gutman, and Elise K. Harrison*   63
Discussion Questions and Activities   67
Suggested Readings   67

CHAPTER 5   POLITICS, ORGANIZATION, AND SCHOOL CHOICE   69

    A Blueprint for Public Education   *John E. Chubb*   70
    Should Market Forces Control Educational Decision Making   *Jack
       Tweedie*   73
    Discussion Questions and Activities   80
    Suggested Readings   81

CHAPTER 6   THE EMANCIPATION OF TEACHING   82

    Teachers as Transformative Intellectuals   *Henry A. Giroux*   83
    Dilemma Language   *Colin Lacey*   89
    Discussion Questions and Activities   90
    Suggested Readings   90

    FURTHER THOUGHTS ON REFORMERS   92

    PART B   INNOVATIONS AND ALTERNATIVES   95

CHAPTER 7   EDUCATIONAL EQUITY THROUGH FINANCIAL REFORM   117

    Rich Schools, Poor Schools: The Persistence of Unequal
       Education   *Arthur E. Wise and Tamar Gendler*   118
    Partial Privatization of Public School Finance   *Thomas G. Fox and
       John Riew*   126
    Discussion Questions and Activities   135
    Suggested Readings   136

CHAPTER 8   PRIVATE SCHOOLS   137

    Quality and Equality in American Education: Public and Catholic
       Schools   *James S. Coleman*   138
    Oranges Plus Apples, Dr. Coleman, Give You Oranges Plus
       Apples   *Joseph Rogers*   147
    Discussion Questions and Activities   150
    Suggested Readings   150

CHAPTER 9   SCHOOL-BASED MANAGEMENT   152

    Synthesis of Research on School-Based Management   *Jane L.
       David*   153
    Unfulfilled Promises   *Betty Malen, Rodney T. Ogawa, and Jennifer
       Kranz*   162

Discussion Questions and Activities   168
Suggested Readings   169

CHAPTER 10   EFFECTIVE SCHOOLS   170

Effective High Schools—What Are the Common
    Characteristics?   *Joseph Murphy and Philip Hallinger*   171
Effective Schools: A Friendly but Cautionary Note   *Larry*
    Cuban   175
Discussion Questions and Activities   178
Suggested Readings   179

CHAPTER 11   MAGNET SCHOOLS   180

In Education, Magnets Attract Controversy   *Mary Haywood*
    Metz   182
Schools of Choice: A Path to Educational Quality or 'Tiers of
    Inequity'?   *Kathleen Sylvester*   192
Discussion Questions and Activities   197
Suggested Readings   197

CHAPTER 12   TEACHER EDUCATION   198

Interesting Times   *Alan H. Jones*   199
Making a Difference in Educational Quality through Teacher
    Education   *Carolyn M. Evertson, Willis D. Hawley, and*
    Marilyn Zlotnik   207
Discussion Questions and Activities   223
Suggested Readings   224

CHAPTER 13   CAREER LADDERS   225

Developing A Career Ladder: Getting down to the Basics   *Thomas*
    Deering   226
The Career Ladder and Lattice: A New Look at the Teaching
    Career   *Timothy J. L. Chandler, Stacey L. Lane, Janice M.*
    Bibik, and Bernard Oliver   230
Discussion Questions and Activities   239
Suggested Readings   239

CHAPTER 14 BILINGUAL EDUCATION   241

Equity, Quality, and Effectiveness in Bilingual Education   *George
    M. Blanco*   242
¡Bilingual—No!   *Muriel Paskin Carrison*   250
Discussion Questions and Activities   256
Suggested Readings   257

CHAPTER 15 MULTICULTURAL EDUCATION   258

Multiethnic Education and the Quest for Equality   *James A.
    Banks*   259
The Limits of Pluralism   *M. Donald Thomas*   266
Discussion Questions and Activities   269
Suggested Readings   269

CHAPTER 16 MAINSTREAMING   271

The Case for Keeping Mentally Retarded Children in Your Regular
    Classrooms   *Martin Tonn*   272
Mainstreaming: A Formative Consideration   *Harry N.
    Chandler*   274
Discussion Questions and Activities   277
Suggested Readings   278

CHAPTER 17 EDUCATING THE GIFTED   279

Reflections on Three Decades of Education of the Gifted   *A. Harry
    Passow*   280
Equity vs. Excellence: An Educational Drama   *James J.
    Gallagher*   287
Discussion Questions and Activities   291
Suggested Readings   292

**FURTHER THOUGHTS ON INNOVATIONS
AND ALTERNATIVES**   293

Appendix   296

Index   299

PREFACE

Education today is in a state of ferment. We hear about the loss of confidence in public education, educational equity through financial reform, widespread changes in education at the state level, schools of choice, the reform of teacher education, career ladders, and the impending technological revolution in education. In light of these and other significant developments, a number of reformers have offered ideas for extricating education from the morass in which it finds itself. These writers are distinguished by their ability to break with tradition and the conventional modes for perceiving educational problems and situations. They have advanced some bold and imaginative proposals for transforming education.

All too frequently the proposals of these reformers are either accepted so uncritically that their ideas become dogmas rather than possible ways of liberating thought and action, or else they are rejected out of hand. In this book, selections by reformers are followed by those of critics in order to overcome this problem. In this way, readers can gain a balance of viewpoints, weigh reformers' strengths and weaknesses, and use the material to help develop their own positions.

Considerable interest is shown today in promising innovations and alternatives in education. They exhibit possibilities for new curricula and instructional patterns as well as a break with traditional forms of school organization and financial support. Both the pros and cons of these innovations and alternatives are presented here.

Thus the book consists of two parts. Part A contains representative selections by today's leading educational reformers. Part B is composed of selections, both pro and con, on the latest and most prominent educational innovations. The innovations presented may include, but are not restricted to, those advocated by the specific reformers in Part A. Introductions precede the main parts, laying the background for the ideas that follow. Readers may find it useful to read over the discussion questions and activities before reading the selections.

The sixth edition features changes in both parts of the book. In Part A some new reformers and critics are introduced, more representative or up-to-date selections by earlier reformers are provided whenever appropriate, and some reformers who once were prominent but have faded have been deleted. New innovations and alternatives in Part B include educational equity through financial reform, school-based management, effective schools, magnet schools, and career ladders. Other features include new selections for some of the innovations and alternatives retained from the fifth edition; updated suggested readings, biographies, and appendix; and new introductions, discussion questions, and activities wherever needed. The numerous teaching methodologies currently in use have not been included but have been left for methods courses.

I wish to thank reviewers for their suggestions, Sean W. Wakely of Allyn and Bacon for his confidence in the project, Philip J. Schwartz for reference assistance, Jana Holzmeier for her thoughtful and efficient secretarial assistance, and Audrey for her support. I have also been encouraged to undertake this edition by favorable informal feedback by the many who successfully used the book in their classes and by the reactions of my own students.

While preparing this edition I have been impressed by the great ferment in education. I hope the reader, too, will be caught up in the intellectual excitement of contrasting ideas and vigorous search for solutions to today's most pressing educational problems.

PART I

EDUCATIONAL REFORMERS AND THEIR CRITICS

Education today is under criticism. Many citizens believe that discipline in schools is far too lax; others believe that schools should return to the basics and fundamentals. Some students are concerned that schools and colleges do not adequately prepare them for the world of work; others find schools to be basically alienating institutions that deny them the freedom to learn as they choose. A number of reformers have joined this criticism with a more penetrating analysis of greater scope that seeks to locate the roots of the malaise. These reformers view many educational practices as anachronistic and dehumanizing and attempt to show how these conditions can be overcome and new ways of educating can be initiated.

Enrollments have declined in some school districts, and funding has been shifted to other needed community services. Many agree that taxes are too high, with some communities even defeating school bond issues. Citizens are demanding that schools become more accountable and that both teachers and students demonstrate requisite competencies.

How should the dissatisfaction toward public education be handled? Reformers have addressed themselves to a wide range of problems and have offered a number of startling recommendations for reconceptualizing, restructuring, and revitalizing education. The essays in this anthology provide viewpoints that should inform, stimulate thought, and encourage readers to reason carefully in order to clarify their own thinking about the topics addressed. If, in fact, readers are able to accept neither the reformers' nor the critics' positions, then it is their task to explore beyond what is provided here. (The suggested readings and discussion questions and activities should help.)

THE TASKS OF EDUCATIONAL REFORM

Generally one thinks the purpose of reform is to amend what is defective, vicious, corrupt, or depraved. It also aims to remove an abuse, a wrong, or errors, and to make changes for the better. Reform, which means to correct, rectify, amend, and remedy by making something right that is wrong, also implies changing something to eliminate imperfections or effect a new form of character, as in changing a policy within an institution.

The two characteristic types of reform are programmatic and systemic. *Programmatic reform* refers to curricula and programs that are used in or influence organized instruction; it also is associated with innovation. An *innovation* is any new idea, method, or device that, in contrast to change, is deliberately introduced for some purpose. One could be an innovator but not a reformer, but every programmatic reformer is an innovator and much more, since he or she goes beyond merely introducing one or more innovations by developing an organized plan for change that may embody various innovations organized to achieve new goals. Thus both the scope and intent of programmatic reform differs from innovation.

Systemic reform pertains to authority relationships and the distribution and allocation of power and resources that control the educational system as a whole. It is often carried out beyond the school, drawing upon social and political forces with which reformers need to be aligned; it calls for a redistribution of power and resources. There has been considerable programmatic reform during this century but a dearth of systemic reform—which is generally understandable because of its threat to the educational power structure.

To perceive what is needed, reformers must be highly sensitive to abuses and imperfections and be dissatisfied and restless once they are uncovered; then they must develop a broad view and a bold vision of what is possible and seek to disseminate new ideas widely in hopes that the proposed reform will be implemented. While it is heartening to have strong organizational support, access to the media, and generous financial backing, few reformers can initially boast of such advantages. Some reformers may feel that their task has been completed once they write and speak to the widest possible audience. Others may go further by setting up learning experiments, teaching in public or private schools, counseling students, working with prospective teachers, raising funds to support reform programs, teaching adults literacy skills, or setting up a free school.

THE CONTINUITY OF EDUCATIONAL REFORM

Today's educational reform is part of a process that began many years ago. Of course current reform has some distinctive features, but it is indebted to a long and colorful history that can only be ignored at our peril. While today's reformers may wear flashy new shoes, they still stand on the shoulders of great thinkers of the past. Many of the earliest reformers' ideas were associated with a movement or an educational philosophy; therefore it may be helpful to see how each reformer relates to these broader patterns. Our survey will selectively focus on twentieth-century American educators but will relate them to European antecedents.

Sense Realism

Early European educational philosophy had an effect on twentieth-century American education by its opposition to formalism and abstraction in instruction, its deductive approach, its emphasis on rote learning, and its reliance upon the teacher's authority and the written word. In opposition to this prevailing system were Wolfgang Ratich (1571–1635), John Amos Comenius (1592–1670), and Johann Heinrich Pestalozzi (1746–1827), who developed different principles of instruction sometimes known as *sense realism.*

Things should be studied before words because words and language itself are more abstract, according to the sense realism theory. For example, in a science demonstration, a thing or experiment would be shown first and then an explanation would follow. Everything was to be learned by an inductive process that Francis Bacon (1561–1626) had advocated. The young, said Comenius, should see real and useful things that can make an impression on the senses and the imagination. If the thing is not available, a representation should be used. Books should have pictures, diagrams, charts; and many pictures should be hung in the classroom. Too often students in traditional schools were required to learn by rote and therefore would not have necessarily understood the material committed to memory; thus rote learning was discouraged by sense realists.

Nature, said Pestalozzi, makes no sudden leaps but unfolds gradually. Consequently, every instructional act should be a small, scarcely perceptible addition to what the learner already knows. Material should become more complex only as the learner's intellectual abilities mature. Each step must be well mastered before the next step is taken. Objects are indispensable, Pestalozzi believed, and must precede pictures. The picture comes later and aids the child in making the transition to drawing, reading, and writing. The child does not just wait passively to receive objects of nature but takes an active role in analyzing and abstracting the qualities of the object. Instruction should proceed from the known to the unknown, from the concrete to the abstract, or from the particular to the general.

Twentieth-century progressives in Europe and America took up the principles of sense realism and combined them with their own ideas. Sense realism, however, was far more suited to elementary than to advanced instruction. It did not develop a sophisticated theory of how the mind works or explain the operations of higher cognitive processes. Nevertheless it was a salutary corrective and an important advance over the inflexible and authoritarian instructional practices of the period.

Romanticism

Sweeping across Western Europe and Russia in the late eighteenth and early nineteenth centuries, *romanticism* became a broad movement that greatly influenced poetry, prose, painting, architecture, music, education, and the tenor of thought. It sought a simpler life, elevated feelings and emotions over intellect, empathized and identified with the poor and downtrodden, deified the child, expressed a love of animals and the beauties of nature, and contrasted these charms to the corruptions and cruelties of urban life. Jean Jacques Rousseau (1712–1778), the leading French romantic, was a highly influential figure in political and educational thought, whose ideas also influenced literary sensibility. Rousseau believed that human beings are born free yet everywhere they are in the chains of corrupt institutions. One approach to removing these chains was to educate the child close to nature by removing him from organized social life. Thus Emile, Rousseau's imaginary pupil, would grow up naturally by letting the laws of nature unfold and not having to perform tasks before readiness was evident. Rousseau attacked the notion of original sin and depravity by declaring that the child is born good. He recognized different stages of growth, explaining how the tutor would relate to Emile at each stage, and the different materials and activities that would be appropriate to introduce in light of the child's naturally unfolding inner development. The program would emphasize activities and experiences, deemphasize book learning, seek to avoid bad habits and instill good ones, and restrict desires so that they are in proportion to the ability to fulfill them. By late adolescence, Emile would have acquired the requisite abilities to return to the larger society, learn from it, but not be corrupted by it.

Child-Centered Progressivism

Developed in America and Western Europe during the early part of this century, *progressivism* was both a movement and a philosophy for educating the child. It was based on placing the child center stage in the educational process, emphasizing the child's needs and interests, striving to develop "the whole child"—not just the child's mind but the emotional, moral, social, and physical characteristics as well. Such educators as Francis W. Parker (1837–1902) adapted curriculum to the needs of individual learners and emphasized more active learning and less dependence on textbooks. William Heard Kilpatrick (1871–1965) opposed a curriculum composed of disparate subjects and instead promoted the use of student projects. For child-centered progressives, the teacher was no longer a taskmaster or authority figure but one who helped guide meaningful learning activities. The subject-matter curriculum, which represents the way scholars organize knowledge, is not consonant with the way the child learns; consequently, programs were based more on the student's needs and interests and on valuable experiences and activities.

The child-centered progressives were influenced by sense realism and romanticism. Learning activities were usually approached inductively and were based upon concrete experiences before any generalizations were drawn. Progressive classrooms usually had many sensory objects—children's drawings, photographs of historical figures, bulletin boards, science displays, with live animals in some instances. Progressives believed in firsthand experiences that included frequent field trips.

As for romanticism, child-centered progressives held that the child was born basically good and therefore there is no need to place many restrictions on the child's self-expression. Although they did not educate the child away from society, they did believe in nature study and readiness for learning. Some progressives were more permissive with children than Rousseau advocated, and the teacher was more of an organizer of learning activities than a fount of knowledge. Pupil-teacher planning was promoted as not only a democratic procedure but also one that would improve learning outcomes.

Child-centered progressivism was criticized by essentialists and other groups. *Essentialism* believes that the goals of education are to develop the mind and prepare people for citizenship responsibilities by having them study essential knowledge embodied in a subject curriculum that is taught by a knowledgeable teacher who expects students to respect authority and exhibit disciplined behavior. Essentialists charged progressives with neglecting basic knowledge, failing to discipline students properly, insufficiently developing their minds, and not preparing them adequately for citizenship responsibilities. Essentialism also rejected romanticism and the romantic view of the child.

Dewey's Pragmatism

Although John Dewey (1859–1952) was also considered a progressive as well as a pragmatist, he was not child-centered and criticized this branch of the movement for alleged excesses. Dewey claimed that one cannot develop a philosophy merely by doing just the opposite of what one is against. In other words, since the traditional teacher was usually authoritarian, the child-centered educator became permissive and laissez-faire; in opposition to subject matter developed in advance and neatly laid out in compartments, were substituted the techniques of teacher-pupil planning and reliance on firsthand experience; and in opposition to external discipline free activity was used.

Dewey sought the relationship between organized bodies of knowledge and the emerging interests and curiosities of the children. He agreed with child-centered educators that one should begin with children's interests but differed from these educators by stating that one should connect these interests to that in which children ought to become interested. The generic method of education, for Dewey, was the scientific method, which he believed could be applied to all areas of human inquiry by teaching problem solving. Reflective thinking or problem solving begins with an indeterminate situation where puzzlement arises, the problem is then defined, and an hypothesis is advanced to guide observation and the collection of data. The hypothesis is then elaborated and sometimes transformed to deal with the problem more expeditiously and effectively, and finally the hypothesis is tested by overt and imaginative action and is either accepted or rejected. If accepted, an indeterminate situation has been made more determinate; whereas if rejected, a new hypothesis will need to be introduced, elaborated, and tested.

Dewey's pragmatism related to his reflective thinking process. Rather than *truth*, Dewey preferred the term *warranted assertibility* to refer to the end result of having hypotheses successfully tested. Once one reaches the final stage of the reflective thinking process and accepts the original hypothesis as fulfilling the conditions of the situation, and once it has been subject to public verification, one is warranted in asserting the statement. *Pragmatism*, in other words, holds that ideas must be referred to their consequences for their truth and meaning. Ideas become instruments for solving problems, attaining goals, and anticipating future experiences.

For Dewey, life is development and development is growth. Because the characteristics of life are growth, education is one with growth. Additionally, since growth is relative to nothing but further growth, education is not subordinate to anything except more education. Education, Dewey says, is a continuous reorganization, reconstruction, and transformation or experience that adds to the meaning of experience and improves the ability to deal with subsequent experience.

Although Dewey achieved a wide following, his ideas were criticized by many different groups and divergent philosophies. Most prominent were those who rejected his pragmatism because it renounced absolute truths and values. Some held that there are some truths that remain true for all times and places, and these are the truths that should constitute the curriculum. And one cannot be considered an educated person until having wrestled with these ideas. Moreover, in contrast to Dewey's emphasis on the educative process, critics insisted on concentrating more on assuring specific learning outcomes that are measurable. More recently, a group of reformers, referred to as romantic naturalists (though they may have had some affinities with progressivism), rejected Dewey's conviction that schools can be sufficiently improved to become fully educative institutions.

Romantic Naturalists

The *romantic naturalists* of the late 1960s and early 1970s shared some beliefs with the early progressives. Like the progressives, they believed that the child rather than the subject matter should be the focal point—the child's needs, interests, and concerns. They also objected to practices that stifled initiative, creativity, and freedom to develop and sought to make the classroom a place where children were free to move about, question, and explore their interests.

But whereas the progressives believed that enlightenment and human progress could be provided by extending the benefits of a more responsive public education to all youth, such romantic naturalists as John Holt, Herbert Kohl, Jonathan Kozol, and the early writing of Neil Postman and Charles Weingartner generally held that school systems have become highly bureaucratic institutions that establish unwarranted constraints over youth, stifling their creativity and alienating them from schools. Some urged open classrooms and free schools; others offered different alternatives.

Paul Goodman, for instance, while seeing a need for compulsory education in the primary grades, opposed its extension to the high school. He recommends that the funds for compulsory secondary education be turned over to youth to establish their own learning communities and enable them to be free to experiment with their own life styles and seek their self-identity. The funds could also be used to promote apprenticeship programs. Ivan Illich goes further by recommending that compulsory schooling be abolished, the whole system be dismantled, and society be deschooled. He proposes instead informal learning arrangements in the larger society that would be based on natural interest and curiosity and entered into voluntarily. Thus the faith that Dewey and the progressives had in innovative organized schooling was, from Illich's viewpoint, seriously misguided.

Although the romantic naturalists have concentrated on how the student can overcome alienating learning conditions, they have made less of a contribution to curriculum theory. How the organizational and administrative structure can be transformed so that their ideas could be effectively implemented is seldom discussed. Thus they have rarely concentrated on the power structure and how it can be changed. Even Illich's deschooled society offers no assurance that the kinds of learning networks envisioned will be successful, because the larger society itself remains essentially unchanged. Romantic naturalists also fall into Rousseau's trap in their belief in the basic goodness and natural curiosity of the child who, once freed from restrictions, will blossom naturally. But what is known about child development today suggests that far more structure and guidance are needed than the romantic naturalists would provide if the child is to develop healthily and become an educated person.

Humanistic Education

Humanistic education was a movement of the 1970s that had more in common with early progressive education than did the views of the romantic naturalists. Humanistic education advocated the principles of treating the student as a person and integrating cognitive learning and affective experience.

Rational beings are people and must not be treated merely as means but also as ends in themselves. Thus the teacher would endeavor to gain an empathetic understanding of the students' feelings and values, and an understanding of how students perceive their schooling. Teachers should become more concerned with the personal development of each student than with acquiring bodies of knowledge. Teachers should seek to understand students as whole persons and avoid labeling them, since those who use labels apply a label to a behavior pattern and then posit the label as the cause of the behavior. Moreover, labeling may legitimize mistreatment and set children apart from one another. Thus such labels as *slow learner, delinquent, troublemaker*, and others may prove self-defeating.

Humanistic educators agree that the affective side of education has been generally neglected by schools, more emphasis should be placed on it, and it should be more fully integrated with cognitive learning. The affective domain includes values, attitudes, feelings, and emotions. Many programs in values education have been instituted to enable students to develop greater awareness of their values and to think more critically and constructively about them so that their decisions will be better informed.

Numerous objections, however, have been raised against humanistic education. It is charged that such programs are likely to neglect the study of organized subject matter and the basics. There is concern by some parents that their children may be indoctrinated or inculcated with a set of values different from their own, and they insist that such matters should be the responsibility of the parents. Some educators claim that most teachers are not adequately prepared to handle affective education programs. Moreover, it is suggested that such programs are difficult to evaluate. Even some of the basic concepts in humanistic education are difficult to agree upon and are extremely complex. Nevertheless, despite these criticisms, the ideals of the early progressives of educating the "whole child" were carried forward effectively by some exceptional humanistic educators such as Carl Rogers.

Freudianism

Sigmund Freud (1856–1939), Austrian neurologist and father of psychoanalysis, had a vast influence on modern thought with his theory of psychoneurosis and his stress on the role of sexuality in human development. Freud believed that there are basic sex and aggressive drives and stated a hard determinism in which early childhood greatly influenced the structure of personality in adulthood. His psychoanalysis sought the roots of neuroses by unearthing from the unconscious repressed wishes and desires of childhood.

Freud's influence on education, though important, was indirect and diffuse. Psychoanalytic theory offered the notion of *sublimation*, which held that the gratification of instinctual impulses, usually of a sexual or aggressive nature, could be achieved by substituting socially accepted behavior for expression of the prohibited drives. Teachers were to recognize unconscious motivation and seek to sublimate the child's repressed desires into socially useful channels. Teachers must also understand their own unconscious in order to improve the way they relate to students.

One example of Freud's ideas in education was Margaret Naumberg's Children's School in New York City in 1915. She thought the child should be weaned from egocentrism but found the task of doing so much more complex than most educators had imagined. Conventional education, she believed, only dealt with symptoms of the basic drives and therefore frequently led to further repression. Thus she sought to bring the child's unconscious to consciousness by permitting greater freedom, especially in the arts, which she thought would bring out the child's inner life. Children would also have to relinquish their dependence on textbooks and teachers and begin to develop independence of thought and action. Other examples of Freudian ideas in education are A. S. Neill's Summerhill.

Freud's theory has been criticized as not being scientific: it is not falsifiable and is unamenable to other canons of scientific experimentation and testing. Although Freud believed that his stages of psychosexual development and other findings were universal, they appear to be not only culturally relative but also relative to certain social classes within a culture. Psychoanalysis itself has proven to be an extremely costly, time-consuming process that has a rather poor record of overcoming patients' psychoneuroses. Moreover, hardly any teachers have the technical preparation to apply Freudian techniques properly. Even if more teachers or guidance counselors developed such skills, one could still seriously question whether the application of psychotherapy is a purpose of schooling.

Reconstructionism

A new educational philosophy emerged during the 1930s under the leadership of George S. Counts and Harold Rugg and was later brought to fruition by Theodore Brameld. *Reconstructionism* recognized that progressivism had made certain advances over traditional education in teacher-pupil relations and teaching methodology, but it charged that progressivism had become fixated on the child and thereby had failed to develop long-range, compelling goals for a society undergoing great social, political, and economic transformations. The crises that gave reconstructionism its urgency were the Great Depression of the 1930s and the earliest dangers of nuclear annihilation in the 1950s. The reconstructionists urged that a new social order be built that would fulfill basic democratic values and harmonize the underlying forces of the modern world. They put forth such ideas as that working people should control institutions and resources if the world is to become democratic. The aim should be the development of an international democracy or world government in which all nations will participate.

An education for a reconstructed society must recognize the interdependence of the world's population (as in cases of ecological and economic problems). Thus students need to study the realities of the modern world and recognize that they live in a global village. The teacher, therefore, critically examines the cultural heritage, explores controversial issues, provides a vision of a new and better world, and enlists students' efforts to promote programs of cultural renewal. The teacher attempts to convince students of the validity of reconstructionist beliefs but employs democratic procedures in doing so.

Although reconstructionism undergirds its beliefs and proposals by drawing upon findings from the social and behavioral sciences, the established empirical conclusions from these disciplines may well be insufficient to use in developing a planned international world order. Thus many of their assertions lack sufficient scientific backing. Reconstructionists have also been accused of indoctrinating students. While Brameld denied the charge, Counts insisted that it is not whether "imposition" will take place but the source from which it will come. Rather than have ruling groups or classes impose ideas on society, teachers, according to Counts, should take the lead in helping to build a new social order. But, one can ask, is this an appropriate goal for education? Reconstructionism does demand a commitment of the educator who in turn tries to bring about strong student commitment. It therefore assumes—probably erroneously—that a consensus can be reached on guiding ideals, goals, and values. In contrast, followers of Dewey would claim that students should be taught to use the scientific method but be free to arrive at their own conclusions.

TYPES OF REFORMERS

As an analogy, let us imagine a situation in which five experts are called in to examine a complex machine that fails to operate properly. After examining the machine *A* and *B* think the breakdown is minor, whereas *C, D*, and *E* consider it serious and of major proportions. *A* says that the machine is a good one and all that is needed is a workable part, which he promptly installs. *B* agrees with *A* that it is a good machine and that the breakdown stems from a defective part; however, *B* believes that the part itself is obsolescent and therefore invents a new type of part that, it is claimed, will work more efficiently. *C, D*, and *E* agree with one another that the entire machine is obsolescent; they disagree, however, over what should be done about it. *C* points out extensive changes in the machine that will make it more effective; whereas *D* argues that the machine should be replaced by one that is different and much better. *E*, on the other hand, contends that all such machines can be abolished and society instead can have individuals and voluntary groups design a device that is not a machine but will provide genuine benefits.

Applying these five types to innovators and reformers, we can distinguish two types of establishment educators: a conventional and an innovative one. They share the view that the system should be both maintained and improved, but established educators place greater emphasis on maintenance. In the previous illustration, Individual *A* is a *conventional establishment educator* who believes that schools are basically good and when things go wrong they can be rectified by rearranging and reorganizing some aspect of the system. *B* shares with *A* a belief in the value of the system; however, *B* is an *innovative establishment educator* who believes that when problems arise innovations should be introduced and effectively implemented. Critics of the reformers would most likely be conventional establishment educators or innovative establishment educators. Some critics, however, may be neither educators nor key establishment members, but they are supportive of the establishment and essentially endorse the same position as *A* or *B*. They could be called *conventional critic* (Type A) or *innovative critic* (Type B). A number of the authors in Part II are innovative establishment educators or innovative critics.

Types *C, D*, and *E* are reformers. They all believe that drastic changes are needed, and they seek to correct abuses; however, they disagree as to what should be done. Type *C* could be called a *system reformer*, one who believes that the school system is salvageable but that extensive and drastic changes may need to be made before it can truly provide quality education. *D* believes that public schools are too defective to offer a quality education and are unlikely to overcome their endemic weaknesses in the near future. *D* is an *options reformer*; he has left the public school to develop options, such as free schools, outside public education. Finally, reformer *E* is a *deschooler*, who usually argues that compulsory schooling should be abolished, support for formal systems be withdrawn, and learning should take place in informal networks within the community.

You may wish to keep these different types in mind while reading the selections in Part I to see whether doing so promotes better understanding of reformers and critics.

REFORM RATIONALES

Reformers may appeal to one or more of the following rationales to justify their arguments: (1) quality, (2) quantity, (3) equity, (4) rights, (5) decision making, and (6) restoration. Reforms that appeal to quality refer either to the outcomes of education or the process. An outcome criterion would focus on desirable outcomes amenable to behavioral formulation and measurement (competency testing, for instance). On the other hand, some reformers appeal to the worthwhileness of the educational process itself and the excitement and stimulation students find in learning (Summerhill and open education).

An appeal to quantity calls for larger appropriations, greater and more extensive facilities, and more specialists. Such appeals were made during the post-World War II period of high birth rates and the later Sputnik era that appropriated more funds for training scientists and engineers in order to surpass the Russians in the space race. It is also seen today in the demand for higher teacher salaries.

Appeals to equity argue for reform on grounds that fairer and more equal distribution of educational resources and more equal access are needed. Such arguments are characteristic of the school desegregation movement and recent school financial reform proposals.

A rationale that appeals to rights usually claims that certain fundamental rights have been denied and a need exists to rectify injustices and protect rights. Examples are arguments to eliminate corporal punishment, enact school dress codes, and protect children's rights.

Those arguments appealing to decision making allege that certain community groups have been denied a voice in decisions about public education. Consequently, reforms are demanded to make decision making more widely shared. The community-control movement, in which minorities seek power to make key decisions in neighborhood schools, is a case in point.

Finally, an appeal to restoration is based on the conviction that present standards and programs are inferior to those of the past. This argument is similar to the quality appeal except that it primarily seeks to restore neglected standards rather than invent new ones. The back-to-basics movement is an example.

Thus, depending on the case, reformers appeal to a rationale of quality, quantity, equity, rights, decision making, or restoration. Deliberations about educational reform are likely to be improved by greater attention to the concept of reform and the rationale of reform arguments.

CHAPTER 1

GOALS AND
CURRICULAR CONNECTIONS

read

Under the sponsorship of the Carnegie Foundation, Ernest L. Boyer and a site-visit team conducted a study of the American high school in which fifteen varied schools from all sections of the country were investigated. He found that "high schools lack a clear and vital mission. They are unable to find a common purpose or establish educational priorities that are widely shared." As a consequence, he recommended that every high school develop clearly stated goals that can be supported by students, and he suggested four goals to guide curriculum development.

Boyer's proposed core curriculum would be structured around those ideas, experiences, and traditions that were significant at a particular time in history. These shared experiences include our history, use of symbols, group and institutional membership, need for well-being, relation to nature, and our dependence on technology. Elective clusters would be introduced in the last two years of high school.

He also indicates in the study how working conditions for teachers can be improved. High school teachers should be limited to a daily load of four regular class sessions; provided a minimum of one daily hour available for class preparation; exempted from monitoring halls, lunchrooms, and recreation areas; and honored annually through recognition and cash awards for outstanding teachers.

In the selection by Boyer, there is an emphasis on the importance of writing and thinking skills, the curriculum core, and strong leadership to fulfill a vital mission. John Martin Rich compares the Boyer Report with two earlier national studies and three more recent studies. He finds that the report's goals lack a sufficient rationale and the proposed core curriculum, among other things, is deficient in providing coherence and integration.

CLARIFYING THE MISSION OF THE AMERICAN HIGH SCHOOL

ERNEST L. BOYER

Ernest L. Boyer (b. 1928) studied at Greenville College (A.B.) and the University of Southern California (M.A., Ph.D., LL.D.). He has served as Chancellor of SUNY, U.S. Commissioner of Education, and is currently President of the Carnegie Foundation for the Advancement of Teaching. He is the recipient of a number of awards and honorary degrees.

While we were preparing our report on secondary education (Boyer, 1983), it became obvious that school improvement was a complicated, demanding task. Indeed, the process must begin with purposes, goals, a clear and vital mission.

In our study, we looked at the education laws in all fifty states and discovered a numbing hodgepodge of rules and regulations. In California, for instance, the education code is four volumes and 3,700 pages long; in New York it occupies five volumes and 4,000 pages.

More troublesome are the vague and wide-ranging mandates the states have imposed on public education. Many of these requirements are pushed by special-interest groups. Frequently, they trivialize the mission of public education and, therefore, are rarely taken seriously by schools. Here is a sampling of what state laws say they should do:

Idaho: "The school program shall be organized to meet the needs of all pupils, the community, and to fulfill the state objectives of the school."

Mississippi: The purpose of education is "to provide appropriate learning experiences to promote the optimum growth and development of youth and adults throughout life."

Oregon: "Each individual will have the opportunity to develop to the best of his or her ability the knowledge, skills and attitudes necessary to function as an individual . . . a learner . . . a producer . . . a citizen . . . a consumer . . . and a family member."

Maine: "The public school must teach virtue and morality for not less than one-half hour per week. This includes "principles of morality and justice and a sacred regard for truth, love of country, humanity, a universal benevolence, sobriety, industry and frugality, chastity, moderation and temperance, and all other virtues that ornament human society."

California: "Each teacher shall endeavor to impress upon the minds of the public the principles of morality, truth, justice, patriotism, and a true comprehension of the rights, duties, and dignity of American citizenship, including kindness toward domestic pets and the humane treatment of living creatures, to teach them to avoid idleness, profanity, and falsehood, and to instruct them in manners and morals and the principles of a free government."

At the district level we found school leaders frequently preoccupied with administrative procedures. Educational goals appeared to be of only marginal concern. In one district, for example, principals were called

From Ernest L. Boyer, "Clarifying the Mission of the American High School," *Educational Leadership* 41, 6 (March 1984): 20–22. Reprinted with permission of the Association for Supervision and Curriculum Development. Copyright © 1984 by ASCD. All rights reserved.

together by the superintendent to produce "performance standards" for the year. All schools in the district were expected to accomplish the following objectives:

- Raise the attendance rate
- Reduce teacher absence to 1.5 days per week, which, incidentally, was less than the sick days allowed in the contract
- Improve parent participation

High schools, to be effective, must have a sense of purpose, with teachers, students, administrators, and parents sharing a vision of what they are trying to accomplish. The vision must be larger than a single class in a single day. It must go beyond keeping students in schools and out of trouble, and be more significant than adding up the Carnegie units the student has completed.

Today many proposals for school reform are heatedly debated. But, unguided by a larger vision, they amount to little more than tinkering with an elaborate and complex system. What is needed is a coherent vision of what the nation's high schools should be seeking to accomplish.

A clear and vital mission is the first requirement for school improvement. However, there are three additional priorities and they too deserve special attention:

> The high school should help all students develop the capacity to think critically and communicate effectively through a mastery of language.
> The high school should help all students learn about themselves, the human heritage, and the interdependent world in which they live through a core curriculum based upon consequential human experiences common to all people.
> The high school requires leadership from superintendents and legislators, of course, but especially from school principals.

TOP PRIORITY: THINKING AND WRITING SKILLS

Focusing on the centrality of language is, therefore, our second priority for excellence in education. The use of complex symbols separates us from all other forms of life. Language provides the connecting tissue that binds society together, allows us to express feelings and ideas, and powerfully influences the attitudes of others. It is the most essential tool of learning. We recommend that all high schools help all students develop the capacity to think critically and communicate effectively through the written and spoken word.

When we speak of language, we first mean mastery of English. We acknowledge the richness of other languages and cultures, and we have proposed the study of a second language for all students. Still, for those living in the United States, the effective use of English is absolutely crucial. Those who do not become proficient in the primary language of the culture are enormously disadvantaged in school and out of school, as well.

Schools should build on the remarkable language skills a child already has acquired. Unfortunately, reading programs in the primary grades often seem to assume that children come to school with limited language and that decoding skills can be separated from comprehension. An approach to reading that builds on the child's own language experience offers a rich alternative that can at once continue language development and build confidence as well. Once young learners have become actively involved in the writing and reading of their own thoughts, they are ready to consider seriously the ideas and writings of others.

During high school, every student should learn to write more clearly, read with greater comprehension, listen with more discrimination, speak with more precision, and, through critical thinking, develop the capacity to apply old knowledge to new concepts. Patricia Albjerg Graham, dean of the Harvard University School of Education, writes: "Literacy is essential both for the individual and the society in the late twentieth century, and the high school is the institution with the unique responsibility to assure it." Therefore, we also recommend that high schools give priority to language study, requiring of all freshman a 3) one-year basic English course, with emphasis on writing.

Clear writing leads to clear thinking; clear thinking is the basis of clear writing. Perhaps more than other forms of communication, writing holds us responsible for our words and ultimately makes us more thoughtful human beings.

Teaching students to write clearly and effectively should be a central objective of the school. But this goal cannot be magically accomplished. Time must be provided to assure that the task is adequately performed. Teachers must have time not only to assign writing but also to critique carefully what students write. We recommend that those who teach English have no more than twenty students in each class, and no more than two such classes should be included within the regular teacher's load.

The high school curriculum should also include a study of the spoken word. As humans, we first use sounds to communicate our feelings. Very early, we combine phonemes orally to express complex ideas. In our verbal culture we speak much more than we write. We use the telephone more frequently than we send letters. Talk is everywhere. Throughout our lives we judge others, and we are ourselves judged by what is said. We therefore need to be as precise in speaking as we are in writing. Therefore, we recommend that high schools give priority to oral communications, requiring all students to complete a course in speaking and listening.

Language defines our humanity. It is the means by which we cope socially and succeed educationally. The advent of the information age raises to new levels of urgency the need for all students to be effective in their use of the written and the spoken word. The mastery of English is the first and most essential goal of education.

A CORE OF COMMON KNOWLEDGE

A third priority is a core of common learning—a program of required courses in literature, the arts, foreign language, history, civics, science, mathematics, technology, and health—to extend the knowledge and broaden the perspective of every student.

Since Sputnik orbited into space, it has become dramatically apparent that we are all custodians of a single planet. When drought ravages the Sahara, when war in Indochina creates hundreds of thousands of refugees, neither our compassion nor our analytic intelligence can be bounded by a dotted line on a political map. We are beginning to understand that hunger and human rights affect alliances as decisively as weapons and treaties. These global changes must be understood by every student.

Today's high school curriculum barely reflects the global view. The world has shrunk, yet American young people remain shockingly ignorant about our own heritage and about the heritage of other nations. Students cannot identify world leaders or the capitals of other countries at a time when all nations are interlocked.

If high schools are to educate students about their world, new curriculum priorities must be set. If a school district is incapable of naming the things it wants high school graduates to know, if a community is unable to define the culture it wants high school graduates to inherit, if education cannot help students see relationships beyond their own personal ones, then each new generation will remain dangerously ignorant, and its capacity to live confidently and responsibly will be diminished.

What, then, do we see as the basic curriculum for all students? Broadly defined, it is a study of those consequential ideas, experiences, and traditions common to all of us by virtue of our membership in the human family at a particular moment in history. These shared experiences include our use of symbols, our sense of history, our membership in groups and institutions, our relationship to nature, our need for well-being, and our growing dependence on technology.

The content of the core curriculum must extend beyond the specialities, and focus on more transcendent issues, moving from courses to coherence. We recommend, first, that the number of required courses in the core curriculum should be expanded from one-half to two-thirds of the total units required for high school graduation. Secondly, in addition to strengthening the traditional courses in literature, history, mathematics, and science, emphasis should also be given to foreign language, the arts, civics, non-western studies, technology, the meaning of work, and the importance of health.

In addition to tightening requirements, we must bring a new interdisciplinary vision into the classroom and the total program of the school. The content of the core curriculum must extend beyond the specialities to touch larger, more transcendent issues.

Teachers must play a key role in making these connections between the disciplines. They must view the curriculum in a more coherent way. We cannot expect students to see relationships that teachers do not see. Teachers also should work together more collaboratively.

Students, too, must begin to seek out connections between the disciplines. It is one thing to teach students that the world is a complicated place; it is another—and more lasting—lesson for them to discover it on their own. Specifically, we recommend that all students, during their senior year, complete what we call a Senior Independent Project, a written report that focuses on a significant contemporary issue—one that draws on the various fields of academic study that have made up the student's program. This assignment is part of core requirements.

To be prepared to live in our interdependent, interconnected, complex world, students must be well informed. They also must have the ability to bring together information from ideas across the disciplines, organize their thoughts, reach conclusions, and, in end, use knowledge wisely. To expect less is to underestimate the capacity of students and diminish the significance of education.

SCHOOL LEADERSHIP

Goals, English proficiency, and a core curriculum in a global context are clearly priorities that are central for achieving excellence in today's high schools. But there is a fourth requirement for the attainment of the first three: leadership.

For years now, studies have pointed to the pivotal role of the principals in bringing about more effective schools. Our own field studies bear out these findings. In schools where achievement was high and where there was a clear sense of community, we invariably found that the principal made the difference. Like a symphony orchestra, the high school must be more than the sum of its parts. If the goals we set forth are to be accomplished, strong leadership will be needed to pull together the separate elements in the school and make them work.

Rebuilding leadership means giving each school more control over its own budget. Specifically, we recommend that the school principal and staff should have authority to allocate funds within guidelines set by the district office. Further, school systems should provide each high school principal with a Discretionary School Improvement Fund to provide time and materials for program development, or provide for special seminars or staff retreats.

Principals also should have more leeway in rewarding good teachers. In most schools they either inherit their staffs or are not consulted when the district decides which teachers should be assigned to which school. Principals we visited expressed frustration about the constraints they have in dealing with teachers under their supervision. "I have no control anymore," said one principal. "We have had five weeks of school, and already fifteen new teachers have come in—and fifteen have left because of 'bumpings,' teachers with seniority removing other teachers. In addition, each year, mostly through inheritance from somewhere else, I get three to five inept teachers."

We recommend that principals, acting in consultation with their staffs, be given responsibility for the final selection of teachers for their schools. In districts where court-ordered mandates are in effect, we urge that principals participate with central office personnel in the assignment of teachers to district schools. In meeting these responsibilities, principals should follow central office policies and civil rights requirements.

In making these recommendations, we recognize that issues of financing and equity, as well as court mandates, have placed heavy burdens on school districts. The impact of federal legislation and the courts on the daily operation of schools has been immense. Many districts have felt overwhelmed by the seemingly endless specifications, regulations, and detail involved in administering federal and state programs. We acknowledge, therefore, the key role of the central office and, particularly, that of the superintendent. District leadership is crucial.

In our school visits, we encountered superintendents who exercised superb leadership by establishing and maintaining high-quality education in their districts. In a number of cases, these superintendents transformed failing school systems into model ones for the nation.

Nonetheless, we believe that principals and staffs of individual schools need far more autonomy and authority to carry out their responsibilities. Heavy doses of bureaucracy are stifling creativity in too many schools and preventing principals and their staffs from exercising their best professional judgment on decisions that properly should be made at the local level.

What we seek are high schools in which the school community—students, teachers, and principals—sees learning as the primary goal. In such a community, the principal becomes not just the top authority but the key educator, too.

Rebuilding excellence in education means reaffirming the importance of the local school and freeing leadership to lead.

In our report entitled *High School*, we identified twelve key strategies for achieving high quality in education: clear goals, the mastery of language, a core of common learning, preparation for work and further education, school and community service, better teachers, improved instruction, effective use of technology, flexible school patterns, strong leadership, connections with colleges and corporations, and a renewed public commitment to the nation's schools.

All of these strategies deserve implementation. However, none are more important to the achievement of quality schools than the four we have identified for special attention—writing and thinking skills, the curriculum core, and strong leadership in the service of a clear and vital mission.

Reference

Boyer, Ernest L. *High School: A Report on Secondary Education in America.* Washington, D.C.: Carnegie Foundation for the Advancement of Teaching, 1983.

EDUCATIONAL GOALS AND CURRICULAR DECISIONS IN THE NEW CARNEGIE REPORT

JOHN MARTIN RICH

The Carnegie Foundation has recently issued another important survey and assessment of American public education (hereafter referred to as the Boyer Report), this time devoted to secondary education and authored by Ernest L. Boyer, president of the Carnegie Foundation and former United States Commissioner of Education (Boyer, 1983).

The purpose of this paper is to examine and evaluate two vital areas of the Boyer Report: educational goals and curricular decisions. First, some comparisons will be made with two earlier Carnegie reports; next, goals and curriculum in the Boyer Report will be evaluated; finally, the Boyer Report will be briefly compared to other contemporary national surveys.

A COMPARISON OF CARNEGIE REPORTS

A two-year study completed in 1959 that attracted national attention was James B. Conant's study of fifty comprehensive high schools in seventeen states (Conant, 1959). Conant found that the comprehensive high school could provide adequate programs of citizenship education, vocational education, and challenging studies for the more able student. Conant identified the more gifted stu-

dents as about 15 percent of the high school population; he recommended that each of these students study three or four years in the basic disciplines, take at least five subjects each year with homework of fifteen hours or more each week. Placement tests would determine the appropriate sections for the academically talented, and effective guidance programs would be needed to assist this group and the rest of the student population, who would take a more limited number of advanced courses in the basic disciplines.

The Conant Report was likely influenced by the cold war, the launching of Sputnik, and the National Defense Education Act; its publication aroused a greater national consciousness about the status of American education. Tying in to the space race with the Soviet Union, it called attention to the need for more academically able girls to enter science and mathematics programs, the neglect of foreign languages, and a more complete education for all students in the comprehensive high school.

In sharp contrast, Charles Silberman's Carnegie-sponsored study, published in 1970, emerged during the upheavals of the civil rights movement, the Vietnam War, and student militancy on campuses. Not surprisingly,

From John Martin Rich, "Educational Goals and Curricular Decisions in the New Carnegie Report," *The High School Journal* 69 (February–March 1986): 222–227. Reprinted with permission from The University of North Carolina Press.

Note: This paper was presented at the American Educational Studies Association in San Francisco, November 9, 1984. The author wishes to thank Joseph L. DeVitis for organizing and chairing the session and suggesting the topic of this paper.

the tone and content differed markedly from the Conant Report.

Silberman (1970) deplored the school's preoccupation with order and control. This preoccupation could be found in a focus on time and the clock (although time frequently was not used productively) and on the demand for silence. The repressiveness he observed was reinforced by parental attitudes that viewed discipline as more important than student self-inquiry. At the root of the problem is "mindlessness," the failure "to think seriously or deeply about the purposes or consequences of education" (Silberman, 1970). Silberman's curricular solution was to promote the growth of open classrooms.

In many respects, the Boyer Report is more similar to the Conant Report, both stylistically and substantively, than to Silberman's. Both in style and tone Boyer and Conant express themselves in an objective, detached, and straightforward manner. In contrast, Silberman is idiosyncratic, digressive, fond of injecting items and case studies, and is given to waxing passionately about his favorite nostrums. Substantively, both Boyer and Conant exhibit essentialist elements, while Silberman is more of a neoprogressive. Conant does not deviate from the subject curriculum, and the Boyer Report largely adheres to it as well.

GOALS AND THE CURRICULUM

The Boyer Report studied fifteen high schools in all sections of the country that varied considerably, including small rural schools, alternative schools, magnet schools, big-city schools, suburban schools, and other types. Educational goals were found to be only of marginal concern at the district level; whereas high schools' written goals were often vaguely stated and generally ignored. Boyer found that "high schools lack a clear and vital mission. They are unable to find common purpose or establish educational priorities that are widely shared" (1983). He recommended that every high school develop clearly stated goals that were understood and supported by students. Here Silberman would heartily agree.

Boyer advocated four essential goals and stated how they could be achieved. First was that of learning to think critically and communicate effectively through a mastery of language. Second, students should learn about themselves, their human heritage, and the world in which they live through a core curriculum. Third, students should be prepared for the world of work and further education through electives. Finally, all students should fulfill their civic and social responsibilities through school and community service.

As for the curriculum, Boyer found that many high schools offered a wide range of electives. He did not object to the numerous electives as long as an academic core was provided. Guidance for students in planning their programs, however, was usually found to be inadequate. The curriculum, moreover, was not discussed by faculty in terms of what should be the content of a high school education and what it means to be an educated person.

The proposed core curriculum would be structured around those ideas, experiences, and traditions that were significant at a particular time in history. These shared experiences include our history, use of symbols, group and institutional membership, need for well-being, relation to nature, and our dependence on technology. This curriculum, Boyer believes, is appropriate for all students.

Boyer believes that the mastery of English is the first and most essential goal of education, because literacy is the most important tool for learning. Thought and language, he holds, are inextricably connected; and with greater proficiency in self-expression, the quality of thinking will improve. Moreover, those not proficient in the primary language of their culture are greatly disadvantaged in school and the larger society. It is recommended that language proficiency be assessed one year prior to entering high school; that teachers of English be limited to twenty students in each class, and that no more than two basic English classes be included within the teacher's load; and that a one-semester speech course be included in the program.

In terms of the core curriculum, all students should begin to develop "cultural literacy." Included in a cultural literacy program would be a one-year course in literature (although not a great books program), some study in the fine arts, and two years of foreign language study. To supply the shared experiences that include our history, Boyer recommended a one-year study of United States history that would provide an understanding at a deeper level, a one-year Western-civilization course, and a one-semester required course that studies a single non-Western nation. The shared experiences of group and institutional membership would consist of a one-year course in American government that explores traditions of democratic thought, government structures, and current political and social issues.

Shared experiences in our relations with nature and technology would include a two-year sequence in the biological and physical sciences, two years of mathematics and additional courses for those qualified to take them, a one-semester course in technology, and a course in health and lifetime fitness.

Vocational education is complicated by a rapidly changing job market and the inability of most schools to offer a sufficient range of courses. Job prospects for vocational students, it was found, are not much better than for those in nonspecified programs, with the exception of secretarial positions. High school vocational programs are caught between the prospects of a job market featuring many low-paying, dead-end jobs for which formal education is not required, and high-tech jobs that require more training than most high schools can supply. Boyer recommends that, as part of the core, a seminar on work be offered that examines its importance in the lives of everyone; that tracking be abolished and replaced with a single-track program; and that only vocational courses be offered that have intellectual substance rather than narrow "marketable" skills.

The required courses of the core would constitute two-thirds of the total units needed for graduation. The last two years of high school would be considered a "transition school" where half the time is devoted to the core and the other half to elective clusters. These clusters would be a carefully planned program for each student consisting of five or six courses that would permit further study of selected academic subjects or explorations of career options, or a combination of both. In order to offer these courses, schools will have to draw more on the resources of the larger society and expect students to assume greater responsibility for their own education. The transition school can include work with mentors, and early college study or apprenticeship outside of school.

In assessing the Boyer Report, one is first struck by the clearly stated goals and the exceptional balance of the curriculum as a whole. Many glaring weaknesses in most high school curriculums have been overcome by requiring a study of vital but neglected areas: fine arts, non-Western cultures, foreign languages, technology, and the world of work and vocations in the lives of people. Moreover, by eliminating the tracking system, invidious discrimination is reduced. And by mixing in a coherent plan of electives with the core curriculum during the last two years, student choice and individual differences are recognized. The reason that the curriculum appears to be exceptionally balanced lies with the broad range of studies in the core, from the fine arts to the sciences; the inclusion of significant but commonly neglected studies; and the opportunity to pursue a meaningful program of electives.

Despite these genuine achievements, real problems remain with both the goals and the curriculum. The emphasis on clearly stated goals is commendable, but it is unclear why this set of goals should be accepted. The goals are baldly stated as though their worth is self-evident; however, no rationale or justification is given other than indirectly through the curriculum as a fulfillment of the goals. But the curriculum should not determine the goals or render the goals a mere curriculum appendage; rather, the goals should help give direction to curriculum decisions. Since innumerable goals are available, why choose these four? Even those readers who find these goals worth adopting will have to search elsewhere for a rationale to support their decision. Thus the Boyer Report, in contrast to its greater attention in providing a curriculum rationale, appeals to authority or intuition rather than reasoned grounds for goal acceptance.

Problems of coherence and integration arise in a varied and complex curriculum. The Boyer Report has made an attempt to handle this problem, but it appears to be insufficient. The report states that teachers must view the curriculum coherently and work together cooperatively. Students will try to make connections by participating in a senior independent project—a written report that deals with a contemporary issue that requires drawing upon various disciplines. But no attention is given to constructing the curriculum around broad themes or major questions that everyone will face. Such themes could include the individual's relation to the environment; the individual's relations to others and institutions; or the individual and social reform. Some examples of the major questions: What is human nature? Does the universe have a purpose? What is the good life?

Another problem with the curriculum is that it is a subject curriculum, which fails to acknowledge much that has been done in curriculum experimentation over the past fifty years. The early progressive education movement broke sharply with the subject curriculum and offered a wide range of new forms, from broad fields to the experience curriculum. Nor does the Boyer Report recognize the structure of the disciplines approach. Even though some emphasis is placed on an inquiry approach in social studies and other fields, a consistent and systematic inquiry approach is not utilized, and the structure of the disciplines model is essentially ignored.

Boyer generally argues convincingly for each discipline introduced in the core, but much less convincingly for the relative weight accorded to each discipline in the overall curriculum: Why, for instance, two years of science and two years of mathematics rather than one year or three years?

An even more serious criticism is the justification of a core or required curriculum. In order to justify such a curriculum, several questions should be answered in the affirmative. Can all students learn and become proficient in the same subjects? Does the core curriculum recognize different learning styles? And does the core curriculum place more emphasis on *what* one learns rather than learning *how* to learn? The Boyer Report does not address these questions. But it does appear that, in light of previous results with required curriculums for all students, insufficient attention is being given to individual differences, varied learning styles, and too much emphasis is placed on what must be learned rather than how to learn more effectively. By providing an elective cluster and a senior independent project, the Boyer Report copes with these problems better than some required curricula but does not do enough within the required courses themselves to offset these problems.

COMPARISON OF CURRENT REPORTS

Among many national commission reports published in the last year or so, the Boyer Report will be briefly compared with three other widely recognized, nationally sponsored reports. These reports include *A Nation at Risk*, under a commission created by Secretary of Education T. H. Bell (1983); Mortimer Adler's *The Paideia Proposal* (1982); and Theodore Sizer's study of high schools titled *Horace's Compromise* (1984).

Although each of the three reports refers, either directly or indirectly, to goals, none of them provides a sufficiently adequate justification for the goals chosen; therefore, our attention will be given to brief comparisons of their curricular proposals with the Boyer Report. An adequate justification of goals should include relating goal choices to a value theory or an educational philosophy, a conceptual analysis of the goal statements, and a delineation of the linkage between the goals and the curriculum.

A Nation at Risk is written in a strident, urgent style employing military metaphors reminiscent of the Sputnik era. Warning that the nation stands on the verge of losing its prominence as a world leader in industry and commerce because of its education failures, the commission recommends a high school curriculum for all students consistent of three years each of English, mathematics, science, and social studies, and one-half year of computer science. The college-bound student would be required to take two years of a foreign language. The commission generally believes that more is better—more homework, a longer school day and school year—although research supporting this claim is not presented.

In comparison, the Boyer Report does not fall into the "more is better" trap, and it offers a broader, better balanced curriculum by recognizing important, neglected subjects and the need for meaningful elective clusters.

The Paideia Proposal attempts to provide a liberal and general education for every student and is a required curriculum that provides no electives or specialized courses. Electives, Adler holds, are appropriate for different forms of preparation for the professions or technical careers at the post-high school level. Adler's curriculum is subject not only to all the criticism made earlier about required curriculums but is probably also inconsistent with Adler's goal of preparation for good citizens by learning to make intelligent choices, in proportion to their maturity and judgment, about critical decisions that affect their lives, which would include some responsibility for curricular choice.

Theodore Sizer visited more than forty American secondary schools, some extensively, some briefly, and relates his intensely personal observations, which stylistically are not unlike Silberman's case study approach. Sizer (1984) asserts that the essential claims in education are literacy, numeracy, and civic understanding; and he believes that the students' work should be focused on using their minds. He would organize a high school into four areas or large departments: inquiry and expression; mathematics and science; literature and the arts; philosophy and history. Sizer attempts to avoid a fragmented view of knowledge, to teach less but to engage students in a few more important ideas more deeply; he is also opposed to master plans that standardize instruction, because no one set of procedures, he believes, can serve all students well.

Of the four current national reports, Sizer's plan has the virtues of simplicity and adaptability to divergent school populations. Yet even those who are generally sympathetic with a broad fields approach and interdisciplinary programs will likely find Sizer's plan too amorphous and underdeveloped to become a functional curriculum design.

Despite the difficulties noted earlier that the Boyer Report does not adequately address, it is still better balanced, more carefully supported in terms of the choice of curriculum content, and the clearest and most incisively designed of the recent national reports considered here. It deserves a wide audience, vigorous discussion, and ample testing in numerous secondary schools.

References

Adler, M. J. (1982). *The Paideia Proposal: An Educational Manifesto*. New York: MacMillan.

Boyer, E. L. (1983). *High School: A Report on Secondary Education in America*. New York: Harper & Row.

Conant, J. B. (1959). *The American High School Today*. New York: McGraw-Hill.

National Commission on Excellence in Education. (1983). *A Nation at Risk: The Imperative for Educational Reform*. Washington, D.C.: U.S. Government Printing Office.

Silberman, C. E. (1970). *Crisis in the Classroom*. New York: Random House.

Sizer, T. R. (1984). *Horace's Compromise: The Dilemma of the American High School*. Boston: Houghton Mifflin.

DISCUSSION QUESTIONS AND ACTIVITIES

1. What are Boyer's priorities, and on what basis were they selected?
2. Boyer proposes a basic curriculum for all high school students. Of what does it consist, and how is it to be organized?
3. How are connections to be made between the disciplines?
4. What is the principal's role in this program?
5. Compare and contrast the Boyer Report with earlier studies made by Conant and Silberman.
6. Has Boyer provided an adequate rationale for the goals of the program?
7. Have the problems of coherence and integration been adequately handled?
8. What are the dangers, if any, of a required curriculum?
9. Compare the Boyer Report with other recent national studies in terms of their curricular proposals.
10. Visit local secondary schools, and gather data on their general education program.
11. Trace the changes in general education programs at the secondary level during the past twenty-five years. Present your findings in class.

SUGGESTED READINGS

Books by Ernest L. Boyer

The Book and Education. Washington, D.C.: Library of Congress, 1980.

College: The Undergraduate Experience in America. New York: Harper & Row, 1988.

Educating for Survival. New Rochelle, N.Y.: Change Magazine Press, 1977. (with Martin Kaplan)

High School: A Report on Secondary Educa-

tion in America. New York: Harper & Row, 1983.

High School/College Partnerships. Washington, D.C.: American Association for Higher Education, 1981.

Higher Learning in the Nation's Service. Washington, D.C.: Carnegie Foundation for the Advancement of Teaching, 1981. (with Fred M. Hechinger)

A Quest for Common Learning: The Aims of General Education. Washington, D.C.: Carnegie Foundation for the Advancement of Teaching, 1981. (with Arthur Levine)

Recent Major Reports on Education

Academic Preparation for College. New York: College Entrance Examination Board, 1983. Seeks to raise college entrance standards and develop national standards in secondary education.

Adler, Mortimer. *The Paideia Proposal.* New York: Macmillan, 1982. See chapter 3.

Boyer, Ernest L. *High School: A Report on Secondary Education in America.* New York: Harper & Row, 1983. See this chapter.

Carnegie Task Force on Teaching as a Profession. *A Nation Prepared: Teachers in the 21st Century.* New York: Carnegie Corporation, 1986. Recommends national certification standards, and seeks to implement it through a nonprofit national board.

Goodlad, John I. *A Place Called School: Prospects for the Future.* New York: McGraw-Hill, 1983. Recommends a comprehensive set of goals for schools, the availability of alternative curriculum designs, and continuing assessment of schools.

Holmes Group. *Tomorrow's Teachers.* East Lansing, Mich.: Holmes Group, 1986. Recommends that the undergraduate education major be replaced with a liberal arts degree and a fifth year of graduate-level preparation.

National Commission on Excellence in Education. *A Nation at Risk: The Imperative for Educational Reform.* Washington, D.C.: U.S. Government Printing Office, 1983. A highly influential report that claims that America is falling behind internationally and therefore prescribes a longer school day and school year with more rigorous courses and requirements.

Sizer, Theodore R. *Horace's Compromise: The Dilemma of the American High School.* Boston: Houghton Mifflin, 1984. See chapter 2.

Task Force on Education for Economic Growth. *Action for Excellence.* Denver: Education Commission of the States, 1983. Seeks to foster a partnership between the private sector and education.

Task Force on Federal Elementary and Secondary Education Policy. *Making the Grade.* New York: Twentieth Century Fund, 1983. Seeks to improve basic skill programs, to increase federal aid for programs for the disadvantaged, and to develop scientific literacy.

Time for Results: The Governor's 1991 Report on Education. Washington, D.C.: National Governor's Association, 1986. Recommends that the state's role in education be expanded.

Evaluations of Major Reports on Education

Felt, Marilyn Clayton. *Improving Our Schools.* Newton, Mass.: Education Development Center, 1985. Summarizes and provides excerpts of thirty-three studies that provide recommendations for local action.

Griesemer, J. Lynn, and Cornelius Butler. *Education under Study: An Analysis of Recent Major Reports on Education.* Chelmsford, Mass.: Northeast Regional Exchange, 1983. Provides synopses of nine major reports.

Gross, Beatrice, and Ronald Gross, eds. *The Great Debate: Which Way for American Education?* New York: Simon & Schuster, 1985. Includes selections by Adler, Boyer, Goodlad, Sizer, and others.

McNett, Ian. *Charting a Course: A Guide to the Excellence Movement in Education.* Washington, D.C.: Council for Basic Education, 1984. Outlines the essential points of nine national commission reports.

Marino, Jacqueline L. "Between the Lines of Boyer, Goodlad, and Sizer." *English Journal* 77 (February 1988): 19–21. Indicates some commonalities implicit in three reports.

Newmann, Fred M. *Educational Reform and Social Studies: Implications of Six Reports.* Boulder, Colo.: Social Science Education Consortium, 1985. Compares the implications of six national reports with past and present practices in the social sciences.

Passow, A. Harry. *A Review of the Major Current Reports on Secondary Education.* New York: ERIC Clearinghouse on Urban Education, Urban Diversity Series Number 88, 1984. Summarizes fifteen commission and study groups on secondary school reform.

Rich, John Martin, and Joseph L. DeVitis. "An Evaluation of the Aims and Curricula Proposals in 'Horace's Compromise'." *Clearing House* 60 (January 1987): 219–222. Evaluates Sizer's study in two areas, and compares it to two earlier Carnegie reports that shaped educational reform.

Spady, William G., and Gary Marx. *Excellence in Our Schools: Making It Happen.* Arlington, Va.: American Association of School Administrators, 1984. Evaluates nine major reports, and summarizes their recommendations.

Thorpe, Steve. "Searching for Social Studies Excellence among the Reports in Schooling." *Social Studies Review* 25 (Fall 1985): 25–34. Explores four reports and their agendas for secondary social studies.

CHAPTER 2

RESTRUCTURING SECONDARY SCHOOLS

Over the past decade, Theodore R. Sizer visited over one hundred schools; and during his two years of field work, he visited over forty American secondary schools. Sizer found that public school teachers are overworked and cannot devote sufficient attention to each student; moreover, they are unable to control their destiny because of a bureaucratic maze.

Sizer states four goals, three of which are essential for responsible citizenship and government. He then divides the curriculum into four areas or large departments and thereby disavows the traditional subject curriculum and its problem of fragmentation. Sizer endorses Whitehead's dictum not to teach too many subjects and that whatever you teach, teach thoroughly. Thus students would learn more while being taught less. Compulsory schooling should end upon demonstration of a "mastery of the minimal"; and since most students can do so before senior high school, schooling at that level would be voluntary. Diplomas would be awarded upon demonstrated mastery rather than after four years of study or the collection of a set number of credits. Students are also likely to be motivated in good schools—schools that have standards and are challenging rather than threatening, stable, clear about their mission, fair, and decent places that deserve loyalty.

In Sizer's selection, he argues against compartmentalization, indicates four areas around which the curriculum can be clustered, and presents a plan for reducing the total number of students for which each teacher has responsibility. Chester E. Finn, Jr., however, warns that in Sizer's plan the "entire heritage of Western civilization is merely an educational option."

THEODORE R. SIZER

ESSENTIAL SCHOOLS: A FIRST LOOK

Theodore R. Sizer (b. 1932) was educated at Yale University (B.A.) and Harvard University (M.A., Ph.D.). He taught at Roxbury Latin School and Melbourne (Australia) Grammar School as well as at the university level. He is a former Dean of Faculty of Education at Harvard and a former Headmaster of Phillips Academy. He is the recipient of honorary degrees and is author of Horace's Compromise *and other books about education. He is presently Professor of Education at Brown University.*

Background in "Private Schools"

A Study of High Schools, cosponsored by NASSP and the Commission on Educational Issues[1] of the National Association of Independent Schools, is in its fourth of five years, the conclusions are beginning to take form, and three books outlining findings and recommendations will be published.[2]

My volume, *Horace's Compromise: The Dilemma of the American High School Today*, will be issued in January 1984. It focuses on teaching and learning—on the excessive compromises that serious school people are all too often forced to make. A history of the American high school since 1940 by Robert Hampel will be published in the spring. And an analysis of schools arising from close observation of fifteen secondary schools across the country during the 1981–82 academic year will appear in the fall, written by Arthur G. Powell, David K. Cohen, and Eleanor Farrar.

No reader of the *Bulletin* will be surprised to hear that we found high schools to be very complicated, rich institutions (far more complicated, and thus fragile, than many policy makers today seem to realize, alas). To reduce our findings and recommendations to a few brief pages, therefore, is difficult, and carries the great risk of glibness, oversimplification, and overgeneralization. However, I will take that risk, at least for my own volume, in order to give NASSP members a first glimpse of what we have found.

At the start, I must emphasize that the focus of our study has been narrow, primarily on the "insides" of schools—on the critical triangle of student, teacher, and subject and on the climate of the school in which this triangle functions. There are, of course, many important problems "outside" of schools—the forms of governmental control, finance, and teacher education, to mention but a few. Consequential though these are, our study has not directly addressed them. We choose to concentrate closely on what we believe is the heart of the matter.

From Theodore R. Sizer, "Essential Schools: A First Look," NASSP *Bulletin* 67 (October 1983): 33–38. Reprinted with permission.

[1]The Commission on Education Issues is a programmatically autonomous unit within NAIS devoted to policy studies affecting American education. Scott Thomson, executive director of NASSP, and John Esty, president of NAIS, are commissioners, as are ten other educators from public and private schools and universities, and journalism.

[2]Houghton Mifflin will publish these volumes in 1984.

SOME OBSERVATIONS

First, some impressions arising from our visits in the field:

• The extent of free high school education in this country is astonishing. The crusade for universal secondary education, envisioned almost 100 years ago, is now a reality. The American high school may be this century's most far-reaching and generous social invention. Unfortunately, and despite well-intentioned, sincere efforts, many schools are not uniformly productive and serve some of their students poorly.

• While community values and populations vary widely across the country, the basic structure of the high school is strikingly common, and it is markedly similar to its 1890 founding model. Students are grouped by age; the substance of learning is organized by academic departments largely akin to those of the 1890s; the primary pedagogy is lecturing in one form or another, in separate blocks of time each of something under an hour; school is in session from Labor Day to mid-June; and student accomplishment is measured in the coinage of credits earned and time spent ("four years of English"). Even the rituals of going to school—proms, athletic events, student organizations—are remarkably consistent across all kinds of schools and across time. Given the size and demographic diversity of this country and changes in American society and in scholarship during the last fifty years, this stubbornly persistent common structure is extraordinary.

• Unfortunately, this structure does not serve its purpose well and is the root cause of the schools' weak productivity.

• While not structural, some key differences among schools are significant and usually follow the income group of the particular students served. Schools for poor youngsters are, on the whole, more troubled and more ne-

glected by the society than those for children of wealthier families. This sad finding should surprise no one and should shame everyone.

• Some groups of students—the honors track, or the athletes, or the special education group, or even the persistently troublesome kids—get relatively intensive individual attention. They are "known" in schools, and their programs often serve them very effectively. The unspecial majority, however, often remains anonymous and relatively unchallenged.

• Just as Charles Silberman found in the late 1960s, our principal conclusion after observing students is their docility in classrooms. While there are, of course, many exceptions, most high school students go along in an unchallenging way with their school's routines. They expect to be entertained as well. Too many are not intellectually engaged, and their ultimate performance, particularly in complex reasoning skills, shows it. However, given the structure of high schools and the loads which most teachers carry, "engaging" students in the academic realm is often very difficult to accomplish. Many students, however, colorfully engage in extracurricular and social realms. The contrast between their behavior in class and outside of it is marked.

• The high school curriculum is overloaded and unwisely values mere coverage more than mastery of intellectual skills. Its division into academic subjects, while hallowed by age and tradition, functions poorly.

• The quality of professional staff is higher than today's media would have us believe, but many teachers and principals are angry and frustrated. Many are also seriously underpaid.

• The current trend toward more centralized direction of schools increases staff demoralization and even lessens the opportunities for principals and teachers to adapt their programs to real and pressing local needs.

• Schools are largely judged on the basis of data which happens to be easy to collect and to manipulate statistically. Taken alone, such data can produce strikingly misleading assessments.

SOME RECOMMENDATIONS

Where does this lead us?

I ask that we consider a substantial restructuring of the high school. Big and politically risky though that task is, it is about time that we tackle it.

The current high school structure dates back to, and arises from, the beliefs of the 1890s. We've learned much and changed much since then, and we can do better than continuing to operate a school designed when Henry Ford's Model T was new.

First must come some changes in the ways that we look at the school and its mission. The metaphors we live by professionally are both subtle and deeply rooted. Altering them will take courage. For example, high school should not primarily be a place where adults "deliver a service" to adolescents. The key workers must be the students; only they can do the learning. We must stop thinking of ways to "give" or "present" material to kids and explore how we can *inspire* them to get it for themselves. The difference between "giving" and "inspiring" is crucial.

Another example is the dependence on "time spent" as the criterion for learning— "four credit hours of science," "two years of mathematics," "at least 180 days a year," "52,000 minutes per year." "Time spent" is but one factor in learning, and there are others, such as motivation and learning style, which are more important.

A further example is age grading. When we meet a youngster, the first question many of us ask him or her is what grade he or she is in. However, we all learn at different rates at different times; to assume all of us at fifteen

are essentially two years from completing secondary education is a serious oversimplification. On the contrary, we must take students where they are, not where somebody else's age-related norm says they should be.

Finally, we must be ready to look across the existing subjects of the curriculum and to find ways of reconstructing knowledge to most aptly conform to current scholarship, the way people learn, and the adolescents' world. Compartmentalization by English, mathematics, science, social studies, foreign language, physical education, et al. is not the most productive way of organizing a high school program. It will take an heroic leap for each of us to escape the entrapment of this manner of organization and the hold on us of our own disciplines.

In a word, we must get our minds open and make sure that the metaphors and constructs by which we live professionally can stand honest criticism.

Given such a frame of mind, what of the structure? There is no one detailed answer. It is no contradiction to say that each school should have its own ethos and individuality and that the structure of all schools should reflect a common set of essential principles. Common ends are desirable and so are appropriately differentiated means.

We should start defining these essentials, the principles by which new high schools can be structured:

1. *No one should enter high school-level studies who has not clearly mastered the basic educational requirements of a citizen in a democracy—literacy, numeracy, and civic understanding.*

These elementary studies should be provided free until each young person masters them. Attendance at school until that mastery is attained must be compulsory. Secondary school studies should focus on more advanced work. No citizen should be compelled to pursue these studies, but all citizens should be guaranteed free access to them for six years, to be taken at any point during their lives. (The practical effects of this will be that no student who does not want to attend will be in high school and that a student whose behavior unmistakably signals that he does not want to work at school can be expelled—with the clear understanding that he can return when he later gets his act together. The momentum of tradition, however, guarantees that most adolescents will attend school.)

2. *The high school should focus on helping adolescents to learn to use their minds.*

It should not attempt to be "comprehensive," but it can properly assist students in learning how to make decisions that arise in their private and work lives. (Technical, vocational, and career education for all Americans should be concentrated for citizens of all ages in special institutions, such as community colleges or existing, but expanded, vocational technical high schools. A cross-age mix of students will benefit all. Part-time enrollment should be encouraged.)

3. *The tone of the high school should be one of unanxious expectation.*

School should be a purposeful place, safe and focused on the tasks at hand. The primary burden for learning should be squarely on the students, and they and their families should be unequivocally clear about this. The school should consciously promote the virtues of *decency*; it should go to lengths to insist on fair, generous, and empathetic behavior.

4. *The diploma should be awarded only upon a student's exhibition of mastery of the high school's program.*

"Time served" and "credits earned" would disappear as criteria for performance. So would age-related promotion. An exhibition should be more than one paper-and-pencil test; there must be a variety of ways and times whereby each student can exhibit his or her mastery. (No practical task will be more diffi-

cult for school staff than designing and administering these exhibitions; none will be more important, as the exhibition will be a specific representation of the goals of the school. An excellent point of departure for construction of an exhibition can be the College Board's recent report, "Academic Preparation for College: What Students Need To Know and Be Able To Do." While prepared for the college bound, it can readily be adapted for all students.)

5. *The primary pedagogy of the high school should be "coaching,"* as defined by Mortimer Adler in his recent *Paideia Proposal.*

The critical intellectual skills that shape effective reasoning depend on this technique, and on sustained questioning. (One cannot *tell* a student to think deeply and inquire wisely; he or she has to learn it personally, albeit assisted by a critic-teacher.) Students should be helped to teach themselves (the practical effect of this policy will be to limit "coverage" of material. The resulting trade-off of breadth to depth is worthwhile: less is more).

6. *The program of study must be simple and universal.*

The complexity and confusion of the existing curriculum must be eased, in order to provide a setting where students can learn a few things well and learn how to learn. All students would be enrolled at all times in all areas, but the obvious need for variety and student choice would be accommodated *within* each of those areas. (A practical example of a simplified course of study is to cluster the curriculum, and its teachers, into but four areas: inquiry and expression, mathematics and science, literature and the arts, philosophy and history.)

7. *Teaching and learning must be personalized to the greatest extent possible.*

No high school teacher should have responsibility for more than eighty pupils. (The practical implications of this are radical, as most teachers today work with almost twice as many students. There are a variety of steps one can take to reduce the student-teacher ratio, such as increasing the percentage of adults in a school who are actively teaching, and expecting cross-subject instruction—one teacher working with 80 students in English and social studies rather than 160 in just one of these fields. There are extra benefits to be found in cross-subject teaching, and the risks can be minimized by team arrangements. The shift toward expecting students to teach themselves more—homework or independent study—can free class time now spent in lecturing, at least to some degree.)

Personalization is the only way to take advantage of our new understanding of differing learning styles. Again, the short-term cost may be to "coverage": the student may have to know fewer dates in history and fewer phyla in biology than heretofore. The long-term gains—in students' confidence, effectiveness, and ability to teach themselves—clearly outweigh the cost, however.

8. *Control of the detailed school program must be given to the principal and teachers at the level of each school.*

While the standards and shape of the culminating exhibitions may properly be largely in the hands of state or school district authorities, the design of the means to reach them must rest with those who best know each particular group of students. Centralized, standardized practice almost always leads to low standards; decentralized authority provokes commitment from school people on the firing line and increases the chances of wise response to the special needs and opportunities that each student has.

CONCLUSION

These eight principles represent a beginning. Many will find them genteel, elitist, and unrealistic. Visiting dozens of schools across this country, however, has convinced me that they

need be none of these things. The greatest insult to young citizens is to assign them to their "appropriate track" early in life (say at age fourteen). To give everyone a chance to learn to use her or his mind well is not gentility, but democracy. A focus on the mind is not elitism, but a necessity in a complex, turbulent culture and economy. It lies at the core of all careers.

An education in how to think rigorously and imaginatively is the ultimate modern vocational education. It is not unrealistic to find some students reacting poorly to academic teaching—because it is poor teaching. It is realistic to assert that there is an academic approach to every adolescent's motivation and learning style. As long as we give some things up in the existing school program, it is realistically possible to get faculty-student ratios down and to improve teacher salaries.

However, it may be unrealistic to think that many educators, students, parents, and school board members will accept our analysis to the degree necessary to attempt to create newly-structured high schools along these principles, ones which can be called Essential Schools. However, and at the same time, an honestly realistic person knows that some other commonly-accepted remedies—a few more dollars added to teachers' salaries, a year or two of this subject or that added to the diploma requirements, and competency tests for teachers—are not going to ignite the fire necessary to make our schools significantly more productive and effective.

Perhaps a middle ground can be found, with school boards and state authorities encouraging a number of communities to establish experimental Essential Schools and run them long enough to test them thoroughly. The best can ultimately serve as models.

America created in the 1890s the design for a secondary school which now is accepted worldwide. Do we have the courage, imagination, and idealism to shape a fresh design, one powerfully attuned to the 1990s?

TEACHING AND LEARNING: THE DILEMMA OF THE AMERICAN HIGH SCHOOL

CHESTER E. FINN, JR.

Chester E. Finn, Jr., formerly Professor of Education and Public Policy at Vanderbilt University, is Assistant Secretary for Educational Research and Improvement and Counselor to the Secretary in the United States Department of Education.

Besieged and benumbed as we already are by proliferating studies of American education, we might fairly wonder what could possibly justify another one. Yet even after nearly two years of commission reports, task forces, presidential hoopla, gubernatorial activism, and a thousand solemn conferences, Theodore Sizer's book is, initially, a refreshing addition to the literature.

For one thing, it acknowledges and celebrates the existence of private schools, institutions which educate more than four million children but which were banished from the pages of all the recent reports on education. For another thing, it is written primarily from the standpoint of the teacher and the student, rather than from atop some public-policy pinnacle, and its glimpses into actual schools and classrooms are far more realistic—and sympathetic—than those offered by the competition. What is more, the prose is brisk, clean, and nearly free of "educationese."

Unfortunately, it is also nearly free of educational content. As with a fizzy drink made from chemical sweeteners, the initial refreshment is not accompanied by much nutrition. The compromising Horace of the title turns out not to be the great Roman poet and satirist so well-remembered by veterans of fourth-year Latin, but one Horace Smith, a fifty-three-year-old suburban high-school English teacher who moonlights at a liquor store. His compromise—a real and painful one skillfully drawn by Sizer—is the balance he has struck between the bottomless instructional needs of his too numerous students and what he is able to supply within the constraints of fifty-minute periods and twenty-four-hour days. Horace is no loafer: as Sizer makes clear, he is in fact an exemplary teacher, severely limited in his pedagogical effectiveness by the circumstances within which he must function.

Such problems are real enough and deeply frustrating to the dedicated teacher. Five classes a day of thirty or so youngsters each; students who function at many different levels of ability, preparation, and motivation; short class periods punctuated by announcements, messengers, and record keeping—this can be pretty discouraging to the person who became an English instructor because he loved literature and wanted to initiate children into its joys.

We instinctively empathize with Horace and want to alter his school both so that he will be able to accomplish more and so that he and others like him will want to continue teaching, mindful as we are that the alterna-

From Chester E. Finn, Jr., "Teaching and Learning: The Dilemma of the American High School." Reprinted from *Commentary* 77 (May 1984): 64, 66, 68, 70, by permission; all rights reserved.

tive is a cadre of practitioners entering the classroom not because they love their subjects but because they weren't smart enough, ambitious enough, or well-enough educated to get better jobs.

But empathy is not enough. The book's troubles begin with the matter of exactly what Horace's students are supposed to end up knowing. What should be the content of a good secondary education? This is never a trivial question, and especially not at the present time, when the intense interest being paid to school reform by governors, legislators, boards of regents, business leaders, even university presidents, has created a rare opportunity to turn the smorgasbord of elective courses in family living and revolutionary movements into some semblance of an orderly curriculum.

Yet Sizer declines to prescribe content. Worse, he comes very close to arguing that the choice of content does not really much matter, that any book or fact or problem or event is as suitable as any other—at least in the hands of a gifted teacher—for coaching an eager pupil in the necessary intellectual plays.

Horace's Compromise is indeed splendid on "cognitive skills," both the simple ones (decoding words on a page, handling number problems) and the important advanced ones like abstract reasoning, clear exposition, and analysis. It borrows heavily from Mortimer Adler's *The Paideia Proposal* and displays comparable sophistication about the nature of various intellectual processes and the pedagogical approaches most apt to develop them. Anyone successfully completing the required part of a secondary education designed by Theodore Sizer would have gained a lot more skills than most high school students acquire today, and would in that sense be better prepared to cope with the challenges of further education and of modern life.

But he would know very little about the society he was entering, about its heritage, its works of art, its internal tensions or its external threats. He would have acquired little or none of what E. D. Hirsch, Jr., has termed "cultural literacy."

This bobtailed education results from an insidious combination: Sizer's beatification of pedagogy itself—the act of teaching—together with a relative indifference to curriculum content, and his minimalist view of "the essential claims of the state" with respect to education. Those claims, he insists, are precisely three: literacy, numeracy, and "civic understanding," the last a welcome addition here defined as "a grasp of the basis for consensual democratic government, a respect for its processes, and acceptance of the restraints and obligations incumbent on a citizen." But that is as far as Sizer goes, at least in compulsory education. "Once those minima are demonstrably reached," he says, "the state has no right whatsoever to compel a citizen to attend school" or "to compel her or him to learn anything else." All subsequent education would thus be voluntary—available, even enticing, but optional.

This vision is as audaciously attractive as it is outrageously inadequate. It may be possible to shrink most of the problems that beset American secondary education by eliminating all youngsters who meet Sizer's "minima" and thereupon decide they have had enough of schooling. And there is no denying that too many people today—working in offices, wandering the streets, and sitting in college classrooms, as well as those still in school—never do attain minimum levels of much of anything. But do the "claims" of society upon its children really stop short of Shakespeare, Emerson, and Frost, of Plato, Locke, and Marx, of Jefferson, Lincoln, and Roosevelt? Leaving aside entirely the demands of technological literacy and scientific competency, are we really prepared to conclude, with Sizer, that history, literature, and philosophy are, strictly speaking, electives, and that the entire heritage of Western civilization is merely an educational option, lying outside the domain of that which the society may reasonably oblige its youngest members to learn? Is it really an "abuse of state power," as Sizer suggests, to require teenagers not only to ponder the implications of the Bill of Rights (which he sensibly advises as a basic text for "civic understanding") but also to read a bit of Melville, a little Conrad, a smidgen of Longfellow, to examine the conceptions of justice and morality in *To Kill a Mockingbird* or the wellsprings of character in *Abe Lincoln Grows Up*?

To be sure, Sizer does not rule out the possibility of such study. He merely excludes it from the compulsory part of education. In truth, his idealized high school, trimmed down to four departments, with far fewer students per teacher, and with the day vastly more flexible than at present, is a beguiling notion, as are his suggestions for the virtual exclusion of vocational training and the deemphasis on athletics and other extracurricular activities. Himself a historian, teacher, and former high school headmaster (as well as one-time dean of the Harvard Graduate School of Education), Sizer depicts a school that would be far more intellectually challenging than most are today. It would be a school populated by outstanding teachers free from the harassments of meddlesome administrators, and by motivated, spontaneously well-behaved students who have already acquired the essential skills and are continuing their studies because they want to.

Some critics have suggested that this imaginary school looks awfully like Phillips Academy, the superb private school that Sizer previously headed. The implication is that *Horace's Compromise* suffers from an advanced case of educational elitism. In fact, I believe, the opposite may be more true: the book reflects an extraordinarily optimistic, even romantic, neoprogressivism that is

slightly reminiscent of A. S. Neill and Summerhill. Sizer appears to believe both that youngsters will only learn that which they want to learn when they are motivated to learn it *and* that, given the right institutional circumstances, practically all youngsters will eventually want to learn practically everything that adults might want them to.

Sizer's feeling for adolescents is deep and sensitive, and his portraits of them as individuals are vivid and affectionate. He correctly points out that a number of schools, blindly following regulations specifying what must be "covered" in which courses, engage in the utter folly—and unintentional cruelty—of handing an 800-page world history textbook to "Dennis," a tenth grader who has never really learned to read; that many a "Miss Romagna" never engage the intellectual participation of "Melissa"; and that it is far too common for "Mr. Brody," slightly intimidated by his students, to enter into a "conspiracy for the least" with them, whereby the teacher makes practically no demands and in return the youngsters refrain from hassling him. But the assumption that seems to underlie the entire book is that (except for those pupils with chronic discipline problems, whom Sizer rightly insists be sent out of school) the institutional arrangements of the high school should accommodate themselves to the impulses and anxieties of the teenage population rather than the knowledge and priorities of the adults who presumably have something to teach. Sizer is ostentatiously nonjudgmental about the students, reporting calmly on his observation of drug deals, libidinous displays, even some ugly peer behavior, in the schools he has visited. The only adolescent trait he explicitly condemns is "docility."

Since the dawn of the twentieth century, American education has been riven by two competing approaches: molding the child to the standards and expectation of the school, or shaping the school to the interest and enthusiasms of the student. *Horace's Compromise* does not fall completely into the latter camp; indeed, one suspects that Horace Smith himself would be uncomfortable there. But it is there that the author's sincere reformist zeal appears to focus, and it is in this crucial respect that Sizer differs from the National Commission on Excellence in Education, from most other contemporary school critics, and certainly from the lay boards and elected officials who are now striving to strengthen the educational systems of their states and communities.

Sizer, too, will have a chance to put his ideas into practice. He is moving to Brown University (an institution whose undergraduate curriculum is celebrated for its lack of requirements) to head the education department and, from that perch, to organize a network of public and private high schools that will voluntarily transform themselves into places where Horace will have to make fewer and less painful compromises. We should wish Sizer and Horace Smith well. We should even consider sending our children to their schools, for the teaching there will be superb and the students will all be eager. But will any of them be motivated to read the poems written two millennia ago by the other Horace? And if not, will any of them be obliged to do so, on the grounds that there are some things every educated person ought to know?

DISCUSSION QUESTIONS AND ACTIVITIES _____

1. According to Sizer, what common structures are found in American high schools? How well do these structures serve their purposes?

2. Why is compartmentalization not the most productive way of organizing a high school program, and what can be done to change it?

3. Why does Sizer believe that the secondary school should focus on advanced work and that no student should be compelled to attend? Explain why you agree or disagree.

4. Sizer says that "school should be a purposeful place, safe and focused on the tasks at hand." Is this not a description of most schools?

5. Do you believe that the curriculum can be successfully clustered into the four areas Sizer enumerates?

6. Does Sizer offer a realistic plan for reducing the total number of students for which each high school teacher has responsibility?

7. Does Sizer fail to prescribe the content of a good secondary school education?

8. Finn, while applauding Sizer's curriculum for teaching valuable skills, warns that, in Sizer's plan, the "entire heritage of Western civilization is merely an educational option." Is Finn's statement accurate?

9. More surprisingly, Finn claims that Sizer's plan is not elitist (as some critics have suggested) but is in the romantic, neoprogressive vein reminiscent of Summerhill. Is this an accurate interpretation?

10. Finn believes that there are some things that every educated person ought to know. Does Sizer? Do you?

11. Compare Sizer's plans with those of Boyer (chapter 1) and Adler (chapter 3).

12. See if you can locate schools that have adopted Sizer's plan and develop a report on your findings.

SUGGESTED READINGS

Works by Theodore R. Sizer

The Age of the Academies (editor). New York: Bureau of Publications, Teachers College, Columbia University, 1964.

"High School Reform and the Reform of Teacher Education." *Journal of Teacher Education* 38 (January–February 1987): 28–34.

Horace's Compromise: The Dilemma of the American High School. Boston: Houghton Mifflin, 1984.

Places for Learning, Places for Joy. Cambridge, Mass.: Harvard University Press, 1973.

"Rebuilding: First Steps by the Coalition of Essential Schools." *Phi Delta Kappan* 68 (September 1986): 38–42.

Religion and Public Education (editor). Boston: Houghton Mifflin, 1967.

A Review and Comment on National Reports: Perspectives. Reston, Va.: National Association of Secondary School Principals, 1983.

Secondary Schools at the Turn of the Century. New Haven, Conn.: Yale University Press, 1964.

"A Visit to an Essential School." *School Administrator* 45 (November 1988): 18–19.

CHAPTER 3

THE PAIDEIA PROPOSAL

Since the philosophy of perennialism underlies Mortimer Adler's educational proposals, a word about that philosophy is in order. Adler holds that there are absolute truths and values that are knowable, many of which are expressed in the *Great Books of the Western World*. The ultimate ends of education are the same for all persons at all times and everywhere; these ends are absolute and universal principles. The ultimate ends are the first principles, and the means in general are the secondary principles.

The problems of education are both theoretical and practical. A theoretical question is one that inquires about the nature of things, as in educational science and history. A practical question asks what should be done. Practical questions have three levels: the first and most specific is practice, which deals with particular cases; the second is policy, which pertains to a class of cases in which rules can be formulated; and the third is the principles, which deal with universals or all cases (the realm of educational philosophy).

Education, for Adler, is a process by which the abilities of human beings are perfected through artistically developed good habits. Education is a cooperative enterprise, and no person can completely educate himself or herself. In other words, the infant is dependent upon adults—learning skills are initially acquired from others.

Adler envisions the goals of schooling to be the same for all students. This rests on his view of human nature: human beings are essentially rational creatures, and rationality is not only a distinguishing trait (from animals) but also one of their best traits. Rationality needs systematic attention and cultivation; this can best be done under a plan of systematic schooling.

Adler's Paideia Proposal provides a more tangible grounding for his educational thought in a specific curriculum. His curriculum consists of three divisions: the first is devoted to acquiring knowledge in three subject areas, the second is designed to develop intellectual skills of learning, and the third is devoted to enlarging the understanding of ideas and values. Different methods of instruction are employed in each division.

The Paideia Proposal differs from others studied in a number of ways: same goals for all students, a required curriculum through twelve grades (except with respect to a second language), and three distinct modes of teaching and learning. Both the common goals and the required curriculum for all are based on Adler's view of a common human nature and the importance of a basic body of knowledge and truth, whereas the three modes of teaching and learning stem from a conviction about the different forms of knowledge and how they can best be understood. Subject matter studied is good not only for its own sake but also for the development of intellectual abilities. The underlying conviction is that equal opportunity is provided by maintaining a quality education for all based on high intellectual standards.

THE PAIDEIA PROPOSAL: REDISCOVERING THE ESSENCE OF EDUCATION

MORTIMER ADLER

Mortimer Jerome Adler (b. 1902) was awarded the Ph.D. by Columbia University and taught at that institution, the University of Chicago, and was a visiting lecturer at St. John's College. It was at the University of Chicago, in conjunction with Robert Maynard Hutchins, that he developed the Great Books program. Professor Adler has been Director of the Institute of Philosophical Research since 1952. Since 1966 he has served as Director of Editorial Planning of the fifteenth edition of Encyclopedia Britannica *and has been Chairman of the Board of Editors since 1974. Since 1945 he has been Associate Editor of the* Great Books of the Western World *and in 1952 developed its Syntopicon. Professor Adler is author and coauthor of more than thirty books, ranging from religious to scientific studies. Philosophically, he is one of the leading perennialists.*

In the first eighty years of this century, we have met the obligation imposed on us by the principle of equal educational opportunity, but only in a quantitative sense. Now, as we approach the end of the century, we must achieve equality in qualitative terms.

This means a completely one-track system of schooling. It means, at the basic level, giving all the young the same kind of schooling, whether or not they are college bound.

We are aware that children, although equal in their common humanity and fundamental human rights, are unequal as individuals, differing in their capacity to learn. In addition, the homes and environments from which they come to school are unequal—either predisposing the child for schooling or doing the opposite.

Consequently, the Paideia Proposal, faithful to the principles of equal educational opportunity, includes the suggestion that inequalities due to environmental factors must be overcome by some form of preschool preparation—at least one year for all and two or even three for some. (See definition and list of participants on page 45.) We know that to make such preschool tutelage compulsory at the public expense would be tantamount to increasing the duration of compulsory schooling from twelve years to thirteen, fourteen, or fifteen years. Nevertheless, we think that this preschool adjunct to the twelve years of compulsory basic schooling is so important that some way must be found to make it available for all and to see that all use it to advantage.

THE ESSENTIALS OF BASIC SCHOOLING

The objectives of basic schooling should be the same for the whole school population. In our current two-track or multitrack system, the learning objectives are not the same for all. And even when the objectives aimed at those on the upper track are correct, the

From Mortimer Adler, "The Paideia Proposal: Rediscovering the Essence of Education." Reprinted, with permission, from *The American School Board Journal* (July 1982): 17–20. Copyright 1982, the National School Boards Association. All rights reserved.

course of study now provided does not adequately realize these correct objectives. On all tracks in our current system, we fail to cultivate proficiency in the common tasks of learning, and we especially fail to develop sufficiently the indispensable skills of learning.

The uniform objectives of basic schooling should be threefold. They should correspond to three aspects of the common future to which all the children are destined: (1) Our society provides all children ample opportunity for personal development. Given such opportunity, each individual is under a moral obligation to make the most of himself and his life. Basic schooling must facilitate this accomplishment. (2) All the children will become, when of age, full-fledged citizens with suffrage and other political responsibilities. Basic schooling must do everything it can to make them good citizens, able to perform the duties of citizenship with all the trained intelligence that each is able to achieve. (3) When they are grown, all (or certainly most) of the children will engage in some form of work to earn a living. Basic schooling must prepare them for this or that specific job while they are still in school.

To achieve these three objectives, the character of basic schooling must be general and liberal. It should have a single, required, twelve-year course of study for all, with no electives except one—an elective choice with regard to a second language, to be selected from such modern languages as French, German, Italian, Spanish, Russian, and Chinese. The elimination of all electives, with this one exception, excludes what *should* be excluded—all forms of specialization, including particularized job training.

In its final form, the Paideia Proposal will detail this required course of study, but I will summarize the curriculum here in its bare outline. It consists of three main columns of teaching and learning, running through the

twelve years and progressing, of course, from the simple to the more complex, from the less difficult to the more difficult, as the students grow older. Understand: The three columns (see chart below) represent three distinct modes of teaching and learning. They do not represent a series of courses. A specific course or class may employ more than one mode of teaching and learning, but all three modes are essential to the overall course of study.

The first column is devoted to acquiring knowledge in three subject areas: (A) language, literature, and the fine arts; (B) mathematics and natural science; (C) history, geography, and social studies.

The second column is devoted to developing the intellectual skills of learning. These include all the language skills necessary for thought and communication—the skills of reading, writing, speaking, listening. They also include mathematical and scientific skills; the skills of observing, measuring, estimating, and calculating; and skills in the use of the computer and of other scientific instruments. Together, these skills make it possible to think clearly and critically. They once were called the liberal arts—the intellectual skills indispensable to being competent as a learner.

The third column is devoted to enlarging the understanding of ideas and values. The materials of the third column are books (*not* textbooks), and other products of human artistry. These materials include books of every variety—historical, scientific, and philosophical as well as poems, stories, and essays—and also individual pieces of music, visual art, dramatic productions, dance productions, film or television productions. Music and works of visual art can be used in seminars in which ideas are discussed; but as with poetry and fiction, they also are to be experienced aesthetically, to be enjoyed and admired for their excellence. In this connection, exercises in the composition of poetry, music, and visual works and in the production of dramatic

The Paideia Curriculum. *know what*   *know how & think clearly*

	COLUMN ONE	COLUMN TWO *critically*	COLUMN THREE
Goals	Acquisition of Organized Knowledge	Development of Intellectual Skills and Skills of Learning	Improved Understanding of Ideas and Values
	by means of	by means of	by means of
Means *lecture*	Didactic Instruction, Lecturing, and Textbooks	Coaching, Exercises, and Supervised Practice	Maieutic or Socratic Questioning and Active Participation *philosophical*
	in these three subject areas	in these operations	in these activities
Subject Areas, Operations, and Activities	Language, Literature, and Fine Arts Mathematics and Natural Science History, Geography, and Social Studies	Reading, Writing, Speaking, Listening, Calculating, Problem Solving, Observing, Measuring, Estimating, Exercising Critical Judgment	Discussion of Books (Not Textbooks) and Other Works of Art Involvement in Music, Drama, and Visual Arts

The three columns do not correspond to separate courses, nor is one kind of teaching and learning necessarily confined to any one class. *(thought & communication)*

works should be used to develop the appreciation of excellence.

The three columns represent three different kinds of learning on the part of the student and three different kinds of instruction on the part of teachers.

In the first column, the students are engaged in acquiring information and organized knowledge about nature, man, and human society. The method of instruction here, using textbooks and manuals, is didactic. The teacher lectures, invites responses from the students, monitors the acquisition of knowledge, and tests that acquisition in various ways.

In the second column, the students are engaged in developing habits of performance, which is all that is involved in the development of an art or skill. Art, skill, or technique is nothing more than a cultivated, habitual ability to do a certain kind of thing well, whether that is swimming and dancing, or reading and writing. Here, students are acquiring linguistic, mathematical, scientific, and historical *know-how* in contrast to what they acquire in the first column, which is *know-that* with respect to language, literature, and the fine arts, mathematics and science, history, geography, and social studies. Here, the method of instruction cannot be didactic or monitorial; it cannot be dependent on textbooks. It must be coaching, the same kind used in the gym to develop bodily skills; only here it is used by a different kind of coach in the classroom to develop intellectual skills.

In the third column, students are engaged in a process of enlightenment, the process whereby they develop their understanding of the basic and controlling ideas in all fields of subject matter and come to appreciate better all the human values embodied in works of art. Here, students move progressively from understanding less to understanding more—understanding better what they already know and appreciating more what they already have experienced. Here, the method of instruction cannot be either didactic or coaching. It must be the Socratic, or maieutic, method of questioning and discussing. It should not occur in an ordinary classroom with the students sitting in rows and the teacher in front of the class, but in a seminar room, with the students sitting around a table and the teacher sitting with them as an equal, even though a little older and wiser.

Of these three main elements in the required curriculum, the third column is completely innovative. Nothing like this is done in our schools, and because it is completely absent from the ordinary curriculum of basic schooling, the students never have the experience of having their minds addressed in a challenging way or of being asked to think about important ideas, to express their thoughts to defend their opinions in a reasonable fashion.

The only thing that is innovative about the second column is the insistence that the method of instruction here must be coaching carried on either with one student at a time or with very small groups of students. Nothing else can be effective in the development of a skill, be it bodily or intellectual. The absence of such individualized coaching in our schools explains why most of the students cannot read well, write well, speak well, listen well, or perform well any of the other basic intellectual operations.

The three columns are closely interconnected and integrated, but the middle column—the one concerned with linguistic, mathematical, and scientific skills—is central. It both supports and is supported by the other two columns. All the intellectual skills with which it is concerned must be exercised in the study of the three basic subject-matters and in acquiring knowledge about them, and these intellectual skills must be exercised in the seminars devoted to the discussion of books and other things.

In addition to the three main columns in the curriculum ascending through the twelve years of basic schooling, there are three adjuncts: One is twelve years of physical training, accompanied by instruction in bodily care and hygiene. The second, running through something less than twelve years, is the development of basic manual skills, such as cooking, sewing, carpentry, and the operation of all kinds of machines. The third, reserved for the last year or two, is an introduction to the whole world of work—the range of occupations in which human beings earn their livings. This is not particularized job training. It is the very opposite. It aims at a broad understanding of what is involved in working for a living and of the various ways in which that can be done. If, at the end of twelve years, students wish training for specific jobs, they should get that in two-year community or junior colleges, or on the job itself, or in technical institutes of one sort or another.

Everything that has not been specifically mentioned as occupying the time of the school day should be reserved for after hours and have the status of extracurricular activities.

Please note: The required course of study just described is as important for what it *displaces* as for what it introduces. It displaces a multitude of elective courses, especially those offered in our secondary schools, most of which make little or no contribution to general, liberal education. It eliminates all narrowly specialized job training, which now abounds in our schools. It throws out of the curriculum and into the category of optional extracurricular activities a variety of things that have little or no educational value.

If it did not call for all these displacements, there would not be enough time in the school day or year to accomplish everything that is essential to the general, liberal learning that must be the content of basic schooling.

THE QUINTESSENTIAL ELEMENT

So far, I have set forth the bare essentials of the Paideia Proposal with regard to basic schooling. I have not yet mentioned the quintessential element—the sine qua non—without which nothing else can possibly come to fruition, no matter how sound it might be in principle. The heart of the matter is the quality of learning and the quality of teaching that occupies the school day, not to mention the quality of the homework after school.

First, the learning must be active. It must use the whole mind, not just the memory. It must be learning by discovery, in which the student, never the teacher, is the primary agent. Learning by discovery, which is the only genuine learning, may be either unaided or aided. It is unaided only for geniuses. For most students, discovery must be aided.

Here is where the teachers come in—as aids in the process of learning by discovery not as knowers who attempt to put the knowledge they have into the minds of their students. The quality of the teaching, in short, depends crucially upon how the teacher conceives his role in the process of learning, and that must be as an aid to the student's process of discovery.

I am prepared for the questions that must be agitating you by now: How and where will we get the teachers who can perform as teachers should? How will we be able to staff the program with teachers so trained that they will be competent to provide the quality of instruction required for the quality of learning desired?

The first part of our answer to these questions is negative: We *cannot* get the teachers we need for the Paideia program from schools of education *as they are now constituted*. As teachers are now trained for teaching, they simply will not do. The ideal—an impracticable ideal—would be to ask for teachers who are, themselves, truly educated human beings.

But truly educated human beings are too rare. Even if we could draft all who are now alive, there still would be far too few to staff our schools.

Well, then, what can we look for? Look for teachers who are actively engaged in the process of *becoming* educated human beings, who are themselves deeply motivated to develop their own minds. Assuming this is not too much to ask for the present, how should teachers be schooled and trained in the future? First, they should have the same kind of basic schooling that is recommended in the Paideia Proposal. Second, they should have additional schooling, at the college and even the university level, in which the same kind of general, liberal learning is carried on at advanced levels—more deeply, broadly, and intensively than it can be done in the first twelve years of schooling. Third, they must be given something analogous to the clinical experience in the training of physicians. They must engage in practice teaching under supervision, which is another way of saying that they must be *coached* in the arts of teaching, not just given didactic instruction in educational psychology and in pedagogy. Finally, and most important of all, they must learn how to teach well by being exposed to the performances of those who are masters of the arts involved in teaching.

It is by watching a good teacher at work that they will be able to perceive what is involved in the process of assisting others to learn by discovery. Perceiving it, they must then try to emulate what they observe, and through this process they slowly will become good teachers themselves.

The Paideia Proposal recognizes the need for three different kinds of institutions at the collegiate level: The two-year community or junior college should offer a wide choice of electives that give students some training in one or another specialized field, mainly those fields of study that have something to do with earning a living. The four-year college also should offer a wide variety of electives, to be chosen by students who aim at the various professional or technical occupations that require advanced study. Those elective majors chosen by students should be accompanied, for all students, by one required minor, in which the kind of general and liberal learning that was begun at the level of basic schooling is continued at a higher level in the four years of college. And we should have still a third type of collegiate institution—a four-year college in which general, liberal learning at a higher level constitutes a required course of study that is to be taken by all students. *It is this third type of college, by the way, that should be attended by all who plan to become teachers in our basic schools.*

At the university level, there should be a continuation of general, liberal learning at a still higher level to accompany intensive specialization in this or that field of science or scholarship, this or that learned profession. Our insistence on the continuation of general, liberal learning at all the higher levels of schooling stems from our concern with the worst cultural disease that is rampant in our society—*the barbarism of specialization.*

There is no question that our technologically advanced industrial society needs specialists of all sorts. There is no question that the advancement of knowledge in all fields of science and scholarship, and in all the learned professions, needs intense specialization. But for the sake of preserving and enhancing our cultural traditions, as well as for the health of science and scholarship, we need specialists who also are generalists—generally cultivated human beings, not just good plumbers. We need truly educated human beings who can perform their special tasks better precisely because they have general cultivation as well as intensely specialized training.

Changes indeed are needed in higher education, but those improvements cannot rea-

sonably be expected unless improvement in basic schooling makes that possible.

THE FUTURE OF OUR FREE INSTITUTIONS

I already have declared as emphatically as I know how that the quality of human life in our society depends on the quality of the schooling we give our young people, both basic and advanced. But a marked elevation in the quality of human life is not the only reason improving the quality of schooling is so necessary—not the only reason we must move heaven and earth to stop the deterioration of our schools and turn them in the opposite direction. The other reason is to safeguard the future of our free institutions.

They cannot prosper, they may not even survive, unless we do something to rescue our schools from their current deplorable deterioration. Democracy, in the full sense of that term, came into existence only in this century and only in a few countries on earth, among which the United States is an outstanding example. But democracy came into existence in this century only in its initial conditions, all of which hold out promises for the future that remain to be fulfilled. Unless we do something about improving the quality of basic schooling for all and the quality of advanced schooling for some, there is little chance that those promises ever will be fulfilled. And if they are not, our free institutions are doomed to decay and wither away.

We face many insistently urgent problems. Our prosperity and even our survival depend on the solution of those problems—the threat of nuclear war, the exhaustion of essential resources and of supplies of energy, the pollution or spoilage of the environment, the spiraling of inflation accompanied by the spread of unemployment.

To solve these problems, we need resourceful and innovative leadership. For that to arise and be effective, an educated populace is needed. Trained intelligence—not only on the part of leaders, but also on the part of followers—holds the key to the solution of the problems our society faces. Achieving peace, prosperity, and plenty could put us on the threshold of an early paradise. But a much better education system than now exists also is needed, for that alone can carry us across the threshold. Without it, a poorly schooled population will not be able to put to good use the opportunities afforded by the achievement of the general welfare. Those who are not schooled to enjoy society can only despoil its institutions and corrupt themselves.

Here's What Paideia Means

The Greek word *Paideia* (pronounced PIE-day-uh) means general, humanistic learning—the learning that should be the common possession of all human beings. That is why we adopted *Paideia* as the name for our project and our proposals.

The Paideia group has spent more than two years thinking about what must be done to rescue our schools from the anything-but-innocuous desuetude into which they have fallen. My summary of the Paideia Proposal in the accompanying article must necessarily omit many details. But I have tried to describe the essentials of our proposals for the reform of basic schooling.

The other participants in the Paideia project include the following:

Jacques Barzun, formerly provost of Columbia University, currently literary advisor of Charles Scribner's Sons;

Otto Bird, formerly head of the program of general studies, University of Notre Dame;

Leon Botstein, president of Bard College, Annandale-on-Hudson, New York;

Ernest Boyer, president of the Carnegie Foundation for the Advancement of Teaching, Washington, D.C.;

Nicholas Caputi, principal of Skyline High School, Oakland, California;

Douglass Cater, senior fellow of the Aspen (Colorado) Institute for Humanistic Studies;

Donald Cowan, formerly president of University of Dallas, and currently fellow of the Dallas Institute for Humanities and Culture;

Alonzo Crim, superintendent of schools, Atlanta;

Clifton Fadiman, director of the Council for Basic Education, Washington, D.C.;

Richard Hunt, director of program, Andrew W. Mellon Faculty Fellowships in the Humanities, Harvard University;

Ruth Love, superintendent of schools, Chicago;

James Nelson, director of the Wye Institute, Queenstown, Maryland;

James O'Toole, professor of management in the Graduate School of Business Administration University of Southern California, Los Angeles;

Theodore Puck, president of the Eleanor Roosevelt Institute for Cancer Research, Denver;

Adolph Schmidt, member of the Board of Visitors and Governors of St. John's College, Annapolis, Maryland;

Adele Simmons, president of Hampshire College, Amherst, Massachusetts;

Theodore Sizer, formerly headmaster of Phillips Academy, Andover;

and finally, my close associates at the Institute for Philosophical Research in Chicago, **Charles Van Doren, John Van Doren**, and **Geraldine Van Doren**.

THE PAIDEIA PROPOSAL: NOBLE AMBITIONS, FALSE LEADS, AND SYMBOLIC POLITICS

WILLIS D. HAWLEY

Willis D. Hawley is Dean and Professor of Political Science at George Peabody College for Teachers, Vanderbilt University. His articles have appeared in a number of education journals.

Any idea that has the support of both Mortimer Adler and Albert Shanker is an idea worth engaging and, some would say, worrying about. *The Paideia Proposal* enjoys the endorsement not only of these two luminaries but of people as diverse in background and commitments as Benjamin Mays, William Friday, Theodore Sizer, Ruth Love, Jacques Barzun, Alonzo Crim, Ernest Boyer, Clifton Fadiman, and Gus Tyler.* It has been the focus of national news magazines and TV talk shows. Bookstores in many parts of the country report that the attractive eighty-four-page "manifesto" is already sold out.

Interest in the Paideia group's proposal seems traceable to the growing national concern that our schools are not preparing our young people for the challenges of what Daniel J. Boorstin calls "the technological republic" and that this failure, especially when compared to the achievements of other nations, threatens our economic prosperity and even our national security.

The Paideia Proposal eloquently urges on us a single-track core curriculum for elementary and secondary schools and certain strategies for teaching those subjects. There is much to admire in the proposal. There is no question that we need to change the curriculum of American schools to make it more rigorous and to ensure attention to more advanced mathematics, science, and language competencies. And, it is surely time that we ask more of youngsters than we are asking and that we insist that the gaps in achievement among and within most schools be reduced dramatically. It is easy to identify with Mr. Adler and his colleagues in the Paideia group when they assert that we should insist on education of superior quality for all Americans, regardless of their social background.

As a call to renewed interest in the quality

From Willis D. Hawley, "The Paideia Proposal: Noble Ambitions, False Leads, and Symbolic Politics." Reprinted with permission from *EDUCATION WEEK,* Volume II, Number 12 (November 24, 1982).

*Benjamin Mays, president emeritus, Atlanta Board of Education; William Friday, president, University of North Carolina; Theodore R. Sizer, chairman, "A Study of High Schools" and former headmaster, Phillips Academy, Andover; Ruth B. Love, superintendent of schools, Chicago; Jacques Barzun, former provost of Columbia University, author, and critic; Alonzo Crim, superintendent, Atlantic Public Schools; Ernest L. Boyer, president, Carnegie Foundation for the Advancement of Teaching; Clifton Fadiman, author and critic; Gus Tyler, assistant president, International Ladies Garment Workers Union.

of our schools, as a stimulant to reexamine what is being taught, and as a challenge to expect more of our schools and of our young people, the Paideia Proposal contributes much to the growing demand for educational change. But as a guide to action, which it purports to be, the proposal leads us down primrose paths and away from the main roads we need to travel if we are to secure, as almost all now agree we must, higher quality education for all the nation's youngsters.

The Paideia Proposal is not a blueprint for a new structure within which we can bring about meaningful change in the effectiveness of our schools. Rather, it is an artist's rendering that pays little attention either to the terrain upon which the new structure will be built or to the practical problems of financing and construction.

Mr. Adler is impatient with those who charge that the proposal is impractical. He has been quoted as saying, "I don't see why our group, having come up with the proposal, should solve all the practical problems." Nice work, if you can get it. But one reason one might want to engage practicalities is that they often suggest important shortcomings of an idea. Educational reformers are well acquainted with windmills, and the lesson of past reform efforts is that the search for "a solution" or "an approach" is futile. If only it were as simple as deciding what it would be nice for everyone to know (which is, according to the Paideia Proposal, *everything* except vocation skills).

But the key to improving our schools is not curriculum reform. Americans have always sought a quick and simple fix to what they have perceived to be the problems of schools. However, meaningful changes will require that we undertake the complicated jobs of improving teaching, dealing with diversity, and ensuring effective management of resources. Better curricula will help, to be sure, but they are not *the* answer.

The inadequacies of our schools mirror the characteristics of our society. Dramatic inequalities of income, racial and social class discrimination, chronic unemployment in some sectors, and the historically low status of education are the causes, not the products, of schools' shortcomings.

The Paideia group's proposal fails us for at least three reasons: the idea of a core curriculum is not only impractical but educationally unsound; its attention to evidence about learning and school effectiveness seems nonexistent; and its emphasis on curriculum as the vehicle for change puts the cart before the horse and seems likely to direct attention away from more promising, but more complicated, solutions.

The single-track core curriculum proposed by Mr. Adler and his colleagues insists that all children learn the same things in schools. For example, all children are expected to know calculus. The first question is: Can all children learn—and become proficient in—the same subjects? It is one thing to say, as many scholars and educators now do, that almost all children can be expected to acquire certain knowledge and skills and to demonstrate reasonably high levels of achievement. It's quite another to neglect the reality that successful efforts to do this require heavy emphasis on a limited number of subjects and the adaptation of the pace and content of learning to the capabilities of students. Never mind that teachers do not know many of the things that the Paideia Proposal says students need to learn. Let me assert that a majority of the nation's brightest college students—or philosophers—could not employ calculus to solve a problem if their lives depended on it. Fortunately, few of us are in such mortal danger or ever will be. The Paideia group wants everyone to learn everything—our language, a foreign language, literature, fine arts, mathematics, natural science, history, geography, and social studies. On top of this, students will take twelve years of physical education as well as industrial arts; they will be involved in drama, music, and the visual arts; and they'll learn how to exercise critical and moral judgments. Let him or her among us . . . cast the first stone.

The second problem with the idea of a core curriculum is that it assumes that all students learn in the same way. What people can learn—even if they have the same capabilities—is related to what they want to learn and to differences in the ways they acquire, process, and integrate information. These differences in interest and "learning style" are affected not only by what goes on in schools, but by differences in genes and in home and community environments.

Third, the Paideia group's heavy emphasis on a core curriculum ascribes more importance to *what* one learns than to the acquisition of an ability to learn and a love of learning. In a society where the average person may change occupations five times and where the ability to use new information may be the most important determinant of success, our concept of what it means to be an educated person will need to change. It will be more important to be a learner than to be learned.

In dealing with the teaching and learning process, the Paideia Proposal imagines that one can divide the things to be learned into three classes and for each of these a particular pedagogical approach is most appropriate. No evidence is offered to support this important assertion. Research on effective teaching suggests that good teachers have a broad repertoire of teaching skills and that while teaching a given subject the teachers easily move from one to another in meeting the needs of their students.

Those who study how children learn will be surprised to find that lectures and description are strongly recommended teaching styles and that the group advocates "coaching" as the major way to ensure that children develop their intellectual skills.

To accept fully the argument of the Paideia group, educators would need to overlook much of the recent research on effective teaching and effective schools because that research directs the quest of better education to concerns largely unaddressed in the proposal.

The history of American education is replete with efforts to find, as the Stanford University scholar David Tyack has put it, the "one best system." We want desperately to make the big play that will, in itself, turn the game around. Whether it is desegregation, open classrooms, technology, or curriculum reform, we persist in searching for *the* solution. In many ways, curriculum reform is the most attractive strategy for change. It is easily explained, can be imposed from above (seemingly), is hard to argue against, and, if properly articulated, holds out hopes for great change. Everyone knows that a better cake can be had through a better recipe. But experience indicates that curriculum reform is illusory. The distance between mandating a curriculum and student learning is great indeed. The "new math," for example, stumbled on teacher incapacity and parental ignorance. The results of the more recent legislatively imposed requirements that economics (especially free enterprise) be taught in schools should provide no sense of security to those who worry about the collapse of our economy or the triumph of democratic socialism.

Curriculum reform is not only difficult to achieve at the classroom level, but the imposition of new structures lulls us into a sense of false security. As Soviet educators know, if people see everyone taking physics courses, they are less likely to ask whether students are learning about physics. And, as university professors know, if the curriculum is rigorous, the blame for student failure can be assigned to students.

The point here is the argument of Murray Edleman (professor of political science at the University of Wisconsin) that many public changes in structures can be thought of as symbolic politics. They create the illusion of real change, which, in turn, dampens the fires of reform and induces quiescence. The Paideia Proposal is patent medicine in this sense. Unfortunately, the formula that will improve the health of the body education is more complicated and, probably, more difficult to sell.

At best, this critique may seem like overkill to many. The goals of the Paideia group are noble ones, after all, and the proposal will surely encourage us to rethink what we are doing. Isn't it all right to set high goals and let others worry about whether it can really work? No, it is not.

First, to pursue the Holy Grail with no certainty of its powers and without a reasonably good map is not likely to be productive. Such a quest, instead, is likely to be frustrating and to engage energies that could be better spent on the pursuit of more promising ways to improve American education.

Second, we have substantially increased our knowledge about effective teaching and effective schools, and it seems important to pursue the directions suggested by this relatively recent research. Some school systems are now engaging successfully in such pursuits, though they are certainly less dramatic than the steps the Paideia group would have us take.

Third, a major obstacle to securing an educational system that produces high academic achievement among all youngsters is the social and economic inequality that distinguishes the United States from most other industrialized nations. The relationship between family income and academic performance is powerful. The Paideia Proposal takes note of this fact by urging a system of preschool education, but it does not emphasize this strategy nor does it recognize that persistent efforts to ex-

pand publicly supported, early-childhood programs, which now serve less than one-third of the children who are legally eligible for (much less need) such services, have been unsuccessful. Nor does the Paideia Proposal grapple with the fact that differences in the wealth of the haves and the have-nots is growing and that the proportion of school children from families *below* the median income is rising. It is not enough to hold high hopes.

A growing body of knowledge about teaching and learning suggests directions for change that can increase the academic achievement of students from different backgrounds. A strategy for change must be of many parts. A core curriculum, much less one taught in specified ways, does not emerge from the accumulated knowledge as a strategy that has worked or is likely to work in the United States.

Instead, the research tells us, among other things, that student learning is fostered by engaging students in intensive success-bringing learning experiences, by using interactive teaching strategies, by refocusing the principal's efforts on instructional support, by restructuring decision making at the school level, by adapting the curriculum to student needs while insisting on high performance and steady progress, by creating school climates that emphasize academic achievement, by promoting change from the bottom up, and by encouraging stability in interpersonal contacts and curricula.

This is not an exhaustive list of promising strategies for school improvement. And, to be sure, we need to know more. But now that we are beginning both to understand systematically how to meet effectively the very diverse needs of students and to have the ability to learn more, it is time to put that knowledge and capacity to work.

There is in the land a sense that the improvement of our schools is not only necessary but possible. But failure to recognize that low achievement is critically related to poverty, to racial, class, and ethnic discrimination, and to the prospect of unemployment upon graduation is a form of national self-delusion. Changes in our educational system could improve the education of almost all children. But even if we make substantial progress in what and how we teach, the fundamental inequalities of income, status, and opportunities created by our economic, political, and social systems make it very unlikely that we will achieve equal outcomes for all.

DISCUSSION QUESTIONS AND ACTIVITIES

1. Does quality education require a one-track system of schooling?

2. How would some of the larger environmental inequalities be overcome in the Paideia Proposal?

3. What is the rationale for a single, required, twelve-year course of study for all?

4. Examine the three broad divisions of the curriculum. What features do you consider necessary? What needs to be added?

5. Adler's curriculum displaces many elective courses presently found in schools, specialized job training, and optional extracurricular activities. Explain why you agree or disagree with him over this decision.

6. Is Adler's plan adequate for selecting and preparing qualified teachers to staff his program?

7. In contrast to Adler, Hawley claims that the key to school improvement is not curriculum reform. What, then, is the key?

8. Can all students learn and become proficient in the same subject?

9. Does the Paideia Proposal assume that all students learn in the same way? Does it also emphasize what one learns more than acquiring an ability to learn and developing a love of learning?

10. What recent findings from research about teaching and learning does the Paideia Proposal neglect?

11. Make a survey of present school systems for programs similar to the Paideia Proposal, and evaluate their success.

12. Explain the recent history of American education for similar programs. Trace and appraise their progress.

13. Organize a classroom debate of the Paideia Proposal and the perennialist philosophy on which it rests.

SUGGESTED READINGS

Works by Mortimer Adler

Adler has written more than thirty books and numerous articles. Listed below are his more important publications about education. See *Books in Print* for his other works.

A General Introduction to the Great Books and to a Liberal Education. Chicago: Encyclopedia Britannica, 1954. (with Peter Wolff)

A Guidebook for Learning: For the Lifelong Pursuit of Wisdom. New York: Macmillan, 1988.

"In Defense of the Philosophy of Education." In *Forty-first Yearbook of the National Society for the Study of Education*, pt. I. Edited by Nelson B. Henry. Chicago: University of Chicago Press, 1942, 197–249.

How to Read a Book, rev. ed. New York: Simon & Schuster, 1972. (with Charles Van Doren)

How to Speak, How to Listen. New York: Macmillan, 1985.

Paideia Problems and Possibilities. New York: Macmillan, 1983.

The Paideia Proposal. New York: Macmillan, 1982.

Philosopher at Large: An Intellectual Autobiography. New York: Macmillan, 1977.

Reforming Education. New York: Macmillan, 1989.

Reforming Education in America. Boulder, Colo.: Westview Press, 1977.

The Revolution in Education. Chicago: The University of Chicago Press, 1958.

Works about the Paideia Proposal and Mortimer Adler's Educational Philosophy

Arnold, Genevieve, and others. "Introducing the Wednesday Revolution." *Educational Leadership* 45 (April 1988): 48.

Aubrey, R. F. "Reform in Schooling: Four Proposals on an Educational Quest." *Journal of Counseling and Development* 63 (December 1984): 204–213.

Blank, Kermit J. "The Paideia Proposal: Adler's Sugar-Coated Elitism?" *Tennessee Education* 13 (Winter 1984): 10–16.

Childs, John L. *Education and Morals.* New York: Appleton-Century-Crofts, 1950, ch. 5. A critique of perennialism.

Delattre, E. J. "The Paideia Proposal and American Education." Eighty-Third Yearbook, pt. II, National Social Studies Education, 1984, 143–153.

Gilli, A. C. "The Role of Vocational Studies and Training in General-Liberal School." *Journal of Industrial Teacher Education* 21 (Spring 1984): 13–24.

Gregory, Marshall W. "A Response to Mortimer Adler's 'Paideia Proposal'." *Journal of General Education* 36, no. 2 (1984): 70–78. A critique.

Hook, Sidney. *Education for Modern Man*, enlarged ed. New York: Knopf, 1963, ch. 3. A critique of perennialism.

Johnson, T. W. "Classicists versus Experimentalists: Reexamining the Great Debate." *Journal of General Education* 36, no. 4 (1985): 270–278.

Laub-Novak, Karen. "The Habits of Art." *Momentum* 17 (September 1986): 25–28. A critique.

Ravitch, Diane, and others. "The Paideia Proposal: A Symposium." *Harvard Educational Review* 53 (November 1983): 377–411.

Smith, Philip L., and Rob Traver. "Program and Prophecy: The Fate of General Studies in Teacher Education." *Educational Theory* 53 (Spring 1983): 73–77.

Socha, Thomas Joseph. "The Paideia Proposal: Implications and Challenges for Communication Instruction." *Journal of Speech Communication* 17 (Spring 1985): 35–44.

Spear, Karen. "The 'Paideia Proposal': The Problem of Means and Ends in General Education." *Journal of General Education* 35, no. 2 (1984): 79–86. A critique.

CHAPTER 4

CULTURAL LITERACY

Public concern about the decline of basic skills has led to the back-to-basics movement. The concern of E. D. Hirsch, Jr., led to his devising a "cultural literacy" approach to learning in his book by that title. He believes that only two-thirds of American citizens are literate, and even among the literate the average level should be raised because it is too low. Cultural literacy, he claims, is more than a skill; it requires large amounts of specific information. Literacy involves not only reading and writing but also effective use of the standard literate language for the purpose of fostering effective nationwide communications. The reading level of a person varies from task to task and depends upon the information processed. Any reader who lacks the knowledge assumed in the selection will be illiterate in that piece of writing. Cultural literacy lies in a middle ground between the everyday levels of knowledge everyone possesses and the knowledge of experts. It includes information that we expect children to gain in school, but they no longer do.

What should be done about these deficiencies? Hirsch believes that literate culture needs to be made known to those who lack it. Traditional literate knowledge would be taught not just as a series of terms but as a system of shared associations. Hirsch and his colleagues have initiated the first steps by providing a list of terms that every American needs to know and by developing tests of general knowledge.

In Hirsch's selection, he outlines the characteristics and rationale for cultural literacy. Thomas Estes, Carol Gutman, and Elise Harrison believe that Hirsch has neglected the importance of constructing meaning and overlooks that students will not remember what they do not understand.

E. D. HIRSCH, JR.

CULTURAL LITERACY: LET'S GET SPECIFIC

E. D. Hirsch, Jr., is William R. Kenan Professor of English at the University of Virginia. He is a graduate of Cornell and Yale Universities, is a member of the American Academy of Arts and Sciences, has held various fellowships, and is President of the Cultural Literacy Foundation.

Let me begin by quoting a letter from a teacher. It is typical of many letters I have received from experienced educators about my book, *Cultural Literacy.*

> *Dear Mr. Hirsch,*
>
> *When I read the first chapter of your book,* Cultural Literacy, *I thought I was hearing a voice from the past—mine—telling everyone I could that what was holding many children back in their reading comprehension was a lack of background information. This hit me over and over again during the years I was a special reading teacher for middle school students in Baltimore City and Baltimore County—both in the inner-city ghetto and in the suburbs.*
>
> *Most of the time I was working with students of average or above-average intelligence. They were usually two or more years behind in their reading grade levels. Except for dyslectic children, many of these children were capable of decoding most of the words they had to read. Day after day children would be confused by terms and concepts that one would expect them to know.*
>
> *I, too, became aware that at the third-grade level, most of the children I had to work with had been reading at or near grade level. When they were retested at the fifth-grade level, they had already fallen behind.*
>
> *I retired from teaching eight years ago, but during the past two years I have been doing some volunteer tutoring, primarily with fifthgraders, at an elementary school near my home. I still find the same deficit—a lack of background information.*
>
> *I agree with you that it is necessary to tackle this problem when the children are very young. It is almost impossible to catch up when the children are in middle school.*

I start off by quoting this person's letter on the assumption that members of the NEA might find the view of an experienced reading teacher more persuasive than the abstract reading research that I cited in the second chapter of my book, or than the ivy-tower pronouncements of a university professor. But sound research and experience always coincide, and I wrote *Cultural Literacy* not from my ivy-tower perch as an English professor but as a parent and a citizen. I began with the premise that achieving functional literacy for all citizens should be the primary focus of educational reform in this country. The evidence is clear that our national literacy has been declining not only among disadvantaged children but also among our top students.

This has been happening at a time in the technological era when truly functional literacy has become ever more important for achieving a wide range of national goals—

From E. D. Hirsch, Jr., "Cultural Literacy: Let's Get Specific," *NEA Today* 6 (January 1988): 15–21. Reprinted with permission.

from promoting social justice to attaining a productive economy and maintaining an effective military.

DEFINING LITERACY

Undoubtedly these reasons for giving functional literacy a top priority are well known to all members of NEA. The theme that my book introduces into the discussion is in its insistence that functional literacy depends on readers' acquiring specific information and associations that can be taken for granted in written and spoken communications. Literacy is far more than the ability to call out words from a page. Functional literacy requires a knowledge of shared, taken-for-granted information that is neither set down on the page nor explicitly stated in oral communications. It provides the necessary frame of reference by which literate people understand the content of their reading. I argue that the core elements of this necessary background knowledge can be identified and systematically taught to all students. If that is done, Americans can and will achieve the functional literacy that is a necessary foundation for further educational, economic, and social improvements.

The book also shows that the chief cause of the recent decline in functional literacy has been the use of "skills-oriented," "relevant" materials in elementary and secondary grades. The disappearance from the early curriculum of traditional literate culture (history, myth, and literature) has been a mistake of monumental proportions. Publishers have been constantly "updating" the content that young children are taught, under the theory that modern, relevant materials will be of greater interest to children and will better teach them the skills of literacy than traditional materials. This theory assumes that reading, writing, and oral communication are formal skills rather than acquired abilities based on specific infor-

mation. Unfortunately, the theory that reading and writing are formal skills is an empirically unsound theory that has had disastrous consequence for national literacy.

Instead of trying to overhaul or update the core content of literate culture—something that cannot be done—publishers and schools should devote their energies to improving the effectiveness with which core literate content is presented. That content is highly stable. Yet most reviews of my book have failed to notice that its third chapter, which explains the stability of literate culture, is probably its most important contribution. The chapter shows why many facts, myths, and stories that were common knowledge a hundred years ago remain common knowledge among literate people today. Later on in this article, I will mention some of the technical reasons for this inherent conservatism of literate culture.

Of course, new material is constantly being added to literate culture. Many of its elements do and should change. History goes on. We try to make moral progress; we have successfully expanded our traditional materials to include the contributions of minorities. But the facts, myths, and stories that belong at the core of literate culture have remained and will continue to remain highly stable. Literate culture does not care a fig about either the exigencies of textbook marketing or the theories of cultural Jacobins.

Although the goal of functional literacy for every citizen by twelfth grade is an ambitious one, it is a goal that we have the means and knowledge to accomplish. We know today, with more precision than ever before, how to achieve that goal. We know that we should start imparting literate knowledge in the earliest grades. And we know, within reasonable limits, what that knowledge consists of. We know enough to make every school an institutional Henry Higgins that, in the course of thirteen years, can transform every Eliza Doolittle into a duchess.

Professor Henry Higgins in Shaw's play *Pygmalion* (later turned into the musical *My Fair Lady*) was modeled on Professor Henry Sweet, who was the most distinguished linguist of late Victorian England. To Shaw, it was critically important for the point he was making that Professor Higgins should be a world-class expert who knew exactly what he was up to. Higgins was effective as a teacher because he was knowledgeable enough to be specific. He was able to focus on the specific phonetic and cultural elements that Eliza needed to know. *Pygmalion* was meant to be and still is a profound statement about education. Shaw wanted to show that the difference in social class between a Covent Garden flower girl and a duchess consisted in a limited body of knowledge that could be taught effectively under expert instruction. Part of this purpose in *Pygmalion* was to demystify social class and, with it, the literate culture that helps constitute social class.

Shaw's conception coincides with our traditional American conception of national education, especially as it held sway in the late nineteenth and early twentieth century. Our schools were meant to transform all comers. Only, instead of turning every Eliza into a duchess, they aimed to turn everyone into an American—a person who, in our lore, was the equal of any person of rank. It was a noble and inspiring ideal, and one that we are in danger of forgetting. To be reminded of it, one cannot do better than visit the Great Hall at the City College of New York, a great cathedral-shaped building that is a kind of temple to the ideal of education as Americanization. Along the nave of this Great Hall are stained glass windows which depict no religious scenes or sentiments, but rather the mottos and seals of American universities. And, behind the altar, where lectures are given, there rises a huge mural which is the focus of the vast room. At the left of this mural, one sees a crowd of huddled masses yearning to be free, and as the scene progresses to the right, one sees the bent and ragged figures being tapped with a wand by the radiant goddess of education. From her touch they emerge on the far right with mortar boards on their heads, upright and beaming. Education has transformed them all into equal citizens.

Or as Shelley said, "The loathsome mask has fallen, the man remains/Scepterless, free, uncircumscribed—but man/Equal, unclassed, tribeless . . . /Exempt from awe, worship, degree, the king/Over himself.''

This inspiring vision of national education has been criticized in recent years as cultural imperialism. Schools, instead of continuing to indoctrinate everyone in the literate natural culture, should encourage and celebrate multicultural diversity. But American literate culture has itself assimilated many of the materials that those who favor multiculturalism wish to include. The ethnic or minority items that people have suggested as additions to the preliminary list that is printed at the back of *Cultural Literacy* have numbered fewer than 50; I do not expect the number to exceed 100. We have been delighted to accept these suggestions, and welcome more of them.* The vague, multicultural conception of education (whatever the term really refers to in concrete terms) omits to notice that an Eliza Doolittle is precisely as multicultural as she might wish to be. She can break into cockney whenever she likes, and, because she has *also* learned the standard literate language, she can communi-

---

*The address of the Cultural Literacy Foundation is 2012-B Morton Drive, Charlottesville, Virginia 22901. The Foundation is a nonprofit tax-deductible organization devoted to the advancement of literacy in the United States.

cate with anyone in the land, effectively and as an equal. She has become enriched, not disenfranchised.

This benefit to Eliza as an individual is multiplied enormously when one considers the benefit to the nation that would ensue if our whole educational system were to operate on Shaw's design. The first consequence would be, of course, universal literacy, whose benefits I have already mentioned. We could all address each other as equals, with understanding and civility. No other national effort that we could make would be more likely to promote the general welfare and insure domestic tranquility. By contrast, no principle is more likely to defeat those fundamental aims of our Constitution than the encouragement of cultural separation, which promotes illiteracy, incivility, class warfare, not to mention low economic productivity.

Having alluded just now to the preamble of the Constitution ("promote the general welfare and insure domestic tranquility"), I wish to make some observations about the relevance of cultural literacy (which is to say functional literacy) to the goal of social justice through education. I want, first of all, to focus on the very misguided claim that cultural literacy is an elitist educational goal.

THE 'LIST' AND ELITISM

No doubt, a casual look at the provisional list of culturally relevant terms printed in the back of my book might give some people an impression of elitism, for two reasons. First, some of the items might be unfamiliar. This quite understandably leads some people to reason as follows: "I'm quite literate, so if I don't know some of the items, the list must be elitist." I am sympathetic to that reaction. I think it is correct in several instances, and we are constantly adapting the list to new comments and suggestions. But I believe that the main basis for the accusation of elitism comes

from the observation that the list seems Waspish and conservative; it seems to enshrine the traditional, British-oriented bias of an earlier day. Yet even if it included all minority and ethnic suggestions and removed all esoteric terms, any index to American literate culture would still remain preponderantly British-oriented and traditional and thus apparently elitist.

It is true that many of the richest and best-educated Americans of the nineteenth and early twentieth centuries were white, Anglo-Saxon, and Protestant, and it's true that the literate culture they possessed is still dominantly present in American literate culture. But to think that literate culture is Waspish and elitist just because the educated people who possessed it happened to be, is to reason *post hoc ergo propter hoc*, which an expert in critical thinking will quickly identify as a logical fallacy. It's true that the WASP elite of America possessed traditional literate culture, but not because they were born to it. As children, they had to be (often unwillingly) educated into it. They had to learn literate culture in order to become literate. And still today, every literate person in India, Scotland, Africa, Wales, Ireland, and Australia, no matter what color or religion, has had to learn that same traditional literate culture of English. Zeus and Athene are not, after all, WASP. St. Augustine is not a WASP. Confucius is not a WASP. In short, literate culture is in essence neither WASP nor elitist. It is simply the traditional knowledge required for literacy in any longstanding literate language—in this case, English.

Linguists have long known that literate culture is inherently traditional in character. Literacy preserves traditional forms and points of reference, because the vast numbers of books and people who use those forms and points of reference endow literacy with an inertia that is difficult to change by mere fiat. Everyone is familiar with the inertia of modern English spelling, which exhibits such oddities as *enough*, *doubt*, and *light*. Yet, very few spelling reforms have taken hold in modern English. Spelling is fixedly conservative. No sane liberal would argue against teaching students traditional spelling. The inertia and conservatism of spelling are but extreme examples of the conservative character of all literate culture.

Every modern nation since the industrial revolution has had to create both a standard literate language and a standard literate culture. The two elements, language and culture, were developed in tandem to create a medium of communication that could be used all over the nation by citizens who were not known to one another. Only the ability of citizens to communicate over time and space through speech and writing has enabled industrialized nations to thrive economically and politically. The linguistic and cultural history of every industrial nation in the world has followed or has attempted to follow the pattern. Wherever it has failed to achieve that aim, as for example in China, it has suffered politically and economically.

Despite the unpalatable sound of *standard literate language* and *standard literate culture*, both history and logic support the idea that a core of cultural and linguistic standardization is necessary. Without it no large industrial nation has worked or could work. It follows that the fewer Americans know our traditional linguistic and cultural norms, the less well our nation works.

Change of the literate culture, desirable as it may be, can take place only within sharp limits. That was a lesson learned by the French Revolutionists as well as by the proponents of the Great Cultural Revolution of China. Both attempts were doomed to fail and did fail, even under autocratic regimes. How much less likely of success are such attempts in a free nation.

Let me repeat the basic reason for this robust conservatism of literacy. After having existed for many centuries, literate culture acquires an inertia that makes it inherently resistant to radical change. Of course, the periphery of literate culture does constantly change. Oliver Norths come and go. But Lincoln and Jefferson remain. The core of shared literate culture has been extended broadly over time and space and is understood by millions of people and millions of books; its central words and traditions are almost as difficult to alter as are its spellings.

THE SCHOOL'S ROLE

And here is another critical fact about literacy that has been common to all industrial nations: The literate national language and culture of every nation has necessarily been a *school-transmitted* language and culture. The chief agents of the modern nation have been not just political and industrial leaders, but schoolteachers. Schoolteachers essentially created the modern nation-state, and schoolteachers alone can perpetuate it and make it thrive. When the schools of a nation cease to transmit effectively the literate language and culture, the unity and effectiveness of the nation will necessarily decline.

It's possible that the American public as a whole has instinctively recognized these connections between nationhood and literate culture. It may be that the astonishing amount of newspaper coverage given to my book reflects an instinctive recognition of the momentous issues at stake in the educational reforms it advocates. So, although my third chapter has not been dealt with in reviews, its implications have been understood intuitively by many people who haven't even opened the book. The letters I have received show that people understand very well the conservatism of literacy and its importance to the nation. They concur in the view that a changeable, untraditional curriculum cannot alter literate culture, but only condemn to illiteracy those students who happen to come from illiterate homes. These correspondents have understood that a so-called progressive, skills-oriented curriculum merely consolidates class distinctions and preserves the status quo.

I'll give just one decisive illustration of the social regressiveness of a progressive curriculum. A few years ago two economists, Finis Welch and James Smith, published a monograph called *Closing the Gap*. The gap they referred to was the income gap between blacks and whites who had finished the same level of education. Welch and Smith showed that this income gap had started to close even before the civil rights movement gathered force. Through careful analysis they also showed that the chief factor in this progress toward social justice has been a gradual equalizing of the quality of education given to whites and blacks. Thus, despite racial prejudice in the early years of this century, those Americans who entered the economy with higher skills (chiefly higher literacy skills) gained higher income regardless of race. As the literacy gap closed, so did the income gap. And the progress was fairly constant up to the 1970s when the analysis of Welch and Smith ended.

WIDENING WAGE GAP

On the basis of the Welch-Smith analysis, I made a prediction. Because the civil rights movement has now given blacks and whites more equal educational opportunities, one would expect the income gap to continue closing, assuming that the education available to all had stayed constant. But we know that the outcomes of education have been declining in the past fifteen years, as indicated by national measures of reading ability.

Because of this decline in literacy during the past two decades, I predicted that the wage gap would start opening up again, because a less effective teaching of literacy would have a more adverse effect on blacks than on whites.

My reasoning was this: A larger percentage of whites than blacks would get literate culture in their homes, to make up for what has been missing in the school curriculum. So, although literacy rates have declined for all students, the decline would be greater for blacks, and this differential would be reflected in the economic sphere. To test the hypothesis, I plotted a year-by-year curve from 1973 to 1983 for the decline in mean SAT verbal scores. For these same years I plotted the mean wage differentials for whites and blacks who went into the workforce with a twelfth-grade education. The year-by-year decline in overall literacy almost exactly paralleled the year-by-year reopening of the wage gap between the races.

The importance of a return to a literate curriculum is not, however, limited to poor or minority students. Far from it. The literacy of middle-class children has also been declining, which means that the country as a whole is becoming less literate, just at a time when advanced technology and the widening of the service economy have made high literacy more essential than in previous eras. The skills curriculum, which has now been dominant for several decades, is gradually creating a second generation of middle-class students who are even less literate than their parents, who studied under the same untraditional skills curriculum. What can we learn from the first generation of progressively educated children, who grew up in households that included more literate culture than their own households now provide their children? Sad but true, they are being deprived of a rich literate culture at home, making the content of the school curriculum more important for the middle class today than it was in previous decades.

Of course, the decline of literacy in the American middle class accounts for a decline in communication skills in the country as a whole. Large companies complain that their younger executives cannot communicate well, even though those affluent young executives still give credibility to the grand old American notion that you don't need good grammar to become rich. But in the modern world, that idea has become less and less realistic. Semiliterate people who happen to be rich or powerful in today's world would be less so if they had to compete with people who could communicate better than they.

That is exactly what has happened in the international sphere vis-à-vis Japan. Our country has become less rich and powerful as it has been forced to compete with better-educated, hence more productive, economies. Despite durable American myths to the contrary, the semiliterate but rich person is a vanishing species in the modern world, including even the United States.

So much for misconceptions about the conservatism and elitism of traditional literate culture. Political liberals, of whom I count myself one, must be alert to the paradox that educational conservatism is in fact a socially progressive policy. Educational liberalism, by contrast, with its emphasis on relevance, diversity, and skills, has *proved* itself to be a socially regressive policy. Once we understand the inherent conservatism of literacy, this paradox is easily explained and the way is open to making education reform a non-ideological project. All parties are constrained by the reality that educational conservatism alone can achieve political, economic, and social progress. We liberals make a bad bargain if we choose pious slogans about multi-culturalism over the realities of the conservatism of literacy. We thereby cede to political conservatives the only really practical policy for educational and social progress, making those conservatives, willy-nilly, more truly progressive than ourselves. As this paradox is more widely understood, curriculum reform should become a more multipartisan effort.

For that effort to succeed, however, we shall have to be specific about the content of literate culture. For reform to work, we need to get down to specifics. We need to identify those elements of literate culture that are known to insiders but not to outsiders. That is to say, we have to create a list that will help make literate culture the province of the dispossessed. These days, the dispossessed comprise not just minorities but also large numbers of the middle class.

Since most discussions of my book have focused on its provisional list, those who favor the cultural literacy project have said that the list is basically sound, while others have gleefully pointed out that the list exhibits some egregious omissions and inconsistencies. Both comments are right. The list is basically sound, and it does exhibit some egregious omissions and inconsistencies. We are continually repairing these errors, and we continue to invite suggestions. But even in its defective state the list has proved to be essentially accurate. Well-educated people make up most of the objectors. Critics of the list are able to make their complaints public, because their public can be expected to recognize that the complaints are valid. Thus, every objection to the details of the list implicitly concedes the principle of shared literate culture. In fact, the most useful comments on the list have come from its critics rather than its supporters.

Other critics of *Cultural Literacy* have voiced a rather more substantial and interesting objection. They accept the *Pygmalion* approach to literate culture but nonetheless predict that when such an approach leaves the covers of my book and enters the sphere of actual practice, it may become prey to abuses that will make the cure worse than the disease. Some have expressed the fear that the net result of demystifying literate culture and bringing it to everyone will be to trivialize it. The schools, they predict, will set aside special cultural literacy hours and will go down the list alphabetically, giving students deadening instruction that will be instantly forgotten.

These prophets of failure paint a picture of nitwit teachers and idiot principals who will propose to teach an incoherent encyclopedia.

I don't deny that such abuses are possible with any educational idea, however soundly conceived. But those who prophesy trivialization should at least read what I have said in my book about putting cultural literacy into practice in the schools. The book makes clear that schools should teach a coherent curriculum—both extensive and intensive—based on the elements of literate culture. What's more, the book also insists that literate culture, like any other knowledge, can only be taught successfully if it is embedded in interesting, coherent, motivational materials. The book makes a discrimination (as the prophets of trivialization do not) between levels of understanding in early and later grades. Obviously, the methods and emphases that motivate learning vary from grade to grade as well as from student to student. But perhaps the most decisive answer to prophets of trivialization is to remind them that there are worse things than trivialization, two of them being fragmentation and widespread illiteracy. Unless naysayers can recommend a better plan for overcoming these two ills, they condemn us to perpetuate them. My challenge is always to say: "Let's get specific."

GETTING SPECIFIC

My colleagues and I have proposed a specific plan to encourage the effective teaching of literate culture. The plan includes creating well-designed tests of general knowledge. Such tests, if widely used, would tend to make the issue of trivialization moot. For only a student who really knew literate culture could perform well on properly designed tests. These tests are now being completed. Twelfth-grade versions of them have been field tested in California and Virginia and will be published next year by the Cultural Literacy Foundation, a charitable foundation to which I have assigned ownership of the tests. In addition, we have prepared a twelfth-grade dictionary of cultural literacy that describes the information students need to know to make *100* of any version of the tests.

In addition to making up these twelfth-grade materials, the Cultural Literacy Foundation has secured the help of scholars and teachers to create a sound sequence for systematically working up to them. When this work is consolidated, the foundation will be able to make further tests and dictionaries for elementary and middle grades. The advantage of these sequenced tests (for third, sixth, and ninth grades) will be two-fold. First, the information on which they are based will be known to everyone in advance, in the form of dictionaries arranged by subject matter. That open-door policy will give everyone a fair shot at the tests and remove the issue of cultural bias. Secondly, the tests will leave schools entirely free to determine the most suitable approaches and emphases for teaching literate culture.

The tests are saying in effect: "We don't care how you manage to make people literate. We don't care what political or moral or ethnic slant you apply to the material. We don't care whether you spend a lot of school time or a little in conveying the information. We only want to be sure that you do convey it effectively so that your students will be literate." The policy of the Cultural Literacy Foundation is not to support any one method for teaching literate culture but rather to describe its elements in a sound sequence, to create a series of dictionaries that define these sequenced contents, and to offer a sequenced series of tests for determining whether literate culture has been successfully taught. We wish to leave specific methods to the wisdom, taste, and expertise of those who teach and those who supervise teaching.

I want to end these remarks with a general observation about our chances of attaining universal functional literacy through effective educational reform. Within the educational establishment I have encountered a certain amount of weary defeatism, along the lines of the first Coleman Report, which was taken to show that the job just can't be done by the schools alone. I have been told by educators that people have always complained about our educational shortcomings, that there never was a golden age of education, that things always have been bad, and probably always will be. Cultural literacy is just another simple-minded panacea doomed to failure like the Checklist for Teachers and the new math. And I have heard other, similarly mournful and defeatist attitudes. One reviewer bluntly said that my book is just too optimistic.

But my reply to all this is that education is the field par excellence for optimists. If we aren't optimists, why are we in teaching at all? We will hardly make progress in education if we believe beforehand that we can't. Most good teachers I know are both realists and at the same time tenacious optimists. It's a puzzle to me why anyone but an optimist would want to devote his or her life to education. And nowadays our optimism is better grounded than ever, in light of significant advances in our understanding of literacy. In a country as rich and vigorous as ours, I see no insuperable barrier to universal national literacy within the lifetime of our children.

FOR FURTHER READING

Becoming a Nation of Readers: The Report of the National Commission on Reading. R. C. Anderson and others. National Institute of Education, 1985.

A short, authoritative description of what current research has taught us about the nature of reading and the best means to teach reading. For scholars, the report provides detailed references to the scientific literature. On the subject of cultural literacy, the report has this to say (p. 61): "Even for beginners, reading should not be thought of simply as a 'skill subject.' It is difficult to imagine, for instance, that kindergartners could be called literate for their age if they did not know *Goldilocks and the Three Bears* or *Peter Rabbit*. For each age there are fables, fairy tales, folk tales, classic and modern works of fiction that embody the core of our cultural heritage."

College-Bound Seniors: Eleven Years of National Data from the College Board's Admission Testing Program, 1973–83. The College Board, 1984.

Although the verbal SAT has been rightly criticized for its negative educational and social influences, it is, from a technical standpoint, a sound test. As John Carroll has pointed out, it is a sensitive measure of a student's vocabulary, and little else. For that reason, despite its harmful side effects, the verbal SAT is a sound measure of a student's literacy level. Breadth of vocabulary has a very high correlation with level of literacy. Since words stand for things, a broad vocabulary attests a broad knowledge of things, not just of words. About a million students take the SAT each year. This report, along with other documents, shows that the actual numbers of students who scored over 600 declined from 11.4 percent to 7.3 percent between 1973 and 1983. Among the best students, having scores over 650, the decline was from 5.29 to 3.0 percent! The decline of the *average* SAT verbal score over the past twenty-five years forms a slope that an Olympic skier would have difficulty skiing down. We know from field tests that scores on the verbal SAT have a high correlation with scores on tests of cultural literacy.

The Court and the Constitution. Archibald Cox. Houghton Mifflin, 1987.

For an insight into why a uniform sphere of discourse as well as uniform set of laws have grown in importance since the nineteenth century, two chapters of Cox's eloquent book can be read with profit: "4. Opening a National Market" and "5.

One Nation Indivisible.'' Cox argues that the economy was the cause of ever greater breadth and uniformity in the application of the Commerce Clause of the Constitution. The argument for a similar commonality in education is similarly compelling.

Mankind, Nation, and Individual from a Linguistic Point of View. Otto Jespersen. Indiana University Press, 1945.

A great linguist's perspective on literacy and standard language in a nation. Jespersen was a strong advocate of bringing people together through linguistic standardization. History showed him that failure to achieve such linguistic unification always causes culture to war against culture and class against class. He pointed out, perhaps before anyone else, that a literate national language was not an elite dialect, but was in fact the least elite and most democratic language and culture of a nation.

Nations and Nationalism. Ernest Gellner. Cornell University Press, 1983.

This learned and illuminating book shows, among other things, why every modern industrial nation has had to create a standard national language and culture. The book is essential reading for anyone who might wish to argue that such standardization is *not* essential to modern nationhood and commerce. Gellner's argument that a modern national economy requires a shared standard culture finds confirmation in United States history, which discloses the growing need for uniformity in laws governing interstate commerce. The two kinds of uniformity are closely allied. To grasp that point, one cannot do better than to read the following book.

Theoretical Issues in Reading Comprehension: Perspectives from Cognitive Psychology, Linguistics, Artificial Intelligence and Education. Rand J. Spiro and others. Erlbaum, 1981.

For those interested in the technical, psychological research into the need for shared background knowledge in communication, this is perhaps the most wide-ranging and detailed compendium. It is recommended primarily for those who have a taste for reading about research and about the kinds of ingenious experiments that have yielded new insights into literacy.

THOMAS H. ESTES, CAROL J. GUTMAN, AND ELISE K. HARRISON

CULTURAL LITERACY: WHAT EVERY EDUCATOR NEEDS TO KNOW

Thomas H. Estes is Associate Professor of the Curry School of Education at the University of Virginia. Carol J. Gutman is a reading teacher at Seminole Elementary School, Madison Heights, Virginia. Elise K. Harrison is an instructor on leave from Hampton University and a doctoral student at Curry School of Education, University of Virginia.

E. D. Hirsch's *Cultural Literacy: What Every American Needs to Know* is a paradox and a contradiction. Hirsch has *a* point, but he misses *the* point; the book is half right in its major implication. The result is that readers, blind either to the book's correct assertions and erroneous implications or to its erroneous assertions and correct implications, are aligning themselves at opposite poles of reaction. We hope to quell this dissonance by recognizing the best of what the book offers and rejecting its contradictions.

LITERACY IN LIST FORM

Readers are undoubtedly drawn to *Cultural Literacy* by its list of some 5,000 items "intended to illustrate the character and range of the knowledge literate Americans tend to share" (Hirsch 1987, p. 146). Knowledge of the items on this list presumably confers membership in the fraternity of literacy. Hirsch is now preparing a dictionary of associations for these thousands of bits of knowledge and test of their acquisition.

It is highly unlikely that information fundamental to literacy can be listed at all, except to cite examples. Hirsch's major argument, however, is based on the assumption that the foundation of literacy is the ability to recall and associate a superficial level of knowledge, knowledge that can be acquired by memorizing the items on his list. By reducing the information necessary for literacy to a list, Hirsch inadvertently represents the basis of literacy as the pursuit of trivia.

LEARNING AS MEMORIZATION

Consider the instructional implications to which this commits Hirsch. He openly endorses the dual proposition that "learned is memorized, memorized is known," at least for information that he calls the foundation of literacy.[1] For example, he points out that children at a very young age know the Pledge of Allegiance and the national anthem because they have memorized them. Thus, he reasons, learners of any age can know anything they can memorize. Further, Hirsch dismisses out

---

From Thomas H. Estes, Carol J. Gutman, and Elise K. Harrison, "Cultural Literacy: What Every Educator Needs to Know," *Educational Leadership* 46, 1 (1988): 14–17. Reprinted with permission of the Association for Supervision and Curriculum Development. Copyright © 1988 by ASCD. All rights reserved.
[1]Personal communication with E. D. Hirsch, Jr.

of hand the idea of developmental readiness. He says we needn't worry about teaching children things for which they are not ready, for "it seems self-evident to me that if they learned it, they were ready for it; if not, they were not ready."[2]

Here "learned" equals "memorized," and understanding *follows* learning. That is, learning (memorization) makes understanding possible; understanding, per se, is irrelevant to learning. It is perhaps on this single issue that educators disagree most with Hirsch.

HIRSCH'S LINE OF REASONING

The major assertion of *Cultural Literacy* is that literacy is on the decline in America; that, true to society's suspicions, young people graduating from high school today are less able to read and write than were graduates of years past. The root cause of this decline, according to Hirsch, is that students today are not taught the basic facts and ideas that are the foundation of learning.

But Hirsch provides no indication that he has surveyed either curriculum guides or instructional practices that determine what is taught in school. He draws primarily on information and implications from two major reports. One is the National Assessment of Educational Progress (1986), conducted by the Educational Testing Service but commissioned by the National Endowment for the Humanities, on whose governing panel Hirsch sits. The other is the report of the College Board on results of its Scholastic Aptitude Test (1984).

Using these reports, Hirsch has defined "the great hidden problem in American education" (Hirsch 1987, p. 1) as the failure to provide students access to the wide-ranging

background information that forms the foundation of literacy. He emphasizes the inability of young people to recall and associate historical and literary facts. His major claim is that this inability is both the cause of and evidence for students' failure to acquire what he has labeled "cultural literacy."

Hirsch also addresses what one needs to know to be literate. Literacy, the ability to read and write, depends on two different insights of the learner. One insight is that words in print are associated in sound and meaning with direct counterparts in speech. Spoken language is encoded into printed language; the job of the reader is to crack the code to get from print to speech. This is correct, as far as it goes, and in fact represents the first and greatest insight the young reader must acquire on the way to literacy.

The other insight learners must gain if they are to be readers might be called "culture cracking." This is the aspect of reading that most concerns Hirsch. The ability to read and write depends on the realization that words are associated with a body of remembered facts and details. In other words, literacy depends critically on the possession of specific information, some part of which all authors must assume in their readers.

Hirsch makes the point that regardless of their code-cracking ability, many of today's high school graduates are unable to understand what they read because they lack access to points of reference and allusion on which the meaning of the text depends. This leads Hirsch to his major educational implication: that possession of a knowledge base common to one's literate culture is critical to literacy, that this information is directly teachable to all students, and that it should constitute the major curriculum for literacy in schools.

Hirsch contends that changes within our society cannot explain the decline in literacy he has described. Rather, many graduates today have not acquired the information essen-

---

[2]Personal communication with E. D. Hirsch, Jr.

tial for literacy because both their curriculum and their instruction lack the rigor of times past. According to Hirsch, there is no longer a core curriculum in schools, nor are academic demands made of students; for example, there is no "firm insistence that students complete significant amounts of homework" (Hirsch 1987, p. 20). Evidently, the proper, but abdicated, job of schools is information transmission; and the role of the teacher is to impart information to learners in something like a catechism of cultural associations.

GREAT IRONIES

Hirsch suggests that the weakening of public education has been caused by a curriculum emphasis on cognitive development. He believes that schools today emphasize the "why" and the "how" in learning and ignore the "what." Certainly, we do not deny that students today are graduating from high school woefully ignorant of much that one might expect them to know. The great irony, however, is that they are so ignorant because they have been taught in precisely the way Hirsch advocates.

Those who support Hirsch's argument assert that children should acquire a great deal of information about their culture in order to be considered educated. We are not disputing this truism, but we must ask how any of us becomes culturally literate. Surely, it is by reading, listening, writing, and speaking well and widely in the mainstream of our culture. By doing so, we integrate tens of thousands of items like those on Hirsch's list. However, such information—even language itself—cannot be learned piece by piece or listed item by item. Rather, it must be acquired in what appears to the learner as gestalt, an awareness of the whole acquired over time, as part of living in and comprehending a world that each learner must both invent and participate in with others.

Nevertheless, Hirsch characterizes literate behavior as something like "list knowing." By implying that such knowledge equals competence, he reverses the process of literacy acquisition: knowing the list becomes the criterion for being literate rather than the result of being literate. With cause and effect thus shifted, Hirsch presents a list that can be directly imparted to students. Students can then be tested periodically to see if they can display not literacy but "list knowing"—that is, can they pass a test on the list?

Over the past thirty years, public education has been dominated by this type of psychometric model: what is *objective* and *measurable* determines the educational agenda from kindergarten through twelfth grade. Not only have test scores become the scale by which students, teachers, and schools are ranked; the tests themselves have become the basis of educational programs: another great irony. If learning is defined as only those things that objective paper-and-pencil tests can measure, then only teaching that produces successful scores on these tests is relevant. Although the blame for this does not lie with Hirsch, his proposal will surely aggravate an already deplorable condition.

BEYOND FACTUAL RECALL

Whether or not he intended it, Hirsch has promoted an egregious error: that the wholesale memorization of a list of words and phrases and the associations that go with them will enable children to understand their culture and to participate fully in it. Already school boards and the general public have begun to consider seriously a reductionistic form of Hirsch's proposal: that reintroducing memorization to the instructional program will result in the academic rigor that will improve education everywhere.

Before a person can acquire culture from information, however, that information must be set in a context. Each discrete piece of information must be placed in the account to which it contributes; and, moreover, the focus must always be on the narrative, not on the separate facts that compose it.

In our attempt to prepare young people to succeed in an increasingly technological society, our instructional materials and practices have too often ignored these sound principles. They have focused upon discrete pieces of information; they have treated natural intelligence as though it were artificial; they have made the computer the ruling metaphor in education; they have asked our children to be information processors. But when students' attention is continually turned toward fragments of information—the data of a discipline or content area or society—the information they acquire is bound to be disjointed. The rich, full, interactive context within which information complements understanding is lost. As John Dewey observed,

> Knowledge, *in the sense of information, means the working capital, the indispensable resources, of further inquiry; of finding out, or learning more things. Frequently, it is treated as an end itself, and then the goal becomes to heap it up and display it when called for. This static, cold storage ideal of knowledge is inimical to educative development (Dewey 1916, p. 158).*

MAKING MEANING IN CONTEXT

The point Hirsch seems to want to make but misses is that whether or not today's students can recall and associate, they almost certainly cannot allude and apply. But teaching culture from a list, using a dictionary of associations and a test of achievement, will not enable students to create a context; in fact, it will only exacerbate their inability to do so.

Today, as always, students must be guided to reinvent the very culture in which they par-

ticipate. A culture must always bear the stamp of its current generation. The hardest lesson for any educator (or parent) to learn is that *telling* is not "teaching," *told* is not "taught." The conception of teaching as transmission— as if parents, teachers and schools were conduits through which culture flows—ignores the central role of the learner in learning.

Meaning derives from the learner's participation in the learning. Most students today undoubtedly view the purpose of their education as information acquisition, while most teachers view their work as information transmission. As a result, students are graduating to the worlds of work and higher education in possession of varying amounts of knowledge but without the understandings that would make the content of instruction memorable. This is what Hirsch and others have observed but have failed to understand.

PARTICIPANTS IN OUR COMMON HERITAGE

It is not the emphasis on cognitive development but the reduction of education to a technology that is responsible for breaking the curriculum into discrete, and often isolated, fragments. These unrelated fragments make too little sense to be of use in allusion and application. The great irony is that Hirsch's proposal, as it is likely to be interpreted, will aggravate the very conditions in education he deplores. The valuable things he would have children learn will be trivialized if teachers ask students to memorize what they do not understand. Moreover, students will not remember this content when they have not attached meaning to it. We must teach students to explore actively the literacy and the culture we want to share with them; only in this way do we empower them as participants in our common heritage. Knowledge, thought, and literacy are malnourished on a diet of scraps with no invitation to the banquet that is culture.

References

The College Board. *College Board Seniors: Eleven Years of National Data from the College Board's Admission Testing Program, 1973–1983.* New York: The College Board, 1984.

Dewey, J. *Democracy and Education.* New York: The Free Press, 1916.

Hirsch, E. D., Jr. *Cultural Literacy: What Every American Needs to Know.* Boston: Houghton Mifflin, 1987.

Kelty, Mary G. *The Beginnings of the American People and Nation.* Boston: Ginn and Company, 1937.

National Assessment of Educational Progress. *The Reading Report Card: Progress Toward Excellence in our Schools, Trends in Reading over Four National Assessments, 1971–1984.* Princeton, N.J.: Educational Testing Service, Rep. No. 15-R-01, 1986.

DISCUSSION QUESTIONS AND ACTIVITIES

1. What, according to Hirsch, is "functional literacy"?

2. Why is the theory unsound that reading and writing are formal skills?

3. Why is it a logical fallacy to charge that his list of terms is "elitist"?

4. "Schoolteachers," he claims, "essentially created the modern nation-state, and schoolteachers can perpetuate it and make it thrive." Explain and evaluate the soundness of this statement.

5. Can valid tests of general knowledge be devised?

6. Examine Hirsch's list of relevant terms in his books (see Suggested Readings), and assess whether they are likely to achieve the objectives he intends.

7. Have Estes, Gutman, and Harrison supported their claim that Hirsch's list of terms represents the basis of literacy as the "pursuit of trivia"?

8. For Hirsch, learning is something like "list knowing"; but for the three authors, students learn in terms of contexts and gestalt. What do they mean by this form of learning?

9. Visit your local school district, gather data about how literacy is promoted, and make a report on your findings to class.

10. Organize a classroom debate: "Cultural Literacy Can Best Be Promoted by Pursuing Hirsch's Model."

SUGGESTED READINGS

Works by E. D. Hirsch, Jr., about Cultural Literacy

" 'Cultural Literacy' Doesn't Mean 'Core' Curriculum." *English Journal* 74 (October 1985): 47–49.

Cultural Literacy: What Every American Needs to Know. New York: Houghton Mifflin, 1987. Random House, 1988 paperback.

The Dictionary of Cultural Literacy: What Every American Needs to Know (coauthor). New York: Houghton Mifflin, 1988.

The First Dictionary of Cultural Literacy. New York: Houghton Mifflin, 1989.

"Hirsch Responds: The Best Answer to a Caricature Is a Practical Program." *Educational Leadership* 46 (September 1988): 18–19.

"The Paradox of Traditional Literacy: Response to Tchudi." *Educational Leadership* 45 (December–January 1987–1988): 63–70.

"A Postscript by E. D. Hirsch, Jr." *Change* 20 (July–August 1988): 22–26.

"The Primal Scene of Education." *New York Review of Books* 36 (March 2, 1989): 29–39. Discussion (April 13, 1989): 50.

"Restoring Cultural Literacy in the Early Grades." *Educational Leadership* 45 (December–January 1987–1988): 68–70.

Evaluations of Hirsch's Cultural Literacy Proposals

Feinberg, Walter. "Foundationalism and Recent Critiques of Education." *Educational Theory* 39 (Spring 1989): 133–138.

Fleming, D. B. "What Every High School Graduate Needs to Know: Trivia or Essentials?" *High School Journal* 73 (February–March 1990): 139–142.

Hitchens, C. "Why We Don't Know What We Don't Know." *New York Times Magazine* (March 13, 1990): 32–33.

Postman, Neil. "Learning by Story." *The Atlantic* 264 (December 1989): 119–124.

Schuster, E. H. "In Pursuit of Cultural Literacy." *Phi Delta Kappan* 70 (March 1989): 539–542.

Schwartz, Gretchen. "A Good Idea Gone Wrong." *Educational Leadership* 45 (December–January 1987–1988): 77.

Seligman, D. "Here Comes Culture." *Fortune* 118 (December 19, 1988): 196.

Squire, James R. "Basic Skills Are Not Enough." *Educational Leadership* 45 (December–January 1987–1988): 76–77.

Tchudi, Stephen. "Slogans Indeed: A Reply to Hirsch." *Educational Leadership* 45 (December–January 1987–1988): 72–74.

Tuttleton, J. W. "Literacy at the Barricades." *Commentary* 84 (July 1987): 45–48.

CHAPTER 5

POLITICS, ORGANIZATION, AND SCHOOL CHOICE

John Chubb and Terry Moe sought to determine why some schools are more successful than others in raising student achievement. Their conclusions are based on the federal study, *High School and Beyond*, that provides data about high school students and their schools. In their book, *Politics, Markets, and America's Schools*, they seek to define the characteristics of an effective school. They also examine how public and private schools are organized and administered, including the relationships of principals and teachers and expectations of students. They found that well-run schools can make a significant difference for students, regardless of their background and ability. Teachers in effective schools were treated as professionals, whereas in ineffective schools they were treated as common civil servants. Effective schools, they observed, experience 20 to 50 percent less interference from superintendents and district-level administrators in areas of curriculum, instruction, and the employment and discharge of teachers.

They propose that statewide tenure laws be eliminated and that collective bargaining be carried out at the school rather than the district level. New minimum criteria would be established by states as to what constitutes a public school, and, in effect, any group or organization could apply and, if they meet the standards, be chartered as a public school and receive public funds. Each school would be self-governing by making basic decisions about educational policy. Parents could choose any public school in the state, assisted by a state-operated "choice office." Existing public schools would have to compete with new schools for students, and schools would be accountable to parents and students.

In the selections, Chubb presents the details of his plan and how it operates. Jack Tweedie finds that the Chubb study does not account for intervening factors on school characteristics, that it fails to recognize the present advantages of private schools and that these advantages may not carry over in a market system, and that the study develops a biased and deterministic model.

JOHN E. CHUBB

A BLUEPRINT FOR PUBLIC EDUCATION

John E. Chubb is a political scientist and a Brookings Institution fellow who is coauthor of Politics, Markets, and America's Schools.

The past decade has been the most ambitious period of school reform in the nation's history. But evidence of school improvement— e.g., in test scores and dropout rates—is almost impossible to find.

How can government work so hard to solve a problem yet make so little progress? The conclusion Stanford Professor Terry Moe and I reached—after analyzing more than 20,000 students, teachers, and principals in a nationwide sample of 500 schools—is that government has not solved the education problem because government *is* the problem.

The public education system functions naturally and routinely, despite everyone's best intentions, to burden schools with excessive bureaucracy, to discourage effective school organization, and to stifle student achievement. Efforts to improve schools are therefore doomed unless they eliminate or sharply curtail the influence of the institutions that cause the schools' problems in the first place.

We consequently propose a new system of public education that will not be governed directly by politics but will be controlled indirectly through markets—through school competition and parental choice. Markets, we found, discourage excessive bureaucracy and promote more effective schools. Because states have primary responsibility for public education, the best way to establish a "choice" system is for states to withdraw authority from existing institutions and vest it directly in the schools, parents, and students—as follows:

THE SUPPLY OF SCHOOLS

The state will be responsible for setting criteria that define what constitutes a "public school" under the new system. These criteria should be minimal, roughly corresponding to the criteria many states now use in accrediting private schools—graduation requirements, health and safety requirements, and teacher certification requirements. Any group or organization that meets these minimal criteria must then be chartered as a public school and granted the right to accept students and receive public money. Existing private and parochial schools (as long as their religious functions are kept separate) will be eligible, and their participation should be encouraged, because they constitute a ready supply of often-effective schools.

Schools districts can continue running their present schools, but they will have no authority over any of the others that may be chartered by the state.

From John E. Chubb, "A Blueprint for Public Education," *The Wall Street Journal* (June 6, 1990): A14. Reprinted with permission of The Wall Street Journal © 1990 Dow Jones and Company, Inc. All rights reserved.

FUNDING

The state will set up a choice office in each district, which, among other things, will maintain a record of all school-age children and the level of funding—the scholarship amounts—associated with each child. This office will directly compensate schools based on the specific children they enroll. Public money will flow from funding sources to the choice office and then to schools.

The state must pay to support its own choice office in each district. Districts may retain as much of their current governing apparatus as they wish, but they have to pay for it out of the scholarship revenue of those children who choose to attend district-run schools.

As it does now, the state will have the right to specify how much, or by what formula, each district must contribute for each child. Our preference is for an equalization approach that requires wealthier districts to contribute more per child than poor districts do and that guarantees an adequate financial foundation to students in all districts.

Scholarships will also take into account special educational needs—arising from economic deprivation, physical handicaps, and other disadvantages—that can be met effectively only through costly specialized programs. State and federal programs already appropriate public money to address these problems. These funds should take the form of add-ons to student scholarships. At-risk students would then receive bigger scholarships than the others, making them attractive clients to all schools and stimulating the emergence of new specialty schools.

CHOICE AMONG SCHOOLS

Each student will be free to attend any public school in the state, with the scholarship—consisting of federal, state, and local contributions—flowing to the school of choice. Most students will probably choose schools close to home, but districts will have no claim on their own residents. To the extent that tax revenues allow, every effort will be made to provide transportation for those who need it, especially the poor and those in rural areas.

To assist parents and students in choosing among schools, the state will provide a parent information center within each local choice office. This center will collect comprehensive information on each school in the district and distribute and collect applications. Its liaisons will meet with parents to help them judge which schools best meet their children's needs.

Schools will make their own admissions decisions, subject only to nondiscrimination requirements. This step is absolutely crucial. Schools must be able to define their own missions and build their own programs, and they cannot do that if their students are thrust on them by outsiders. They must be free to admit as many or as few students as they want, based on whatever criteria they think relevant.

Schools will set their own "tuitions." They may choose to do so explicitly, say, by publicly announcing the minimum scholarship they are willing to accept. They may also do it implicitly by allowing anyone to apply for admission and simply making selections, knowing in advance what each applicant's scholarship amount is. In either case, schools are free to admit students with different-sized scholarships and to keep the entire scholarship that accompanies each student they admit. That gives schools incentives to attract students with special needs, since these children have the largest scholarships.

While it is important to give parents and students as much flexibility as possible, we think it unwise to let them supplement their scholarships with personal funds. Such add-ons threaten to produce too many inequalities within the system, and many citizens would regard them as unfair.

The application process must guarantee each student a school, as well as a fair shot at getting into the school he most wants. We suggest the following. The parent information center will be responsible for seeing that applications are submitted by a given date. Schools will then be required to make their admissions decisions within a set time, and students who are accepted into more than one school will be required to select one. Students who are not accepted anywhere, as well as schools that have yet to attract enough students, will participate in a second round of applications, after which unaccepted students (there should be few) will be assigned to schools by the choice office.

GOVERNANCE AND ORGANIZATION

The state must grant each school sole authority to set its own governing structure. A school may be run entirely by teachers or even a union; may vest all power in a principal; may be built around a committee that guarantees representation to the principal, teachers, parents, students, and community members. Or it may do something completely different.

The state will also do nothing to tell the schools how they must be internally organized. It will not set requirements for career ladders, advisory committees, textbook selection, in-service training, preparation time, homework, or anything else.

Statewide tenure laws will be eliminated, allowing each school to decide for itself whether to adopt a tenure policy and what the specifics will be. This change is essential if schools are to have the flexibility to build well-functioning teams of professionals. Some schools may rely solely on pay and working conditions to attract teachers, while others may offer tenure as a means of compensating and retaining their best teachers.

Teachers will continue to have a right to join unions and engage in collective bargaining, but the bargaining unit will be the individual school or, as in the case of the district government, the organization that runs the school.

The state will continue to certify teachers, but requirements will be minimal. Individuals should be certified to teach if they have a bachelor's degree and if their personal history reveals no obvious problems. Whether they are good teachers will be determined in practice, as schools decide whom to hire; observe their own teachers in action; and make decisions about merit, promotion, and dismissal.

The state will hold the schools accountable for meeting the criteria set out in their charters, for adhering to nondiscrimination laws, and for making available to the public, through the parent information center, information on their mission, their staff and course offerings, standardized test scores (which we would make optional), parent and student satisfaction, and anything else that would promote informed educational choice.

The state will not hold the schools accountable for student achievement or other dimensions that call for assessments of the quality of school performance. When it comes to performance, schools will be held accountable from below, by parents and students who directly experience their services and are free to choose.

CHOICE AS A PUBLIC SYSTEM

These changes have nothing to do with privatizing the nation's schools. The choice system we outline would be a truly public system—and a democratic one.

Nothing in the concept of democracy requires that schools be subject to direct control by school boards, superintendents, central offices, departments of education, and other arms of government. Nor does anything in the concept of public education require that schools be governed in this way. There are many paths to democracy and public education. The path

America has long been treading is exacting a heavy price—one the nation and its children can ill afford to bear, and need not.

JACK TWEEDIE

SHOULD MARKET FORCES CONTROL EDUCATIONAL DECISION MAKING?

Jack Tweedie is a professor of political science at State University of New York at Binghamton.

In "Politics, Markets, and the Organization of Schools," John Chubb and Terry Moe (1988) examine institutional choice in education, specifically the issue of whether political control or market responsiveness results in better schools. They report the descriptive results of a survey of private and public schools' organizational and environmental characteristics. They argue that market controls in private schools are superior to political controls in public schools because the need to meet parents' concerns results in more effective school-level organization. Governance in public schools interferes with effective organization because it imposes restraints on school-level autonomy. They conclude that market controls produce more effective schools and advocate institutional reforms shifting schools away from direct democratic control and toward a decentralized system based on parental choice.

These conclusions are not justified by the argument and evidence that Chubb and Moe present. Their case for market control of schools goes wrong at three levels. First, they do not develop an adequate explanation for the different organizational characteristics of private and public schools in the current system because they do not examine the influence of intervening factors on schools' organizational characteristics. They treat all schools' environmental and organizational characteristics, including the purposes of schooling, as endogenous and then fail to examine this assumption. Second, they infer directly from the current system of private and public schools to the institutional logics of market and political control without recognizing that their findings are contingent on the special character and advantages of private schools in the current system. Their empirical findings about private schools tell us little about market con-

From Jack Tweedie, *American Political Science Review* Vol. 84, no. 2 (June 1990): 549–554, 565–567. Reprinted with permission.

trol of schools, given their failure to examine how supply and parental demand in a universal market system relates to supply and demand in the current private system. Third, and most fundamentally, they focus exclusively on the choice between politics and markets and develop biased and deterministic models of educational governance within those systems. They define away the complex and interactive processes of institutional development that result in substantial variance within the systems and, in some cases, mixed modes of governance. These flaws, taken together, strongly undermine Chubb and Moe's conclusions about public and private schools and market and political systems of control in education.

COMPARING PRIVATE SCHOOLS AND PUBLIC SCHOOLS

Chubb and Moe's primary aim is to evaluate market and political institutions of control in education. At the empirical center of this evaluation, however, is a comparison of private and public schools' organizational characteristics: school-level autonomy, intraschool relations, and school goals and practices. They find that in private schools principals have greater authority and exercise more leadership, parents are more interested in their children's education and more involved with the school, the schools' goals are clearer and more focused, and teachers have greater influence and are more satisfied.[1] They point out that these findings reinforce other research reporting that private schools are more effective than public schools (Coleman and Hoffer 1987; Coleman, Hoffer, and Kilgore 1982).[2] Chubb and Moe recognize that many factors influence schools' organization, such as school size, the homogeneity of student bodies, and the self-selection of parents who send their children to private schools. They explicitly choose not to control for these fac-

tors in interpreting their survey findings. They argue that these factors provide the basis of appeal to parents and that it is the market that gives private schools the incentive to maintain them. In short, the organizations of schools and their relations with their environments are endogenous to the system of institutional control, and it would be inappropriate to control for those differences (pp. 1071–1073).

This grand assumption follows from their exclusive focus on the institutional choice between politics and markets in education. Given this focus, incorporating the features of the private and public school systems within their models is valid, at least as a working assumption.[3] However, for reasons I explain in the third section, this focus defines away key theoretical and empirical questions about the development of institutional arrangements in education. The deterministic models they use simply assert without examination that all organizational characteristics are endogenous to the choice between markets and politics. Their decision not to examine the influence of other environmental factors on school organization also undermines using the results reported here for the more limited purpose of comparing the organizations of private and public schools directly. Their approach precludes the examination of alternative explanations and intervening forces in the organization of private and public schools.

In addition, they treat the *ends* of education as endogenous. They assert neutrality on the issue of purposes for education, explaining that choosing between parents' concerns and society's goals would require "a fundamental judgment about what the schools ought to be doing" (p. 1070). However, in choosing not to impose their own values for education, they are also rejecting the role of public deliberations concerning the purposes of education and denying the character of education as a public good. Some parents' concerns are outside the scope of public concern, such as children's religious training; and other parents' concerns are counter to public policy, such as desires for racial segregation or religious intolerance. Their point of view is troubling precisely because abdication of collective determination of purposes and the notion of education as a private good is inherent in the market control of schools they advocate (Gutmann 1987).

USING EMPIRICAL RESEARCH TO ADDRESS INSTITUTIONAL QUESTIONS

Chubb and Moe's conclusions address the institutions of market and democratic control, but their research findings are contingent on the current system of private and public education. Private schools have important advantages over public schools in the current system. Most children attend public schools and parents who choose private schools tend to be more active and interested in their children's education as well as better off financially (Coleman, Kilgore, and Hoffer 1982). In addition, private schools' student bodies are more homogeneous than those in public schools. These advantages influence the survey results, but they are not inherent in the market system of control. Even if we were to accept their conclusions about the superiority of private schools' organization in the current system, that tells us little about how schools would operate under a universal system of market control.

Reasoning from current observations to a more inclusive or universal market system in education requires taking into account both the supply of schools and parents' demand for them. Chubb and Moe's survey of schools does not provide an empirical basis for such an extrapolation of the institutional logic of markets.[4] Supply and demand are closely related. Indeed, market theorists argue that supply would rise to meet parents' school demands. For that reason, and because we know

more about parents' demands for education, I will focus on the question of demand. Prior to that, however, it is important to recognize that we know little about how the supply of education would work in a universal market system. In particular, we do not know how the existing public schools system would evolve under market control. It seems unlikely that there would be sufficient interest on the part of school entrepreneurs and parents to result in new schools with the organizational characteristics of current private schools that would serve all children (or that sufficient pressure would be put on public schools that they would act like private schools). Some children would not have access to these "better" schools and would be left in schools like those they currently attend or (more likely) schools depleted by the exit of interested parents and able children (Hirschman 1970).

In using current private schools to advocate market control for schools, Chubb and Moe must assume that all parents are like (or would become like) parents who currently send their children to private schools and therefore that parental demand in a universal market system would result in schools that look like current private schools. However, as they point out, the fact that parents in the current private system are more interested and active in their children's education is one key factor that makes private schools better. Projecting how the universe of parents would choose if given the opportunity (without cost) involves trying to answer several difficult questions: What kinds of factors would parents consider important? What proportion of parents would consider alternative schools? How many alternatives would be considered? How would parents obtain information about schools? Parental choice of schools has been adopted in only limited circumstances in the United States, so we do not know the answers to these critical questions. However, parents in Scotland have been given strong rights of choice within the public school system. I want to use the findings of research in Scotland concerning parents' school choices to raise questions about how such a system might work.[5]

In 1982, legislation essentially gave Scottish parents rights to send their children to any public school as long as the school had not reached its physical capacity. Few parents in rural areas made school requests, as alternative schools were usually some distance away. Within towns and urban areas, substantial numbers of parents (between 10 percent and 25 percent) requested schools other than their district school. Even in these areas, most parents did not *consider* schools other than the district school. Of those who did consider an alternative school, most stayed with the district school anyway. And for parents requesting an alternative school, the most common reasons involved the nearness of the school and the attendance of the child's friends and siblings at the alternative school. Parents' requests have resulted in several popular schools being filled to capacity. Other schools have become seriously underenrolled, receiving less than a hundred new students a year, two-thirds the number considered the minimum for a viable school. These schools are expensive to run, they must offer restricted curricula, and they have lost many of their more able pupils, thus depriving the remaining pupils of important stimuli for learning. At the same time, parents of children still at those schools strongly resist attempts to close the schools.

What is more, there is little evidence that the more popular schools are more effective schools. Parents' concerns for the convenience of travel to the school act as a strong constraint on the operation of demand. Only a minority of parents choosing schools cited concerns about the schools' educational records or discipline at the schools or other reasons related to school effectiveness. Even here

"success" was often primarily a matter of the kinds of pupils who resided in the school's district or the history of the school (Willms 1986). Schools cited for poor examination results and discipline problems were invariably located in economically and socially disadvantaged areas. Schools cited favorably were usually located in the more well-to-do areas and had been selective schools before Scottish schools had been reorganized along comprehensive lines. (Indeed, some parents explicitly choose schools to avoid the "bad children" who attend their district school.) These surveys raise serious doubts about the validity of concluding that popular schools are "good" schools that should be rewarded or that unpopular schools are "bad" schools that should be penalized. Such a policy would likely result in increased disparities between schools in well-to-do areas and those in less-advantaged areas (Adler, Petch, and Tweedie 1989).

In sum, Chubb and Moe tell us something about the differences between market and political controls in current conditions; but they are not in a position to extend those conclusions to the operation of the market (or democratic controls) outside of that context. They do not give us any empirical basis on which to predict the crucial behavior of parents or school entrepreneurs as we move away from the current system of public and private education. Predicting their behavior requires reliance on other sources of data, and these suggest that market control of schools holds significantly less promise than Chubb and Moe claim.

FRAMING INSTITUTIONAL QUESTIONS

Chubb and Moe frame the question of institutional choice in education exclusively in terms of reliance on politics or markets. They also pack a great deal into their institutional logics of market and democratic control. According to Chubb and Moe, the choice between markets and politics determines all lesser decisions about education policy and school organization: school-level autonomy, principal-teacher-parent relations, and school goals. Their approach fundamentally mischaracterizes the nature of institutional choices in educational governance. It also excludes inquiry into the development of organizational structures and practices in education and the various influences of politics, markets, and other factors on those structures and practices.[6]

Chubb and Moe's analysis of private schools is driven by the idea of the market. Their emphasis on the market leads them to exclude discussion of other elements in the institutional structure of private education that would seem to be vital, such as the Catholic church's doctrine and hierarchy and the professional ideology of the teaching profession. In their approach, market control results in principals' being given autonomy; and responding to parents' concerns, principals' decisions determine the structure and operation of the organization. Surely this misses much, if not most, of what is institutional about private schools. Their discussion of democratic control in public schools takes a broad range of considerations into account—bureaucracies, teacher's unions, and interest groups, for instance. However, even in this discussion, they attribute the entire institutional structure of public schools to the initial choice of democratic control. School-level autonomy and policy coherence are eliminated by the self-interested actions of the various parties involved in schooling—bureaucrats; teachers and their unions; and associations representing minorities, handicapped children, and textbook publishers, among others.

In addition to being deterministic, these models of market and democratic control are biased. In democratic control, participants' selfish motives always undermine educational quality. Bureaucrats, politicians, teachers' unions, and other interest groups all pursue their own agendas; and those agendas are seemingly never related to improving education. Parents are always frustrated in this system. Parents' concerns and the responsiveness of school officials to those concerns are portrayed more benevolently in the market model. The market for education seems to work flawlessly, harnessing the self-interest of parents and school officials to produce efficiency and the common good. Chubb and Moe present no evidence to justify this strong characterization of politics and markets.

While we should aspire to address basic questions concerning the effects of market and politics, Chubb and Moe err in treating that choice as the sole causal factor rather than as part of a complicated and interactive process out of which come the varied institutional structures of private and public education. At the very least, the burden is on them to demonstrate that the choice between markets and politics explains so much of schools' organizational characteristics that it is justified to focus exclusively on those factors. They do not examine this question and instead report the differences between private and public schools as if they were confirmation of that point of view.

Institutions have recently become an important focus of inquiry in political science (Knott and Miller 1987; March and Olsen 1984; Smith 1988). However, compared to Chubb and Moe, others addressing the "new institutionalism" adopt a different, more detailed focus. For instance, March and Olsen stress the importance of political structure—the "collection of institutions, rules of behavior, norms, roles, physical arrangements, buildings, and archives that are relatively invariant in the face of turnover of individuals and relatively resilient to the idiosyncratic preferences and expectations of individuals" (1984, 741). Smith (1988) also emphasizes the importance of cognitive structures, such as popular belief systems and professional ideologies. These authors emphasize the importance of examining the origins and development of these institutional structures, recognizing the importance of strategic action, history, chance, and the influence of other institutions.

Describing the governing institutions in education, their origins, and how they affect the operation of schools involves considerably greater richness and complexity than Chubb and Moe's approach allows. For instance, the relative autonomy of school principals is an important element of an institutional understanding of schools. Principals' autonomy is not determined by whether the school is private or public but varies considerably within those types of schools. (This alone would seem to challenge Chubb and Moe's simple focus on markets and politics.) In part it is determined by structural factors such as state education law, union bargaining, church doctrine, and teachers' professional norms and by policy decisions about such issues as school size and curriculum. To some extent, it is also a matter of choice. Educational policy makers argue for greater school-level autonomy in public schools (Finn 1984). And despite Chubb and Moe's pessimism about the prospect of political reforms (p. 1085), the logic of democratic control does not preclude the possibility of deliberate institutional change.[7] In looking at the governing institutions of education, we should be focusing our investigations on these and other factors that influence principals' autonomy, not only whether schools are controlled by market or political institutions.[8] Indeed, all of the organizational structure and patterns of practice that Chubb and Moe look at in private and public education fit within the scope of this institutional focus. Their origins as well as their effects should be the focus of detailed study that looks at a much broader set of factors than questions of market and political systems of control.

CONCLUSION

Chubb and Moe have raised fundamental questions about the roles of markets and political institutions in education. These questions are particularly important because of the ongoing debates about parental choice in education and the growing emphasis on market institutions in the study of public policy. Chubb and Moe's study of organizational structures and patterns of practice in private and public schools provides important new data with which to address these questions. However, they are mistaken in looking at these results and educational governance solely in terms of their models of politics and markets. Instead, we should bring Chubb and Moe's perspective—especially their empirical study of schools' organizations—into the more detailed and focused studies of organizational structures and patterns of practice in education and their effects on the operation of schools and the education received by students.

Notes

1. Their survey findings generally support these conclusions, though there are some exceptions, particularly where findings for Catholic schools, elite private schools, or other private schools are not statistically significant for particular measures. I will not focus on these inconsistent results, although the inconsistencies weaken the argument that it is market control that produces the differences between public and private schools.

2. Chubb and Moe note several articles that challenge these studies' conclusions and then simply assert that they have, in their judgment, withstood the challenges (1988, 1086).

3. They acknowledge that this assumption should be examined further, but they do not carry out this examination. Looking at the influence of school size, student body homogeneity, region, and rural-

suburban-urban location would be particularly helpful in the interpretation of their results.

4. Some relevant evidence does exist, but Chubb and Moe do not use it. Several studies have been conducted of voucher experiments and choice within public school systems. These plans have been limited in scope (often focused on achieving voluntary desegregation), and studies of them have found mixed results; but they raise some doubts about the advantages of voucher plans and the workings of market systems in education (Cohen and Farrar, 1977; Murname, 1986; Nault and Uchitelle, 1982; Rossell and Glenn, 1988).

5. The following two paragraphs state the conclusions of a study of parental choice in Scotland conducted by Adler, Petch, and Tweedie (1989). See also University of Glasgow Department of Education (1986) and Tweedie (1989). This research can be used only to examine the operation of parental demand as local authorities maintained control over the supply of education in Scotland.

6. By framing the institutional choice as one of politics *or* markets, they exclude consideration of mixed systems, such as allowing parents to choose within the public school system and alternative ways of structuring democratic or market control of schools.

7. Their pessimism is contradicted by the adoption of strong rights of parental choice in Scotland and more limited schemes of parental choice in many U.S. jurisdictions, including Minnesota and Cambridge, Massachusetts. For a survey of the wide variety of schemes that exist, see Raywid (1985). In addition, there is growing support for similar plans in many other locations, as well as a myriad of institutional arrangements in local education that are not consistent with their depiction of democratic control.

8. A second key issue involves examining how principals use their autonomy. Chubb and Moe state that given the discipline of the market, principals hire effective teachers. They emphasize external restrictions on principals' influence in public school hiring and how this interferes with leadership, the selection of effective teachers, and incentives for good teaching (pp. 1082–84). They ignore possible beneficial effects of job security and protection from political and personal favoritism and bias.

References

Adler, Michael, Alison Petch, and Jack Tweedie. 1989. *Parental Choice and Education Policy*. Edinburgh: Edinburgh University Press.

Brigham, Frederick, H., Jr. 1989. *United States Catholic Elementary and Secondary Schools: A Statistical Report on Schools, Enrollment, and Staffing*. Washington: National Catholic Education Association.

Chubb, John E., and Terry Moe. 1988. "Politics, Markets, and the Organization of Schools." *American Political Science Review* 82:1065–1087.

Chubb, John E., and Terry Moe. 1990. *Politics, Markets, and America's Schools*. Washington: Brookings.

Cohen, David, and Eleanor Farrar. 1977. "Power to the Parents? The Story of Education Vouchers." *Public Interest* 48:72–97.

Coleman, James, and Thomas Hoffer. 1987. *Public and Private High Schools*. New York: Basic Books.

Coleman, James, Thomas Hoffer, and Sally Kilgore. 1982. *High School Achievement*. New York: Basic Books.

Domanico, Raymond. 1989. "Model for Choice: A Report on Manhattan's District 4." New York: Manhattan Institute for Policy Research. Typescript.

Finn, Chester. 1984. "Toward Strategic Independence: Nine Commandments for Enhancing School Effectiveness." *Phi Delta Kappan* 65:518–524.

Fliegel, Sy. 1989. "Parental Choice in East Harlem Schools." In *Public Schools by Choice*, ed. Joe Nathan. St. Paul: Institute for Learning and Teaching.

Gutmann, Amy. 1987. *Democratic Education*. Princeton: Princeton University Press.

Hirschman, Albert. 1970. *Exit, Voice, and Loyalty*. Cambridge: Harvard University Press.

Knott, Jack, and Gary Miller. 1987. *Reforming Bureaucracy: The Politics of Institutional Choice*. Englewood Cliffs: Prentice-Hall.

Kraushaar, Otto F. 1972. *American Nonpublic Schools: Patterns of Diversity*. Baltimore: Johns Hopkins University Press.

March, James, and Johan Olsen. 1984. "The New Institutionalism: Organizational Factors in Political Life." *American Political Science Review* 78:734–49.

Murname, Richard. 1986. "Family Choice in Public Education: The Roles of Students, Teachers, and System Designers." *Teachers College Record* 88:169–89.

National Catholic Education Association. 1985. *The Catholic High School: A National Portrait.* Washington: NCEA.

National Catholic Education Association. 1989. "Enrollment by Ethnic Group." Computer printout.

National Center for Education Statistics. 1988. *Digest of Education Statistics.* Washington: GPO.

Nault, Richard, and Susan Uchitelle. 1982. "School Choice in the Public Sector: A Case Study of Parental Decision Making." In *Family Choice in Schooling,* ed. Michael Manley-Casimir. Lexington, MA: Lexington Books.

Purkey, Stewart C., and Marshall Smith. 1983. "Effective Schools: A Review." *Elementary School Journal* 83:427–52.

Raywid, Mary Anne. 1985. "Family Choice Arrangements in Public Schools: A Review of the Literature." *Review of Educational Research* 55:435–67.

Rossell, Christine, and Charles Glenn. 1988. "The Cambridge Controlled Choice Plan." *Urban Review* 20:75–93.

Smith, Rogers. 1988. "Political Jurisprudence, the New Institutionalism, and the Future of Public Law," *American Political Science Review* 82:89–108.

Tweedie, Jack. 1989. "Parental Rights and Accountability in Education: Special Education and Choice of School." *Yale Law and Policy Review* 7:396–418.

U.S. Bureau of the Census, *Statistical Abstract of the United States: 1988* (108th ed.). Washington, 1987.

University of Glasgow, Department of Education. 1986. *Parental Choice of School in Scotland.* Glasgow: University of Glasgow.

Willms, J. Doug. 1986. "Social Class Segregation and Its Relationship to Pupils' Examination Results in Scotland." *American Sociological Review* 51:224–41.

DISCUSSION QUESTIONS AND ACTIVITIES

1. How do markets discourage excessive bureaucracy and promote better schools?

2. Are Chubb's criteria adequate for what constitutes a public school? What would be the educational consequences of defining public schools in this manner?

3. How would his plan work in terms of parental choice, state funding, school governance, and accountability?

4. Chubb claims that his plan would be a "truly public system—and a democratic one." Do you believe that his assessment is accurate? Explain why.

5. Does Chubb's approach preclude examining alternate explanations and intervening forces?

6. Does the market-control-of-school model consider education as a private good that denies education as a public good?

7. Private schools, according to Tweedie, have important advantages over public schools, and these advantages influence the Chubb study, but they are not inherent in the market system of control. Explain why.

8. Tweedie utilized data from Scotland. Can these findings be validly applied to American education?

9. Is Chubb's market-control model "deterministic" and "biased"? Is choice treated as the sole causal factor?

10. Investigate various states (Minnesota and others) that have initiated school-choice plans, and report your findings.

11. Read *Politics, Markets, and America's Schools* by Chubb and Moe (see Suggested Readings), and make an oral presentation and evaluation of the book in class.

SUGGESTED READINGS

"Brookings Institute Calls for Open Market." *Education Week* (June 6, 1990): 1.

Chubb, John. "Making Schools Better: Choice and Educational Improvement." *Equity and Choice* 5 (May 1989): 5–10.

Chubb, John. "The Theory: The Rationale for Educational Choice." In *Education Policy Paper No. 2*. New York: Center for Educational Innovation, Manhattan Institute for Policy Research, 1989.

Chubb, John, and Terry Moe. *Politics, Markets, and America's Schools*. Washington, D.C.: Brookings Institution, 1990.

Chubb, John E., and Terry M. Moe. "Politics, Markets, and the Organization of Schools." *American Political Science Review* 82 (December 1988): 1065–1077.

Hechinger, Fred M. "Put Schools on the Free Market and Let Parents Choose, Two Authors Propose." *New York Times* (June 20, 1990): B9.

Olson, Lynn. "Prescription for a Revolution." *Teacher Magazine* (August 1990): 46–52.

"Wrong Surgery for Sick Schools." (Editorial). *New York Times* (July 3, 1990): A14.

CHAPTER 6

THE EMANCIPATION OF TEACHING

Although heavily influenced by Marxism, Henry A. Giroux is highly critical of deterministic and structural tendencies within contemporary Marxist philosophy and its failure to develop a theory of subjectivity. He seeks to develop a theory for a radical pedagogy. This is undertaken by seeking an in-depth psychology to understand the mechanism of domination and the process of liberation. Giroux develops a concept of critical discourse within a post-Marxism framework that brings together the Frankfurt School on the one end and Paulo Freire on the other.

He does not see radical teachers as free-floating revolutionaries but as persons within and outside of schools who might develop educative practices outside of established institutions. Giroux wants schools to participate in recreating a new society; he views schools as potent vehicles for social change. Key players in this drama are teachers and students. The school will seek to unite theory and practice as it provides unified cognitive and affective characteristics that will liberate the individual and bring about social reconstruction.

In the selections that follow, Giroux shows the dangers of the technocratic approach in education and proposes that these dangers can be overcome by restructuring the nature of teacher work so that teachers become transformative intellectuals. Colin Lacey offers three serious criticisms of Giroux's ideas.

TEACHERS AS TRANSFORMATIVE INTELLECTUALS

HENRY A. GIROUX

A former high school history teacher, Henry A. Giroux (b. 1943) has taught at Boston University and is currently Associate Professor of Education at Miami University, Oxford, Ohio. Among his books are Ideology, Culture, and the Process of Schooling *and* Theory and Resistance in Education. *He is also a contributor to education and social-theory journals. His primary focus is on the roles that schools play in promoting success and failure among different classes and groups of students, especially the way schools mediate values and messages that result in special privileges for some groups.*

The call for educational reform has gained the status of a recurring national event, much like the annual Boston Marathon. There have been more than 30 national reports since the beginning of the twentieth century, and more than 300 task forces have been developed by the various states to discover how public schools can improve educational quality in the United States.[1] But unlike many past educational reform movements, the present call for educational change presents *both* a threat and challenge to public school teachers that appears unprecedented in our nation's history. The threat comes in the form of a series of educational reforms that display little confidence in the ability of public school teachers to provide intellectual and moral leadership for our nation's young. For instance, many of the recommendations that have emerged in the current debate either ignore the role teachers play in preparing learners to be active and critical citizens, or they suggest reforms that ignore the intelligence, judgment, and experience that teachers might offer in such a debate. Where teachers do enter the debate, they are the object of educational reforms that reduce them to the status of high-level technicians carrying out dictates and objectives decided by "experts" far removed from the everyday realities of classroom life.[2] The message appears to be that teachers do not count when it comes to critically examining the nature and process of educational reform.

The political and ideological climate does not look favorable for teachers at the moment. But it does offer them the challenge to join in a public debate with their critics as well as the opportunity to engage in a much-

From Henry A. Giroux, "Teachers as Transformative Intellectuals," *Social Education* 49 (May 1985):376–379. Reprinted from *Social Education* with permission of the National Council for the Social Studies.

[1]K. Patricia Cross, "The Rising Tide of School Reform Reports," *Phi Delta Kappan*, 66:3 (November 1984), p. 167.

[2]For a more detailed critique of the reforms, see my book with Stanley Aronowitz, *Education Under Siege* (South Hadley, MA: Bergin and Garvey Publishers, 1985); also see the incisive comments on the impositional nature of the various reports in Charles A. Tesconi, Jr., "Additive Reforms and the Retreat from Purpose." *Educational Studies* 15:1 (Spring 1984), pp. 1–11; Terrence E. Deal, "Searching for the Wizard: The Quest for Excellence in Education," *Issues in Education* 2:1 (Summer 1984), pp. 56–67; Svi Shapiro, "Choosing Our Educational Legacy: Disempowerment or Emancipation?" *Issues in Education* 2:1 (Summer 1984), pp. 11–22.

needed self-critique regarding the nature and purpose of teacher preparation, in-service teacher programs, and the dominant forms of classroom teaching. Similarly, the debate provides teachers with the opportunity to organize collectively so as to struggle to improve the conditions under which they work and to demonstrate to the public the central role that teachers must play in any viable attempt to reform the public schools.

In order for teachers and others to engage in such a debate, it is necessary that a theoretical perspective be developed that redefines the nature of the educational crisis while simultaneously providing the basis for an alternative view of teacher training and work. In short, recognizing that the current crisis in education largely has to do with the developing trend toward the disempowerment of teachers at all levels of education is a necessary theoretical precondition in order for teachers to organize effectively and establish a collective voice in the current debate. Moreover, such a recognition will have to come to grips not only with a growing loss of power among teachers around the basic conditions of their work but also with a changing public perception of their role as reflective practitioners.

I want to make a small theoretical contribution to this debate and the challenge it calls forth by examining two major problems that need to be addressed in the interest of improving the quality of "teacher work," which includes all the clerical tasks and extra assignments as well as classroom instruction. First, I think it is imperative to examine the ideological and material forces that have contributed to what I want to call the proletarianization of teacher work; that is, the tendency to reduce teachers to the status of specialized technicians within the school bureaucracy, whose function then becomes one of managing and implementing curricula programs rather than developing or critically appropriating curricula to fit specific pedagogical concerns. Second, there is a need to defend schools as institutions essential to maintaining and developing a critical democracy and also to defending teachers as transformative intellectuals who combine scholarly reflection and practice in the service of educating students to be thoughtful, active citizens. In the remainder of this essay, I will develop these points and conclude by examining their implications for providing an alternative view of teacher work.

TOWARD A DEVALUING AND DESKILLING OF TEACHER WORK

One of the major threats facing prospective and existing teachers within the public schools is the increasing developing of instrumental ideologies that emphasize a technocratic approach to both teacher preparation and classroom pedagogy. At the core of the current emphasis on instrumental and pragmatic factors in school life are a number of important pedagogical assumptions. These include a call for the separation of conception from execution; the standardization of school knowledge in the interest of managing and controlling it; and the devaluation of critical, intellectual work on the part of teachers and students for the primacy of practical considerations.[3]

---

[3]For an exceptional commentary on the need to educate teachers to be intellectuals, see John Dewey, "The Relation of Theory to Practice," in John Dewey, *The Middle Works, 1899–1924*, edited by Jo Ann Boydston (Carbondale, Southern Illinois University Press, 1977), [originally published in 1904]. See also, Israel Scheffler, "University Scholarship and the Education of Teachers," *Teachers College Record*, 70:1 (1968), pp. 1–12; Henry A. Giroux, *Ideology, Culture, and the Process of Schooling* (Philadelphia: Temple University Press, 1981).

This type of instrumental rationality finds one of its strongest expressions historically in the training of prospective teachers. That teacher training programs in the United States have long been dominated by a behavioristic orientation and emphasis on mastering subject areas and methods of teaching is well documented.[4] The implications of this approach, made clear by Zeichner, are worth repeating:

> *Underlying this orientation to teacher education is a metaphor of "production," a view of teaching as an "applied science," and a view of the teacher as primarily an "executor" of the laws and principles of effective teaching. Prospective teachers may or may not proceed through the curriculum at their own pace and may participate in varied or standardized learning activities, but that which they are to master is limited in scope (e.g., to a body of professional content knowledge and teaching skills) and is fully determined in advance by others, often on the basis of research on teacher effectiveness. The prospective teacher is viewed primarily as a passive recipient of this professional knowledge and plays little part in determining the substance and direction of his or her preparation program.[5]*

The problems with this approach are evident in John Dewey's argument that teacher training programs that emphasize only technical expertise do a disservice both to the nature of teaching and to their students.[6] Instead of learning to reflect upon the principles that structure classroom life and practice, prospective teachers are taught methodologies that appear to deny the very need for critical think-ing. The point is that teacher education programs often lose sight of the need to educate students to examine the underlying nature of school problems. Further, these programs need to substitute for the language of management and efficiency a critical analysis of the less obvious conditions that structure the ideological and material practices of schooling.

Instead of learning to raise questions about the principles underlying different classroom methods, research techniques, and theories of education, students are often preoccupied with learning the "how to," with "what works," or with mastering the best way to teach a *given* body of knowledge. For example, the mandatory field-practice seminars often consist of students sharing with each other the techniques they have used in managing and controlling classroom discipline, organizing a day's activities and learning how to work within specific time tables. Examining one such program, Jesse Goodman raises some important questions about the incapacitating silences it embodies. He writes:

> *There was no questioning of feelings, assumptions, or definitions in this discussion. For example, the "need" for external rewards and punishments to "make kids learn" was taken for granted; the educational and ethical implications were not addressed. There was no display of concern for stimulating or nurturing a child's intrinsic desire to learn. Definitions of good kids as "quiet kids," workbook work as "reading," on-task time as "learning," and getting through the material on time as "the goal of teaching"—all went unchallenged. Feelings of pressure and possible guilt about not keeping to time schedules also went unexplored. The real*

---

[4]See, for instance, Herbert Kliebard, "The Question of Teacher Education," in D. McCarty (ed.) *New Perspectives on Teacher Education* (San Francisco: Jossey-Bass, 1973).

[5]Kenneth M. Zeichner, "Alternative Paradigms on Teacher Education," *Journal of Teacher Education* 34:3 (May–June 1983), p. 4.

[6]Dewey, op. cit.

concern in this discussion was that everyone "shared." [7]

Technocratic and instrumental rationalities are also at work within the teaching field itself, and they play an increasing role in reducing teacher autonomy with respect to the development and planning of curricula and the judging and implementation of classroom instruction. This is most evident in the proliferation of what has been called "teacher-proof" curriculum packages. [8] The underlying rationale in many of these packages reserves for teachers the role of simply carrying out predetermined content and instructional procedures. The method and aim of such packages is to legitimate what I call management pedagogies. That is, knowledge is broken down into discrete parts, standardized for easier management and consumption, and measured through predefined forms of assessment. Curricula approaches of this sort are management pedagogies because the central questions regarding learning are reduced to the problem of management, i.e., "how to allocate resources (teachers, students, and material) to produce the maximum number of certified . . . students within a designated time." [9] The underlying theoretical assumption that guides this type of pedagogy is that the behavior of teachers needs to be controlled and made consistent and predictable across different schools and student populations.

What is clear in this approach is that it organizes school life around curricular, instructional, and evaluation experts who do the thinking while teachers are reduced to doing the implementing. The effect is not only to deskill teachers, to remove them from the processes of deliberation and reflection, but also to routinize the nature of learning and classroom pedagogy. Needless to say, the principles underlying management pedagogies are at odds with the premise that teachers should be actively involved in producing curricula materials suited to the cultural and social contexts in which they teach. More specifically, the narrowing of curricula choices to a back-to-basics format and the introduction of lock-step, time-on-task pedagogies operate from the theoretically erroneous assumption that *all* students can learn from the same materials, classroom instructional techniques, and modes of evaluation. The notion that students come from different histories and embody different experiences, linguistic practices, cultures, and talents is strategically ignored within the logic and accountability of management pedagogy theory.

TEACHERS AS TRANSFORMATIVE INTELLECTUALS

In what follows, I want to argue that one way to rethink and restructure the nature of teacher work is to view teachers as transformative intellectuals. The category of intellectual is helpful in a number of ways. First, it provides a theoretical basis for examining teacher work as a form of intellectual labor, as opposed to defining it in purely instrumental or technical terms. Second, it clarifies the kinds of ideological and practical conditions necessary for teachers to function as intellectuals. Third, it helps to make clear the role teachers play in producing and legitimating

---

[7]Jesse Goodman, "Reflection and Teacher Education: A Case Study and Theoretical Analysis," *Interchange* 15:3 (1984), p. 15.

[8]Michael Apple, *Education and Power* (Boston: Routledge & Kegan Paul, Ltd., 1982).

[9]Patrick Shannon, "Mastery Learning in Reading and the Control of Teachers and Students," *Language Arts* 61:5 (September 1984), p. 488.

various political, economic, and social interests through the pedagogies they endorse and utilize.

By viewing teachers as intellectuals, we can illuminate the important idea that all human activity involves some form of thinking. In other words, no activity, regardless of how routinized it might become, can be abstracted from the functioning of the mind in some capacity. This is a crucial issue, because by arguing that the use of the mind is a general part of all human activity we dignify the human capacity for integrating thinking and practice, and in doing so highlight the core of what it means to view teachers as reflective practitioners. Within this discourse, teachers can be seen not merely as ''performers professionally equipped to realize effectively any goals that may be set for them. Rather [they should] be viewed as free men and women with a special dedication to the values of the intellect and the enhancement of the critical powers of the young.''[10]

Viewing teachers as intellectuals also provides a strong theoretical critique of technocratic and instrumental ideologies underlying an educational theory that separates the conceptualization, planning, and design of curricula from the processes of implementation and execution. It is important to stress that teachers must take active responsibility for raising serious questions about what they teach, how they are to teach, and what the larger goals are for which they are striving. This means that they must take a responsible role in shaping the purposes and conditions of schooling. Such a task is impossible within a division of labor in which teachers have little influence over the ideological and economic conditions of their work. This point has a normative and political dimension that seems especially relevant for teachers. If we believe that the role of teaching cannot be reduced to merely training in the practical skills but involves, instead, the education of a class of intellectuals vital to the development of a free society, then the category of intellectual becomes a way of linking the purpose of teacher education, public schooling, and in-service training to the very principles necessary for developing a democratic order and society.

I have argued that by viewing teachers as intellectuals those persons concerned with education can begin to rethink and reform the traditions and conditions that have prevented schools and teachers from assuming their full potential as active, reflective scholars and practitioners. It is imperative that I qualify this point and extend it further. I believe that it is important not only to view teachers as intellectuals, but also to contextualize in political and normative terms the concrete social functions that teachers perform. In this way, we can be more specific about the different relations that teachers have both to their work and to the dominant society.

A fundamental starting point for interrogating the social function of teachers as intellectuals is to view schools as economic, cultural and social sites that are inextricably tied to the issues of power and control. This means that schools do more than pass on in an objective fashion a common set of values and knowledge. On the contrary, schools are places that represent forms of knowledge, language practices, social relations, and values that are representative of a particular selection and exclusion from the wider culture. As such, schools serve to introduce and legitimate *particular* forms of social life. Rather than being objective institutions removed from the dynamics of politics and power, schools actu-

---

[10]Israel Scheffler, op. cit., p. 11.

ally are contested spheres that embody and express a struggle over what forms of authority, types of knowledge, forms or moral regulation, and versions of the past and future should be legitimated and transmitted to students. This struggle is most visible in the demands, for example, of right-wing religious groups currently trying to institute school prayer, remove certain books from the school library, and include certain forms of religious teachings in the science curricula. Of course, different demands are made by feminists, ecologists, minorities, and other interest groups who believe that the schools should teach women's studies, courses on the environment, or black history. In short, schools are not neutral sites, and teachers cannot assume the posture of being neutral either.

In the broadest sense, teachers as intellectuals have to be seen in terms of the ideological and political interests that structure the nature of the discourse, classroom social relations, and values that they legitimate in their teaching. With this perspective in mind, I want to conclude that teachers should become transformative intellectuals if they are to subscribe to a view of pedagogy that believes in educating students to be active, critical citizens.

Central to the category of transformative intellectual is the necessity of making the pedagogical more political and the political more pedagogical. Making the pedagogical more political means inserting schooling directly into the political sphere by arguing that schooling represents both a struggle to define meaning and a struggle over power relations. Within this perspective, critical reflection and action become part of a fundamental social project to help students develop a deep and abiding faith in the struggle to overcome economic, political, and social injustices, and to further humanize themselves as part of this struggle. In this case, knowledge and power are inextricably linked to the presupposition that to choose life, to recognize the necessity of improving its democratic and qualitative character for all people, is to understand the preconditions necessary to struggle for it.

Making the political more pedagogical means utilizing forms of pedagogy that embody political interests that are emancipatory in nature; that is, using forms of pedagogy that treat students as critical agents; make knowledge problematic; utilize critical and affirming dialogue; and make the case for struggling for a qualitatively better world for all people. In part, this suggests that transformative intellectuals take seriously the need to give students an active voice in their learning experiences. It also means developing a critical vernacular that is attentive to problems experienced at the level of everyday life, particularly as they are related to pedagogical experiences connected to classroom practice. As such, the pedagogical starting point for such intellectuals is not the isolated student but individuals and groups in their various cultural, class, racial, historical, and gender settings, along with the particularity of their diverse problems, hopes, and dreams.

Transformative intellectuals need to develop a discourse that unites the language of critique with the language of possibility, so that social educators recognize that they can make changes. In doing so, they must speak out against economic, political, and social injustices both within and outside of schools. At the same time, they must work to create the conditions that give students the opportunity to become citizens who have the knowledge and courage to struggle in order to make despair unconvincing and hope practical. As difficult as this task may seem to social educators, it is a struggle worth waging. To do otherwise is to deny social educators the opportunity to assume the role of transformative intellectuals.

COLIN LACEY

DILEMMA LANGUAGE

Colin Lacey is a faculty member at University of Sussex, England.

Henry Giroux's book *Ideology, Culture and the Process of Schooling* has the benefit of an almost adulatory preface by Stanley Aronowitz who describes his approach as a "far cry from all previous theory" and as a "fecund work of *immanent critique*." In addition, according to Aronowitz, it contributes the "absolutely singular breakthrough in American literature" by offering us a critique of schooling within a framework which makes pedagogy an emancipatory activity.

In fact the introduction and six essays that make up the book are long on criticism and synthesis and short on new theoretical approaches. The critique, in each case, is developed within a now familiar framework. Giroux tells us that functionalism has been disposed of by the newer critical approaches of phenomenology and humanistic Marxism . . . Giroux points out [that] the neo-Marxist or economistic view, which provides [the] theory of class domination, presents an overdetermined view of correspondence between the effects of schooling and the economic structure.

Giroux wishes to produce a synthesis by demonstrating the contradictions within existing institutions and pointing to the degrees of autonomy that these contradictions confer within a class-dominated society. He thus deals with an exceptionally important topic and certainly reminds us of the inadequacies of our understanding of many aspects of the school system. He reminds us of the degree to which many of our present practices and educational programs support the class domination that many of us complain about. He reminds us of the importance of developing within our education, whether it be for our pupils or teachers in training, a critical awareness of the commonsense assumptions that legitimize existing practices and forms of knowledge, that bolster this domination. He reminds us that the present crisis in education was not produced by education. It is a political and economic crisis with its roots outside the education system, which must not accept the blame for it.

Finally he proposes training programs that will produce a new radical pedagogy welded to a new radical content, in which the learner and teacher collaborate in producing a new relationship and a new understanding of the multiple socioeconomic and ideological connections "that mediate between schools and the wider social structure." The revolution in education, he argues, must begin now but teachers will need to fight in each future generation for a better and more just society.

Despite my sympathy for the task he sets himself and the hard work he has put into reading, synthesizing, and referencing the theoretical works of many writers, my view is that he fails either to advance our theoretical understanding to any extent or to popularize the works of the writers on whom he depends for most of his concepts and ideas. It is in fact not at all clear whether he is writing for an

From "Dilemma Language," Reviews by Colin Lacey. © *Times Educational Supplement*, 1982.

academic audience or producing a popularizing account of the theoretical works of others meant to inform radical educators. The result is a text studded with terminology which often obscures and sometimes damages the analysis. For example, the term *cultural capital* is useful if it is used sparingly for those aspects of culture that resemble the use of capital by the capitalist class. If the term is used as synonymous with *culture*, it loses any analytical quality and unnecessarily complicates the text.

A second major problem lies in the large gap left by the analysis between the theoretical debate and the problem and constraints of the classroom. In fact the author fails to identify these practical problems and frequently talks of the classroom as if it were a theoretical entity.

Although he acknowledges the important work done by sociologists studying the classroom, he fails to make use of their findings. As a result many educationists will feel just as baffled by his suggestions as by the "pessimistic" "Orwellian" "economistic" sociologists whom he criticizes for trying to persuade educationists that change is not possible within education.

This last point leads to my third major criticism. Giroux's claim to a new synthesis of radical pedagogy and radical content depends on an intimate understanding of the classroom and the culture of the learner. Yet he makes absolutely no progress toward deepening our understanding of what this might mean. We are left with exhortation. As learners we have a right to be disappointed.

DISCUSSION QUESTIONS AND ACTIVITIES

1. Describe the technocratic approach in both teacher education and classroom pedagogy.

2. What are the shortcomings of the technocratic approach?

3. Collect information about your own teacher education program, and observe the extent to which it follows a technocratic model. Which of the technocratic practices should be kept and which ones eliminated?

4. Why does Giroux believe it is better to conceptualize the teacher's role as a "transformative intellectual"?

5. Schools, it is said, are "contested spheres" that are "inextricably tied to the issues of power and control." What does that mean?

6. How can we make the "pedagogical more political and the political more pedagogical"? Do you think that it is important to do so?

7. Lacey claims that Giroux's writing is replete with terminology that obscures analysis and that it is not clear for what audience he is writing. What is an author's responsibility to his or her audience?

8. Does Giroux fail to bridge the gap, as Lacey claims, between theory and practical classroom problems and constraints?

9. Does Giroux's attempt at a synthesis of radical pedagogy fail to provide "an intimate understanding of the classroom and culture of the learner"?

SUGGESTED READINGS

Books by Henry A. Giroux

Critical Pedagogy, the State, and Cultural Struggle (editor). Albany: State University of New York Press, 1981 (with Peter McLaren).

Education under Siege: The Conservative, Liberal, and Radical Debate over Schooling. Westport, Conn.: Bergin & Garvey, 1985 (with Stanley Aronowitz)

The Hidden Curriculum and Moral Education. Berkeley, Calif.: McCutchan, 1983 (with David Purpel)

Ideology, Culture, and the Process of Schooling. Philadelphia: Temple University Press, 1981. 1984 paperback.

Popular Culture, Schooling, and Everyday Life. Westport, Conn.: Bergin & Garvey, 1989 (coauthor with others)

Postmodern Education: Politics, Culture, and Social Criticism. Minneapolis: University of Minnesota Press, 1990 (with Stanley Aronowitz)

Postmodernism, Feminism, and Cultural Politics: Rethinking Education Boundaries (editor). Albany: State University of New York Press, 1991.

Schooling and the Struggle for Public Life: Critical Pedagogy in the Modern Age. Minneapolis: University of Minnesota Press, 1988.

Theory and Resistance in Education. Westport, Conn.: Bergin & Garvey, 1983.

Teachers as Intellectuals: Toward a Critical Pedagogy of Learning. Westport, Conn.: Bergin & Garvey, 1988.

FURTHER THOUGHTS ON REFORMERS

Boyer states that high schools should have a clear and vital mission; develop thinking, writing, speaking, and listening skills; and provide a core of common knowledge. He reemphasizes the role of general education at the secondary level. Some may question whether sufficient options would be built into his program to provide adequately for individual differences and diverse interests and aspirations.

In contrast to Boyer's subject curriculum, Sizer divides the curriculum into four broad areas as a more productive way to organize the high school program. It is better, he believes, not to teach too many subjects but to teach them more thoroughly. Despite curriculum flexibility, whether the cultural heritage can best be transmitted in such a curriculum is open to question.

Mortimer Adler is a perennialist. *Perennialism* derives its aims for education from human nature, holding that human nature is the same everywhere, both today and in the past; human beings are, above all, rational animals. Since this theory stems from human nature, the function of persons is the same in every age and in every society. Rationality is the highest attribute, and, therefore, this attribute should be developed to its fullest extent. It can best be developed through educational institutions, whereas other attributes—morality and spirituality—can best be developed in different institutions (e.g., family and church). *Perennialism* holds that truth is absolute, and it is the task of education to impart these truths. These truths can largely be found in the great books of the past. Since the truth is the same everywhere and everyone is a rational being, all students study the same curriculum, as is the case with the Paideia Proposal. The reader is more likely to accept the proposal once the underlying philosophical grounds are accepted. Adler's reform rationale appeals to restoration by prescribing past ideals and standards and by reinstating a required curriculum.

Hirsch believes that cultural literacy is much more than recognizing words on a page; it requires a knowledge of shared, taken-for-granted information. The disappearance of this traditional literate culture has been an egregious mistake, but he believes that this core background of necessary knowledge can be identified and taught successfully. Hirsch's position is that of an essentialist. *Essentialism* emphasizes the value of transmitting the cultural heritage to all youth, of seeing that they study the basic disciplines. Subjects should be studied in terms of a logical, chronological, or causal approach rather than organized along the lines of activities and projects based on the immediate needs of students (as progressives had done). Only in this way will students develop a sound grasp and appreciation of the heritage, and only in a curriculum that stresses these elements will they develop their minds, become educated persons, and exhibit good citizenship practices.

John Chubb believes that the educational system functions to discourage effective school organization and stifle student achievement. He insists that the use of market forces—competition among schools and parental choice—will likely overcome these problems. Doing so would mean that many nonpublic schools could be chartered as a public school and receive public funds, and each student would be free to attend any public school in the state with the aid of scholarships. One of Chubb's assumptions is that public schools constitute a monopoly, and consequently, a market plan would open many new options for parents. The marketplace analogy suggests that its application to education would do for it what free enterprise has done for the economy and its productivity. Schools, however, are relatively decentralized and do compete with private schools and with each other, in their sports program and for teachers, appropriations, special projects, and so forth. The market analogy is misleading insofar as profit-making firms sell their products to anyone who has cash or credit, whereas private schools are selective and not open to everyone. Moreover, rather than a free marketplace of competition, American capitalism features an oligopoly of big government, big business, and large labor unions, with various tensions and alliances between them. Laws and regulations have been passed to restrict monopolies, price-fixing, and other abuses; a pure marketplace of competition exists only in a theoretical model of capitalism and falls woefully short in actual practice.

Giroux wants schools to participate in developing a new society, and he sees teachers and students playing a key role in this process. One way that this is done is for teachers to avoid becoming technocrats and opt for a transformative intellectual role in which they can understand and relate the pedagogical and political spheres. Giroux's reform rationale appeals to decision making. One needs to decide what the aims of education should be and, consequently, whether the aims proposed by Giroux are justifiable. How are aims determined? A number of approaches have been employed: (1) derive the aims from values deemed to be of greatest worth (a hierarchy may be established, as Herbert Spencer did); (2) derive aims from human nature (as perennialists do); (3) develop aims to meet societal needs; and (4) draw out aims from a preferred philosophy of education. Another approach, as suggested by R. S. Peters, is to claim that the search for aims is misguided because one is not asking for a statement of ends extrinsic to education; one is seeking instead to initiate the young into worthwhile activities that are intrinsic to the educational process. Dewey, even earlier, developed an intrinsic position: because the characteristic of life is growth, education is one with growing. Since growth is relative to nothing but further growth, education is not subordinate to anything except more education.

The reformers can be understood in various ways. How do they define education? In what respects do they differ in their conception of education? What educational aims are most important? What reasons are given for adopting a set of aims? Notice that some reformers seek to liberate the learner. What are they liberating the learner from, and what will the learner be able to do as a result of such liberation? What sort of institutions will nurture the type of person they believe education should develop?

PART II

INNOVATIONS AND ALTERNATIVES

Recent years have been marked by widespread dissatisfaction with public education and numerous attempts to find more successful approaches to educating the young. Not surprisingly, educators have sought to offer innovations and alternatives. Innovation is the introduction of any new idea, method, or device to improve some aspect of the educational process. The idea could lead to a new way of handling gifted or handicapped learners. The innovation may be the project method or the initiation of team teaching, and the device could range from educational television to microcomputers. In contrast, educational alternatives are systems and plans, both inside and outside public education that are different from the typical public school model.

Alternatives first appeared outside of public education as different types of schools (such as free schools), as new organizational plans for redistributing educational resources (vouchers), or plans for home instruction. Alternatives were developed in public education during the 1970s and ranged from schools for performing arts to the back-to-basics alternative.

Although there can be no innovation or alternative without change, most changes are not innovations or alternatives. Change is when something or someone becomes different and may be accidental. An innovation, since it is brought about by human agency to serve a particular purpose, rules out changes in nature and human changes that are unintentional. It is true that some innovations, just as scientific discoveries, are serendipitous. In such cases, however, it is still necessary to make the connection between the discovery and an educational goal and then visualize the innovation within an educational context. Thus, by the time the discoverer finishes, the process has become highly deliberate.

But how novel does something have to be before it is counted as an innovation? Usually it will require some distinctive feature in at least one of the following aspects: rationale, organization, curriculum, or instruction. For instance, the rationale for accountability differs perceptibly from traditional rationales for school organization and evaluation; the organizational procedures of mainstreaming represent a sharp departure from earlier practices in handling handicapped children; and bilingual education differs significantly in curricula and instruction from traditional practices. Although innovations that are highly original are likely to leave a lasting impression, such innovations are also likely to meet with greater resistance from those that require less change. The following survey of key innovations and alternatives of the recent past will clarify these points.

THE CONTINUITY OF INNOVATIONS AND ALTERNATIVES

Early Innovations in Instruction, Curriculum, and Organization

The Dalton Plan.   This is a study plan based on instructional contracts for students. It was named after Dalton, Massachusetts, the district in which it was first introduced in 1920 by Helen Parkhurst. The plan actually attracted more followers overseas—in Europe, China, and Japan—than in the United States.

The plan called for a series of classrooms that were allocated to certain subjects. The classrooms were designated as laboratories and pupils as experimenters. In the English laboratory, pupils had access to significant literary works, and in the geography laboratory, the teacher helped pupils use models, maps, charts, and globes. Thus there was a laboratory for each subject taught in school.

The pupil was given a mimeographed guide sheet that listed all the work to be done for the month. The pupil then signed a contract to complete the assignments on the sheet by specified dates. There was no class teaching and pupils could move from one room to another as they chose in fulfilling their contract. It was initially thought that ideally each pupil would receive his or her own assignment sheet, but the burden proved too great for most teachers. One assignment sheet was usually compiled for everyone. Slower learners and indolent pupils required more supervision and direction. Some Dalton followers set aside afternoons for games, gymnastics, and social activities. Enrichment of English was through debates, public speaking, and histrionics; history was supplemented by discussion of current politics, the customs and manners of earlier eras, and other topics.

Despite greater freedom and individual attention than in traditional classrooms, the Dalton Plan came under criticism for insufficient socialization practices and lack of social education. This criticism, however, was more applicable to the original Dalton Plan and not to those that sprang up in various parts of the world where some attempt was made to balance individual learning with social education. Another criticism was that it did not actually individualize instruction because the assignments were not geared to the needs of each student. Nor did it break from the traditional subject curriculum, which some progressives deplored. The plan was suited for a subject curriculum and could be used with any standard subject, except perhaps with foreign languages.

The Winnetka Plan.   This plan was initiated in 1919 by Carleton Washburne (1889–1968) in Winnetka, Illinois, as a means of individualizing instruction at the elementary level. The curriculum was divided into two parts: the *common essentials*, the three Rs, sciences, and social studies; and *cultural and creative experiences*, which were taught in a group setting.

The common essentials were individualized at the beginning of the term by evaluating the child in each subject and then establishing assignments that were adjusted to the child's needs. Class recitation was discarded. Instead, pupils would read for the teacher one at a time while the others studied. Once a portion of their work was completed, they could ask the teacher for a test and then move on to the next assignment whenever the test was successfully passed. In the Winnetka Plan, children neither skipped grades nor failed. Thus studies were divided by the teachers into tasks and goals, and each child was given simple directions for proceeding independently.

Half the morning and half the afternoon sessions were dedicated to individual work with the common essentials, while the remaining half of the morning and afternoon was devoted to such cultural and creative experiences as plays, open forums, school journals, self-government meetings, workshops, excursions, shop work, music, and art.

The Winnetka Plan was more genuinely individualized than the Dalton Plan; it enabled students to proceed at their own pace, whereas the Dalton Plan insisted that a pupil could not proceed in any subject until the entire monthly assignment was completed. Studies of the Winnetka Plan under Washburne's direction showed favorable results in terms of student performance or standardized tests, except in spelling where they lagged behind. Washburne used the Winnetka Plan for two decades. However, when adopted elsewhere, it was usually modified considerably to bring it more into line with traditional practices.

Some questions were also raised over what constituted "the common essentials" and whether these subjects were the ones that could best be individualized. Additionally, questions arose over how the two major areas of the program could be connected.

The Activity or Experience Curriculum.   This curriculum emerged in elementary schools during the progressive movement in the 1930s. It was based on the assumption that children learn best by experiencing things, rather than by the presentation of subject matter to them. Furthermore, units of study were constructed from a knowledge of their needs and interests. It was also based on the conviction that learning is an active affair, and involvement in activities will overcome the child's passivity and lack of motivation found in traditional schools. The program usually called for some pupil-teacher planning in which teachers ask children about their needs. Teachers and pupils worked together by using a problem-solving approach in planning, focusing on children's interests for organizational purposes.

This program was aimed at overcoming the interest and motivation problem in the subject curriculum, perhaps meeting some additional needs, and keeping students actively involved. One serious mistake, however, was the assumption that because learning is an active affair, then activity itself will lead to effective learning. One may learn by doing, but not all doing results in learning. Activity may be a necessary condition for some forms of learning but not a necessary and sufficient condition. Moreover, an activity curriculum tends to confuse overt activity with doing. Thinking, however, involves an active role by the learner but may not be observable. Another weakness is that since the child's range of experience is extremely limited, it is incumbent upon the school to broaden interests rather than stick to present ones. Finally, to use needs as a basis for curriculum planning may be untenable. To say that a need exists and that it should be fulfilled is to recognize that it exists to fulfill some objective. Whether or not an objective is desirable is determined by a set of values or the school's philosophy—not an appeal to needs.

The Project Method.   William Heard Kilpatrick (1871–1965) believed that the activities found in agriculture and extension work could be applied to other aspects of life through projects. His notion of a project, however, was much broader than the conventional one: "The presence of a dominating purpose." Thus building a boat, making a dress, or staging a play were considered projects, as well as any other activity with a dominating purpose. It was important, in Kilpatrick's view, that any given project would lead to other worthwhile projects, and it was better for each student to choose the project and plan it with teacher guidance, when needed. The Project Method, Kilpatrick believed, is valuable not just to sustain student interest but because life itself is composed of a series of projects, and, therefore, this way of learning will be a suitable preparation for life.

Kilpatrick's definition of the Project Method, however, was too broad since it tended to equate any goal-directed behavior with a project, even though much of this behavior involved no project in the conventional sense of the term. Furthermore, the Project Method lacked structure, sequence, and organization; it was difficult to build a curriculum on the basis of projects. Moreover, classroom management was a problem because too many divergent activities were taking place simultaneously. Moving from one project into another was not always easy, and children became bored and restless. Many projects may also tap only lower-level cognitive abilities. The bulk of organized knowledge, as well as skill development, was in danger of being lost with projects as the basis of curriculum. Today the curriculum is not built on projects alone; however, the "pure" Project Method can still be found in industrial arts, vocational agriculture, and the sciences.

The Platoon System.   Many American school districts adopted the Platoon System early in this century. The first system was organized by William Wirt (1874–1938) in Bluffton, Indiana, in 1900, where Wirt served as school superintendent. The Platoon System divided the school population into two groups. While one group (Platoon A) received instruction in the three Rs for two hours daily, the second group (Platoon B) studied subjects in specially equipped facilities (shop, gym, art room) for the same length of time. Both groups exchanged places at a predetermined time. This was designed to achieve a balance between academic work and social-creative activities. Even the elementary grades followed this compartmentalized plan. This system increased pupil capacity by 40 percent without hiring additional teachers.

In 1907, Wirt became superintendent in Gary, Indiana, and established the Gary Plan. In addition to the Platoon System, Wirt adopted Dewey's idea of education as an embryonic community life in which the different community occupations were reflected in art, history, and science. Not only would the school provide greatly expanded educational opportunities in art and music rooms, swimming pools, gardens, and the like, but the school would become the community's center for intellectual and artistic life. The schools were open all day, twelve months each year, to persons of all ages, for the ultimate objective of bringing about community improvement.

A team of evaluators commended the Gary Plan for its boldness, organizational innovations, the application of democratic principles to school conduct and discipline, and the enrichment of community life through the schools. But it was also criticized for not always working well in practice: Some activities wasted time, others were enjoyable but not educative. School records were often inaccurate; instruction in the subjects was not well organized in many cases, sufficient in content, or presented other than conventionally. Despite these criticisms, over 200 cities had adopted the Gary Plan by 1929.

Early Alternative Schools

Francis W. Parker School.   An educational reformer who was credited by Dewey as the "father of progressive education," Francis W. Parker (1837–1902) became school superintendent in Quincy, Massachusetts, in 1873, and set about reforming the schools. Parker was a child-centered progressive: he sought to move the child to the center of the educative process and to make the curriculum convey greater meaning to the child. Parker's deification of the child suggests that this philosophy is closer to Rousseau's than Dewey's.

Parker abolished the formalities of the traditional classroom that insisted the child remain perfectly still and quiet and substituted instead observation, laboratory work, and the use of ideas in practice (as in the teaching of arithmetic). Inductive methods were employed in arithmetic; geography was taught by field trips as well as formal study. The emphasis was on observing, describing, and gaining a grasp of things before being introduced to more conventional studies. The program, which was dubbed the "Quincy System," achieved considerable recognition before Parker moved to the Cook County Normal School in Illinois. Here he continued his opposition, first expressed at Quincy, to traditional teaching and stressed instead activity, creative self-expression, the scientific study of education, and prepared special teachers for these subjects. In 1901, the Francis W. Parker School was founded in Chicago, staffed by many teachers prepared by Parker; it continued for more than thirty years.

Parker was a founding father of progressive education in the United States and set an example for others to follow. Criticisms of his approach are essentially those made earlier about progressivism of the child-centered variety.

The Dewey Laboratory School.   This experimental elementary school began in Chicago in 1896, reached its peak of 140 pupils in 1902, and closed in 1904 after a disagreement with the University of Chicago over the administration of the school. Whereas the Parker School began with practice and later moved to theory, Dewey sought to test theory in the Laboratory School. The school was an experiment in "cooperative living" whereby both individual interests and social life could be satisfied. Dewey sought to reconcile a host of dualisms in the larger culture: interest and effort, individualism and collectivism, work and play, labor and leisure, school and society, the child and the curriculum. The school was experimental, and children were allowed to explore, create, and make mistakes in testing ideas.

The organizational focus for the Laboratory School was social occupations. Studying occupations, it was thought, not only would promote the social purposes of the school but also would greatly enliven the school's activities and make the learning of routine skills more interesting. It would also promote a balance between intellectual and practical activities. Since, for Dewey, education was not a preparation for life but was life itself, children were to learn directly about life by the school producing in miniature the conditions of social life. And since many of the children would later become manual workers, they needed an understanding of industrial processes. School subjects in the conventional sense were dispensed with, and even the three Rs grew out of the child's activities. The social occupations represented human concerns about food, clothing, shelter, household furnishings, and the production, consumption, and exchange of goods. Four- and five-year-olds learned about preparing lunch before going home at midday; by the age of seven, the emphasis had changed from occupations in the home and neighborhood to an historical approach that traced the emergence of occupations beginning with earliest culture; finally, by the age of thirteen, the emphasis shifted to current events.

The Dewey Laboratory School was a bold experiment and represented the most salient ideas on the leading edge of the progressive movement. It was criticized because it was difficult to achieve a balanced focus on both the individual (the child) and society. The individualistic or freedom side may have been given greater attention. Systematic follow-up studies were not conducted of the school's graduates and therefore no record is available of the school's impact on their lives. Yet from the records of the school and the extant examples of student work, it appears to have been a soundly managed school with quality teachers.

The Montessori School.   Maria Montessori (1870–1952), the first woman in Italy to receive an M.D. degree, worked with mentally defective children and then turned to normal children. Montessori believed that the child needs to escape from the domination of parents and teachers. Children in modern society are victims of adult suppression that compels them to adopt coping measures foreign to their real nature. Teachers must change their attitudes toward children and organize an environment in which children can lead lives of their own.

In Montessori schools children are placed in a stimulating environment where there are things for them to do and things to study. This environment should be free of rivalry, rewards, and punishments; instead, learning is to be experienced through interesting activities. Teachers become directors who see that activities proceed according to a master plan; in fact, Montessori believed that one teacher could handle as many as forty-five children if necessary, but a class of thirty is more desirable. Special materials are used by children in a carefully organized environment. Through regular, graded use of didactic material, children gain skills of manipulation and judgment, and the special senses are separately trained by use of apparatus: Cubes of various sizes are used to build a tower so that children can learn about volume; several kinds of wooden insets exhibit breadth, depth, and volume; sticks of graduated length and cylinders of different sizes are to be placed in the correct blocks. Children learn to develop neuromuscular mechanisms for writing by pouring rice and picking up beans; they learn their letters through a combination of senses: visual, tactile, and auditory. And they learn to associate the sound of the word (sounded phonetically) with an object. In geography, children are given a sandpaper globe, tangible objects, and pictures of people from different cultures. Geography activities lead to the study of history, while learning one's language leads to the study of both subjects. Science, mathematics, and foreign languages are outgrowths of learning one's native language.

The Montessori system spread to many parts of the world prior to World War I, lapsed during the war but had a brief recovery in the 1920s, and was revived again in the United States in the 1950s. Despite their achievements, Montessori schools have been criticized for using equipment too complex and intricate for children, for failure to stimulate the imagination because no imaginary tales are used, for using overly planned and structured learning, and for not promoting social learning sufficiently.

Waldorf Education.   Rudolf Steiner (1861–1925), the founder of Waldorf education in 1913, believed in theosophy, a religious movement that originated in India that teaches about God and the world on the basis of mystical insight. Steiner later called his philosophy *anthroposophy*. It was his objective to provide a program of education from a spiritual point of view that recognized the child's physical, emotional, and intellectual development as manifested in three successive stages of growth in seven-year cycles. The first stage is characterized by imitation and expression in active movement. It is inappropriate, Steiner believed, to teach the three Rs at this stage. The second stage, from years seven to fourteen, features the development of feelings and imagination and is the period when basic skills are acquired. The third stage is where the pupil's thinking ability is emphasized through formal study.

During the first two stages, no specialization is permitted and pupils are grouped according to age and intelligence. The greatest need of the child, according to Steiner, is security; therefore, one teacher remains with a group of children throughout the first stage; similarly, another teacher remains throughout the second stage; and only in the final stage, when subject matter specialists are needed, is this pattern altered. No examinations are used because Steiner considered them of no educational value. In addition to traditional subjects, Waldorf education places emphasis on mythology, art, and eurhythmics (a music-based method of physical training). The Waldorf program strives to develop intellectual and manipulative skills, cultivate social conscience, promote self-expression, and encourage spiritual development. Waldorf schools have a non-denominational Christian outlook. By the 1980s, more than eight of these schools were established in Europe and the United States.

Waldorf education offers a broad view of education, is holistic, and recognizes different stages (and suitable materials) of pupil development. It may not be appropriate for public education, not only because teachers are unprepared to handle this type of program but also because it might raise questions about religious teaching in public schools. Steiner's stages of development do not reflect the latest research findings, and the practice of one teacher remaining with a group of pupils for many years is problematic on pedagogical grounds.

RECENT INNOVATIONS IN INSTRUCTION AND CURRICULUM

Instructional Innovations

Behavioral Objectives.   Behavioral objectives arose during the 1960s to move away from high-sounding educational goals on which performance could not be measured. Instead, behavioral objectives (or "instructional objectives," as they were later called) provide precise, observable, measurable statements of goals. Behavioral objectives state exactly what students can be expected to do after completing designated learning activities. (For example, after four weeks in an introductory typing course, students should be able to type at least twenty words per minute on a ten-minute typing test with no more than four errors.) Those planning a course are able to select materials designed to accomplish the objectives. Thus the teacher is able to plan more effectively as well as assess course effectiveness with greater precision. It also means teachers are more accountable for instructional activities, and the student is better informed about what is expected of him or her.

Behavioral objectives, however, have been criticized on a number of grounds. Since objectives for courses are set in advance, they make it difficult for teachers to change plans in the face of special learning needs. This leaves out much learning of an effective, aesthetic, and moral nature that cannot be stated as an objective. Although convergent thinking may in many cases be stated behaviorally, it is far less likely that divergent thinking can be stated or measured precisely (though it could be evaluated). Thus many of the more important objectives cannot be stated behaviorally. Emphasis on behavioral objectives may lead to neglect of principles, broad concepts, and understandings that give meaning to behavior. Even if behavioral objectives are sound, they are not feasible because of the enormous amount of time required for teachers to compose innumerable objectives.

Programmed Instruction and Computer-Assisted Instruction.   The first teaching machine was developed in the 1920s by Sidney L. Pressey and was revived in the 1950s by B. F. Skinner in the form of programmed materials. These materials use a carefully planned sequence of learning tasks by breaking the material down into its smallest meaningful units. Students are expected to show mastery of each exercise before proceeding to the next one. Once the exercise is completed, the student knows if he or she has mastered the knowledge because the correct answer is given. If the student's answer is incorrect, he or she restudies the material (in a linear program) or is assigned a new exercise, as in alternate or branching programs developed by Norman Crowder.

Programmed instruction has some advantages over traditional teaching. Students have greater recall of material through programmed instruction, master knowledge and skills more rapidly than in traditional instruction, and enjoy the benefits of individualized learning through the use of branching. (Branching is when a learner temporarily ceases work with the main sequence of frames to study a subsidiary or remedial program.)

The disadvantages of programmed instruction are that these materials have not been used to teach higher-order skills and knowledge; students tend to become bored once the novelty has worn off; it is expensive (fifty or seventy-five hours of programming are needed for each student hour of instruction); it does not satisfy students whose learning objectives differ from the material; and it is atomistic and mechanistic.

Computer-assisted instruction (CAI) operates on similar principles of learning as programmed instruction. Students work individually with a programmed computer by typewriter, touch-manipulation board, or electronic pointer. The computer responds via typewriter, television, slides, recordings, or print. CAI can be used to individualize instruction, supplement classroom demonstrations, promote independent study, and diagnose student learning difficulties.

The advantages of CAI are that students learn faster than by using other methods; it may reduce student drop-out rates; it allows students to study at their own pace; students generally react favorably toward it; it is effective for students who do not perform well in traditional instruction; and it aids students to complete courses satisfactorily.

The disadvantages of CAI are that it is expensive; it is difficult to exchange programs because of many different computer languages; it is impersonal and lacking human interaction; student excitement over CAI is not easily sustained; teachers generally resist it; and it operates on an atomistic rather than a holistic model of learning.

Mastery Learning. This form of learning is based on the assumption that the mastery of a topic or a human behavior is theoretically possible for anyone given the optimum quality of instruction appropriate to each individual and given the time needed for mastery. Mastery learning began with the work of Henry C. Morrison in the 1920s and continued in the 1960s with further studies by J. B. Carroll and Benjamin S. Bloom.

Carroll's model uses five variables: aptitude, perseverance, ability to understand instruction, quality of instruction, and opportunity for learning. Taken together, these variables predict the degree of student learning for a particular learning task, and they also play an important role in Bloom's strategy for mastery learning. A mastery strategy involves deciding what will constitute mastery for a particular course, determining appropriate procedures, and deciding how mastery will be evaluated. Bloom supplements regular instruction with frequent evaluation to determine student progress and uses alternative methods and materials. Objectives are

Sounds very good but not whole answer

stated behaviorally; a preassessment of students is used before instruction to determine interest and ability; instruction is adapted to the learner; difficulties are frequently diagnosed; prescriptions for improvement are made; and postassessments are undertaken. A variety of instructional procedures are selected. Some are discarded and new ones added, based on feedback from ongoing instruction. Those students who fail to achieve mastery need to be assessed to determine the problems they are having and given more time to gain mastery.

Mastery learning has the advantage of being workable for virtually any level of schooling for any subject; potentially 90 percent of students can master a course; students can have a role in developing objectives; it can enhance a student's self-concept with a sense of accomplishment; and it promotes cooperation rather than competition for grades.

The disadvantages of mastery learning are that it is more appropriate for learning technical skills; it is unfair if most of the students receive the same grades because grades then become meaningless; teachers are unprepared for master learning because of the scarcity of reliable tests to assess the five variables; it is overly teacher-centered by ignoring credit for student effort not reflected on tests; and it overemphasizes outcomes to the detriment of learning processes.

Discovery Learning.   This learning is inductive. The student is expected to formulate a rule, devise a formula, and recognize a generalization as a result of first-hand experience with cases or instances of some phenomena. Discovery learning was first advocated by Jerome S. Bruner, who held that the most uniquely personal learning is that which the individual discovers for himself or herself. The student, for instance, can discover the generalization that lies behind a particular mathematical operation. Discovery is a process of going beyond the data to develop new insights. This process not only encourages mastery of fundamental ideas about a subject but promotes intellectual excitement about discovery and confidence in one's ability to perceive previously unrecognized relationships. Thus it helps the student acquire information in ways that make it more readily applicable; the student becomes less motivated by external rewards or fear of failure; the act of discovery provides a mode of inquiry in future learning; and the knowledge is more likely to be retained because it is organized in terms of learner interest.

Discovery learning has an outward similarity to Dewey's problem-solving or scientific method insofar as both promote independent, reflective thinking. Dewey's problem solving, however, is more structured, utilizing a step-by-step sequence, whereas discovery learning is not highly structured and more fully recognizes insight and intuition in the discovery of new knowledge.

One of the basic weaknesses in this area is that researchers have not specified what is to be discovered by the student. In some situations the student is left with almost no cues to discover a simple principle, but without cues it is unlikely that the student can arrive at the principle. However, if intensive cues are needed by the student, very little discovery will take place. In contrast to an expository approach (in which the teacher provides background information and the correct answer), discovery learning is far more time consuming. It is probably true, though, that discovery methods are preferable to expository teaching if large amounts of time are not consumed by greater learning activity and involvement. Discovery, however, is only one way this involvement can be brought about. Expository teaching could be used to impart basic knowledge, and then students would become more actively involved by applying the knowledge to new situations.

Television Instruction.   This form of instruction uses live or prerecorded television lectures or demonstrations in courses. It is used to enlarge slides, documents, and pictures; to provide off-campus instruction; to share first-hand field experiences; to provide short demonstrations for videotapes; to observe one's own behavior, as in teaching, in order to improve performance; and to offer professionally prepared educational programs. Besides these uses, television instruction has certain advantages: It provides instruction to those unable to attend classes (in conjunction with a study guide or syllabus); the broadcasts can be aired repeatedly at convenient times; students generally prefer television instruction to regular lectures; and it enables viewers to see specimens, documents, and pictures more clearly.

Instructional television has some disadvantages: Except in the early grades, students prefer small-group discussion; it is essentially a one-way medium that provides no interaction or opportunity to raise questions (unless special provisions are made); it is inferior to other media for music broadcasts; it requires a large audience to be cost effective; and some teachers are averse to using it. When instructional television offers students an opportunity to raise questions and interact, it is at least as effective as other media and methods.

Curriculum Innovations

Structure of the Disciplines Approach.   This approach originated with scholars in the 1950s and 1960s as a response to their findings of obsolete content and instructional practices in the subject curriculum. While retaining subjects as a framework for organization, the scholars revised and updated content, introduced discovery learning, and deemphasized rote learning in favor of teaching students how to grasp the structure of a discipline. This meant that fundamental axioms, concepts, and other building blocks of a discipline became the focus of learning so that students could comprehend the underlying structure, attempt to generate fruitful hypotheses, and perceive how scholars generate new knowledge. The concept of readiness was reassessed, and it was found that students could grasp concepts earlier if the concepts were formulated in terms of the student's cognitive development and how students learn best at different ages and levels of maturity. This led to earlier grade placement of subjects and concepts (in mathematics, for instance, set theory was introduced earlier).

The structure of the disciplines approach has certain advantages over the traditional subject curriculum: Revision and updating and curriculum content are undertaken more frequently; the emphasis is on undertaking a discipline's structure rather than learning facts for their own sake; stress is placed on critical thinking and intuitive judgment (in discovery learning); concepts are mastered earlier; and, as a consequence of these features, there is a greater likelihood of effective transfer of training.

Despite the promise of this approach and genuine progress in curriculum revision during the 1960s, some shortcomings should be noted. Students face problems in their daily lives that are not restricted to disciplines—problems of relations between the sexes, marriage and the family, racial matters, war and peace, ecology, shortages of economic resources, and numerous others that are better approached through interdisciplinary perspectives. Second, a subject or discipline approach to curriculum, as opposed to an interdisciplinary one, discourages examination of the curriculum as a whole in order to develop concepts progressively and provide proper continuity and articulation from one grade to the next. Third, this approach emphasizes cognitive learning and neglects social, emotional, and moral development. Stress on cognitive learning slants the approach to the more academically talented and is, in fact, used with highly motivated children in superior schools. A fourth difficulty is that children do not think like researchers in the disciplines, yet the program establishes models of this type of thinking and inquiry. Finally, this curriculum innovation gives little attention to goals and their justification, other than assuming that a mastery of disciplines is the most desirable end—an assumption that is not self-evident and needs to be demonstrated.

Compensatory Education.   These are programs that seek to overcome the educational disadvantages of children that arise from personal history, social background, or economic conditions. Research has indicated that retardation may be long lasting or permanent unless intervention occurs at an early age; consequently, early childhood education programs such as Head Start have been developed. Compensatory education leaves responsibility for physical handicaps, brain damage, and genetic limitations to special education. Among the many approaches used in compensatory education are health programs, reading readiness and remediation programs, emphasis on developing a positive self-concept, expanded guidance services, and curriculum enrichment.

Compensatory education programs were funded under Title I of the Elementary and Secondary Education Act (ESEA) passed by Congress in 1965. This immediately provided $1 billion in Title I funds to supplement and improve the education of poor and minority-group children. By 1965 funds totaled $2 billion per year, or approximately $200 more for each disadvantaged child.

Despite ample funding and federal support, most of these programs were ineffective in raising the cognitive level of disadvantaged children. Numerous reasons account for these early failures: inadequately prepared teachers, a piecemeal approach, consultant fees paid for work improperly done, unethical methods of awarding grants, vague objectives, increased quantity of services without improved quality of program content, and poor evaluation procedures. Results since 1975 have been more favorable as some of these earlier deficiencies have been corrected, better monitoring procedures have been implemented, greater funding has been provided from state and local levels, and program evaluation has improved. Thus programs such as Head Start and Follow-Through have begun to succeed as student achievement in low-income schools in several metropolitan areas is shown to match or exceed the national average. Some studies of early childhood education programs have revealed that they have a lasting effect in raising achievement and IQ scores. The cost, however, of compensatory education is high—$3,000 annually per student—and it is questionable whether funds of this magnitude will be available during a recession or that the public will be willing to provide this level of support.

Organizational Innovations

Middle Schools.   During the 1960s the middle school was developed not only as a new form of organization but as a new approach for educating pupils in the sixth, seventh, and eighth grades. (In some instances the fifth and ninth grades were also included.) Proponents of the middle school believe that the junior high school has not been entirely effective and propose that a separate building and special programs be used to educate pupils in these grades. The middle school is designed to serve as a bridge between childhood and adolescence, a transitional period where existing programs are not suitable for this age group. Thus the middle school seeks to establish its own identity and mission. The program stresses such features as individualized study, team teaching, integration of extracurricular activities into the formal curriculum, use of a nongraded plan, and development of interdisciplinary programs.

One of the dangers is that the middle school will be little different than the conventional junior high school. In some cases middle schools have been used to accommodate excessive enrollments by transferring students to less overcrowded middle schools. Besides the problem of providing a distinctive program and recruiting teachers with the requisite abilities and interests, school buildings geared to these special programs are not always available. Considering it took junior high schools nearly fifty years to acquire buildings adequate for their programs, the likelihood of obtaining buildings does not appear promising. Additionally, the middle school movement has met considerable resistance from proponents of the junior high school; these proponents believe the criticisms of the junior high school are at best superficial. Middle school advocates, however, point to the junior high school as largely an administrative reorganization of secondary education that belatedly developed a curricular rationale, whereas the middle school is a curriculum response to the special needs of this age group. Moreover, the junior high school movement lacks a sufficiently broad research base to validate its effectiveness, whereas the middle school movement has recently accumulated greater data to support its claims.

Nongraded Schools.   These schools are a newer form of curricular and instructional organization and are found principally at the elementary level. Grade levels and all expectations associated with separate grades are eliminated. The goals are to individualize instruction and permit each student to learn at his or her own rate of speed. The problem of promotion and retention is overcome, instruction no longer has to be geared to the average student, and student progress is not delayed because of slower classmates. Different age groups work together and learn from one another. For example, a child may be advanced in arithmetic but slower to grasp social studies; consequently, this student will be placed with others of similar abilities in each subject and will work with them in large and small groups and spend some time working alone.

Nongraded plans, however, are no panacea for curricular and instructional problems. It is still necessary to have teachers adequately prepared for this form of organization and to have sufficient and appropriate curricular materials (which, generally, are in short supply). Without these two essential ingredients, it would be better to remain with graded plans. Moreover, in some schools the actual organizational pattern required has not been actually put into operation, though teachers and administrators usually assume the plan is nongraded. Other than different reading levels, many so-called nongraded plans are little different than graded ones. Thus many of these plans are conventional homogeneous groupings of pupils within the same grade; curriculum organization and instruction remain the same.

Despite these criticisms, research studies indicate that nongraded school children's achievement scores are significantly higher than those of graded children. Additionally, fewer children are retained, and nongraded schools are especially beneficial for blacks, underachievers, and boys. Most research on nongraded schools, however, was conducted in the early 1970s, and little research has been available since 1973.

Differentiated Staffing.   This is a plan for structuring the teaching faculty so that instruction can be individualized by utilizing teachers in different types of assignments according to their competencies. Differentiated staffing is especially suited to merit plans. Public school teachers generally have little differentiation in assignments and responsibilities. People performing the same type of tasks are paid different rates in regular schools, whereas in differentiated staffing, teachers receive merit pay but for different types of responsibilities and tasks.

One model of differentiated staffing divides the staff into paraprofessionals and professionals. The paraprofessionals consist of clerical assistants and proctors, technical assistants and instructional assistants, instructional associates, and research assistants. These people serve as the supporting staff to provide clerical and proctoring services, assist in classroom management, supervise the school building and grounds, prepare transparencies and slide presentations, and carry out numerous other tasks that would allow the teacher to concentrate on instruction.

The professional staff consists of the intern teacher, probationary teacher, staff teacher, master teacher, and teacher specialist. The intern teacher is noncertified and teaches part-time or full-time, depending on the school system. The probationary teacher is equivalent to today's certified teachers who have yet to be awarded tenure. The staff teacher would be tenured and have a fifth year of preparation but not necessarily a master's degree. The master teacher has demonstrated ability to assume leadership in teaching. This teacher has a master's degree and assumes leadership on curriculum committees, serves as a team-teaching leader, assists in training of probationary and intern teachers, and undertakes related responsibilities. Finally, the teacher specialist has a doctorate or post-master's degree work and is responsible for research in the area of specialization, planning programs systemwide, demonstrations in experimental teaching situations, and related duties. The teaching specialist is employed on a twelve-month basis, whereas the master teacher is employed on a ten- or eleven-month basis.

Differentiated staffing, according to proponents, breaks the lockstep of traditional plans, affords far better staff utilization, and is more likely than traditional staffing to provide students with superior teaching and services. It also offers greater incentives and rewards for superior teaching, and it relieves teachers of more routine chores so that they can concentrate on professional activities.

Critics, however, say that there are problems in determining the different levels of responsibilities, assigning duties to these levels, and assessing competence. The plan also seems to be a surreptitious way of initiating merit pay. If this is the case, a genuine plan of merit pay, based on performance, would be preferable to one based on roles assumed, degrees held, and the like. Second, differentiated staffing fosters specialization and moves the system away from a child-centered approach to one that is subject-centered. Third, the competent teacher is not necessarily the skillful supervisor or coordinator. Thus the Peter Principle may be operating here. Finally, some teachers resent a meritocratic system and a hierarchical arrangement. Although differentiated staffing enlists greater teacher participation in policy making, some administrators are reluctant to support such changes. If administrators are to make the plan work, they will need to involve teachers in organizing it, demonstrate that competencies can be accurately and impartially assessed, and clearly designate the specific types of responsibilities expected in each position.

Team Teaching.   This instructional arrangement breaks from the one-teacher-per-class system by involving two or more teachers who plan instruction and evaluation cooperatively for a group of students usually the size of two to five conventional classes. The class may range in size from 50 to over 180 students, two to six teachers may participate, and the class may be organized at times as one group, several small groups, or for individual instruction. Teams may be selected on the basis of the teacher's specialization or teachers who have special talents that complement one another. Usually a team leader with organizational and curriculum-development abilities is selected. Differentiated staffing employs team teaching, but this hierarchical model is not a prerequisite for using team teaching, as some plans use teachers of equal or similar status. The ability of competent team members to work together cooperatively, agree upon objectives, and delegate responsibilities is essential for successful team teaching.

Among the advantages of team teaching are: it allows greater utilization of personnel, space, material, and equipment; it offers students an opportunity to find a teacher with whom they relate effectively; it permits students to work in large groups, small groups, and engage in individual study; and it is more likely to provide a more perceptive diagnosis of learning difficulties and a more objective evaluation of achievement because two or more teachers are involved. Teachers benefit as well. They receive stimulation from observing their colleagues, by being observed, and by sharing ideas. Teachers also prepare more carefully and exert greater effort when under observation, and it is an opportunity for more experienced teachers to help less experienced ones.

Yet despite these advantages, many difficulties have arisen in team teaching. One problem lies in organizing the team. Able team leaders and team members are hard to find; large amounts of time are required for preparation and planning and are not always available; and confusion arises at times over the team leader's role—whether to supervise teachers or instruct students. As for students, they may take advantage of different expectations of teachers and pit them against one another. Students may also find that members of the team have different grading practices.

Open Education.   This innovation emerged in Great Britain about twenty-five years ago and was popularized in the United States during the 1970s. It drew upon the findings of Susan Issacs and Jean Piaget. The term *open* may be somewhat misleading because it suggests large undivided spaces and removable partitions; however, open education can be conducted in classrooms that are traditional in a physical sense.

A number of characteristics are shared by open education classrooms. In the open classroom, the teacher may observe patterns of growth outlined by Piaget. The teacher instructs and guides learning in small groups or individually rather than instructing the class as a whole. Flexible scheduling is used, with many activities progressing simultaneously. And the abolition of a required curriculum permits children to make some decisions about their work. It is also characteristic that grading is deemphasized, that children learn at their own pace and in terms of their own learning style, and that the teacher's role is that of diagnostician, guide, and stimulator. Above all, the whole child is recognized—intellectually, emotionally, morally, socially, and physically.

Although open education shares similarities with the early progressive movement in the United States, it differs insofar as it is used more in public than in private schools, is more structured, provides an active role for the teacher, and offers more of a planned environment than child-centered progressive schools. Open education also diverges from free schools (which are discussed shortly) by usually placing more emphasis on cognitive development, providing greater curriculum structure, affording a more direct leadership role for teachers, and circumscribing more precisely the range and types of choices given to children.

The chief difference between open-space schools and open education is in the flexible architectural arrangements. Research evidence, however, does not support real differences in learning or teaching outcomes. Changes in architectural design in and of themselves do not make a difference. In open education, affective factors such as self-concept, creativity, independence, attitude toward school, and curiosity do show measurable improvement. Nevertheless, the divergent definitions of open education and the evaluative criteria are too varied to arrive at conclusive evidence that open classrooms are better than traditional ones.

Recent Alternatives

Education Vouchers.   Dissatisfaction with public education has led to alternative proposals for the use of resources. The voucher plan would finance elementary and secondary education through certificates given by the government to parents of school-age children. The parents select the school of their choice—public, private, or parochial—and present the certificate as payment for instruction in the chosen school; the school then presents the voucher to the government and receives a check for a stipulated amount based on a formula.

Early voucher plans were essentially unregulated and posed threats of violating the separation of church and state and increasing segregated schooling. In contrast, Christopher Jencks and others have developed a highly regulated voucher plan that seeks to overcome the serious shortcomings of the earlier proposals.

Jencks's plan would create an Education Voucher Agency (EVA) at the community level for receiving government funds for financing schools. It would be locally controlled and would resemble a board of education except that it would not operate any schools of its own; responsibility for operating schools would be retained by public and private school boards. The EVA would determine the eligibility of public and nonpublic schools to participate in the plan.

The purposes of the voucher plan are to provide more education options, break the "monopoly" of the public schools, and enable poor parents to have the same choice as wealthy parents as to where they can send their children to school. The vouchers would offer each applicant roughly an equal chance of admission into any school by taking each student who applied to a particular school, except when the number of applicants exceeded the number of places, in which case a lottery would be used to fill half of its places. Each school would have to show that it had at least accepted as high a proportion of ethnic-group students as had applied. Vouchers from children of lower-income families would have higher redemption value because their education would likely be more costly. Additionally, EVA would pay the transportation costs of all children in order that low-income families would not be inordinately burdened. EVA would also disseminate information about all schools in the area, enabling parents to make intelligent choices.

The Office of Economic Opportunity made grants to several communities to study the feasibility of the voucher plan, but only the community of Alum Rock, California, with the aid of a federal grant, decided to try it. Alum Rock's plan, however, differed from Jencks's plan by using only public schools and providing alternative programs within them, and using the board of education in lieu of EVA. After four years of operation, it was found that teachers, students, and parents liked the plan but standardized test scores were either equivalent to national norms or, in some instances, were below them. In any case, the Alum Rock program does not actually test the original plan; it explores a new option instead.

Excluding Alum Rock, a number of serious deficiencies can be found in voucher plans. A basic tenet of voucher proponents is that public schools constitute a monopoly, and, consequently, the use of vouchers would open many new options to parents. Voucher advocates frequently use the free-marketplace analogy that vouchers would do for education what free enterprise has done for the economy and its productivity. Schools, however, are relatively decentralized and do compete with private schools and with each other: in their sports programs, for teachers, appropriations, special projects, and the like. The market analogy is misleading insofar as profit-making firms sell their products to anyone who has cash or credit, whereas private schools are selective and not open to everyone. Moreover, for the voucher system to result in the benefits it purports to offer, nonpublic schools would have to be far more innovative and experimental in their programs and organizations; as of now only a small number exhibit these characteristics.

Furthermore, once nonpublic schools accept substantial state funds, they are likely to be more thoroughly regulated. It may mean that parochial schools would no longer be able to offer sectarian religious courses, and all nonpublic schools would be subject to desegregation rulings. Voucher plans make no provision for eliminating discrimination in the hiring of teachers. Nonpublic schools may also be required to observe judicial standards of academic freedom.

Public schools, under a voucher plan, would not likely receive additional tax funds but nonpublic schools would be free to increase their endowments, thereby leading to greater inequities. The voucher system could increase public costs by paying nonpublic-school tuitions, staffing and operating the EVA, creating new buildings and facilities for private schools, and underusing those of public schools (because of decreased enrollment, increased transportation costs, and inefficient use of tenured public school teachers). Thus, in view of the substantial shortcomings of the voucher plan, it may be wiser to offer greater curricular alternatives in public schools.

Performance Contracting.   This innovation, which rose and fell in the early 1970s, was one manifestation of the widespread concern that schools should be more accountable to the public at large. Performance contracting is a procedure by which a school system enters into an agreement with a private firm to take over from the school certain instructional tasks in order to achieve a set of designated objectives. The school system can contract with the firm to teach such subjects as reading and mathematics or to assume responsibility for the instructional program of an entire elementary or secondary school. For a stipulated sum of money, the firm guarantees certain results within a designated time period. Should the company fall short of its goals, a lesser amount is paid; whereas, when goals are exceeded, some contracts award bonuses. An independent audit team is employed by the local education agency to monitor execution of the contract and certify results to the agency for purposes of payment.

In 1969, a Texarkana, Arkansas, school district entered into a contract with a private firm to take over part of their instructional program. Gary, Indiana, received a four-year grant in 1970 in excess of $2 million to experiment with performance contracting in an effort to overcome "gross underachievement." A number of the other school districts throughout the country have initiated performance contracting. The Office of Economic Opportunity (OEO) in 1970 sponsored eighteen experiments in performance contracting at a cost of $5 million to $6 million. The test results at the end of the year for the experimental and control groups show that both groups did equally poorly in terms of overall averages, but these averages, with very few exceptions, are very nearly the same in each grade for the best and worst students in the sample. Thus the future of performance contracting as a means of insuring accountability—at least in its present form—is seriously in doubt.

Free Schools.   As a response to the call for a new type of learning environment, free schools sprang up across the country in the late 1960s. Using city storefronts, old barns, barracks, abandoned churches, and even people's homes, these schools attempted to bring about greater freedom of learning through humanistic principles. Many of the directors of these schools believed that freedom was good, even though "freedom" was not always clearly defined or examined.

Although the majority of these schools are organized by middle-class white parents and attended by their children, occasionally integrated school settings can be found—in fact, there are a few free schools with little or no tuition located in economically depressed neighborhoods. The free schools utilize both early and neoprogressive methods, borrow ideas on child development from Piaget, and mix in here and there some practices from the English infant schools. Schools range from a Summerhill-type atmosphere to that of a more structured one, but generally children are not pushed to acquire basic skills before they show a readiness to learn.

The precarious financial basis upon which most free schools rest results in an average life span of about eighteen months—scarcely a beginning and surely no time to test a program. Financial instability, joined with the more independent, idiosyncratic personalities who are drawn to establishing free schools, engenders a further basis for their transience. Additionally, free schools have been criticized for being accessible primarily to middle-class whites and for giving little emphasis to basic skills and vocational training that ethnic groups might find useful for their survival. With the emergence during the 1970s of alternatives within public schools, there has been less incentive to establish free schools and the movement has rapidly declined.

PLACING INNOVATIONS IN PERSPECTIVE

Educational Theories

Three educational theories that have been influential during the past several decades are behaviorism, essentialism, and progressivism. Proponents of each of these theories have contributed certain perspectives and sponsored or opposed certain innovations.

Behaviorism.   Behaviorism has been the dominant American psychology since the militant behaviorism was first enunciated by John B. Watson in 1913. It spread into education through intelligence testing and then through a larger measurement movement that sought to make education scientific, as in the case of Edward Lee Thorndike, who sought to propound laws of learning. Behaviorists study overt behavior and only those human and animal phenomena subject to measurement; thus they reject introspection and mentalistic concepts and rely instead on observing stimulus-response patterns. One of the chief applications of behaviorism in therapeutic situations is the rise of behavior modification.

In education, behaviorists have sponsored teaching machines, programmed learning materials, computer-assisted instruction, competency testing, some forms of accountability, and homogeneous groupings and tracking. One need not be a behaviorist to support one or more of these innovations; it is just more likely that a behaviorist would do so than someone who espouses a different theory or who is not entirely clear what theory to support. In seeking scientific precision, behaviorists are atomistic rather than holistic in approach; they seek to break things down into their smallest meaningful components for either study or educational use. Response patterns can be as simple as finger twitches or knee jerks. Similarly, programmed materials break learning bits to their smallest meaningful units. Since behaviorists also attempt to make accurate measurement of human abilities, they are usually interested in the classification of abilities and placing students in learning situations with peers of similar abilities. Thus they believe that homogeneous groupings will more likely insure that no one will be held back by slower classmates or have to move more rapidly than they are able to do. Other behavioristic programs include competency education (which is based upon the assumption that human competencies can be identified), student acquisition of designated competencies, and tests designed to measure their attainment.

Essentialism.   Essentialism, one of the older theories in the history of education, was prominent in American education during the 1930s and 1950s and then again in the 1970s in the back-to-basics movement. Essentialism emphasizes transmitting the cultural heritage to all students, seeing that they are soundly trained in the fundamentals, and insuring that they study the basic disciplines. In this way students will become educated persons and good citizens. Students, however, cannot always study what strikes their immediate interest but must study what they need to enable them to assume responsible adult roles. This means that discipline and sound study habits should be stressed in order to master fundamental disciplines. Essentialists believe these disciplines are best grasped in a subject curriculum rather than vitiated in a broad fields curriculum or interdisciplinary programs.

The back-to-basics movement, since it focuses largely on the three Rs and firm disciplinary standards, is actually a truncated essentialist program because it fails to give equal weight to the other elements in the cultural heritage. In other words, it is generally consonant with essentialist principles but underdeveloped. Moreover, some back-to-basics programs advocate corporal punishment whereas some prominent essentialists would not do so. Essentialists would also want schools to be accountable, but the operational principles of accountability follow behavioristic lines more closely.

Progressivism. Progressivism in American education began slowly around the turn of the century; as a formal movement it reached its zenith in the late 1930s, only to decline precipitously by the mid-1950s. It rose again in the late 1960s in different forms and under new rubrics; it was largely submerged, however, by the overriding emphasis on accountability during the 1970s. Early progressives stressed the needs and interests of children and the importance of placing them in a learning environment where they could develop naturally, be free to express themselves, and nurture their creative development. This meant that the progressive teacher would shape learning experiences to students rather than the converse, that the subject curriculum would be modified to take into consideration individual differences, and that the teacher would be a guide, a facilitator of learning, rather than an authority figure.

Essentialists did not appreciate the progressives' departure from exact studies in the disciplines and their alleged abandonment of rigorous standards of scholastic achievement for projects based on immediate interests. Behaviorists found the atomistic approach in conflict with the holistic approach of humanistic education (a form that progressivism took during the 1970s). Rather than precise measurement of abilities and achievement in homogeneous groups, the neo-progressives stressed heterogeneous classrooms and evaluations of a qualitative type. Besides interdisciplinary programs and other departures from the subject curriculum, neo-progressives support open classrooms, free schools, nongraded schools, alternatives within public schools, and various types of individualized instructional plans.

Ideologies in Education

Among the ideologies in education, meritocracy and egalitarianism have special bearing on innovations. Both of these ideologies have long been prominent in education, but egalitarianism has grown since the civil rights movement and the Elementary and Secondary Education Act of 1965.

The rewards in the meritocratic system go to those who achieve through demonstrated performance, rather than on the basis of race, religion, nationality, seniority, family background, politics, and other artificial distinctions commonly found in most societies. Instead, the abilities, skills, and types of performance are evaluated by merit. And those abilities most prized would be determined by the society's highest values and priorities. A meritocratic system is based on equal access to educational resources and opportunities so that those students with the potentials most valued by a given society would be in a position to best develop them and subsequently be rewarded for their use. Educational institutions are one of the chief mechanisms used by advanced industrial societies to screen and sort out those best qualified to assume careers and tasks that are highly esteemed and that demand greater abilities, responsibility, and leadership. Tomorrow's leaders will be sorted out through the process of schooling by its competitive system of grading, promotion, honors, and awards. Those who fail will be notified that they were given a fair chance and must now assume societal roles consonant with demonstrated abilities.

The meritocrat would want to maintain equal access to education to assure that all talented youth have an opportunity to be identified and developed; therefore, programs for the gifted and talented would be encouraged and competency education, if not construed too narrowly, would assure that certain measurable outcomes would be achieved. Meritocrats may at times join forces with essentialists in upholding standards, though the meritocrat would be more closely attuned than the essentialist to various sectors of society—government, business, industry, the military—to determine the standards needed.

Egalitarianism as an ideology renounces the policy of equal access because it fails to consider the handicaps and discrimination suffered by racial and ethnic minorities; thus equal access continues to give children of the white majority an unequal chance to advance. Egalitarians would either favor equal outcomes or substantive equality or both. Equal outcomes would assure that the overall average achievement scores of the different school populations are essentially the same, whereas substantive equality would require a redistribution of wealth in order to abolish poverty (just how this would be handled would depend on the particular plan). Those egalitarians who have not given up working with public education favor some compensatory education programs, community control of schools, bilingual education, multicultural education, and in some cases vouchers and free schools. These programs and plans, they believe, would best help the less advantaged and help to make society more just and egalitarian. The meritocrat would object to most of these proposals because they allegedly would result in the loss of a nation's talent and a subsequent rise of mediocrity. This would also bring about a leveling process whereby individual initiative and the achievement motive would be discouraged.

Whatever the respective merits of these theories and ideologies, one may want to look more closely at the basis for accepting or rejecting an innovation. It is no longer necessary to choose on an ad hoc basis if one wishes to adopt one of these theories or ideologies.

CHAPTER 7

EDUCATIONAL EQUITY
THROUGH FINANCIAL REFORM

A school financial-reform movement began with court decisions in the 1970s and continued to be implemented in the 1980s. An early principle underlying the movement, based on a study by John Coons, William Clune, and Stephen Sugarman (see Suggested Readings), is that quality of public education should not be a function of wealth other than the total wealth of the state. A power equalizing formula would be designed to insure that each district would be able to secure an equivalent volume of educational spending for the same fiscal effort, thereby assuring equivalent educational offerings.

The California Supreme Court in 1971 concluded in *Serrano v. Priest* that the state's public school financing system produces substantial disparities in revenue available for education and thereby denies pupils the equal protection of the laws (as enunciated in the Fourteenth Amendment). The Court cited two school districts within the same county where the local assessed property valuation per child was thirteen times greater in the wealthier district. The system of school finance was found to be unconstitutional, and the California legislature responded to the decision by substantially altering the school finance system.

In *San Antonio v. Rodriguez* (1973), the United States Supreme Court reversed a three-judge federal panel in deciding that Texas school financing violated constitutional guarantees of equal protection. The Court held that the Constitution does not explicitly or implicitly create a fundamental right to an education. In *Rodriguez* the view prevailed that the Court should limit itself to interpreting the Constitution rather than making new law.

The decision shifted financial reform to the states. Some states were not persuaded that school taxes and funding disparities are unconstitutional. But in addition to California, courts in Connecticut, Kentucky, Montana, New Jersey, Texas, Washington, and West Virginia declared their financial system unconstitutional and mandated the legislature to undertake reforms. Five states have adopted full state funding as a result of these decisions, and eighteen states have adopted some form of power-equalizing plan.

Arthur Wise and Tamar Gendler review the school financial-reform movement and respond to criticisms directed against it. Instead of state financial reform, Thomas Fox and John Riew consider the considerable benefits that accrue to students from public education and recommend that parents, on the basis of an income scale, make a direct financial contribution.

The court turned for solution to the legislature, which passed an act designed to equalize funding across the state. On its face, the law appeared reasonable and appropriate, but, as we will see, it was never fully implemented, and in 1988 New Jersey's courts were once again called upon to review the state's school finance system.

The second court affirmation of school finance reform came several years later from the other side of the continent; in 1976 the California Supreme Court concluded a series of decisions known as *Serrano v. Priest* by declaring the state's system of school finance to be in violation of both the Fourteenth Amendment of the federal Constitution and the state's own equal-protection clause—assurances that guarantee citizens equal protection under the law. By making the quality of education a child received a function of the local school district's taxable wealth, California's school finance system was denying equal protection to children from poorer districts. Declared the court: "We have determined that this funding scheme invidiously discriminates against the poor because it makes the quality of a child's education a function of the wealth of his parents and neighbors."[14] But other public goods are a function of the wealth of one's parents and neighbors, such as the quality of a municipality's Fourth of July fireworks display or the state of repair of a municipality's sidewalks. The court distinguished between less essential goods and the fundamental right to an education:

> First, education is essential in maintaining what several commentators have called "free enterprise democracy"—that is, preserving an individual's opportunity to compete successfully in the economic marketplace, despite a disadvantaged background . . . Second, education is universally relevant . . . Third, public education continues over a lengthy period of life—between ten and thirteen years . . . Fourth, education is unmatched in the extent to which it

> molds the personality of the youth of society . . . Finally, education is so important that the state has made it compulsory—not only in the requirement of attendance, but also by assignment to a particular district and school.[15]

The court, finding education a fundamental right, ruled California's system of school finance unconstitutional.[16]

LEGISLATIVE RESPONSES TO EARLY LITIGATION

Throughout the 1970s, prodded by actual or threatened lawsuits, many states passed laws aimed at reducing the vast discrepancies in funding among districts. But soon thereafter, inflation, fiscal constraints, politics, and self-interest took their tolls. By the end of the decade, many of the reforms that had been instituted had been rendered nearly ineffectual, and, during the 1980s, while the world focused on excellence, inequality in finance grew. In "Reforming School Finance in Illinois," James Gordon Ward observed a pattern that has been repeated in a number of states:

> The 1973 reform did seem to increase equity in school spending through the state . . . [but] changes in the formula later in the 1970s weakened the equalization elements and by 1980 the state of Illinois had reverted to a "politics-as-usual" approach to funding public schools.[17]

In states where watchfulness continued, the results of school finance legislation were dramatic. In New Mexico,

> The 1974 equalization guarantee formula has continued a trend toward financial equalization which began in the 1930s . . . The intent of this reform legislation, "to equalize financial opportunity at the highest possible revenue level and to guarantee each New Mexico public school student access to programs and services appropriate to his educational needs regardless of geographic or local economic conditions," has

been realized. Fiscal neutrality is nearly a reality, as revenues and expenditures are no longer closely related to district wealth . . . School finance reform has been and continues to be a priority for the state of New Mexico.[18]

California, which twelve years ago was chastised by its supreme court in *Serrano v. Priest*, has equalized finances so that "95.6 percent of all students attend districts with a per-pupil revenue limit within an inflation-adjusted 100-dollar band (now $238) of the statewide average for each district type."[19] Students in California now receive nearly an equal share of the state resources to develop their individual abilities.

THE RECENT ROUND OF LITIGATION: MONTANA, TEXAS, NEW JERSEY

Despite these successes, the realization of how rapidly the effects of reform can be eroded has been sobering. New lawsuits have had to be brought in states where the issue seemed resolved a decade ago. Despite the practical lessons of the past fifteen years, the fundamental legal issues have not changed. In 1988 alone, three major decisions mandating school finance reform have been handed down in Montana (*Helena v. Montana*), Texas (*Edgewood v. Kirby*), and New Jersey (*Abbot v. Burke*). Each uses one or both of the basic arguments established in *Robinson* and *Serrano*: that denying equal educational opportunity violates the state's constitutional obligation to provide a thorough and efficient education for all children, or that since education is a fundamental right, denying equal educational opportunity violates children's rights to equal protection under the law. Since these decisions were handed down, the Texas decision has been overturned by an appeals court but is now on its way to the state's highest court. The Montana decision has been affirmed by the Montana Supreme Court,

thus making the decision final. The New Jersey decision has been rejected by the state education commissioner in an unusual proceeding and will ultimately be reviewed by the state supreme court.

THE DECLINE OF THE LOCAL-CONTROL ARGUMENT

In the *Rodriguez* decision, Texas had argued that the inequities in funding across school districts were an unfortunate by-product of the compelling interest in local control of schools. In *Edgewood*, the defense offered a similar argument, but the court found that

local control of school district operations in Texas has diminished dramatically in recent years, and today most of the meaningful incidents of the education process are determined and controlled by state statute and/or state board of education rule, including such matters as curriculum, course content, textbooks, hours of instruction, pupil-teacher ratios, training of teachers, administrators, and board members, teacher testing, and review of personnel decisions and policies.[20]

The state regulates not only administrative procedures, such as how many times each day a school may broadcast announcements over the public address system,[21] how many hours of state-approved training all school board members must have,[22] what routes school buses must follow,[23] and how grades should be recorded on report cards,[24] but also basic features of the curriculum.

"The state board of education has promulgated 350 pages of regulations that detail the content of every course in every year in every school district in the state."[25] These regulations include requirements that prekindergarten students "develop pincher control" and that homemaking students learn to "identify principles of pleasing interior decoration," and to "recognize commitments made in marriage vows."[26] Districts may select only textbooks that have been adopted by the state board of education (generally five per subject area),[27] teach only courses approved by the Texas Education Agency,[28] and must devote a certain number of minutes each week to specific elementary school subjects, such as language arts and social studies.[29]

Clearly, local districts have lost much of their historical control over the content of their educational offerings. In fact,

the only element of local control that remains undiminished is the power of wealthy districts to fund education at virtually any level they choose, as contrasted with the property-poor districts who enjoy no such local control . . . because of their inadequate property tax base; the bulk of the revenues they generate are consumed by the building of necessary facilities and compliance with state-mandated requirements.[30]

The myth that local control justifies vast discrepancies in spending among districts is thus discredited in two ways. First, the possibility of meaningful local control is in fact enhanced by a funding system that insures equalized opportunity for districts to fund educational programs, for it allows all districts, not just those with large tax bases, to exercise options in financing their schools. But Texas has demonstrated that it does not even truly value local control; a state that regulates and standardizes as Texas does can hardly claim that its commitment to local control compellingly outweighs the need to abide by the constitutional guarantees of equal opportunity and the right of all students to an efficient education.[31]

THE DEFENDANTS' ARGUMENTS

Throughout the history of school finance reform, opponents of change have offered three arguments. In states without an explicit education clause, they have tried to show that education is not a fundamental right and is therefore not subject to the close scrutiny implied by the equal-protection clause. This argument has been accepted by courts in Idaho, Oregon, Ohio, New York, Georgia, Colorado, and Maryland,[32] which used it as a basis for a judgment not to inquire too deeply into the inequities that the plaintiffs set forth. In states such as New Jersey that have a "thorough and efficient" clause, and in states such as Montana that accept education as a fundamental right, the defense has relied on two other major arguments: that local control outweighs the rights of districts to equal funding and that financial input has no effect on the quality of the education a district is able to offer.

The issue of local control has already been discussed in the context of Texas, whose regulation of its local schools is typical of Sun Belt states. But many states in the pursuit of excellence since 1980 have aggressively tried to improve and control local schools through regulation; some have even gone so far as to enact takeover legislation through which they would govern local school systems from the capital. By their actions, states have shown that standardized tests, statewide curriculums, uniform textbooks, and consistent teacher evaluation all outrank local control.

Two empirical justifications are offered for the contention that financial input and quality of education are unrelated. The first is that low-cost attitudinal and administrative changes, such as Ron Edmond's effective schools formula, contribute more to the quality of education than the amount of money a district is able to spend on its schools. Although this argument is appealing, closer examination shows it to be irrelevant. It is reassuring to know that schools can overcome, to some extent, the handicaps of dilapidated classrooms, textbook shortages, high student-teacher ratios and limited library facilities, but that does not justify such conditions. Nor has any research been able to show that a school with high expectations and no German teacher will produce students who speak German, or that a school with orderly classrooms and no laboratory facilities will train its students to be good scientists.

The second defense offered is that statistical studies have not been able to show a direct correlation between dollar input and school output. In 1966 James Coleman's *Equality of Educational Opportunity Report* offered the conclusion ''that schools bring little influence to bear on a child's achievement that is independent of his background and general social context.''[33] This report shaped the education policy debate of the 1970s, as supporters and detractors argued whether schools can affect achievement, and whether there is any correlation between the cost of education and its quality. Unfortunately, available research has been crude and therefore inconclusive; the factors affecting a child's development are many, and the resources devoted to research meager. Causal relationships are entangled (Do poor schools attract poor teachers? Do good students create good schools?) and measures of effectiveness (Should we look for higher reading scores or a more self-directed

learning?) may be indeterminate or contradictory. And since analyses of the problem have depended upon existing schools and school systems, they necessarily describe what has been and not what might be.

This being so, the controversy over whether differences in expenditures can be empirically demonstrated to affect the outcomes of schooling is unlikely to be resolved any time soon. To a certain extent, this is not surprising. Money does not buy everything; there are good schools in poor districts, bad schools in wealthy districts. But by commonly accepted standards, it is clear that resources do affect educational quality. Districts that spend more money can build nicer buildings, supply more staff, pay their teachers more, and thereby attract better teachers. A recent study of Pennsylvania school districts (see table below) confirms this.

The author of the study concludes: ''The pattern was consistent. On every measure, high-spending districts had the most or best, next came the middle-spending districts, and the last were the low-spending districts.''[35] The examples cited by the judges in Montana, New Jersey, and Texas provide further evidence for the correlation between funding and

Money and Quality in Pennsylvania Schools[34]

	HIGH SPENDING	MIDDLE SPENDING	LOW SPENDING
Average per-student expenditures	$ 4,298	$ 2,759	$ 2,266
Student-teacher ratio	15.7	19.2	21.0
Student-services ratio	158.3	217.1	246.3
Student-administrator ratio	245.6	349.6	378.5
Teacher salaries	$28,065	$22,345	$20,474
Educational level (years)	5.8	5.5	5.4
Years of experience	17.3	15.5	5.4
Administrator salaries	$41,625	$35,638	$32,891
Education level (years)	7.2	6.8	6.8
Years of experience	23.9	23.0	22.1

facilities and between resources and offerings, as does even a cursory visit to an inner-city or wealthy suburban public school.

Both of the arguments made by defendants of the status quo are thus refuted by both empirical and theoretical considerations. And, as the recent decisions in Montana, New Jersey, and Texas have shown, these refutations can be accepted by the courts. Given that current schemes are unconstitutional, what should states do?

ENFORCING EQUAL EDUCATIONAL OPPORTUNITY

It is not the job of the courts to design new systems for equalizing education; their responsibility is only to guarantee a constitutional right. Implementation is a matter for legislative action. Typically, the court charges the state legislature with developing an equitable finance scheme, reserving for itself the right to review it after implementation.

Although there is no one best funding scheme, choices available to the legislature will shape education in the state. Does the legislature want to create incentives to focus on the basic skills, or does it want to encourage a variety of educational goals? Does it want to micromanage teachers in their classrooms, or does it want to unleash their creative potential? Does it want to weaken local control or strengthen state control?

If a state regulates outputs, it may create an obsessive concern with test-score performance. As multiple-choice, predictable tests become the driving force of the curriculum, their subject matter and question format become classroom fixtures. Teachers spend hours drilling students on identifying antonyms, multiplying fractions, and filling in answer sheets, focusing on little that is richer, broader, or deeper. Thus the legislature's effort to produce equal education ends up degrading learning for all. Individuality, cre-

ativity, and depth are lost; all that is retained is uniformity, conventionality, and trivial skills.

If a state regulates process, it becomes embroiled in regulating nearly every aspect of what goes on in schools. Local boards and teachers are left no choice but to slavishly implement the minutiae dictated from above. Citizens are frustrated that they have no input into their child's education; teachers become discouraged because their professional judgment is overruled or unused; students become bored or dispirited because the fare they are fed is inappropriate to their personal needs. Again, the legislature's effort to provide equal education produces nothing but a great deal of frustration and superficial consistency.

If a state regulates inputs, however, it satisfies the constitutional command while encouraging local initiative. It equalizes the capacity of poor districts to secure the services of a sufficient number of teachers, even to bid for the services of highly qualified teachers. It permits schools from poor districts to exercise the same choice—Shall we offer Latin or Russian? Shall we buy computers or microscopes?—that schools from wealthy districts now enjoy. It insures, to the extent that is possible, that educational opportunity is independent of the wealth of one's parents and neighbors.

Improving education for children in poor school districts would benefit them and the nation. A future physicist is as easily born in Jersey City as in Princeton, a future pianist in Edgewood as in Alamo Heights. But it is not only potential luminaries that are lost; it is part of an entire generation of citizens whose potential contributions are stunted by the inadequacy of the education they are provided. School finance reform cannot solve all of the problems of education, but it can equalize the opportunities that the state provides. To continue to distribute better education to children in rich districts and worse education to children in poor districts is only to exacerbate the inequalities that children bring to school. To equalize educational opportunity is to redress some of the accidents of birth.

References

1. *Edgewood v. Kirby*, slip opinion, p. 25.
2. See ref. 1, p. 16.
3. See ref. 1, p. 19.
4. See ref. 1, p. 22.
5. *Abbot v. Burke*, slip opinion, p. 145.
6. See ref. 5, p. 112.
7. See ref. 5, p. 114.
8. See ref. 5, p. 131.
9. See ref. 5, p. 156.
10. See ref. 5, p. 165.
11. See ref. 5, p. 150.
12. Arthur E. Wise, *Rich Schools, Poor Schools: The Promise of Equal Educational Opportunity*, Chicago: University of Chicago Press, 1967; Arthur E. Wise, "Is Denial of Equal Educational Opportunity Constitutional?" *Administrator's Notebook*, XIII (February 1965), pp. 1–4.
13. *Robinson v. Cahill*, 303 A. 2d 273. 294 (1971).
14. 487 P. 1241. 1244.
15. *Serrano v. Priest*, 487 P. 2d 1241 (1971).
16. See ref. 15.
17. James Gordon Ward, "In Pursuit of Equity and Adequacy: Reforming School Finance in Illinois," *Journal of Education Finance* 13:1, Summer 1987, p. 109.
18. Richard A. King, "Equalization in New Mexico School Finance," *Journal of Education Finance* 9:1, Summer 1983, pp. 77–78.
19. James W. Guthrie et al., "Conditions of Education in California 1988: Summary of a Report by Policy Analysis for California Education," Berkeley, Policy Analysis for California Education, 1988, p. 10.
20. See ref. 1, p. 41.
21. See ref. 1, p. 44.
22. See ref. 1, p. 45.
23. See ref. 1, p. 47.
24. See ref. 1, p. 48.
25. See ref. 1, p. 49.
26. See ref. 1, p. 49.
27. See ref. 1, p. 51.
28. See ref. 1, p. 52.
29. See ref. 1, p. 52–53.
30. See ref. 1, p. 41.
31. On December 14, 1988, the Court of Appeals for the 3rd District of Texas overturned the District Court's opinion. The original plaintiffs have announced their intention to appeal the decision to the Texas Supreme Court.
32. Richard A. Rossmiller, "School Finance Reform Through Litigation: Expressway or Cul-desac?" *School Law Update 1986*, p. 196.
33. James S. Coleman et al., *Equality of Educational Opportunity*, Washington, DC: U.S. Government Printing Office, 1966, p. 325.
34. William T. Hartman, "District Spending Disparities: What Do the Dollars Buy?" *Journal of Education Finance* 13:4, Spring 1988, pp. 443, 447, 450, 451.
35. See ref. 34, p. 459.

THOMAS G. FOX AND JOHN RIEW

PARTIAL PRIVATIZATION OF PUBLIC SCHOOL FINANCE

Thomas G. Fox and John Riew are Professors of Economics at Pennsylvania State University.

The basic circumstances of earlier years, which led so inevitably to the system of public financing and public operation of elementary and secondary schools in the United States, have undergone considerable changes. The industrial revolution, the rapid expansion of trade and commerce, and the development of science and technology have led to public recognition not merely of the importance of elementary and secondary education but also of the need for higher education and more diversified types of education better adapted to the demands of a highly developed industrial society. Undoubtedly, the gradual universalization of free public elementary and secondary education has contributed greatly to this realization. Concomitant with the change in public attitudes toward education, the twentieth century economic progress among western nations—especially after their recovery from World War II—has drastically improved the average living standards in those nations. Changes in social and economic conditions have been so revolutionary, one may now justifiably question the rationale of the traditional system of free public education. Is there a plausible case to be made that parents with school-age children attending public schools should be given additional responsibility to finance their children's education?

The institution of free public schools has existed within the United States for many decades. During these long periods, the basic concept of free provision has gone largely unquestioned. Even though the grave and recurring financial crises that have racked many public school systems in recent years have induced a host of tentative solutions to be set forth, the very principle of general tax financing of the public schools remains to be addressed.[1]

This paper will examine the economic rationale of the system of free public education and weigh the merits of a partial privatization of public school financing. A brief sketch of the evolution of public schools in part of Europe and the United States follows in section 2 to provide background perspective. Section 3 summarizes the principal arguments for public financing of public schools. Then, in section 4, the problems of equity and resource allocation associated with free education are discussed as are the probable ramifications under a scheme of a partial privatization of school financing. Implications of the proposed scheme for the fiscal postures of state

From Thomas G. Fox and John Riew, "Partial Privatization of Public School Finance," *Journal of Education Finance* 10 (Summer 1984): 103–120. Reprinted with permission.

[1]The current public finance debate focuses on which level of government should be primarily responsible for the public finance required and how much and how the tax revenues should be raised.

and local governments and for school budgets and educational standards are presented in sections 5 and 6. Ramifications for low-income households are noted in section 7 and the conclusions follow in section 8.

ORIGINS OF THE PUBLIC SCHOOLS[2]

The modern movement toward the education of the general population via the public sector began with the French Revolution. The explicit aim was to provide for both individual and national well-being.[3] Talleyrand, in 1791, drafted a bill to create a system of public education, one aim of which was to make citizens happier and more useful by eliminating their ignorance.[4] Subsequently in 1792, Condorcet offered a bill enacting a new education objective—equality of opportunity for the full development of the ability of individuals.[5] Following the French, the right of the state to require education also was asserted in Prussia in 1794 and adopted later in other German states.[6] The growth of political, military, and economic nationalism served to strengthen state control of education.

While in these early periods France and Germany "proceeded on the theory that the provision of education is the inherent right of the state, England has never looked kindly on it and has proceeded on the doctrine of laissez-faire in education as in other aspects of social control."[7] A large segment of the English were opposed to the provision of public education on the ground that education would make the lower classes restless and discontent. Another segment accepted, however, the argument by Smith and Malthus that England "enforce compulsory education with public financial support for schools for the poor, but that those who could afford it should pay for their own education."[8] Part of Smith's plea for public education for the poor was "to secure decency and order."

The public education movement in the United States was extensively influenced by eighteenth century French political philosophy and practical considerations. In the American colonies, public education was considered pragmatically. Professor Roe L. Johns, one of the great scholars of American educational finance and one of those responsible for directing the recent National Educational Finance Project, states in his 1972 Horace Mann lecture on "The Early History of School Financing":

> *Public education was not started in this nation from altruistic motives: in New England, for example, religious indoctrination was the primary purpose for its establishment. . . . Public education was inaugurated primarily because it benefited business and industry, it promoted*

---

[2]For an overview, *see* "Public Education" by I. L. Kandel in the Education section of the *Encyclopaedia of the Social Sciences* (New York: Macmillan Co., 1963), pp. 414–21.

[3]Ellwood P. Cubberly, *The History of Education: Educational Practice and Progress Considered as a Phase of the Development and Spread of Western Civilization* (Boston: Houghton Mifflin Co., 1920), p. 508.

[4]I. L. Kandel, *Comparative Education* (Boston: Houghton Mifflin Co., 1933), p. 48.

[5]I. L. Kandel, *The New Era in Education: A Comparative Study* (Cambridge, Mass.: The Riverside Press, 1955), p. 89. Neither Talleyrand's nor Condorcet's bills were actually passed, but both profoundly influenced subsequent legislation passed to implement a declaration of the then new 1791 French Constitution. The ideas of Rousseau, La Chalotais, Rolland Mirabeau, among others, also were influential. *See* Kandel's *Comparative Education*, ch. III; Cubberly, *The History of Education*, ch. XX.

[6]Kandel, *Comparative Education*, p. 49.

[7]Kandel, "Public Education," *Encyclopaedia of the Social Sciences*, p. 416.

[8]Ibid.

law and order, and, as suffrage was extended, it was deemed necessary for the safety of the nation under a system of popular government. Prior to the beginning of the twentieth century, public education was provided primarily to benefit and protect the adult society, not the children. The needs of adults, not the needs of children, were the principal determinants not only of whether free public education was provided but also of what was taught in the public schools and how it was taught.[9]

In this country, social agitation for tax-supported, tuition-free public schools with compulsory attendance continued through the second half of the nineteenth century and well into the first half of the twentieth century.[10] Thus, by 1887, twenty-four states had passed a compulsory attendance law; but (as of 1889) these laws often were ineffective.[11] By 1915 all but six southern states had some provision for compulsory attendance; Mississippi, in 1920, was the last state to adopt such a measure—at least for elementary schooling. By 1935 most states required compulsory attendance of children up through the eighth grade or between sixteen and eighteen years of age.[12]

THE CASE FOR PUBLIC FINANCE OF SCHOOLING

The "free" public schools were initially promoted on the belief that education of the masses contributes to the attainment of objectives embodied in such phrases as national welfare, decency and order, loyalty to republican ideals, good citizenship, elimination of ignorance and poverty, and cultural stimulation. And the case for "free" public schools has been amply developed in the school finance literature.[13] Whatever the specific objectives, if schooling of all children was considered necessary for achieving a social goal, the cause for public financing of the public schools appeared compelling in the face of massive lack of public interest in education and the pervasiveness of poverty in that earlier era. Parents who were unwilling for lack of interest or for economic reasons (the practice of child-labor continued well into the twentieth century) have been forced by compulsory attendance laws to send their children to school.

Historically, it is interesting to note that before the mid-nineteenth century both private and public schools operated in the United States, charged fees or tuition to students, and private schools were predominant in terms of enrollments, expenditures, and educational quality. Children from the poorest families were allowed to attend the public schools without paying fees or were sent to "pauper schools" maintained at public expense.[14] The "good education" that now legendary educational leaders, such as Horace Mann, believed

---

[9]Roe L. Johns, *Full State Funding of Education: Evolution and Implications* (Pittsburgh: The Horace Mann Lecture Series, The University of Pittsburgh Press, 1973), pp. 6–7.

[10]In his *Encyclopaedia* article, p. 417, Kandel notes: "It took nearly three-quarters of a century . . . to overcome such obstacles as opposition to taxation for free schools; the elimination of the charity school and the demands of sectarian schools for state aid; and the deep rooted tradition of localism, which was opposed to state control or supervision."

[11]August W. Steinhilber and Carl J. Sokolowski, *State Laws on Compulsory Attendance*, United States Office of Education, OE-23044, Cir. No, 793 (Washington: United States Government Printing Office, 1966), p. 3 and Table 2.

[12]Ibid.

[13]Proponents of public schools also invoke the existence of economies of scale in education to economically rationalize public schools. See the excellent discussion of publically operated versus privately operated schools by Charles S. Benson in his *The Economics of Public Education* (Boston: Houghton Mifflin Co., 1969), pp. 320–32.

[14]Johns, *Full State Funding of Education.*

should be each child's birth right, however, was not being obtained in the public schools. Most families with children in school were simply too poor, given the general pervasiveness of poverty and the extremely unequal distribution of income of the times, to pay tuition fees high enough to permit quality public education. Apparently the needed educational upgrading of the public schools could only be financed via adequate public tax support. By the late nineteenth century, the common schools were created, public education was in the process of being substantially improved, and public schooling became "free" for all.[15]

The contemporary economic rationale for public financing of schools adds to the argument such concepts as "externalities" or "merit" goods. These concepts are not totally separable from the social objectives presented above that comprise the earlier rationale for free public education, but they enable one more readily to delineate the economic benefits of education accruing to the society at large from the private benefits that accrue to those being educated. While pointing to the external benefits (manifested in an informed and productive citizenry) and the meritorious redistributive effects of schooling, the concepts also imply the presence of internalized or private benefits—appropriable by those being educated.

For the purposes of this discussion, the contemporary argument noted above as an economic rationale for free public schools has one basic weakness. If education is a social good because of its associated externalities and its attributes as a merit good, there is nothing in public finance theory to indicate that the public sector should bear the full costs of schooling. It simply points to the problem of underprovision of elementary and secondary education if one were to ignore external benefits and leave all education decisions to the private market mechanism (even if financial capital markets were "perfect"). An important fact remains that schooling generates substantial private personal benefits (economic and otherwise) to those being educated[16] and that many parents in this relatively affluent age (in spite of contemporary economic reversals) have a keen appreciation of the value of education and high effective demand for it as well.

THE PROBLEMS OF EQUITY AND RESOURCE ALLOCATION

From an economic perspective, the institution of free public schooling entails serious inequities. Public education, which represents a major economic burden to state and local communities, becomes essentially free to fam-

---

[15]Of course, schooling still was not completely "free" as long as families must make school-related personal expenditures for such things as special clothing, school supplies not publically provided but required for use in school, or the income foregone for children attending school. The latter is now relatively unimportant for children below ages 14–16 as society has institutionally limited employment prospects for young children, thereby substantially reducing the earnings foregone while children are in school.

[16]*See* Gary S. Becker, *Human Capital: A Theoretical and Empirical Analysis, with Special Reference to Education* (New York: National Bureau of Economic Research, 1967); Martin Carnoy and Dieter Marenbach, "The Return to Schooling in the United States, 1939–69," *Journal of Human Resources* X (Summer 1975):312–31; W. Lee Hansen, "Total and Private Rates of Return to Investment in Schooling," *Journal of Political Economy* 71 (April, 1963):128–40. For an introduction to the literature on rates of return to investment in education, *see* Elchanan Cohn, *The Economics of Education* (Cambridge, Mass.: Ballinger Publishing Co., 1979), ch. 6 and the literature cited therein.

ilies sending children to public schools.[17] The equity problem here is that the children being educated derive significant private or personal benefits, apart from the indirect benefits of education that accrue to all members of the community. Whatever general tax bases are used as sources of public funds, free public education would entail inequity between large families and small families, between families with children and childless families or single adults. Given the value of the private benefits and the enormous volume of tax revenue used to support public schools, the issue here is indeed of major importance. The presence of external benefits, significant as they undoubtedly are, ought not to blind one to this fact that under the present arrangements, local and state tax systems are used to finance private appropriable benefits.

The current system of public school finance also distorts consumer preferences and leads to an allocational distortion. The system often leads to a situation in which coalitions of parents of school-age children, teachers, and public school administrators vigorously seek certain "improvements" in school operations and education programs that may not carry the values commensurate with their economic costs from the viewpoint of the society as a whole. These primary beneficiaries may find it expedient to organize to obtain more benefits, while taxpayers are unable to voluntarily organize effective representation of their interests, except under the most extreme circumstances. In the absence of a direct linkage between personal financing responsibility and the direct private benefits of schooling, school enrichment, improvement, or program continuation may be demanded without careful deliberation as to whether the value of the

implied educational benefits is worth the additional costs to society.

It should be noted that in a school district with declining enrollments, for example, the advantage of a reduced tax burden to parents (whose children attend a neighborhood school) of closing a severely underutilized school is so negligible relative to their benefits of retaining the school open that they almost invariably oppose the school closure. For similar reasons, teachers assigned to that school may oppose it also. Parents and others may speak of the great educational advantages of retaining the neighborhood school and try to force its continued operation. The linkage between who pays for educational program changes and who benefits or loses may become irrelevant in the eyes of the decision makers. Thus, those charged with the stewardship of resources provided to finance public education in concert with teachers and the families with children in school may have little incentive to evaluate educational programs in terms of economic benefits and costs to society.

It also may be worth noting in this context that while regular public elementary and secondary enrollment declined by 10.7 percent from 1970 to 1980, the number of classroom teachers increased by 5.2 percent. During this same period, the total current expenditures increased 144.4 percent (from $39.6 billion to ($96.8 billion), or by 12.3 percent in constant 1980–81 dollars. This, in view of declining enrollments, meant a 25.8 percent increase in per pupil expenditures in constant dollars. Moreover, note that over this same eleven year period the average level of Scholastic Aptitude Test achievement for high school seniors declined from 460 to 424 on the verbal test and from 488 to 466 on the mathematical

---

[17]Granted, families with children in public schools pay real property and other taxes to support public schools. But, under the existing system, these taxes must be paid anyway, even if a family chooses to transfer children from public schools to private schools.

test.[18] Various other factors undoubtedly influence the SAT achievement scores, but it is interesting to observe that the substantial decrease in average pupil-teacher ratios and the 25.8 percent increase in real expenditures per pupil were unable even to sustain the past level of achievements during this time interval.

That elementary and secondary education is available as a "free public good" must have had a profound effect on the composition of many household budgets and most likely has had a major impact on family size for a large number of households. Free public education no doubt constitutes one of the greatest sources of financial relief for families with children. Indeed, the system of public schools as currently financed can be said to be one of the most pronatal of all social institutions that exist in the United States.[19] According to estimates of the National Center for Educational Statistics, the aggregate expenditures for all public elementary and secondary schools of the nation amounted to $96.0 billion for all purposes for the school year 1980–81, with a total public school enrollment of 40.9 million.[20] On the basis of these figures, the average expenditure per pupil per annum for all purposes was about $2,400. This then gives a crude estimate of the annual cost of elementary and secondary public education per child,

for a duration of thirteen years, that parents under the present school finance system are allowed to disregard in their family planning and family budget allocation decisions.[21]

What rationale can be offered today (when the population growth is still a controversial issue) to defend a public finance mechanism that grants such major premiums to family units whose "consumer preferences" lead to the choice of another child, which may be its third or fourth, rather than that of an improvement of the quality of education for other already born members of the family or, for that matter, of any other amenities of life for the family? In view of the magnitude of resources involved, the present system of public schools and mode of finance is expected to lead to a substantial distortion of consumer preference patterns and resource allocation in the manner noted above.

One may reasonably and plausibly argue that a portion of the costs that may be related to private benefits associated with elementary and secondary education and recognized as such should be financed by fees imposed on the individual beneficiaries. Indeed, many public services contain substantial elements of both private and social benefits and are now or could be, insofar as feasible, financed through a combination of general public sup-

---

[18]Data are from United States Department of Education, National Center for Education Statistics, *Projections of Education Statistics to 1990–91* (Washington, D.C.: United States Government Printing Office, 1982), Table 4, p. 32, Table 17, p. 80, Table 26, p. 105, Table 25, p. 101. SAT scores are from United States Bureau of the Census, *Statistical Abstract of the United States: 1982–83.* 103d ed. (Washington, D.C.: United States Government Printing Office, 1982), p. 157. During this period, 1970–80, high school graduation rates and the reduction in dropout rates either remained unchanged or declined slightly. The large favorable improvements in the values of these indices occurred during the 1950s and 1960s.

[19]Deductibility of interest paid on home mortgages, deduction of property taxes, welfare and assistance (AFDC-type) programs, food stamps, personal exemptions, among others, also may be regarded indirectly as pronatal to various degrees.

[20]*Digest of Education Statistics 1982*, Table 68, p. 78 and Table 28, p. 38. These figures include some post-high school students and expenditures.

[21]This is true, provided that "expecting" parents were not planning to send their children to private schools. Of course, on the average, a year of elementary school costs less than a year of secondary school.

port and direct payments or user-fees levied on the direct beneficiaries. It is important to note that to a very modest extent during the last thirty years or so this has been done in the area of public education in those states where students' families supply paper and pencils, gym clothes, band instruments; pay lab fees for certain courses, materials fees for projects in shop classes, fees for driver education, and travel costs associated with selected school activities. It also is common in many school districts for "booster clubs" of parents to be encouraged to raise financial resources to support school-system programs their children participate in (e.g., marching band). Partial privatization of public school finance that incorporates a rational application of the "benefit-received" principle together with a careful consideration and appropriate accommodation of poor households, should promote greater equity and lead to improved allocational efficiency in the use of society's limited resources.[22]

THE FISCAL POSTURES OF STATE AND LOCAL GOVERNMENTS

Much of what is commonly referred to as state and local fiscal problems today are basically associated with local fiscal problems and the increasing involvement of the states in their aid to the local jurisdictions coupled with changing federal-state-local fiscal relationships (and, of course, the current major recession). In 1980, for example, the estimated state payments to local governments in the United States amounted to $81.3 billion. This repre-

sented 47 percent of the states' general expenditures. Of these state payments, transfers to school districts were $45.1 billion in 1979, by far the largest item of the state transfers, accounting for 55 percent.[23]

From the school districts' vantage point, state school aid in 1980 constituted about 46 percent of their total expenditures. Dividing the benefits of public schools between public external and private internal benefits and apportioning the costs between the general public sector and parents of public school children would be extremely difficult. If, however, the cost of public education is arbitrarily imputed evenly between the public and private sectors, the direct payments by parents would roughly equal the present level of state transfers to local districts. If such an even splitting of costs seems impractical, perhaps such a cost-sharing arrangement as one-third private and two-thirds public may be more politically feasible. In any event, direct payments by families should not exceed the average value of private marginal benefits expected from that level of education. Initially, cost sharing should be restricted to current expenditures. How school facilities such as buildings and equipment should be most equitably financed deserves further study as part of an intertemporal equity problem. Moving from the existing system to the suggested partial privatization of public school finance should be done gradually. That such a cost-sharing system would have far-reaching effects on state and local fiscal postures, however, is beyond question.

It is ironic that as the nation has achieved vast improvements in private standards of liv-

---

[22]For an interesting discussion of related efficiency aspects of local school finance, see the articles appearing in Symposium on Efficiency Aspects of Local School Finance, in *Journal of Policy Economy* 81, no. 1 (January/February 1973):158–202.

[23]*Statistical Abstract of the United States: 1982–83*, Table 470, p. 270, and Table 466, p. 276; United States Department of Education, National Center for Education Statistics, *Digest of Education Statistics, 1982* (Washington, D.C.: United States Government Printing Office, 1982), Table 14, p. 21.

ing since World War II, the public can allow the state and local governments to fail in providing quality services that are vital and will not be adequately handled by the private sector. A partial transfer of the burden of supporting public schools to individual parents of public school children would be one way of bringing about a better balance between private-sector consumption and investment and local public-sector services. The estimated 1980 expenditures ($96.0 billion) for the nation's public schools represented 42.9 percent of the total general expenditures of local governments ($223.6 billion), which includes school budgets themselves, and 25.3 percent of the combined state and local direct general expenditures.[24] Leaving a sizeable portion—such as one-third or even a quarter—of the total annual costs of public schools to private responsibility could free a significant amount of general tax revenues to be used for local and state tax rate reductions. The partial privatization of financing the public schools, in addition to the direct effect of reducing the required public funds for school purposes, would have the long-run effect of further relieving the public tax burden via a decline in fertility and in the dependent-taxpayer ratio.[25]

The numerous reports in recent years of closing or threatened closing of parochial schools has obvious implications on the added burden to the public school systems. Partial privatization of public school finance is likely to modestly strengthen support of the parochial and other private schools. Under the present system, parents switching their children from nonpublic schools to public schools find such a move financially advantageous. A system that requires a private payment of part of the costs of the public schools would reduce such advantages. To the extent that the inflow of parochial pupils into public school systems is reduced under the proposed system, it would mean a further reduction in the expenditures of the public schools, without apparent changes in external benefits to society.

SCHOOL BUDGETS AND EDUCATIONAL STANDARDS

The absence of any current and direct link between the benefits of public education and financing responsibilities, it may be argued, contributes to the much observed voter apathy toward proposed school improvements. Rising costs of schools as well as ever increasing property taxes add to the aggravation of public attitudes.[26] This lack of current benefit-payment linkage is probably one of the most important factors contributing to the failure to provide a generally high standard of public education in many areas of the nation today.

To the extent that tuition fees are directly borne by parents for children enrolled in the public schools, the general resistance of the tax-paying community to programs promoting higher quality educational services should be lessened. On the other hand, one would

---

[24]*Digest of Educational Statistics, 1982*, Table 14, p. 21; *Statistical Abstract of the United States: 1982–83*, Table 466, p. 276, and Table 473, p. 281.

[25]The proposed scheme may have only a negligible effect on the bearing of the first or the second child, but its effect on the marginal decisions for subsequent childbearing could be considerable if the school cost borne by the parents reaches such a significant proportion as one-third, for example.

[26]For discussion of the tax revolt, see Milton Friedman, "The Limitations of Tax Limitation," *Policy Review* 5 (Summer 1978):7–14; Daniel Orr "Proposition 13: Tax Reform's Lexington Bridge," *Policy Review* 6 (Fall 1978):57–67; Katharine L. Bradbury and Helen F. Ladd, with Claire Christopherson, "Proposition 2½: Initial Impacts, Part 1," *New England Economic Review* (January/February 1982):13–24.

suspect that the scheme of direct family financial support could lead to more cautious and selective parental demand for improvement in educational programs and more careful monitoring of public education planning and budgeting. But as long as the parents bear only a fraction of the full cost of elementary and secondary education, this restraining effect is more likely to be beneficial than perverse.

It may be argued that private payments for the support of public schools will lead to an increase in enrollment in nonpublic schools since this reduces the net cost of sending children to nonpublic schools.[27] If one reasons, however, that resort to private schools also may be attributable to the current low standards within some public schools, the potential positive effect of parental economic contributions on public educational standards could, at least partially, offset the advantages of the reduced net cost for private schooling.

At present, parochial and other private schools are more numerous in urban areas because the families that constitute either the "economic elite" who can afford private schools or the religious groups preferring parochial schools are numerous enough in these urban areas to allow for efficient-size schools: many central cities facing serious financial problems are unable to provide public schools of a satisfactory standard, thus creating the demand for nonpublic schools. Considering the vital role that central cities play in the economic life of metropolitan areas and their inevitable fiscal disadvantages (low tax bases and high expenditure needs relative to their surrounding suburbs), measures to relieve fiscal problems of the cities may well be in order. Through such an accommodation, the public school systems in the cities may be brought up to standards that are more acceptable to the concerned parents, competing more effectively with other school alternatives.[28]

RAMIFICATIONS FOR LOW-INCOME FAMILIES

One major problem of a proposal to partially privatize school finance is that it may cause severe hardships on low-income families. This can be overcome by providing tuition remission grants on a sliding scale adjusted for family income as well as for the number of children attending school in each family. School systems have extensive experience with the free and reduced-cost lunch programs that are based on such a scheme. With a compassionate system of tuition remission grants, all children within a school district will have access to public elementary and secondary schooling, independent of family socioeconomic background. Because of the social significance of the partial shifting of public school finance to the private sector and the burden this will place on low-income families, it is emphatically asserted that a fair system of tuition remission grants has to be a vital feature of the proposal. The current system should not be substantially altered as suggested unless an enlightened and fair accommodation of perverse economic implications is incorporated into the changes. The poor should not be made any worse off than they already are under the proposed scheme.

---

[27]The basic question of the merit of a plural educational system at the elementary and secondary levels is beyond the scope of this paper.

[28]It is assumed that states continue to provide constitutionally appropriate equalization of public school finance revenue transfers. The appropriate role of state governments in financing education is not addressed in this paper. The focus of the article is primarily on private versus public finance. The intergovernmental division of responsibility for education would require a separate study.

Considerations of intertemporal equity as well as possible financial hardships resulting from the proposed change would point to the need for a cautious, gradual transition. Thus, the ultimate parental share of say a third (or whatever other fraction) of the full cost of schooling may be borne only after a substantial period of transition. Commencing with an initial family assumption of several percentage points of the burden of the full cost and gradually reaching the level desired over a period of a decade, or even longer, would seem to be a reasonable approach.

CONCLUSION

At a time when society perceived merits in education, while the general population was poor and uninformed of its value, the institution of free public schools was a highly desirable arrangement for furthering the cause of the general enlightenment and welfare of the society. The situations that led to the now traditional system of free public schools, however, have undergone great changes. Widespread public recognition of the importance of education and the immense improvement of family economic status (during nonrecessionary periods) now allows one to evaluate the current system of school financing in a new perspective.

This paper attempted to show that the full public fiscal support of public schools is no longer necessary and suggested that the system bears adverse effects in terms of equity and allocation efficiency. It points out that partial privatization of the finance of the public schools would help correct some of these problems and has other salutary effects in mitigating fiscal plights of the state and local governments. That such a plan also may have a profound demographic effect is not without merit in view of the prominence of the contemporary concern directed at environmental control and population growth.

Lest the poor be adversely affected, the proposal calls for a scheme whereby parental payments would range from zero (for the poor) to a specified fraction (such as one-third) of the full cost for middle-income families, based on a sliding scale. In the interest of minimizing undesirable effects on locational preferences and migration, the scheme of partial privatization of school finance should flow from a state mandate, not as a decision by an individual local education authority.

Innovation of this proposal should commence during an era of national economic health, not during a major recession. The question of continued public financing of benefits which accrue directly to individuals (the students) and increase their lifetime earning expectations, as opposed to a new form of partial private and partial public finance, is worth careful consideration. Through partial privatization of public school finance by more directly linking the outlays to the individuals who are the primary beneficiaries, and should be the ones to pay, a better use of society's limited resources should be obtained which leads to an improvement in general social and economic welfare.

DISCUSSION QUESTIONS AND ACTIVITIES

1. What, according to Wise and Gendler, were the grounds for the *San Antonio v. Rodriguez* decision? What were its consequences?
2. Why were some of the early funding reforms rendered nearly ineffectual?
3. What are the arguments commonly used against school finance reform? Assess the validity of each one.

4. Can states equalize funding and still avoid overregulation of local school districts? Explain.

5. According to Fox and Riew, why was American education initiated?

6. Is there an equity problem because those being educated derive significant personal and private benefits apart from indirect benefits to the community?

7. Does the present system of public school finance lead to consumer distortion and distortions in the allocation of benefits to society?

8. What would be the benefits of "partial privatization" of financing public schools? Would the benefits outweigh the shortcomings?

9. Survey three groups: a group of parents with children in public schools, parents with children in nonpublic schools, and married couples without children. Present Fox and Riew's partial privatization plan. Record the responses and note any differences in the three groups.

10. Organize a classroom debate on partial privatization of public school funding.

11. Gather data from states that have upheld the constitutionality of their state finance plan and those states where school plans were found unconstitutional. Examine the legal grounds for the decisions.

SUGGESTED READINGS

Coons, John E., William H. Clune, III, and Stephen D. Sugarman. *Private Wealth and Public Education.* Cambridge, Mass.: Harvard University Press, 1970.

Doyle, Denis P., and Chester E. Finn, Jr. "American Schools and the Future of Local Control." *The Public Interest* 77 (Fall 1984): 77–85.

Glickman, Carl D., and Ray E. Bruce. "Altering the Role of Public Education." *The Educational Forum* 47 (Winter 1984): 151–159.

Hanley, Robert. "The New Math of Rich and Poor." *New York Times* 139 (June 10, 1990): Sec. 4, E6.

LeMorte, Michael W., and Jeffrey D. Williams, "Court Decisions and School Finance Reform." *Educational Administration Quarterly* 21 (Spring 1985): 59–89.

Melvin, Leland D. "The Law of Public School Finance." *Contemporary Education* 55 (Spring 1984): 149–155.

Natale, Jo Ann. "Just Deserts." *American School Board Journal* 177 (March 1990): 20–25, 42.

Odden, Allan. "A School Finance Agenda for an Era of Education Reform." *Journal of Education Finance* 12 (Summer 1986): 49–70.

Ward, James G. "An Inquiry into the Normative Foundations of American Public School Finance." *Journal of Education Finance* 12 (Spring 1987): 463–477.

Wise, Arthur E. *Rich Schools, Poor Schools: The Promise of Equal Opportunity.* Chicago: The University of Chicago Press, 1967.

Wood, R. Craig, and Robert W. Ruch, "Challenges to Financing Education." *School Business Affairs* 52 (July 1986): 31–35.

CHAPTER 8

PRIVATE SCHOOLS

A number of parents are removing their children from public schools and placing them in private and parochial schools. Some do so on academic grounds, others do so for religious reasons, and still others wish to avoid integration. Those who favor financial aid to private schools generally believe private schools offer a better education than public schools.

The percentage of all students who attend nonpublic schools (secular private and parochial) has remained fairly stable since 1970. Enrollment in nonpublic schools is 8.9 percent, with the largest percentage at the elementary level. Public high schools average 750 students, Catholic schools average 500 students, and other nonpublic schools average only 150 students. Pupil-teacher ratios in public and Catholic schools are similar, but the ratio is only about half as large as public schools in other nonpublic schools.

A study by James S. Coleman and others compares public schools with Catholic and other nonpublic schools in terms of discipline, problems of students, homework, achievement test scores, academic demands made on students, and aspirations for higher education. The study also evaluates the degree of religious segregation and economic segregation in American secondary schools. It concludes that Catholic schools have higher quality on the average and greater equality than public schools.

The public school, Coleman has said elsewhere, is no longer a "common" institution because residential mobility has brought about a high degree of racial segregation in education as well as segregation by income. He does not believe that the public interest in common institutions is an overriding public interest. Rather, it is relatively weak compared to helping all children, especially the disadvantaged, receive a better education. Others disagree, citing the vital role that a public educational system can play in a democratic society.

In terms of policy, Coleman opposes the practice of assigning students on the basis of residence because it harms the nonaffluent and increases inequalities in opportunity. He prefers communities based on interests, values, and educational preferences. To support these plans he would expand the different types of education supported by public funds.

QUALITY AND EQUALITY IN AMERICAN EDUCATION: PUBLIC AND CATHOLIC SCHOOLS

JAMES S. COLEMAN

James S. Coleman (b. 1926) took his Ph.D. at Columbia University, taught at Johns Hopkins University, and is now Professor of Sociology at the University of Chicago. He is a member of the National Academy of Education, American Academy of Arts and Sciences, National Academy of Sciences, and the American Philosophical Association. His writing includes The Adolescent Society, High School Achievement *(coauthor), and the landmark USOE study,* Equality of Educational Opportunity *(coauthor).*

The report, "Public and Private Schools," of which I was an author, has raised some questions about certain fundamental assumptions and ideals underlying American education.[1] In this article, I shall first describe briefly the results that raise these questions. Then I shall examine in greater detail these fundamental assumptions and ideals, together with changes in our society that have violated the assumptions and made the ideals increasingly unattainable. I shall then indicate the negative consequences that these violations have created for both equality of educational opportunity in United States public schools and for the quality of education they offer. Finally, I shall suggest what seems to me the direction that a new set of ideals and assumptions must take if the schools are to serve American children effectively.

A number of the results of "Public and Private Schools" have been subjected to intense reexamination and reanalysis. The report has occasioned a good deal of debate and controversy, as well as a two-day conference at the National Institute of Education and a one-day conference at the National Academy of Sciences, both in late July. Part of the controversy appears to have arisen because of the serious methodological difficulties in eliminating bias due to self-selection into the private sector. Another part appears to have arisen because the report was seen as an attack on the public schools at a time when tuition tax-credit legislation was being proposed in Congress.

I shall not discuss the controversy except to say that all the results summarized in the first portion of this article have been challenged by at least one critic; I would not report them here if these criticisms or our own further analyses had led me to have serious doubts about them. Despite this confidence, the results could be incorrect because of the extent of the methodological difficulties involved in answering any cause-and-effect question when exposure to the different treatments (that is, to the different types of schools) is so far from random. Most of my comparisons will be between the Catholic and the public schools. The non-Catholic private schools constitute a

From James S. Coleman, "Quality and Equality in American Education: Public and Catholic Schools," *Phi Delta Kappan* 63 (November 1981): 159–164. Reprinted by permission.

much more heterogeneous array of schools; our sample in those schools is considerably smaller (631 sophomores and 551 seniors in twenty-seven schools), and the sample may be biased by the fact that a substantial number of schools refused to participate. For these reasons, any generalizations about the non-Catholic private sector must be tenuous. Fortunately, the principal results of interest are to be found in the Catholic schools.

There are five principal results of our study, two having to do with quality of education provided in both the public and private sectors and three related to equality of education.

First, we found evidence of higher academic achievement in basic cognitive skills (reading comprehension, vocabulary, and mathematics) in Catholic schools than in public schools for students from comparable family backgrounds. The difference is roughly one grade level, which is not a great difference. But, since students in Catholic schools take, on the average, a slightly greater number of academic courses, the difference could well be greater for tests more closely attuned to the high school curriculum. And the higher achievement is attained in the Catholic schools with a lower expenditure per pupil and a slightly higher pupil/teacher ratio than in the public schools.

The second result concerning educational quality must be stated with a little less certainty. We found that aspirations for higher education are higher among students in Catholic schools than among comparable students in public schools, despite the fact that, according to the students' retrospective reports, about the same proportion had planned to attend college when they were in the sixth grade.

The first two results concerning equality in education are parallel to the previous two results; one concerns achievement in cognitive skills and the other, plans to attend college.

For both of these outcomes of schooling, family background matters less in the Catholic schools than in the public schools. In both achievement and aspirations, blacks are closer to whites, Hispanics are closer to Anglos, and children from less well-educated parents are closer to those from better-educated parents in Catholic schools than in public schools. Moreover, in Catholic schools the gap narrows between the sophomore and senior years, while in the public schools the gap in both achievement and aspirations widens.

It is important to note that, unlike the results related to educational quality, these results related to equality do not hold generally for the public/private comparison. That is, the results concerning equality are limited to the comparison between public schools and Catholic schools. Within other segments of the private sector (e.g., Lutheran schools or Jewish schools) similar results for educational differences might well hold (though these other segments have too few blacks and Hispanics to allow racial and ethnic comparisons), but they are not sufficiently represented in the sample to allow separate examination.

The final result concerning educational equality is in the area of racial and ethnic integration. Catholic schools have, proportionally, only about half as many black students as do the public schools (about 6 percent compared to about 14 percent), but internally they are less segregated. In terms of their effect on the overall degree of racial integration in United States schools, these two factors work in opposing directions; to a large extent they cancel each other out. But of interest to our examination here, which concerns the internal functioning of the public and Catholic sectors of education, is the lesser internal segregation of blacks in the Catholic sector. Part of this is due to the smaller percentage of black students in Catholic schools, for a general conclusion in the school desegregation literature is that school systems with smaller proportions of a disadvantaged minority are less segregated than those with larger proportions. But part seems due to factors beyond the simple proportions. A similar result is that, even though the Catholic schools in our sample have slightly higher proportions of Hispanic students than the public schools, they have slightly less Hispanic/Anglo segregation.

These are the results from our research on public and private schools that raise questions about certain fundamental assumptions of American education. Catholic schools appear to be characterized by *both* higher quality, on the average, *and* greater equality than the public schools. How can this be when the public schools are, first, more expensive, which should lead to higher quality, and, second, explicitly designed to increase equality of opportunity? The answer lies, I believe, in the organization of public education in the United States, and that organization in turn is grounded in several fundamental assumptions. It is to these assumptions that I now turn.

FOUR BASIC IDEAS AND THEIR VIOLATION

Perhaps the ideal most central to American education is the ideal of the common school, a school attended by all children. The assumption that all social classes should attend the same school contrasted with the two-tiered educational systems in Europe, which reflected their feudal origins. Both in the beginning and at crucial moments of choice (such as the massive expansion of secondary education in the early part of this century), American education followed the pattern of common, or comprehensive, schools, including all students from the community and all courses of study. Only in the largest eastern cities were there differentiated, selective high schools, and even that practice declined over time, with new high schools generally following the pattern of the comprehensive school.

One implication of the common-school ideal has been the deliberate and complete exclusion of religion from the schools. In contrast, many (perhaps most) other countries have some form of support for schools operated by religious groups. In many countries, even including very small ones such as the Netherlands and Israel, there is a state secular school system, as well as publicly supported schools under the control of religious groups. But the melting pot ideology that shaped American education dictated that there would be a single set of publicly supported schools, and the reaction to European religious intolerance dictated that these be free of religious influence.[2]

The absence of social class, curriculum, or religious bases for selection of students into different schools meant that, in American schooling, attendance at a given school was dictated by location of residence. This method worked well in sparsely settled areas and in towns and smaller cities, and it was a principle compatible with a secular democracy. Two factors have, however, led this mode of school assignment to violate the assumptions of the common school. One is the movement of the United States population to cities with high population densities, resulting in economically homogeneous residential areas. The other is the more recent, largely post-World War II expansion of personal transportation, leading to the development of extensive, economically differentiated suburbs surrounding large cities.

The combined effect of these two changes has been that in metropolitan areas the assumptions of the common school are no longer met. The residential basis of school assignment, in an ironic twist, has proved to be segregative and exclusionary, separating economic levels just as surely as do the explicitly selective systems of European countries and separating racial groups even more completely. The larger the metropolitan area, the more true this is, so that in the largest metropolitan areas the schools form a set of layers of economically stratified and racially distinct schools, while in small cities and towns the schools continue to approximate the economically and racially heterogeneous mix that was Horace Mann's vision of the common school in America.

In retrospect, only the temporary constraints on residential movement imposed by economic and technological conditions allowed the common-school ideal to be realized even for a time. As those constraints continue to decrease, individual choice will play an increasing role in school attendance (principally through location of residence), and the common-school assumption will be increasingly violated. Assignment to school in a single publicly supported school system on the basis of residence is no longer a means of achieving the common-school ideal. And, in fact, the common-school ideal may no longer be attainable through *any* means short of highly coercive ones.

The courts have attempted to undo the racially segregative impact of residential choice, reconstituting the common-school ideal through compulsory busing of children into different residential areas.[3] These attempts, however, have been largely thwarted by families who, exercising that same opportunity for choice of school through residence, move out of the court's jurisdiction. The unpopularity and impermanence of the court-ordered attempts to reinstitute the common school suggest that attempts to reimpose by law the constraints that economics and technology once placed upon school choice will fail and that, in the absence of those naturally imposed constraints, the common-school ideal will give way before an even stronger ideal—that of individual liberty.

It is necessary, then, to recognize the failure of school assignment by residence and to reexamine the partially conflicting ideals of American education in order to determine which of these ideals we want to preserve and which to discard. For example, in high schools distinguished by variations in curriculum—one form of which is a type of magnet school and another form of which is the technical high school—a more stable racial mix of students is possible than in comprehensive high schools. As another example, Catholic schools are less racially and economically segregated than are United States public schools; this suggests that, when a school is defined around and controlled by a religious community, families may tolerate more racial and economic heterogeneity than they would in a school defined around a residential area and controlled by government officials.

A second ideal of American education has been the concept of local control. This has meant both control by the local school board and superintendent and the responsiveness of the school staff to parents. But these conditions have changed as well. The local school board and superintendent now have far less control over education policy than only twenty years ago. A large part of the policy-making function has shifted to the national level; this shift was caused primarily by the issue of racial discrimination, but it has also affected the areas of sex discrimination, bilingual education, and education for the handicapped, among others. Part of the policy-making power has shifted to the school staff or their union representatives, as professionalization and collective bargaining have accompanied the growth in size of school districts and the breakdown of a sense of community at the local level.

The loss of control by school boards and superintendents has been accompanied by a reduced responsiveness of the school to parents. This too has resulted in part from the breakdown of community at the local level and the increasing professionalization of teachers, both of which have helped to free the teacher from community control. The changes have been accompanied and reinforced by the trend to larger urban agglomerates and larger school districts. And some of the changes introduced to overcome racial segregation—in particular, busing to a distant school—have led to even greater social distances between parent and teacher.

A result of this loss of local control has been that parents are more distant from their children's school, less able to exert influence, less comfortable about the school as an extension of their own child rearing. Public support for public schools, as evidenced in the passage of school tax referenda and school bond issues and in the responses to public opinion polls, has declined since the mid-1960s, probably in part as a result of this loss of local control. Even more recently, in a backlash against the increasingly alien control of the schools, some communities have attempted to counter what they see as moral relativism in the curriculum (e.g., the controversy over the content in *Man: A Course of Study*) and have attempted to ban the teaching of evolution.

Technological and ecological changes make it unlikely that local control of education policy can be reconstituted as it has existed in the past, that is, through a local school board controlling a single public school system and representing the consensus of the community. Individuals may regain such local control by moving ever farther from large cities (as the 1980 census shows they have been doing), but the educational system as a whole cannot be reconstituted along the old local-control lines. Again, as in the case of the common-school ideal, present conditions (and the likelihood that they will persist) make the ideal unrealizable. One alternative is to resign ourselves to ever-decreasing public support

for the public schools as they move further from the ideal. Another, however, is to attempt to find new principles for the organization of American education that will bring back parental support.

A third fundamental assumption of American public schooling, closely connected to local control, has been local financing of education. Some of the same factors that have brought about a loss of local control have shifted an increasing portion of education financing to the state and federal levels. Local taxes currently support only about 40 percent of expenditures for public schooling; federal support amounts to about 8 percent or 9 percent, and state support, slightly over half of the total. The shift from local to state (and, to a lesser extent, federal) levels of financing has resulted from the attempt to reduce inequalities of educational expenditures among school districts. Inequalities that were once of little concern come to be deeply felt when local communities are no longer isolated but interdependent and in close social proximity. The result has been the attempt by some states, responding to the *Serrano* decision in California, to effect complete equality in educational expenditures for all students within the state. This becomes difficult to achieve without full statewide financing, which negates the principle of local financing.

Yet the justification for student assignment to the schools within the family's taxation district has been that the parents were paying for the schools *in that district*. That justification vanishes under a system of statewide taxation. The rationale for assignment by residence, already weakened by the economic and racial differences among students from different locales, is further weakened by the decline in local financing.

A fourth ideal of American public education has been the principle of in loco parentis. In committing their child to a school, parents expect that the school will exercise comparable authority over and responsibility for the child. The principle of in loco parentis was, until the past two decades, assumed not only at the elementary and secondary levels but at the college level as well. However, this assumption vanished as colleges abdicated the responsibility and parents of college students shortened the scope of their authority over their children's behavior from the end of college to the end of high school.

Most parents, however, continue to expect the school to exercise authority over and responsibility for their children through the end of high school. Yet public schools have been less and less successful in acting in loco parentis. In part, this is due to the loss of authority in the society as a whole, manifested in high school by a decreasing willingness of high school-age youths to be subject to *anyone's* authority in matters of dress and conduct. In part, it is due to the increasing dissensus among parents themselves about the authority of the school to exercise discipline over their children, sometimes leading to legal suits to limit the school's authority. And, in part, it is due to the courts, which, in response to these suits, have expanded the scope of civil rights of children in school, thus effectively limiting the school's authority to something less than that implied by the principle of in loco parentis.

There has been a major shift among some middle-class parents—a shift that will probably become even more evident as the children of parents now in their thirties move into high school—toward an early truncation of responsibility for and authority over their adolescent children. This stems in part from two changes—an increase in longevity and a decrease in number of children—which, taken together, remove child rearing from the central place it once held for adults. Many modern adults who begin child rearing late and end early are eager to resume the leisure and consumption activities that preceded the

child-rearing period; they encourage early autonomy for their young. But the high school often continues to act as if it has parental support for its authority. In some cases it does; in others it does not. The community consensus on which a school's authority depends has vanished.

An additional difficulty is created by the increasing size and bureaucratization of the school. The exercising of authority—regarded as humane and fair when the teacher knows the student and parents well—comes to be regarded as inhumane and unfair when it is impersonally administered by a school staff member (teacher or otherwise) who hardly knows the student and seldom sees the parents. Thus there arises in such large, impersonal settings an additional demand for sharply defined limits on authority.

This combination of factors gives the public school less power to exercise the responsibility for and authority over students that are necessary to the school's functioning. The result is a breakdown of discipline in the public schools and, in the extreme, a feeling by some parents that their children are not safe in school. Again, a large portion of the change stems from the lack of consensus that once characterized the parental community about the kind and amount of authority over their children they wished to delegate to the school—a lack of consensus exploited by some students eager to escape authority and responded to by the courts in limiting the school's authority. And, once again, this raises questions about what form of reorganization of American education would restore the functioning of the school and even whether it is possible to reinstate the implicit contract between parent and school that initially allowed the school to act in loco parentis.

The violation of these four basic assumptions of American education—the common school, local control, local financing, and in loco parentis—together with our failure to establish a new set of attainable ideals has hurt both the quality and the equality of American education. For this change in society, without a corresponding change in the ideals that shape its educational policies, reduces the capability of its schools to achieve quality and equality, which even in the best of circumstances are uncomfortable bedfellows.

Next I shall give some indications of how the pursuit of each of these goals of quality and equality is impeded by policies guided by the four assumptions I have examined, beginning first with the goal of equality.

The organization of United States education is assignment to school by residence, guided by the common-school, local-control, and local-financing assumptions, despite those elements that violate these assumptions. In a few locations, school assignment is relieved by student choice of school or by school choice of student. But, in general, the principle observed in American education (thus making it different from the educational systems of many countries) has been that of a rigid assignment by residence, a practice that upholds the common-school myth and the local-control and local-financing myths.

It is commonly assumed that the restriction of choice through rigid assignment by residence is of relative benefit to those least well off, from whom those better off would escape if choice were available. But matters are not always as they seem. Assignment by residence leaves two avenues open to parents: to move their residence, choosing a school by choice of residence; or to choose to attend a private school. But those avenues are open only to those who are sufficiently affluent to choose a school by choosing residence or to choose a private school. The latter choice may be partially subsidized by a religious community operating the school, or, in rare cases, by scholarships. But these partial exceptions do not hide the central point: that the organization of

education through rigid assignment by residence hurts most those without money (and those whose choice is constrained by race or ethnicity), and this increases the inequality of educational opportunity. The reason, of course, is that, because of principles of individual liberty, we are unwilling to close the two avenues of choice: moving residence and choosing a private school. And although economic and technological constraints once kept all but a few from exercising these options, that is no longer true. The constraints are of declining importance; the option of residential change to satisfy educational choice (the less expensive of the two options) is exercised by larger numbers of families. And in that exercise of choice, different economic levels are sorted into different schools by the economic level of the community they can afford.

We must conclude that the restrictions on educational choice in the public sector and the presence of tuition costs in the private sector are restrictions that operate to the relative disadvantage of the least well-off. Only when these restrictions were reinforced by the economic and technological constraints that once existed could they be regarded as effective in helping to achieve a "common school." At present, and increasingly in the future, they are working to the disadvantage of the least well-off, increasing even more the inequality of educational opportunities.

One of the results of our recent study of public and private schools suggests these processes at work. Among Catholic schools, achievement of students from less-advantaged backgrounds—blacks, Hispanics, and those whose parents are poorly educated—is closer to that of students from advantaged backgrounds than is true for the public sector. Family background makes much less difference for achievement in Catholic schools than in public schools. This greater homogeneity of achievement in the Catholic sector (as well as the lesser racial and ethnic segregation of the

Catholic sector) suggests that the ideal of the common school is more nearly met in the Catholic schools than in the public schools. This may be because a religious community continues to constitute a functional community to a greater extent than does a residential area, and in such a functional community there will be less stratification by family background, both within a school and between schools.

At the same time, the organization of American education is harmful to quality of education. The absence of consensus, in a community defined by residence, about what kind and amount of authority should be exercised by the school removes the chief means by which the school has brought about achievement among its students. Once there was such consensus, because residential areas once *were* communities that maintained a set of norms, reflected in the schools' and the parents' beliefs about what was appropriate for children. The norms varied in different communities, but they were consistent within each community. That is no longer true at the high school level, for the reasons I have described. The result is what some have called a crisis of authority.

In our study of high school sophomores and seniors in both public and private schools, we found not only higher achievement in the Catholic and other private schools for students from comparable backgrounds than in the public schools, but also major differences between the functioning of the public schools and the schools of the private sector. The principal differences were in the greater academic demands made and the greater disciplinary standards maintained in private schools, even when schools with students from comparable backgrounds were compared. This suggests that achievement increases as the demands, both academic and disciplinary, are greater. The suggestion is confirmed by two comparisons: Among the public schools, those that have academic demands and disciplinary standards at the same level as the average private school have achievement at the level of that in the private sector (all comparisons, of course, involving students from comparable backgrounds). And, among the private schools, those with academic demands and disciplinary standards at the level of the average public school showed achievement levels similar to those of the average public school.

The evidence from these data—and from other recent studies—is that *stronger academic demands and disciplinary standards produce better achievement.* Yet the public schools are in a poor position to establish and maintain these demands. The loss of authority of the local school board, superintendent, and principal to federal policy and court rulings, the rise of student rights (which has an impact both in shaping a "student-defined" curriculum and in impeding discipline), and, perhaps most fundamental, the breakdown in consensus among parents about the high schools' authority over and responsibility for their children—all of these factors put the average public school in an untenable position to bring about achievement.

Many public high schools have adjusted to these changes by reducing their academic demands (through reduction of standards, elimination of competition, grade inflation, and a proliferation of undemanding-courses) and by slackening their disciplinary standards (making "truancy" a word of the past and ignoring cutting of classes and the use of drugs or alcohol).

These accommodations may be necessary, or at least they may facilitate keeping the peace, in some schools. But the peace they bring is bought at the price of lower achievement, that is, a reduced quality of education.

One may ask whether such accommodations are inevitable or whether a different organization of education might make them unnecessary. It is to this final question that I now turn.

ABANDONING OLD ASSUMPTIONS

The old assumptions that have governed American education all lead to a policy of assignment of students to school by place of residence and to a standard conception of a school. Yet a variety of recent developments, both within the public sector and outside it, suggest that attainment of the twin goals of quality and equality may be incompatible with this. One development is the establishment, first outside the public sector and then in a few places within it as well, of elementary schools governed by different philosophies of education and chosen by parents who subscribe to those philosophies. Montessori schools at the early levels, open education, and basic education are examples. In some communities, this principle of parental choice has been used to maintain more stable racial integration than occurs in schools with fixed pupil assignment and a standard educational philosophy. At the secondary level, magnet schools, with specialized curricula or intensive programs in a given area (e.g., music or performing arts), have been introduced, similarly drawing a clientele who have some consensus on which a demanding and effective program can be built. Alternative schools have flourished, with both students and staff who accept the earlier autonomy to which I have referred. This is not to say, of course, that all magnet schools and all alternative schools are successful, for many are not. But if they were products of a well-conceived pluralistic conception of modes of secondary education, with some policy guidelines for viability, success would be easier to achieve.

Outside the public sector, the growth of church-operated schools is probably the most prominent development, reflecting a different desire by parents for a nonstandard educa-tion. But apart from the religious schools, there is an increasingly wide range of educational philosophies, from the traditional preparatory school to the free school and the parent-run cooperative school.

I believe that these developments suggest an abandonment of the principle of assignment by residence and an expansion of the modes of education supported by public funds. Whether this expansion goes so far as to include all or part of what is now the private sector or is instead a reorganization of the public sector alone is an open question. The old proscriptions against public support of religious education should not be allowed to stand in the way of a serious examination of this question. But the elements of successful reorganization remain, whether it stays within the public sector or encompasses the private: a pluralistic conception of education, based on "communities" defined by interests, values, and educational preferences rather than residence; a commitment of parent and student that can provide the school a lever for extracting from students their best efforts; and the educational choice for all that is now available only to those with money.

Others may not agree with this mode of organizing education. But it is clear that the goals of education in a liberal democracy may not be furthered, and may in fact be impeded, by blind adherence to the ideals and assumptions that once served United States education—some of which may be unattainable in modern America—and by the mode of school organization that these ideals and assumptions brought into being. There may be extensive debate over what set of ideals is both desirable and attainable and over what mode of organization can best attain these ideals, but it is a debate that should begin immediately. Within the public sector, the once-standard curriculum is beginning to take a variety of forms, some of which search for a new mode of organizing schooling. And an increasing (though still small) fraction of youngsters are in private schools, some of which exemplify alternative modes of organizing schooling. These developments can be starting points toward the creation of an educational philosophy to guide the reorganization of American schooling in ways fruitful for the youth who experience it.

Endnotes

1. The other two authors are Thomas Hoffer and Sally Kilgore. A first draft of "Public and Private Schools" was completed on 2 September 1980. A revised draft was released by the National Center for Education Statistics (NCES) on 7 April 1981. A final draft is being submitted to NCES this fall. A revised version of the April 7 draft, together with an epilogue and prologue examining certain broader issues, is being published this fall by Basic Books as *Achievement in High School: Public and Private Schools Compared.*
2. It has nevertheless been true that in many religiously homogeneous communities, ordinarily Protestant, religious influence did infiltrate the schools. Only since the Supreme Court's ban on prayer in the schools has even nonsectarian religious influence been abolished.
3. The legal rationale for these decisions has been past discriminatory practices by school systems; but, in fact, the remedies have constituted attempts to overcome the effects of residential choice.

ORANGES PLUS APPLES, DR. COLEMAN, GIVE YOU ORANGES PLUS APPLES

JOSEPH ROGERS

Joseph Rogers, formerly a principal in Hudson, Ohio, is Superintendent of Windham Exempted Village Schools in Windham, Ohio.

James Coleman's 1981 research comparing private and public education, *Public and Private Schools*, leaves me frustrated and disheartened. Having worked in both systems, I could not help but feel that Coleman lacked insight into private and parochial education.

Whether the matter to be considered is quality, equality, or something else, it seems natural to compare private and public education as two sides of a similar reality. And therein lies the problem! Comparing them is not looking at two closely related variants.

From Joseph Rogers, "Oranges Plus Apples, Dr. Coleman, Give You Oranges Plus Apples," *NASSP Bulletin* 67 (October 1983): 107–109. Reprinted by permission.

Rather, it is an attempt to span a chasm kindred to that of cultural difference.

Coleman's research indicates that Catholic and other private school students have higher academic achievement in the basic cognitive skills. And that should be the case! Because private schools have traditionally had more applicants than openings, applicants were screened and the academic cream accepted. During the 1970s, tuition costs challenged the appeal of Catholic schools, and they were faced with adopting more liberal admission policies. The result was the admittance of less able, but still significantly superior, students. On the other hand, public schools must educate all who have residential claim—regardless of academic achievement. Thus, Catholic and other private schools should be expected to surpass public schools in the area of purely academic achievement.

Coleman's study found that Catholic schools have a lower per pupil expenditure than public schools. And well they should! The lion's share of per pupil expenditure in public schools goes to salaries. Most Catholic schools have some religious members on the faculty and/or staff who do not have to support a family. Their salaries border on what the government cites as the poverty level. The salary of lay educators in Catholic schools is usually below that of public educators as well, even though public school educators are not highly paid. When Coleman commends Catholic education for its low per pupil expenditure, he overlooks this important difference.

Coleman notes that a large number of Catholic and other private school graduates go on to college. However, the number of these graduates who are college bound has nothing to do with the effectiveness of public education.

Seventy-five percent of Hudson (Ohio) High School's graduating class traditionally attends college. In fact, many of them are admitted to the most demanding and exclusive colleges and universities. That does not make

Hudson better than the surrounding schools. Rather, it says that we have an unusual student body for a public school district.

Catholic schools, for the most part, are oriented toward preparation for college. They should be expected to achieve their stated purpose.

"In both achievement and aspirations, blacks are closer to whites, Hispanics are closer to Anglos, and children from less well-educated parents are closer to those from better-educated parents in Catholic schools than in public schools," writes Coleman. Again, I have to wonder at Coleman's amazement. Two factors of private and Catholic education coalesce to insure this result—greater homogeneity of student body and greater parental investment. Most Catholic high schools maintain entrance requirements that insure much greater student body homogeneity than any public high school could ever have. This homogeneity is furthered by the fact that a student who is admitted but is unable to maintain the expected standards, can and will be removed— for all the right reasons. That student can receive more assistance in the public schools, which are better prepared—at least theoretically—to work with a wide range of abilities.

That Catholic and other private schools are doing a good job does not mean that public schools are not. All it indicates is that private and parochial schools are successful within their realm.

Even more ludicrous is Coleman's position that public schools, especially when compared with Catholic schools, have violated the four basic ideals of American education: common schools, local control, local funding, and in loco parentis.

Coleman maintains that public schools today are no longer the common schools that they once were and are still meant to be. Residential restrictions, he contends, have made public schools segregated and exclusionary. Although there are public schools and school districts devoid of racial mix, there are few that lack a diversified student body. That a district has few minority students does not violate the concept of the common school.

Coleman alleges that local control of public education has been lost in the wake of state and federal funding. I would suggest that if the loss really has occurred, it has been more the result of the impact of teacher organizations, court interference, and escalating inflation than of state and federal funding. Residential or neighborhood schools help insure some measure of real local control. The spread of student residence in many Catholic schools far exceeds what would be even loosely termed "the neighborhood." The typical Catholic high school would be hard pressed to specifically define its boundaries, let alone its neighborhood. Local control is, by necessity, surrendered to a board of trustees at best and the administration—diocesan or local—at worst.

The increasing need for and/or acceptance of outside funding does, however, affect the basic assumption that schools are supported by the neighborhood they serve. Coleman bemoans the loss of local financing for public schools. But is it really a loss of local financing when taxes paid by the residents of a district are returned to that district in the form of state or federal funding? If Coleman is correct in his contention that such funding damages the principle of local financing, what makes the violation any less when Catholic and private schools engage in the same pursuit?

Coleman contends that the ideal of in loco parentis has been lost to public schools for a variety of reasons. Chief among these is the current authority crisis and the size of public schools. It is hard to understand how public education can be faulted for a situation it did not create. Further, this crisis of authority is unquestionably on the wane. The appeal and ready acceptance of "assertive discipline" by both public schools and parent groups attests

to this. There are, indeed, many overly large public high schools; however, many Catholic high schools have larger student enrollments than do the public schools. The challenge of in loco parentis and creative response enhances rather than diminishes this principle.

RENEWAL: THREE FORMS

The basic principles of American education have not been violated. Rather, they have developed as all vital and dynamic principles must. The major forces of American history—positive and negative—have influenced these principles. That they have taken on nuances absent from or only suggested in the original form is a tribute to a dynamic society and a sensitive system of public education. Public education does need assistance and renewal. That renewal, however, will not arise from a comparison with Catholic schools, but from serious introspection. Such renewal of public education must take three forms: reestablishment of the priority of education; development of alternatives to the present handling of due process and educational malpractice suits; and a resurgence of professionalism and public support of that professionalism.

Coleman, through his research, has explained why Catholic schools perform admirably and laudably. However, he has not told public education anything relevant. Oranges are not apples. Catholic schools are not public schools. Coleman has, however, provoked needed reflection. Now is the time for the American public and public school educators to look hard at the apple that is public education and to provide it the polish it needs and deserves. Making education a real priority, taking schools out of the courtroom, and intensifying the meaning of being an educational professional are, I believe, giant steps toward polishing the apple that is public education.

DISCUSSION QUESTIONS AND ACTIVITIES

1. In the Coleman study reported, do public-school or private-school students have higher expectations and aspirations?

2. Does being in a private school make any difference in educational achievement?

3. What are the characteristics of private schools that influence positive achievement?

4. Are private schools divisive along economic, religious, or racial lines?

5. Identify the different types of private schools in your community, and visit one of each type. Describe each school's objectives, policies, and programs, then make comparisons with the public schools.

6. What are the methodological weaknesses of the Coleman study?

7. What effect will the tuition tax credit that Coleman advocates likely have on the redistribution of students and financial problems?

8. What are the dangers that race and class inequality in American society will be maintained or even increased?

9. Why are Coleman's proposals not useful for improving the public schools? What does Rogers advocate to bring about improvement?

10. Organize a class discussion involving three groups of students: those who attended a parochial school, a secular private school, and a public school. Ask participants to compare school characteristics and evaluate the quality of their educational experiences.

SUGGESTED READINGS

Proponents

Coleman, James S. *Equality and Achievement in Education.* Boulder, Colo.: Westview Press, 1990, Pt. 4.

————. "Public Schools, Private Schools, and the Public Interest." *The Public Interest* 64 (Summer 1981): 19–30.

————. "Response to Paige and Keith." *Educational Researcher* 10 (August–September 1981): 18–20.

————. "Response to Taueber-James, Cain-Goldberger, and Morgan." *Sociology of Education* 56 (October 1983): 219–234.

————. "Social Capital and the Development of Youth." *Momentum* 18 (November 1987): 6–8.

Coleman, James S., and others. "Achievement and Segregation in Secondary Schools: A Further Look at Public and Private School Differences." *Sociology of Education* 55 (April–July 1982): 162–182.

————. "Cognitive Outcomes in Public and Private Schools." *Sociology of Education* 55 (April–July 1982): 65–76.

Coleman, James S., and Thomas Hoffer. *Public and Private High Schools: The Impact of Communities.* New York: Basic Books, 1987.

Coleman, James S., Thomas Hoffer, and Sally Kilgore. *High School Achievement:*

Public, Private, and Catholic Schools Compared. New York: Basic Books, 1982.

"Reflections on the 1981 Coleman Study." *Momentum* 12 (October 1981): 4–13. Consists of three articles generally favorable to the Coleman study.

Criticisms and Evaluations

Bickel, Robert. "Achievement and Social Ascription: A Comparison of Public and Private High Schools." *Youth and Society* 18 (December 1986): 99–126.

Breneman, David W. "Coleman II and the Credibility of Social Science Research." *Change* 13 (September 1981): 13.

Crain, Robert L., and Willis D. Hawley. "Standards of Research." *Society* 19 (January–February 1982): 14–21.

Culucci, Nicholas. "Should Public Schools Be Judged by Criteria Which Symbolize 'Private School'?" *Capstone Journal of Education* 2 (Winter 1981–1982): 18–28.

Goldberger, Arthur S., and Glen G. Cain. "The Casual Analysis of Cognitive Outcomes in the Coleman, Hoffer, and Kilgore Report." *Sociology of Education* 55 (April–July 1982): 103–122.

Haertel, Edward YH., Thomas James, and Henry M. Levin, eds. *Comparing Public and Private Schools.* Philadelphia: Taylor and Francis, 1987.

McPartland, James M., and Edward L. McDill. "Control and Differentiation in the Structure of American Education." *Sociology of Education* 5 (April–July 1982): 77–88.

Ornstein, Allan C. "Public and Private School Comparisons: Size, Organization, and Effectiveness." *Education and Urban Society* 21 (February 1989): 192–206.

Page, Ellis B. "The Media, Technical Analysis, and the Data Feast: A Response to Coleman." *Educational Researcher* 10 (August–September 1981): 21–23.

Ravitch, Diane. "The Meaning of the New Coleman Report." *Phi Delta Kappan* 62 (June 1981): 718–720.

"Report Analysis: Public and Private Schools." *Harvard Educational Review* 51 (November 1981): 481–545. The colloquium presents seven analyses of the report, *Public and Private Schools*, together with responses by the report's authors.

Wolfle, Lee M. "Enduring Cognitive Effects of Public and Private Schools." *Educational Researcher* (May 1987): 5–10.

CHAPTER 9

SCHOOL-BASED MANAGEMENT

While the state has always been an agent of education legislation, the control over education during the seventeenth and eighteenth centuries resided almost exclusively at the local level. The state's role in education began to grow during the late nineteenth century, but it was not until the twentieth century that the state assumed its primary role in education. The enlarged role was undertaken because of dereliction in local responsibility and the need to assure minimum standards, to eliminate irregularities and erratic local practices, and to secure a more equitable financial base.

With the rise of centralized metropolitan school districts, the growth of large bureaucracies, and decision making from the top down, some communities began to emphasize decentralization and directed criticism at large-city school systems. Decentralization delegates more authority to people in the field closer to the action.

School-based, or site-based, management breaks with the traditional ideology that control rests exclusively with management. Schools participate in school-based management on a voluntary basis, and governance is controlled by the professional staff. It involves managers and teachers in joint planning, development of goals, and redefinition of teacher roles. School-based management reduces centralized control over schools and empowers teachers to participate in decision making.

Thirty-two out of 280 schools in Dade County, Florida are involved in school-based management. Participating schools are expected to devise ways for principals and teachers to run the school together, and whatever changes are made must have measurable benefits for students. In Rochester, New York, schools, with greater teacher participation in decision making and large salary increases, teachers are held more accountable for student achievement, attendance, and related outcomes. The New York City school system divides authority between a central board and thirty-two community boards. It has also added a school-based management plan, involving 117 of the city's 984 schools, in which committees comprising the principal, teachers, and parents engage in shared decision making. School districts in Georgia, Virginia, Illinois, Maryland, and other states have also adopted school-based management. School administrators and teachers are generally favorably disposed toward it, but principals and teachers may need first to undergo a training program before it can operate successfully.

SYNTHESIS OF RESEARCH ON SCHOOL-BASED MANAGEMENT

JANE L. DAVID

Jane L. David is Director of the Bay Area Research Group in Palo Alto, California.

Dade County, Florida, has made front-page headlines with its pilot School-Based Management/Shared Decision-Making Program. The Montgomery County School Board in Maryland has approved a similar plan for spring 1989. In Baton Rouge, Louisiana, school-based management is coupled with parental choice as part of an unusual desegregation strategy. Santa Fe, New Mexico, is implementing school-based management with teacher-led school improvement teams. The list goes on.

School-based management is rapidly becoming the centerpiece of the current wave of reform. The growing number of districts restructuring their schools, as well as commentary from the National Governors' Association, both national teachers' unions and corporate leaders—all make reference to some form of increased school autonomy.

Yet there is surprisingly little empirical research on the topic. Searches of education indexes yield numerous references for school-based management, but virtually all are conceptual arguments, how-to guides, and testimonials from practitioners. There is, nevertheless, an abundance of relevant research. Topics ranging from school improvement to corporate innovation bear directly on school-based management. Their relevance can be

seen when we look at why districts are turning to school-based management today.

SCHOOL-BASED MANAGEMENT TODAY

In the 1960s and 1970s, certain forms of school-based management, usually called *decentralization* and *school-site budgeting,* had a wave of popularity. These were adopted in order to give political power to local communities, increase administrative efficiency, or offset state authority (e.g., Wissler and Ortiz 1986). In the late 1980s, however, school-based management is a focus of attention for quite different reasons. Districts are implementing school-based management today to bring about significant change in educational practice: to empower school staff to create conditions in schools that facilitate improvement, innovation, and continuous professional growth (e.g., Goodlad 1984, Carnegie Forum 1986). Current interest is a response to evidence that our education system is not working and, in particular, that strong central control actually diminishes teachers' morale and, correspondingly, their level of effort (Meier 1987, Corcoran et al. 1988).

Bolstered by analogous research findings in corporations, districts are turning to management structures that delegate more author-

From Jane L. David, "Synthesis of Research on School-Based Management," *Educational Leadership* 46 (May 1989): 45–47, 50–53. Reprinted with permission of the Association for Supervision and Curriculum Development. Copyright © 1985 by ASCD. All rights reserved.

ity and flexibility to school staff (e.g., Kanter 1983). Under school-based management, professional responsibility replaces bureaucratic regulation; districts increase school autonomy in exchange for the staff's assuming responsibility for results (Cohen 1988). Two specific accountability mechanisms often accompany school-based management proposals and practices. One is an annual school performance report. The other is some form of parent choice or open enrollment; schools that do not produce results lose enrollment (Garms et al. 1978, Raywid 1988).

Delegating authority to all schools in a district distinguishes school-based management practices from school improvement programs. Both approaches share a school-based, schoolwide orientation to improvement and, usually, a mechanism for shared decision making (David and Peterson 1984). But school-based management has a broader scope; it represents a change in how the district operates—how authority and responsibility are shared between the district and its schools. It not only changes roles and responsibilities within schools but has implications for how the central office is organized and the size and roles of its staff (Elmore 1988). School improvement programs, on the other hand, usually have no special authority, do not have a separate budget, and involve only a small number of schools (although they can be districtwide).

Once school-based management is understood in the context of empowering school staff to improve education practice through fundamental change in district management functions, the relevant research topics are easy to identify. They include school improvement programs, organizational change, efforts to stimulate innovation, participatory decision making, and effective practices in many areas, from teacher selection to staff development. Next I draw on the literature on these topics, as well as the handful of studies of school-based management itself, to describe (1) how school-based management works in theory and in practice and (2) the connections between changing management structures and achieving improvement goals.

SCHOOL-BASED MANAGEMENT = AUTONOMY + SHARED DECISION MAKING

The rationale for school-based management rests on two well-established propositions:

1. The school is the primary decision-making unit; and, its corollary, decisions should be made at the lowest possible level (e.g., Smith and Purkey 1985).

2. Change requires ownership that comes from the opportunity to participate in defining change and the flexibility to adapt it to individual circumstances; the corollary is that change does not result from externally imposed procedures (e.g., Fullan 1982).

In practice, these propositions translate into two policies that define the essence of school-based management: (1) increasing school autonomy through some combination of site budgetary control and relief from constraining rules and regulations; and (2) sharing the authority to make decisions with teachers, and sometimes parents, students, and other community members (e.g., Garms et al. 1978).

School Autonomy

The backbone of school-based management is delegation of authority from district to schools; without autonomy, shared decision making within schools has little meaning. Analysts of school-based management describe autonomy as decision-making authority in three critical arenas: budget, staffing, and curriculum (Garms et al. 1978, Clune and White 1988). In practice, these distinctions blur because (1) staffing is by far the largest part of a school's budget, and (2) decision-making authority is a matter of degree, constrained by district, union contract, state, and even federal rules and regulations (as well as historical practice).

Budget. Under school-based management, schools receive either a lump-sum budget or some portion of the budget, usually for equipment, materials, supplies, and sometimes other categories such as staff development. Because money usually equals authority, budgetary authority sounds like the most important manifestation of granting authority to schools. But this is misleading because whether or not school-site budgeting equals autonomy depends on how much freedom from restrictions is allowed. For example, a school can receive a lump-sum budget for all expenditures including staff yet have no decision-making authority because of rules governing class size, tenure, hiring, firing,

assignment, curriculum, objectives, and textbooks.

Beyond allotments for staffing (see below), the budgets that districts delegate to schools are typically discretionary funds based on a per-pupil allocation (Clune and White 1988). With staffing, building repairs, and textbook costs removed, each school's budget is the small amount left for materials and supplies, sometimes augmented by district funds for staff development and related categories. Exceptions are found in districts with a large number of federal and state programs that can be passed on to schools without restrictions (David 1989).

Staffing. Typically, schools receive budgets for staffing in terms of "staffing units," which are based on the average cost of a teacher, including benefits. There are two very different types of decision making about staff: defining positions and selecting people to fill them. Once the number of certificated

---

To Shift to School-Based Management, Districts Should:

- Build strong alliances with the teachers' union
- Delegate authority to schools to define new roles, select staff, and create new learning environments
- Demonstrate and promote shared decision making
- Communicate goals, guiding images, and information
- Create direct communication links between school staff and top leaders
- Encourage experimentation and risk taking
- Provide for waivers from restrictive rules
- Motivate principals to involve teachers in school-site decisions
- Promote creation of new roles in schools and central office
- Create new forms of accountability with school staff
- Provide broad range of opportunities for professional development
- Provide time for staff to assume new roles and responsibilities
- Reduce size of central office
- Promote role of central office as facilitator and coordinator of school change
- Match salaries to increased responsibilities

teachers is determined on the basis of enrollment, school staff can choose to spend residual dollars (usually very few) on another teacher, several part-time specialists, instructional aides, or clerical support. Some districts achieve the same effect by allocating one full-time equivalent to each school to be used at the school's discretion (David 1989).

The second area of discretion lies in filling vacancies due to retirements, transfers, or increasing enrollment. Under school-based management, the principal and the teachers select from among applicants, often from a pool screened by the district (Clune and White 1988). Officially, the principal makes a recommendation with advice from teachers; the district still does the hiring. This practice, however, is not limited to districts with school-based management and is, in fact, a characteristic of effective teacher selection practices (Wise et al. 1987).

Curriculum. Under school-based management, teachers are encouraged to develop curriculum and select or create instructional materials, usually within a framework of goals or core curriculum established by the district or the state (David 1989). Clearly, this cannot occur in districts with highly prescribed curriculums, required textbooks, and mandated testing. On the other hand, because students move from school to school, some degree of coordination across schools is required. Districts with a history of decentralization have established effective lines of communication among schools and between schools and the district; and they tend to reflect an ebb and flow regarding control of curriculum. Delegating control of curriculum to schools stimulates the creation of new ideas and materials, which in turn requires new lines of communication and districtwide committees of teachers to coordinate curriculum (David 1989, Wissler and Ortiz 1988).

Most teachers have neither the desire nor the time to create or adapt curriculum beyond what they normally do within their classrooms. Nor does typical participation require formal school-based management. Many districts have committees of teachers who play an active role in choosing textbooks and defining curriculum; more comprehensive curriculum development usually occurs over the summer by paid staff (e.g., David 1989, Sickler 1988). Under school-based management and other forms of decentralization, the primary difference is that school staff, instead of district staff, initiate and lead the efforts (Guthrie 1986). For example, one highly decentralized district, which does not characterize its practices as school-based management, has formally transferred control of curriculum to teachers. The district funds ten districtwide subject-area committees, with representatives from each school, and a Curriculum Master Plan Council composed of the elected heads of each committee. The Curriculum Council makes final decisions on new curriculums subject to the school board's approval (Sickler 1988).

Beyond Budget, Staffing, and Curriculum

Authority to make decisions about budget, staffing, and curriculum goes only part way toward school-based management's goal of empowering staff to create more productive workplaces and learning environments. The images guiding today's reforms and the rhetoric of school-based management include, for example, schools characterized by teacher collegiality and collaboration, schools within schools, ungraded classes, and creative uses of technology. These images require changes beyond staffing and curriculum, such as the school calendar, scheduling, criteria for pupil assignment and promotion, the allocation and

mentation, and Issues for Further Research. Madison, Wis.: Center for Policy Research in Education.

Cohen, M. (1988). *Restructuring the Education System: Agenda for the 1990s.* Washington, D.C.: National Governors' Association.

Corcoran, T. B., L. J. Walker, and J. L. White. (1988). *Working in Urban Schools.* Washington, D.C.: Institute for Educational Leadership.

Cuban, L. (1988). *The Managerial Imperative and the Practice of Leadership in Schools.* Albany, N.Y.: State University of New York Press.

David, J. L. (1989). *Restructuring in Progress: Lessons from Pioneering Districts.* Washington, D.C.: National Governors' Association.

David, J. L., and S. M. Peterson. (1984). *Can Schools Improve Themselves?: A Study of School-Based Improvement Programs.* Palo Alto, Calif.: Bay Area Research Group.

Elmore, R. F. (1988). "Early Experiences in Restructuring Schools: Voices from the Field." Washington, D.C.: National Governors' Association.

Fullan, M. (1982). *The Meaning of Education Change.* New York: Teachers College Press.

Garms, W. I., J. W. Guthrie, and L. C. Pierce. (1978). *School Finance: The Economics and Politics of Public Education.* Englewood Cliffs, N.J.: Prentice-Hall.

Goodlad, J. I. (1984). *A Place Called School.* New York: McGraw-Hill.

Guthrie, J. W. (1986). "School-Based Management: The Next Needed Education Reform." *Phi Delta Kappan* 68: 305–309.

Johnson, S. M. (1988). "Pursuing Professional Reform in Cincinnati." *Phi Delta Kappan* 69: 746–751.

Kanter, R. M. (1983). *The Change Masters.* New York: Simon & Schuster.

Kolderie, T. (1988). "School-Site Management: Rhetoric and Reality." Minneapolis: Humphrey Institute, University of Minnesota. Unpublished manuscript.

Meier, D. (Fall 1987). "Success in East Harlem: How One Group of Teachers Built a School that Works." *American Educator:* 36–39.

Miles, M. (1981). "Mapping the Common Properties of Schools." In *Improving Schools: Using What We Know,* edited by R. Lehming and M. Kane. Beverly Hills, Calif.: Sage Publications.

Raywid, M. A. (1988). "Restructuring School Governance: Two Models." Hempstead, N.Y.: Hofstra University. Unpublished manuscript.

Sickler, J. L. (1988). "Teachers in Charge: Empowering the Professionals." *Phi Delta Kappan* 69: 354–358.

Smith, M. S., and S. C. Purkey. (1985). "School Reform: The District Policy Implications of the Effective Schools Literature." *Elementary School Journal* 85: 352–390.

Wise, A. E., L. Darling-Hammond, and B. Berry. (1987). *Effective Teacher Selection: From Recruitment to Selection.* Santa Monica, Calif.: The RAND Corporation.

Wissler, D. F., and F. I. Ortiz. (1986). "The Decentralization Process of School Systems: A Review of the Literature." *Urban Education* 21: 280–294.

Wissler, D. F., and F. I. Ortiz. (1988). *The Superintendent's Leadership in School Reform.* Philadelphia: The Falmer Press.

BETTY MALEN,
RODNEY T. OGAWA,
AND JENNIFER KRANZ

UNFULFILLED PROMISES

Betty Malen and Rodney T. Ogawa are Associate Professors, and Jennifer Kranz is a doctoral student in the Department of Educational Administration, College of Education, University of Utah.

Among the many reforms in education today, site-based management is one of the hottest.

Numerous commissions, task forces, organizations, and individual leaders are advocating site-based management as a viable approach to education reform. A number of state legislatures and local districts are experimenting with versions of this reform.

Due to the keen interest, we analyzed evidence regarding the ability of site-based management to achieve its stated objectives and highlighted the implications of this analysis for educators and policy makers.

From our review of nearly 200 documents describing current and previous attempts to use site-based management in the United States, Canada, and Australia, we must conclude site-based management in most instances does not achieve its stated objectives.

While there may be exceptions, in most cases a variety of factors prevents site-based management from fulfilling its proponents' promises.

LIMITED EVIDENCE OF OPERATION

While we reviewed a large number of documents, evidence about the actual operation of site-based management plans is limited in several ways.

First, there are only eight systematic studies of site-based management programs.

These studies rely on the experiences of a relatively small number of elementary and secondary schools (from six to thirty-two) located in such diverse settings as California, New York, Utah, Florida, Minnesota, and Australia. They examine different versions of site-based management and focus on its different dimensions.

Second, most writings on site-based management are either project descriptions, status reports, or advocacy pieces. These sources tend to rest on the impressions of a single individual and emphasize the exceptional cases, such as the achievements attained in a small number of the most successful pilot schools.

Despite these limitations, the available information is instructive. It provides a basis for assessing the ability of site-based management to achieve its stated objectives and a basis for identifying issues that warrant special attention as educators and policy makers consider this reform option.

We attempted to summarize the major conclusions and implications that can be drawn from the documents reviewed.

DEFINING TERMS

Basically, site-based management is a form of decentralization. It identifies the individual school as the primary unit of improvement

From Betty Malen, Rodney T. Ogawa, and Jennifer Kranz, "Unfilled Promises," *The School Administrator* 47 (February 1990): 30, 32, 53–56, 59. Copyright © 1990 American Association of School Administrators.

and relies on the redistribution of decision-making authority as the primary means through which improvements might be stimulated and sustained.

While site-based management plans vary, the general approach can be characterized in the following manner:

- Some formal authority to make decisions in the central domains of budget, personnel, and program is delegated to the school site.

- The formal authority to make decisions may be delegated to the principal or distributed among principals, teachers, parents, and others. In most cases, the authority is broadly distributed.

A formal structure (council, committee, team, board) often composed of principals, teachers, parents, and, at times, students and community residents, is created so these actors can be directly involved in schoolwide decision making.

- The formal authority granted site participants may be circumscribed by existing policies, procedures, contractual agreements, or accountability provisions, but site participants are afforded substantial discretion.

Although site-based management is advanced as a robust remedy for a wide range of problems, the rationales rest on several sets of assumptions regarding the manner in which site-based management engenders school improvement.

Essentially, proponents contend site-based management will improve schools because it

- Enables site participants to exert substantial influence on school policy decisions
- Enhances employee morale and motivation
- Strengthens the quality of schoolwide planning processes
- Stimulates instructional improvements
- Fosters the development of characteristics associated with effective schools
- Improves the academic achievement of students

For a number of reasons, site-based management does not succeed in meeting its objectives.

POLICY UNTOUCHED

Proponents suggest principals, teachers, and parents should be able to exert significant influence on matters of budget, personnel, and programming through a transfer of authority from the central office.

This promise is rarely realized. Although site-based management creates opportunities for site participants to be involved in schoolwide decision making, they rarely exert substantial influence on school policy decisions. Three themes illustrate this assessment.

First, site participants rarely address central, salient policy issues in their school council or committee meetings. Teachers and parents frequently characterize the subjects councils and committees consider as "routine," "blasé," "trivial" or "peripheral."

Council members do address topics related to the operation of the building or the implementation of district directives.

For example, council members develop procedures for handling disruptive student behavior, set times for parent conferences, adjust school schedules, sponsor fund-raising projects, make facility improvements, and augment extracurricular activities. They also determine how reduction in work force directives might be implemented or how utility costs might be reduced.

But even on the more tangible, tangential matters, council members typically characterize their involvement as "listening," "advising," "endorsing the decisions others have already made," taking "rubber stamp" or "token" action.

Second, on councils composed of teachers and principals, teachers do not exert meaningful influence primarily because principals control council meetings. By virtue of their position in the school, principals are inclined to protect their managerial prerogatives and able to use low cost, routine strategies to control interactions.

In most instances, principals control the agenda content, meeting format, and information flow. The principals' capacity to exert control is enhanced by the tendency of teachers to defer to the principal. Even when teachers identify issues they would prefer to discuss, they permit the principal to set the agenda.

During discussions, teachers tend to "accept the boss's opinion" or "take the principal's lead." When responses are selected, teachers often "approve what the principal wants."

In short, the propensity of principals to protect their prerogatives and the reluctance of teachers to challenge this dynamic allows principals to fundamentally control decision processes and thereby decision outcomes.

Third, on councils composed of principals, teachers, and parents, professional-patron influence relationships are not substantially altered primarily because principals and, at times, principals and teachers control council meetings.

Since professionals can set the agenda, manage the meeting time, disperse the information, and shift potentially contentious issues to more private arenas, they essentially control decision processes and ultimately control decision outcomes.

Parents are reluctant to challenge this dynamic. As a result, the traditional pattern wherein administrators make policy, teachers instruct, and parents provide support is maintained.

PARTICIPANTS HANDCUFFED

Several factors combine to restrict site-based management from increasing the influence of teachers and parents on school policy decisions.

One set of factors relates to the composition of councils. Councils tend to be, at least on demographic dimensions, relatively homogeneous groups.

Members bring information-service expectations to the group. They tend to view participation in councils as an opportunity to acquire information and provide service, not an opportunity to redefine roles and make policy.

A second set of factors relates to norms. Schools have deeply ingrained norms, well-established unwritten rules that guide and govern behavior.

Even though site-based management plans stipulate that teachers and parents can affect decisions in the central domains of budget, personnel, and program, ingrained norms dictate that district officials and school administrators set policies, teachers deliver instruction, and parents provide support.

Site-based management plans grant participants the formal right to challenge and change this presumption. But well-established norms nullify that option.

A third set of factors relates to the nature of site-based management provisions. Site-based management plans often are ambiguous. They also frequently are circumscribed by the need to keep council decisions consistent with existing policies.

As a result, it's difficult to determine what decision-making authority site participants have been given and how that differs from prior arrangements.

Given these conditions, site participants are uncertain of the parameters of their formal power. They are unconvinced they have been given greater power. They become skeptical of the new arrangements and inclined to accept decision-making roles that conform to familiar practice.

A fourth set of factors relates to capacity. While school systems do delegate formal decision-making authority, they tend not to address participant capacity. Sponsoring systems rarely infuse councils with critical resources (e.g., time, technical assistance, inde-

What Are the Steps to Success in Site-Based Management?

Precise prescriptions for addressing the various factors that hamper site-based management cannot be derived from the available literature. However, general guidelines can be identified.

The guidelines relate to the content and specificity of site-based management plans, the provision of resources, and the development of strategies for changing participant orientations and organizational norms.

First, site-based management plans must specify what authority is delegated to site participants, how that authority is distributed, and the manner in which the discretion of site participants is conditioned and constrained by contractual agreements, by district, state or federal policies, procedures, and/or accountability provisions.

Without this detail, site participants have no basis for determining what they can and cannot do. They have no basis for determining whether they have greater discretion or greater opportunity to make policy decisions.

When site participants are not clear on the parameters of their power or when they are not convinced that they have been given greater power, they become frustrated by the ambiguity, skeptical of the new arrangements, and inclined to adopt decision-making roles that conform to familiar practice.

Second, site-based management plans must provide site participants adequate resources, namely time, training, technical assistance, and supplemental funds. Without these critical resources, site-based management plans do not achieve their intended objectives.

Third, site-based management plans must recognize the orientations of site participants and the norms of schools can nullify the impact of formal policy provisions. Site-based management plans must address these factors.

These factors can be addressed in several ways. Plans could include provisions that school council membership reflect the diversity of the school community and incorporate strategies to enlist participants with different backgrounds, orientations, and points of view.

Plans also could include provisions for training programs that address individual attitudes and school norms. Such training could redefine the roles administrators, teachers, and parents play in decision making and the development of skills needed to carry out these new roles.

Continuous, systematic assessment is essential. While the existing literature on site-based management identifies factors that impede the ability of this reform to achieve its stated objectives, there are no guarantees site-based management will fulfill its promises, even if some or all of these factors are addressed.

Therefore, continuous, systematic assessments of site-based management programs must be conducted to determine the conditions under which site-based management might be able to achieve its objectives and improve the performance of schools.

Given the widespread interest in and reliance on site-based management as a reform strategy, those interested in site-based management have both the opportunity and the responsibility to carry out these assessments.

---

pendent sources of information, continuous, norm-based training, funds to assess current programs or develop new programs).

In addition, sponsoring systems rarely redistribute existing resources in ways that might balance the positional advantages of principals vis-à-vis teachers or the positional advantages of professionals vis-à-vis parents.

MORALE BOOST FLEETING

Proponents claim site-based management will improve the morale and motivation of school employees primarily because principals and teachers are given greater opportunity to be involved in and exert influence on school policies and operations.

Site-based management appears to have an initial, energizing impact on some participants. While individuals often are skeptical and workplace tensions clearly are present, some principals are excited by the prospects.

Some teachers are eager to tackle the important issues facing schools. Some teachers feel "truly professional."

However, the initial, energizing effects of site-based management often are offset by factors such as the

- Time-consuming character of the process
- Confusion, anxiety, and contention as site participants and district employees attempt to define their new roles
- Dissonance created as committee demands compete with teaching responsibilities
- Complexity of the problems site participants are supposed to solve
- Resentment generated if site participants perceive they have only modest influence on marginal matters
- Frustration produced by fiscal constraints

PLANNING UNAFFECTED

Proponents claim site-based management will improve the quality of planning because it capitalizes on the expertise of site participants and the benefits of group interaction.

While site-based management may direct attention to aspects of schoolwide planning in some settings, there is little evidence it stimulates interest in or enhances the quality of that process in a significant number of settings.

Various factors prevent site-based management from improving the planning process. In most instances, site participants simply do not have the time, technical assistance, or logistical support to carry out the full range of planning activities in a substantive and coordinated fashion.

As such, there is a pronounced tendency to go through the recommended or required procedural motions (e.g., surveying the faculty or parents to assess needs, writing a plan, preparing reports, and rehearsing presentations for review team visitations).

INNOVATION LACKING

Proponents claim site-based management will foster the implementation of instructional improvements for two reasons.

First, site participants are free to design innovative instructional programs that meet the unique needs of students in their schools.

Second, since they are involved in designing these programs, they will be more likely to implement them.

While site-based management precipitates a wide range of activities, such as student recognition programs, discipline policies, workshops, and newsletters, there is little evidence that it stimulates the development or enhances the implementation of major instructional changes.

Site participants rarely address subjects central to the instructional program in their school council or school committee meetings. Where instructional program issues are discussed, it often is difficult to see how the plans depart from or improve upon existing practices.

Where instructional changes are proposed, they rarely are implemented in classrooms. Where teachers incorporate the recommended adjustments, they tend to "drift back to conventional practice" in a fairly short period of time.

Moreover, in some cases the move to site-based management impedes the development and installation of instructional improvements. It diverts attention from teaching and learning as site participants take on activities and responsibilities that only remotely are related to instruction.

Various factors restrict the ability of site-based management to produce substantial improvements in instruction.

At times, teachers are prone to define instructional improvement as an individual responsibility rather than a collective pursuit. Thus, they are reluctant to address or assess the school's instructional program.

In some cases, district and/or state requirements are viewed as so extensive or confining that site participants focus more on compliance than improvement. In most instances, site participants lack the time, technical assistance, requisite skills, and supplemental funds to develop major changes.

In many cases, these conditions prompt site participants to develop plans to "keep their day-to-day operations intact."

Even where instructional innovations are proposed, they rarely are implemented for many of the same reasons. The initial enthusiasm gets "outstripped" by the gaps in knowledge (i.e., how to translate enthusiasm into action, how to convert interesting ideas into teaching behaviors) and the failure to recognize that change is "a costly process." Sizable and stable financial allocations to procure instructional materials and provide training experiences and professional development programs are required to sustain substantial instructional improvements.

LIMITS TO AUTONOMY

Proponents argue that because site-based management grants schools greater autonomy, it facilitates the development of characteristics associated with effective schools.

While these characteristics seem to be more pronounced in schools with considerable autonomy, there is no clear evidence that greater autonomy will produce these characteristics.

Some studies indicate when site participants are asked to develop school improvement plans which address the elements of effective schools, their efforts are constrained by state and/or district regulations, priorities, and pressures.

Other studies demonstrate that where these constraints are relaxed and site participants have both considerable latitude and extensive involvement in designing plans (albeit not formal authority for determining those plans), the features of effective schools do not become more pronounced.

These studies suggest if the objective is to engender the characteristics of effective schools, factors related to capacity (e.g., number and types of demands on the system, technical assistance, staff development, time to discuss and develop alternatives, funds for new program costs, district response to requests for assistance) are at least as important as factors related to autonomy.

ACHIEVEMENT UNAFFECTED

Proponents maintain site-based management can improve the academic achievement of students. Their arguments often rest on the ability of site-based management to fulfill the promises already discussed.

Yet again there is little evidence that site-based management improves student achievement. Although some documents claim site-based management produced improved scores on achievement tests, the requirements for making these causal claims are not met.

First, these sources do not address the issue of temporal order. They fail to establish that gains in achievement followed the move to site-based management and, in some cases, acknowledge achievement scores already were improving before site-based management was in place.

Second, these sources do not address the issue of rival explanations: They fail to demonstrate that site-based management is a contributing factor, let alone the critical factor affecting student achievement.

The fact that achievement gains occur in only a small number of select pilot schools over a short period of time is a sign that site-based management is not the critical factor. If it were, one would expect achievement gains to be more widespread and more stable.

Only two systematic studies examine the relationship between site-based management and student achievement. While there are exceptions on both ends of the spectrum (a few schools improve and a few schools decline), these studies conclude that most schools maintain their previous level of performance. Student achievement does not appear to be either helped or hindered.

ISSUES NEEDING ATTENTION

Since there is little evidence site-based management plans achieve their stated objectives, several issues warrant attention. Educators and policy makers may want to pay particular attention to the following:

- The viability of site-based management as a reform strategy
- The conditions necessary for site-based management to be successful
- The need for continuous, systematic assessments of site-based management programs

Educators and policy makers need to carefully consider whether they wish to invest in a reform strategy that has not been able to achieve its objectives in most settings where it has been attempted.

Perhaps site-based management simply is not an effective approach to education reform. However, it is also possible site-based management has not been given a full or fair test.

It may be premature to dismiss site-based management on the basis of only eight systematic studies, particularly when some of these studies indicate isolated instances where site-based management appears to be approaching, if not achieving, its stated objectives.

Policy makers and educators may need to give site-based management a more complete test by designing plans that attend to those inhibiting factors. Perhaps if these factors were addressed, site-based management could become an effective approach to education reform.

DISCUSSION QUESTIONS AND ACTIVITIES

1. What is the rationale for school-based management?
2. What are teachers' responsibilities in terms of budget, staffing, and curriculum under school-based management?
3. Identify the beneficial changes that have resulted from this form of management.
4. What type of problems are likely to arise in implementing such management plans, and how can these problems best be handled?
5. According to Malen, Ogawa, and Kranz, why do teachers and parents fail to exert significant influence in site-based management activities?
6. What factors prevent site-based management from improving planning and innovation?

7. Evaluate the evidence that such management promotes greater school autonomy and fosters higher student achievement.

8. Visit a school district in which school-based management is used. Make observations, conduct interviews with key personnel, and collect pertinent data. Organize and evaluate your findings.

9. Identify school districts in your state or region where school-based management has been implemented. Develop a questionnaire and submit it to each district in order to gather data. Report on your findings to class.

10. Invite to class a principal or teacher who has been involved in such management to speak about their experiences.

SUGGESTED READINGS

Caldwell, Sarah D. "School Improvement—Are We Ready?" *Educational Leadership* 46 (October 1988): 50–53.

Carr, Rex A. "Second-Wave Reforms Crest at Local Initiative." *School Administrator* 45 (August 1988): 16–18.

Clune, William H., and Paula A. White. *School-Based Management.* New Brunswick, N.J.: Center for Policy Research in Education, 1988.

Conley, Sharon C., and Samuel B. Bacharach. "From School-Site Management to Participatory School-Site Management." *Phi Delta Kappan* 71 (March 1990): 539–544.

Heller, Robert W. "You Like School-Based Power, But You Wonder If Others Do." *Executive Educator* 11 (November 1989): 15–16, 18.

Lindquist, Karin M., and John L. Mauriel. "School-Based Management: Doomed to Failure?" *Education and Urban Society* 21 (August 1989): 403–416.

Murphy, Jerome T. "The Paradox of Decentralizing Schools: Lessons from Business, Government, and the Catholic Church." *Phi Delta Kappan* 70 (June 1989): 808–812.

Sirotnik, Kenneth A., and Richard W. Clark. "School-Centered Decisions Making and Renewal." *Phi Delta Kappan* 69 (May 1988): 660–664.

White, Paula A. "An Overview of School-Based Management: What Does Research Say?" *NASSP Bulletin* 73 (September 1989): 1–8.

CHAPTER 10

EFFECTIVE SCHOOLS

Recent literature on school effectiveness shows that schools do affect students' academic achievement. This literature challenges earlier studies that found unequal academic achievement a function of family background.

The following school-level characteristics promote higher achievement in basic skills: First, a school climate conducive to learning—it is free from disciplinary problems and embodies high expectations for student achievement. Second, a schoolwide emphasis on basic skills. Third, the development of a system of clear instructional objectives for monitoring and assessing students' performance. Finally, a school principal who is a strong programmatic leader, sets high standards, frequently observes classrooms, and creates learning incentives. The elements of school effectiveness must be considered in relationship to all the other elements and in terms of the situation in which found; they cannot meaningfully be considered in isolation from one another.

But researchers do not know whether these characteristics are the cause of school effectiveness, nor have these characteristics been ranked in importance. Evidently these multiple characteristics in combination with one another would need to be implemented to insure desired results.

Since the characteristics above are related to success in imparting basic skills, the characteristics of effective schools are stated somewhat differently: (1) the principal's leadership ability and emphasis on the quality of instruction, (2) a broad and pervasive instructional focus, (3) a safe, orderly climate conducive to teaching and learning, (4) teachers who promote at least minimum mastery, and (5) program evaluation based on measures of student achievement.

Joseph Murray and Philip Hallinger present effective school characteristics, the prevailing learning environment, the careful attention to each student, and the differences between effective elementary and effective secondary schools. Larry Cuban, though generally sympathetic with the effective school movement, highlights some pronounced weaknesses and limitations that need to be overcome.

JOSEPH MURPHY
AND PHILIP HALLINGER

EFFECTIVE HIGH SCHOOLS— WHAT ARE THE COMMON CHARACTERISTICS?

Joseph Murphy is Associate Professor, Department of Administration, Higher, and Continuing Education, University of Illinois, Champaign. Philip Hallinger is Assistant Professor, Department of Educational Administration, St. John's University, Scarsdale, New York.

What constitutes an effective school? Researchers undertook a study of schools in California that was designed to answer that question.

CURRICULAR AND CLIMATE VARIABLES

Analysis of questionnaires completed by administrators of schools identified as effective[1] reveals the recurring presence of eight general factors:

- A clear sense of purpose
- A core set of standards within a rich curriculum
- High expectations
- A commitment to educate each student as completely as possible
- A special reason for each student to go to school
- A safe, orderly learning environment
- A sense of community
- Resiliency and a problem-solving attitude.

Clear Sense of Purpose

A very clear sense of mission, with a specific emphasis on high academic performance, was identifiable in the effective schools. There was total dedication to academic excellence. Unlike many of the effective elementary schools identified in earlier studies, these schools did not often translate their sense of purpose into levels of achievement sought on standardized achievement tests. Rather, there was a prevailing norm that guided decision making and other important activities in the school which can best be described as "academic press"— the sense that all activities combine to create an environment of academic rigor (Murphy, et al., 1982).

Core Set of Standards within a Rich Curriculum

One of the most interesting findings had to do with the curriculum content. On the one hand, as would be expected from reviews of effective schools (Levine, 1982; Cooley and Leinhardt, 1980), these schools had a core set of curriculum standards which all students were expected to master. On the other hand, contrary to what has sometimes been suggested, this core program did not limit the scope of course offerings at the schools.

From Joseph Murphy and Philip Hallinger, "Effective High Schools—What Are the Common Characteristics?" *NASSP Bulletin* 69 (January 1985): 18–22. Reprinted with permission.

[1]Effective schools were identified in a nationwide government-sponsored study. California schools so identified were then screened by the writers to locate the eighteen "most effective" high schools in the state.

Each of the schools in this study had rich and diverse academic programs, with intensive and extended course content available in almost all subject areas. There was also some evidence of schools' trying to integrate the common core standards into a wide range of courses.

High Expectations

Permeating the atmosphere in all of these schools was the expectation of academic achievement and educational excellence. This was obvious in a number of ways. First, administrators and teachers in these schools held high expectations for themselves and took responsibility for what students accomplished. Second, the school mission of academic achievement created a strong press for academic excellence. Third, these schools were characterized by a number of policies and practices which conveyed the importance of high achievement. These included such things as regularly assigned and graded homework, policies that permitted participation in cocurricular activities only if grades were high, and quick and regular notification of parents when expectations were not being met.

Somewhat surprisingly, however, the expectations of these schools in terms of formal graduation requirements were not particularly high. The average number of years of each subject needed for graduation were: math—1.6; English—3.5; social studies—3.2; science—1.3; foreign language—0. It seems that, as with goals or mission, expectations tended to be reflected in a norm of academic press rather than in high targets for performance.

One of the most interesting aspects of high expectations was that they spilled over into almost every activity the schools undertook. That is, these schools not only developed students who won numerous academic awards and honors and scored well on tests, but they also regularly produced award-winning sports, music, and art programs as well.

Commitment to Educate Each Student as Completely as Possible

One of the most exciting aspects of effective elementary schools is that they see to it that every student in the school progresses. Selected groups of students are not forgotten about or relegated to a second-class academic citizenship. This factor was also abundantly evident in the high schools in this study. In addition to a rich and diverse general curriculum, these schools had excellent remedial and advanced placement courses and programs. They had, on an average, almost 30 percent of their students working in advanced placement courses.

On the other hand, they were leaders in developing a variety of programs and strategies to insure that no students fell through the cracks because of academic or adjustment problems; and to insure that students with special needs received programs consistent with mainstream core curriculum standards. The schools developed an especially effective array of methods for monitoring and working with the following groups of students: limited English proficient, special education, remedial, school-age mothers, and potential dropouts.

Very few of the students in these schools failed to graduate because of academic deficiencies, and the drop-out rates were extremely low. Contrary to popular belief, it may be that high expectations reduce rather than increase dropouts.

Special Reason for Each Student to Go to School

In addition to insuring that each student progressed as fully as possible academically, these schools all created rich environments where there were multiple opportunities for student responsibility and meaningful involvement. These schools had a wide variety of sports teams, an array of interest and curriculum clubs, opportunities for students to work in the larger community, and a number of ways for students to take responsibility through student government. These various activities captured a high percentage of the students.

Responses in the questionnaires indicated that two factors were primarily responsible for both the depth of the cocurricular program and the high level of student involvement. First, there were strong efforts on the part of the entire school community to bring new students into the programs. Second, there was the commitment of dedicated staff pushing for the same levels of excellence in these activities that they required in the classroom.

Safe, Orderly Learning Environment

In all of the eleven schools, a great deal of attention was devoted to creating effective learning environments. Attendance rates were generally high and increasing, while dropout rates were generally low and decreasing. There were five key elements of the discipline policies and practices in these schools. First, school rules and standards for behavior were clearly specified. Second, the rules and consequences for breaking them were systematically communicated to parents and students.

Third, the consequences were incremental in nature. Fourth, the rules were fairly and consistently enforced everywhere on the school campuses. Fifth, a great deal of thought and energy went into the enforcement of school rules. Specifically, regular telephone contacts with parents, high administrator visibility on campuses, and innovative disciplinary programs in lieu of suspension were common characteristics in these schools.

Sense of Community

Three factors combined to create a strong sense of community in these schools. First, they enjoyed strong support from the parents and the communities in which they were located. There was a good deal of parent participation in these schools and involvement in advisory and decision-making bodies. Second, these schools maintained an internal atmosphere of professional collegiality. There were strong indications of groups working together, making decisions, resolving conflicts, and so forth, in pursuit of a common goal—academic excellence. Third, there was evidence of cohesion and support among professional staff and students. There was a feeling of mutual respect throughout these school communities.

Resiliency and a Problem-Solving Attitude

Since Proposition 13 was passed in California, the level of financial support for schools has decreased dramatically. While once among the top ten states in school support, California is now fiftieth in percent of personal income provided for education. This decline has caused serious hardships on many of the schools in the state.

One of the interesting things about the schools in this study was the way they responded to these hardships. There was a sense of resiliency in these schools as they bounced back from such difficulties as mergers, the loss of funds for special programs, and reductions in personnel. The schools did not allow these difficulties to become excuses for failure but, rather, treated them as problem-solving opportunities.

For example, in one school, a merger was translated into new organizational arrangements for greater academic rigor; in another, a loss in funds was offset by the development of a foundation, which also helped bind the community and school closer together; in a third, the elimination of counselors meant the development of an administrator-adviser program to insure that students could still receive needed services.

CONCLUSION

One of the tentative conclusions that can be drawn from this study is that the suggested differences between effective elementary and effective secondary schools may be more apparent than real. That is, both types of schools share a number of common characteristics such as a clear mission, high expectations, a commitment to fully educate each student, a sense of community, and a safe, orderly learning environment. Where secondary schools seem to move beyond this common definition is in the richness of the curriculum and the complexity of the social system.

Although the effective secondary schools in this study had a core set of standards, these were embedded in a rich and diverse curriculum. These schools also differed from effective elementary schools in relying less on the parenting aspect of teacher-student relations and more on the involvement of students in the social system in which they functioned. In both cases, the differences appear to be due less to a basic difference between effective practices in elementary and secondary schools than to greater organizational complexity at the high school level.

References

Cooley, W., and Leinhardt, G. "The Instructional Dimensions Study." *Educational Evaluation and Policy Analysis* 2 (1980): 7–25.

Levine, D. "Successful Approaches for Improving Academic Achievement in Inner-City Elementary Schools." *Phi Delta Kappan* 63 (1982): 523–526.

Murphy, J.; Weil, M.; Hallinger, P.; and Mitman, A. "Academic Press: Translating Expectations into School Level Policies and Classroom Practices." *Educational Leadership* 40 (1982): 22–26.

9. Obtain a list of effective schools, select some from which to gather information, and present your findings to class.

10. Invite a teacher from an effective school to make a presentation in your class.

SUGGESTED READINGS

Clayron, Constance. "Children of Value: We 'Can' Educate All Our Children." *The Nation* 249 (July 24, 1989): 132–135.

Contreras, A. Reynaldo. "Use of Educational Reform to Create Effective Schools." *Education and Urban Society* 2 (August 1988): 399–413.

Creamers, Bert P. M., and Jaap Scheerens, eds. "Development in School Effectiveness Research." *International Journal of Educational Research* vol. 13, no. 7 (1989): 685–825.

Duignan, Patrick. "Research on Effective Schooling: Some Implications for School Improvement." *Journal of Educational Administration* 24 (Winter 1986): 59–73.

Garten, Ted, and Jerry Valentine. "Strategies for Faculty Involvement in Effective Schools." *NASSP Bulletin* 73 (March 1989): 1–6.

Levine, Daniel U., and Allan C. Ornstein. "Research on Classroom and School Effectiveness and Its Implications for Improving Big City Schools." 21 *Urban Review* (June 1989): 81–94.

Lezotte, Lawrence W., and Barbara O. Taylor. "How Closely Can Magnet Schools Be Aligned with the Effective School Model?" *Equity and Choice* 5 (February 1989): 25–29.

Mann, Dale. "Effective Schools as a Dropout Prevention Strategy." *NASSP Bulletin* 73 (September 1989): 77–83.

Moody, Charles D., Sr., and Christella D. Moody. "Elements of Effective Black Schools." *Urban League Review* 11 (Summer–Winter 1987–1988): 177–186.

Rossmiller, Richard A. "Achieving Equity and Effectiveness in Schooling." *Journal of Education Finance* 12 (Spring 1987): 561–577.

Steller, Arthur W. *Effective Schools Research: Practice and Promise* (Fastback 276). Bloomington, Ind.: Phi Delta Kappan Educational Foundation, 1988.

Teddlie, Charles, and others. "Effective Versus Ineffective Schools: Observable Differences in the Classrooms." *American Journal of Education* 97 (May 1989): 221–236.

Wilson, C. Dwayne, and Esther Onaga Fergus. "Combining Effective Schools and School Improvement Research Tradition for Achieving Equity-Based Education." *Equity and Excellence* 24 (Fall 1989): 54–65.

CHAPTER 11

MAGNET SCHOOLS

Alternative schools arose in public education during the 1970s to provide options to the traditional model or comprehensive high school in order to serve diverse educational needs within the community. Alternative schools tend to have more comprehensive goals than traditional schools, provide greater curricular flexibility, and usually are smaller and less bureaucratic than comprehensive high schools.

A 1976 amendment to the federal Emergency School Aid Act (ESAA) authorized grants to school districts involved in desegregation. It stimulated widespread options (in contrast to one or two alternative schools in a metropolitan district), and since 1976 magnet schools became a significant part of urban school desegregation. In districts with enrollment of 20,000 or more, there are more than 1,000 magnet schools; these schools are numerous in the West, Midwest, and Northeast.

Magnet schools also offer alternatives and options to traditional programs and, in this sense, are alternative schools. Magnet schools attract voluntary enrollment by offering special programs designed to appeal to students of various backgrounds and in differing neighborhoods. They were initially established as an alternative to forced busing to promote voluntary school desegregation. Magnet schools seek to attract students from diverse backgrounds and draw upon community resources (as in cooperative programs with local businesses); some seek to serve the needs of local markets. Houston established a magnet school to prepare workers for the petrochemical industry, and Atlanta developed a school to serve the financial district.

Magnet schools seek to offer quality programs that emphasize certain curricular specialties. A magnet school may specialize in the performing arts, business, science, or a college preparatory program. Other magnet school specialties include applied technology, health professions, law and public administration, communications and media, computer data processing, small business management, and others.

Magnet schools face funding problems as well as the need to develop acceptable desegregation plans. Mandatory desegregation plans, although they evoke greater resistance among various groups, achieve greater racial balance than voluntary plans; therefore, desegregation cannot be left to magnet schools alone. Some administrators of neighborhood schools believe that magnet schools siphon off the brightest children and thereby foster elitism. Magnet schools also must insure that students receive an adequate general education and basic skills. This is accomplished in some cases by taking courses for part of the day in a traditional school and then spending the remainder of the day in a magnet school.

Mary Haywood Metz describes the characteristics of magnet schools, their effect on desegregation, and their benefits to students who have previously resisted school or done poorly. Kathleen Sylvester's article explores schools of choice, including magnet schools, and assesses the advantages and dangers of such schools.

MARY HAYWOOD METZ

IN EDUCATION, MAGNETS ATTRACT CONTROVERSY

*Mary Haywood Metz is Professor of Education at the University of Wisconsin at Madison.
Her book,* Different by Design: The Context and Character of Three Magnet Schools, *explores the characteristics of three formerly traditional middle schools and their transition to magnet schools.*

Magnet schools simultaneously address two important social needs—desegregation and educational innovation. They are being established in increasing numbers and are attracting lively interest from policymakers across the country. Magnets are schools with educational innovations for which students volunteer; spaces are filled within racial quotas so that the schools will be desegregated. Magnet schools thus reward students for participating voluntarily in desegregation by offering them an innovative education. They can convert parents who might otherwise be reluctant to send their children to desegregated schools into eager participants in desegregation programs.

The innovative charter of magnet schools allows these schools to design programs that accommodate the economic, cultural, and academic diversity common in student bodies of desegregated schools. This charter also frees the magnet schools from standard formulas for education—formulas that have not been working well with increasing proportions of students—and gives them license to develop distinctive educational approaches. Last, but not least, parents and students participate voluntarily and may leave a magnet school without changing their residence. This relationship can generate some of the same enthusiasm and commitment to the school found in the voluntary bond private schools are able to forge with students and parents.

If magnet schools can do all these things, one would expect them to be universally endorsed and to be taking our nation's cities by storm. In fact, magnets are popular, and they are spreading. But they are also resisted and resented—a subject of hot political debate in many communities. Magnet schools run afoul of some established, powerful organizational and political forces in public schooling. They also challenge a strong and pervasive myth—the idea that equal educational opportunity requires that the same education, in effect a standardized education, be offered to all students.

WHY MAGNET SCHOOLS?

Magnet schools are important because both racial desegregation and educational innovation are crucial if we are to provide a sound education to the generation of students now in our public schools. Despite continuing debate, there is widespread evidence that desegregated schools improve minority students' achievement—at least when the students attend de-

From Mary Haywood Metz, "In Education, Magnets Attract Controversy," *NEA Today* 6 (January 1988): 54–60. Reprinted with permission.

segregated schools from the earliest grades—without hurting white achievement.

Less attention has been paid to the long-term social effects of desegregation. It leads minority children to increase their participation in mainstream white institutions when they are older—to participate in "white" colleges, work settings, and neighborhoods. In other words, desegregation gives minority students a better education and a better opportunity to make their way into the mainstream of society.

But desegregation is not just a social good for the minority children who participate. White America needs to realize that the coming generation is one-third minority. When those minority children are adults, it will be necessary not only for their welfare, but for society's, that this third of our population have the technical skills and social confidence to participate fully in all sectors of the economy and polity. For this to happen, not only must minority children be prepared—their white contemporaries must learn to be at ease with people of color, to consider them their equals (and in many specific contexts, such as supervisor and worker, their superiors), and to cross the cultural boundaries created by different ethnic backgrounds.

White students raised in the isolation of all-white, or nearly all-white, small towns, suburbs, and city neighborhoods simply do not acquire the knowledge or attitudes that will allow them to participate constructively in the multiracial society they will face as adults. In short, for the good of the society, white children need to be in desegregated schools—or better yet, desegregated neighborhoods—just as much as minority children do. Though the issues are slightly different, similar arguments can be made for schooling that brings together more fortunate children with the one-fourth of school children, a large proportion of them white, who live in official poverty.

Innovation in education is a necessity for all students in a rapidly changing industrial society. In our society, it seems especially important for students whose families are excluded from the mainstream because of minority racial status, poverty, or both. These children generally achieve poorly in schools as they presently exist. Social scientists, such as anthropologist Shirley Brice Heath, have vividly demonstrated that schools are often radically discontinuous with the home life of poor children, both minority and white. Many such children feel forced to choose between the world of home and peers and that of the school. Not surprisingly, many choose their home worlds.

Older students may disengage from the school as their peer group questions the reality of the benefits school promises. John Ogbu, an anthropologist, has written extensively about this phenomenon among minority youth. Minority students learn from the experience of older relatives who have found that education has not brought steady employment or income for them as it has for their white contemporaries.

As our economy contracts, the discontinuity between life and school is beginning to spread beyond minorities. Much of the reform literature written about high schools suggests that a majority of students, those not heading toward somewhat selective colleges, is growing doubtful of the value of more than minimal compliance with schools' educational demands. Authors such as Michael Sedlak persuasively argue that the schools must make some significant changes if the large middle of our society is to be willing to become engaged with high school education.

From the progressive movement of the early 1900s to the local school initiatives of the 1960s, schools in our country have a long history of successfully using unconventional methods and content to engage students outside the mainstream in school learning. Magnet schools have the potential of carrying this history of innovation into the next century.

MAGNET POTENTIAL

I first became interested in magnet schools after completing a study, published as *Classrooms and Corridors: The Crisis of Authority in Desegregated Secondary Schools*, in the course of which I spent a year in two desegregated junior high schools. I found that the teachers in those schools taught very differently when working with high-track, mostly upper middle-class students, and with low-track, mostly poor students. Teachers with differing philosophies of teaching made similar adjustments in response to the behavior and skills of the students. In the low tracks, these adjustments often had more to do with control than with teaching.

In analyzing these schools, I argued that the physical setting, daily routines, and set curriculum engendered control problems. These were easily manageable with children who arrived at school with faith in school learning and whose faith was reinforced by success. But control problems were severe with those children who lacked trust in the significance of school knowledge or skill in acquiring it. Common solutions to these control problems undercut teachers' and students' engagement with learning, especially in the lower tracks.

After studying these desegregated, traditional junior highs, I was eager to look at magnet schools—to see what effects might result from changes in some of the nearly universal parameters of American schooling, such as the daily routine and the set curriculum. I was able to undertake this study of magnet schools in a large midwestern city I call Heartland. The study, reported at length in *Different by Design: The Context and Character of Three Magnet Schools*, encompassed in-depth observation of the interior

lives of three magnet middle schools, as well as consideration of the school district policies and politics shaping the development of Heartland's magnet schools over a seven-year period.

Two of Heartland's three magnet middle schools did indeed create significant changes in the traditional forms of schooling. As a result, the teachers and students in these two schools were able to develop much more constructive social relationships in support of their academic work together than were those in other schools I had seen—or most I had read about.

One of the magnet middle schools, Adams Avenue, had a student body that almost perfectly reflected Heartland, a blue-collar city, except that it was somewhat poorer. Well over half the Adams Avenue students were eligible for free lunch, and half of those entering sixth grade were reading at levels comparable to the bottom third of a national sample. At Jesse Owens, another of the Heartland magnets, more than two-thirds of the students were eligible for free lunch, and almost half were reading at a level comparable with the bottom quarter of a national sample (though math scores were somewhat stronger).

Both these magnet middle schools enrolled fewer than 400 students, and both modified traditional curriculum, grading practices, and classroom activities. Jesse Owens also had a modified daily schedule. Though they both altered traditional patterns in these common ways, their educational philosophies and curricular approaches were quite different.

Adams Avenue offered individually guided education. In practice this meant that students progressed through a curriculum of carefully defined, skill-oriented objectives at their own pace, working in small groups with other children at the same level of skill. Students of all skill levels were assigned to each classroom, and then were divided into five or six skill-based groups. Teachers spent most of their time circulating among the groups. The skill-oriented curriculum was balanced with a set of learning activities that cut across subject areas, and with a rich extracurricular program in which the majority of students participated. Grades reflected progress and effort, with separate notations of a student's absolute level of accomplishment.

Jesse Owens offered open education. Students spent most of their day in self-contained, multi-aged classes; they kept the same teacher throughout their middle school careers. Working with this teacher, each student developed individual long-term and short-term goals and programs of activity to meet those goals. Activities sometimes included working with others in a group. Projects integrating subjects were encouraged, and during much of the day students could move about the school using varied resource centers with staff available to assist them. Grades were given in the form of narrative progress reports.

Both Adams Avenue and Jesse Owens enabled low-achieving students to make more sense of their education, and to experience greater academic success, than had similar students in the other desegregated schools I had studied earlier. Teachers also felt more successful. They came to know their students better as persons and were able to develop a more supportive, less discipline-oriented relationship with them than had been possible in the other schools.

Students at Adams Avenue and Jesse Owens came from diverse social backgrounds. There were students at both schools who were academically successful from entrance onward. Both teachers and students felt, for the most part, that these students' needs could be met along with those of the low achievers because the curriculum and structure of teaching and learning activities were designed to accommodate students with diverse backgrounds, knowledge, and speeds and styles of learning. Relations between children of different races were relaxed and positive. At Adams especially, there were many racially mixed groups in voluntary activities and many genuine friendships that crossed racial lines.

THE STRENGTH OF TRADITION

Adams Avenue and Jesse Owens strongly suggest that departure from traditional models of schooling can benefit children who have resisted school and done poorly. The schools also show that it is possible to educate these children together with those who have been more successful—with benefit to both groups. Adams Avenue and Jesse Owens demonstrate that magnet school innovations can have definite positive effects. They show that such schools can desegregate across lines of social class, achievement, and race—and serve all their students well.

Not all magnet programs make changes that affect students' alienation—pressures to maintain traditional educational forms are strong. The third school in the Heartland study, a school for the gifted and talented, made no serious alterations in traditional school routines, curriculum, grading, or classroom activities. Nor was it supposed to, according to the blueprint given it by the central office. This school had more difficulty than Adams or Owens, both in reaching its lower achievers (most of whom would have been average or above in the other two schools) and in interracial relations.

Last year, as part of the work of the National Center on Effective Secondary Schools at the University of Wisconsin, I was a member of a team that visited eight "ordinary" schools in diverse communities for two to three weeks each. We discovered, consistent with the reform literature, that teachers in low- and middle-income schools were experiencing a lot of frustration with the unwillingness or inability of large numbers of students to apply themselves to the traditional high school curriculum—and in some cases to comply with the schools' behavioral expectations. Virtually all the teachers and administrators were concerned with ways to change the students to fit the schools' routines and curriculums—which varied very little between settings despite enormous variation in the students' experiences, skills, and interests. Except in small changes at the margin, the administrators and teachers did not feel it appropriate to consider changing the schools' routines or curriculum to fit the students.

The teachers and administrators in these "ordinary" schools seemed to be voicing a deep-seated cultural assumption that the routines and curriculum that are generally standard across high schools form a definition— or at least a floor—for a "real" high school education. To innovate in ways that significantly alter either curricular substance or the organization of daily school life is to offer a second-rate, counterfeit education. As I consider what we learned in these schools, I see that something like magnet schools, with their official license and obligation to innovate, will be needed to create any serious innovation in high schools.

It would be naive, however, to expect a great change through magnet schools. There must be good reasons why so many innovations that seemed effective in the 1960s and earlier have quietly disappeared. Strong social and political forces are pushing for standardized traditional schools—and against significant innovation. It is at least as likely that these forces will turn magnet schools into forms that differ little from other schools as that magnet schools will become dominant or have diversifying effects on other schools.

These forces are at work already. Many school systems define magnet schools as schools that emphasize a certain curricular area—rather than as schools that change the social structure, daily activities, or overall curricular approach of traditional schools. Heartland's Jesse Owens became ineligible for federal magnet school funds because it changed the style of education rather than the content. After the magnet schools were established, the Heartland school board sought to improve education throughout the system by requiring various pieces of standard "good practice." For example, they increased system-wide testing and adopted a single reading series to be used in all schools—decisions that severely undercut the magnet schools' ability to be innovative or distinctive.

Magnet schools are often designed for students who achieve best and are organized around curricular emphases more likely to appeal to elites than to a cross section of citizens. In many communities, all or most magnets developed are schools for the gifted and talented, or high schools stressing math and science, or at best schools for the performing arts. These magnets have entrance requirements. In Heartland, however, planners made a real effort to develop a series of magnet schools that, as a group, would attract children from all walks of life. On the whole they succeeded, though a few of the magnets did draw a definitely more affluent and highly achieving clientele than a cross section of the city.

SCHOOLS' SOCIAL ROLE

If it's true that culturally different children, children from low-income families, and, increasingly, even children from solid blue-collar families do not prosper in traditional schools, why is there such resistance to adopting successful alternative patterns of schooling? Why should educators and the public shrink from the thoroughgoing educational change the magnet school idea can legitimate? Why should they often turn the magnets' potential for helping urban children in sore need of help into a way of enriching traditional schools for the more privileged children of a city? And when magnet schools are established, why are they so often resented and politically opposed by those not directly involved with them?

When educators discuss public schooling, they think of it as instilling the content of the curriculum and some of the social graces required to be a member in good standing of a school community. But education plays another very important role for society—it prepares the young to enter into adult roles. Schooling sorts the group of babies born in any year, looking very much alike in their hospital cribs, into a set of eighteen-year-olds divided into groups labeled as suited for very different kinds of occupational futures.

Imagine what would happen if some year the end that schools supposedly seek was actually accomplished. If all the graduates of all of the high schools in the country were successfully educated. If all scored in the 99th percentile on standardized tests and made perfect scores on the Scholastic Aptitude Test, not to mention having perfect "A" records throughout their schooling. Chaos would ensue: colleges would not have room for all these students, but they would have little ground on which to accept some and reject others. Employers looking for secretaries, computer programmers, waiters, bus drivers, and factory workers would have jobs unfilled as every student considered such work beneath his or her accomplishments.

Good education, or students' success at education, must remain a scarce commodity as long as education is used to rank young people and sort them into occupational futures that yield substantially different intrinsic as well as monetary rewards. Society's recruitment of a work force proceeds more smoothly if only a relatively few students excel while others have varied success in school. Those who perform well have less competition when large numbers of others do not.

In the United States, we do not believe in passing privilege from parent to child. We expect individuals to earn the favored slots in society through talent and hard work; the schools are expected to be the judges of that talent and diligence. Thus it is important to our national sense of a fairly ordered social system that all children have an equal opportunity through education. The poorest child must have access to as good an education as the richest if we are to be able to say that educational success is a just criterion by which to award young adults a slot in the occupational hierarchy.

At the same time, education in this country is formally decentralized, officially the province of the states, and in many ways shaped by local school districts, which number in the hundreds in each state. How then to guarantee an equal education? By guaranteeing the *same* education. Educators have built a social reality around the idea of progress through the grades. It is supported by nationally distributed textbooks keyed to particular grades and nationally normed tests that report children's progress in grade equivalents.

We feel we are talking about something real when we say a child reads at the third grade level. Formally, a child who completes the fourth grade anywhere in the country should be able to move into the fifth grade in a different community without serious difficulty. In the same vein, our high schools have remarkably similar curriculums and requirements. Schools in quite different communities use the same textbooks for widely taught courses like geometry, American history, biology, and English literature.

To deviate from this pattern to design an educational setting around children's needs, interests, prior knowledge, or special aspirations creates two problems. It risks offering the child less than full educational opportunity. To deviate also risks offering less than a satisfactory credential—employers or colleges will not know how to judge graduates against those from other schools. The result may disadvantage ambitious graduates and confuse college admissions and industrial personnel departments.

At the same time that schools are officially declared equal, middle-class parents and alert working-class parents diligently strive to place their children in schools where the education will be more than equal. It is widely recognized by such parents that schools are not in fact the same—that children changing schools may find the next grade much more, or much less, demanding in a different community.

SCHOOLS AND PRIVILEGE

Parents usually regard schools that draw students from a higher social class as better. Peers are a crucial resource for each individual child, as teachers must teach to the level of the class. Both research and conventional wisdom indicate that group levels of achievement rise as social class rises and fall as it falls. Schools with budgets sufficient to provide additional visible resources or activities, often those serving higher socioeconomic groups, are also attractive.

That schools are not the same, despite the appearance of standardization, is such an open secret that realtors advertise houses according to their school-attendance area when the school has a local reputation for high quality. Houses in such neighborhoods can cost thousands of dollars more than equivalent structures in neighborhoods where schools have a less sterling reputation.

Separate suburban school districts allow their residents far more control over the means to create superior schools based on the social class of the student body and the availability of funding. Ordinances requiring certain sizes for lots, or only single-occupancy housing, can keep out lower-income families. Fair-housing groups across the country document the continued practice of racial steering by real estate agents; it can be used to keep suburban communities all or mostly white. Suburban districts also can take advantage of their higher tax base to offer higher salaries for teachers, small class sizes, richer stores of materials, and special programs in their "standard" schools.

Through my visits to secondary schools in a wide variety of communities, it is clear to me that the internal lives of high schools differ dramatically according to the socioeconomic status of their communities. Though the schools might offer the same courses—and even have the same books available—the substance of daily work, the stuff of classroom interaction, and the kinds of questions asked on tests are in no way comparable. The subtler stuff of atmosphere and expectations are worlds apart.

I am not suggesting that students alone determine the character of these schools; they emphatically do not. Teachers play a major role, one that can significantly improve the situation for low- and middle-income children. Still, the makeup of the student body is a major condition of school life that deeply affects teachers' and administrators' actions.

Differences between the schools of communities of differing social class are a reality that is widely recognized but rarely mentioned in public discourse about education, except by those trying to get access to a better education for disenfranchised children.

As a political entity, Americans seem to live with this contradiction between officially equal education based on standardization of curriculum and activities, on the one hand, and tremendous variety in the quality and content of education arising from the linkage of public education to housing that is segregated by social class as well as race, on the other. In a process that political scientist Murray Edelman argues is common in many areas of our political life, we rarely see, let alone

choose one of the district's junior highs of choice.

These twenty-three junior highs are the miracle schools of Spanish Harlem. While they began as a radical notion suitable for an experiment in a failing school system, they have become a model for change in a nation looking for a way to make schools better. "Choice has taken off and become wildfire," says Alvarado, "because everyone always looks for simplicity and for the magic bullet, the one or two things that will solve the problem."

Choice is also very seductive in its political appeal. Once, it was a conservative idea closely linked to the idea of "vouchers," or tuition tax credits—allowing tax dollars to follow students to any school, public or private. The voucher idea is being held in abeyance for the moment, but even in its more limited form, conservatives say they like choice. They insist that a free market, competitive approach to education is the best way to reward good schools and weed out bad ones.

And in the wake of success such as District 4, liberals like it too. Many are calling choice "empowering," a way, within the public school system, to extend to all the freedom wealthy families have always had: choosing where and how their children will be educated.

There is an irony in all of this consensus, however. Just as enthusiasm builds for choice, some of its biggest proponents are urging caution.

Choice, Alvarado says vehemently, should not be viewed as a panacea, "or else in three years everybody will say how we have again failed." Absent a broader plan for working on the "blood and guts of education," he says, "choice is meaningless."

Charles Glenn, director of the Massachusetts education department's Office of Educational Equity, cautions that "by and large, the way choice has worked in education is against poor kids."

And choice advocate May Anne Raywid, a professor of education at New York's Hofstra University, warns that when choice plans are not carefully implemented, "they can create tiers of inequity."

What choice accomplishes depends largely on which of its many forms it takes. It can provide choice for a limited number of students, as it does when selected students are allowed to choose magnet schools designed to allow them to hone their special talents. It can be expanded to provide choice for all students, as it does in Spanish Harlem. And in its most extreme form, it could mean allowing students to opt out of the public school system with vouchers. The Reagan administration supported vouchers, and although President Bush has refrained from explicitly endorsing that idea, he said earlier this year that expansion of choice is a "national imperative."

As a concept, its vagueness makes it very popular. Because choice means whatever politicians want it to mean, they are endorsing it in droves. The Education Commission of the States reports that as many as twenty-five states debated choice-related proposals this year. While Minnesota has the only mandatory statewide open enrollment plan, a number of other states, including Iowa, Arkansas, and Hawaii, have adopted limited programs modeled on Minnesota's. Illinois approved a choice plan for Chicago, and Washington State has a plan aimed specifically at dropouts. In New Jersey, the education department developed a pilot plan to take effect in September 1991 if the legislature approves it. Well over half of the states now have at least some limited form of choice—in a county or a city or a single school district—operating within their borders.

Choice can achieve three very important goals. It can revitalize school programs by giving teachers the freedom to be creative. It can make schools better places for children to be. Finally it can break down the barriers of segregation because of its power to draw students across political and economic boundaries.

Choice is also dangerous. It can "resegregate" schools when choices are limited or available only to the elite. It can create new kinds of inequities by funding schools unequally or segregating students within schools by "tracking" them by ability. Most troubling, it can lull politicians and educators into believing they have found the answer to the problems of education.

One of the best examples of how choice works well for both teachers and students comes from District 4's Isaac Newton.

Just ask Manny Kostakis. He came to Isaac Newton when it was created six years ago as one of four choice schools in the old Benjamin Franklin High School building. Today, he still teaches math, but he also serves as the school's "director," which means that he runs Isaac Newton without extra pay. The building still has a "principal," who serves as a building manager, but the junior highs in the building are run by their directors.

Zigzagging constantly between his classroom and his administrative duties, Kostakis still calls his job "refreshing." John Falco says that most of the teachers of District 4 feel that way. "It's been a renaissance for many," he says. "People who were completely burned out, ready to chuck it all, did a complete turnaround when they were put in an environment where they were useful again."

Kostakis' feelings about his school are obvious. He proudly points out the school's new computer lab, built by teachers who brought in tools, put up a wall to create the space, then held a fund raiser to buy the computers. Kostakis is very matter-of-fact about the reasons that he and other teachers take on extra responsibilities: It is their school. "That wall was put up by the teachers because if we waited for the Board of Education, it just wouldn't get done." Making the school better

is a matter of professional pride. It's also a matter of professional pride that Isaac Newton doesn't turn away "tough" kids. "We take students who have problems," he says with a grin. "If we motivate the kids, they're not going to misbehave. . . . We've given them that sense of they can do it . . . and they're doing it. They're really benefiting."

Children are also benefiting in Minnesota, home of the country's first statewide choice program. Access to Excellence is the three-part brainchild of Democratic Governor Rudy Perpich. The program began modestly in 1985, when the legislature approved a plan to allow eleventh- and twelfth-grade students to take classes in colleges and vocational schools with state funding following them. Next came the High School Graduation Incentives plan, aimed at dropouts and potential dropouts. It allows students from the ages of twelve to twenty-one to enroll in a school outside their district if they haven't succeeded in their local public school, unless such a change would hurt desegregation efforts. Even more ambitious is the state's Enrollment Options plan, which by the fall of 1991 will allow any public school student to attend any school in the state—with state tax dollars following the student—unless the move would harm desegregation plans.

There are some signs of success. The Post-Secondary Options program has quadrupled to 5,700 participants since it began in 1985; 700 dropouts have taken advantage of the graduation incentives program and come back to get their diplomas. This year 440 students, or only about 0.4 percent of those eligible, are taking part in the Enrollment Options plan, but state officials say they think that will increase as word spreads through satisfied parents.

Barbara Zohn, who runs the state's choice hotline, answering queries about the programs, reports that many formerly complacent school systems—now worried about losing students and the state tax dollars that go with them—are beefing up programs. She speaks of rural superintendents who are improving teachers' training and buying new books for their libraries, and of local officials who are finding the political will to raise taxes.

But the Minnesota plan also raises a number of concerns. One is the idea of applying the free market approach to education. Zohn says the state is betting that "market forces will inspire districts and schools" to do better or lose their students. Although no schools have actually closed for lack of business, it could happen. That makes Tony Alvarado cringe. Education, he says, can't be run through a competition "in which this business succeeds and another business dies. We are providing a public service, and when one [school] dies, it is kids who are dying."

Another issue is whether there is enough "real" choice in Minnesota. Raywid, the Hofstra professor, says that a critical difference between choice that works and choice that doesn't is "whether there really is legitimate choice. If you can choose among ten brown ties, then that really isn't choice." She suggests that unless schools are given the means to make their programs better and more distinctive, parents won't be opting for good schools; they will simply be opting for the school that is the least bad.

Alvarado wonders too whether a statewide choice system is manageable. "It's hard enough to do it well locally," he says. "When you broaden the parameters to state parameters, you get some real negative things happening all over the place." It may, he suggests, become more bureaucratic and less effective.

Zohn says simply that it's too soon to tell about these issues. "We are still in the early stages, still evaluating."

It is certainly easier to implement choice on a smaller scale. One of the testimonials to that comes from the schools of Cambridge, Massa-

chusetts. Concerned early on that their plan could work against poor families if they didn't take precautions, educators in Cambridge began a "controlled choice plan" in 1982–83 that included several strategies to avoid making choice a program for the elite only.

Like New York's District 4, the Cambridge plan requires every student to choose a school. But to make sure that all families have the same opportunity in making a choice, Cambridge launches a massive public outreach campaign every spring. A bilingual hotline is set up, counselors are available to all parents, a special effort is made to visit all welfare families, and even grocery bags are imprinted with messages about choice.

Glenn, of Massachusetts' Office of Educational Equity, says it is most important for every student to be required to make a choice and for the school system to impose adequate controls to assure equal access and racial integration. He adds that in order to make choice valid, "there must be a strategic effort to create options" in all of the schools. "Otherwise, what you get are a few groovy magnet schools where everyone sings and dances and knows calculus," while the rest of the schools are left to languish.

In fact, the most striking examples of how choice systems can create inequities come from some of the nation's large cities.

Donald R. Moore, president of a children's research and advocacy organization in Chicago called Designs for Change, recently completed a study that reached some disturbing conclusions. Moore looked at high school choice programs in four large school systems: Chicago, Philadelphia, Boston, and New York (where high schools are run by the city, not community school districts, and choice for students is optional, not mandatory). Moore's study found that "in these school systems, loosely implemented school choice programs have become a new form of segregation, in which students are segregated based on a combination of race, income level, and previous school performance."

Moore labeled these choice programs "a new, improved method of student sorting in which schools pick and choose among students" because they are allowed to reject the ones they don't want. In the process, the study concludes, "schools sort out black and Hispanic students and students with poor English proficiency." The result of choice is that these high-risk students don't have a choice.

Even when schools operate on a first-come, first-served basis, there are inequities. Joyce Charles, a PTA activist from Prince George's County, Maryland, is not happy with her county's much-acclaimed magnet school system. "There are lines of people wrapping around Largo High School for days," she says, "and they still don't get their kids into the school they choose." The result: "Some children in Prince George's County get a premium education; others get a discount education." There's nothing fair about that, says Charles, who feels that "every school should offer the same quality the magnet schools offer."

One of the reasons that parents in Prince George's County don't always get their choices is that the county is operating under a court-ordered desegregation plan. The administrative strategies required to achieve racial balance often put severe limitations on real choice; when the right numerical racial balance is achieved, choice often comes to a screeching halt. In Minneapolis, for example, no minority students are being permitted to transfer into city schools this year, and no white students are being permitted to leave city schools for the suburbs. Zohn says simply that "sometimes the needs of society must come before the needs of individuals. When you have a desegregation plan, that must come first."

There is some consensus developing about what makes choice work well. Most educators agree that the most significant factor is that choice must be real. If students and parents are to choose among schools, then all schools must provide valid educational options. "Every school ought to be a school of choice," says Charles Glenn, "or there's no equity." Next, Glenn says, "you have to figure out how to get people in the schools to take initiative. You don't want teachers who just punch time clocks, but creative, entrepreneurial thinkers, and it ain't easy in a deadening bureaucracy."

Raywid suggests that the final factor is parental involvement. Parents, she says, are tired of not having any more say than what day the cake sale ought to be." There is no better way to get parents involved than giving them a role in choosing their children's schools.

New York City's Alvarado, who after leaving District 4 was chancellor of the city's schools until he stepped down in 1984 because of personal financial problems, now runs District 2 in midtown Manhattan along the East Side. Looking back on District 4's success, he worries that choice will be a "hot item for two or three years and everybody will think that they're doing a wonderful job, and it will keep attention off some of the nastier educational failures that we continue to promulgate."

What are the problems that are left? "The essential problems of education," he says. "The nature of the teaching act; the development of the skills of the people who have to work with those kids." And finally, "What it is that education's supposed to be."

Alvarado believes in choice, but he hopes that what he helped to start doesn't become a distraction. "Education is particularly vulnerable to it because we're such a reflection of the society, which is the search for the quick fix and the latest fad diet: Give me the quickest menu for success. Everyone knows that there is none of that, but if someone says, 'These are the five things to do to insure success,' the only thing you can be sure of is that doing those five things is not going to result in it."

DISCUSSION QUESTIONS AND ACTIVITIES _____

1. Identify the distinctive characteristics of magnet schools.

2. What, according to Metz, are the effects of desegregation on minority students and on whites?

3. Can magnet schools benefit students who have previously resisted school and done poorly?

4. Magnet schools have been criticized for receiving extra resources and drawing the better students from a city's other schools. Are these criticisms warranted?

5. According to Sylvester, do schools of choice, including magnet schools, work against poor students and create inequities?

6. What are the advantages of schools of choice? The dangers?

7. Visit a magnet school. Observe and record its distinctive characteristics. Interview students, teachers, and administrators in order to evaluate the school's effectiveness.

8. Invite a teacher from a magnet school to class to convey the differences between teaching in a magnet school and a traditional school.

SUGGESTED READINGS _____

Alternative Education. Report No. 085-4. Sacramento: California State Department of Finance, 1985.

Ascher, Carol. *Using Magnet Schools for Desegregation: Some Suggestions from the Research.* New York: Columbia University Teachers College ERIC Clearinghouse on Urban Education, 1987.

Chabotar, Kent John. "Measuring the Costs of Magnet Schools." *Economics of Education Review* 8, no. 2 (1989): 169–183.

Clinchy, Evans. "Looking inside Schools of Choice: Eight Portraits." *Equity and Choice* 2 (May 1986): 17–75.

Lezotte, Lawrence W., and Barbara O. Taylor. "How Closely Can Magnet Schools Be Aligned with the Effective School Model?" *Equity and Choice* 5 (February 1989): 25–29.

Metz, Mary Haywood. *Different by Design: The Context and Character of Three Magnet Schools.* New York: Routledge & Kegan Paul, 1986.

Moore, Donald R., and Suzanne Davenport. "High School Choice and Students at Risk." *Equity and Choice* 5 (February 1989): 5–10.

Murname, Richard J. *Family Choice in Public Education: Possibilities and Limitations.* Cambridge, Mass.: Harvard University Press, 1984.

Raywid, Mary Anne. "Family Choice Arrangements in Public Schools: A Review of the Literature." *Review of Educational Research* 55 (Winter 1985): 435–467.

Roselle, Christine H. "The Carrot or the Stick for School Desegregation Policy?" *Urban Affairs Quarterly* 25 (March 1990): 474–499.

CHAPTER 12

TEACHER EDUCATION

The first systematic arrangement for teacher preparation in the United States was the founding of the first normal school in Lexington, Massachusetts, in 1839. Normal schools spread slowly and grew at a rate of about twenty-five new schools each decade until after the end of the century. As the programs multiplied, a pedagogical literature developed in which study required two years beyond the high school level. The teacher college was founded in the 1890s in New York State by converting the normal schools into four-year programs and by offering greater work in general education. Yet it was not until the 1920s that there were more teachers' colleges than normal schools in the country. Teacher preparation was also introduced in the late nineteenth century as a part of state university programs, yet because of resistance it was not until the 1920s that most universities undertook such programs.

This century has witnessed the establishment of accrediting bodies for teacher education, state certification of teachers, national teacher examinations, the development of tenure provisions for teachers, and the growth of sophistication in educational research. Despite these developments, a number of critics have charged that teacher education programs are inadequate. Arthur Bestor, Admiral Hyman Rickover, and other critics during the 1950s claimed that teachers are generally weakly grounded in their subject matter because their programs are overly crowded with education courses on *how* to teach rather than *what* to teach. One dominant solution would be to have all prospective teachers thoroughly educated in the liberal arts and greatly reduce or eliminate their requirements in education courses. The solution, as advocated by James Koerner in the 1960s, was to immerse the student in his or her specialty and in liberal arts studies.

In contrast, national studies by James B. Conant and Charles Silberman recognized responsibility by all parties: teacher educators, liberal arts faculty, and the public schools. Conant, along with most critics other than Silberman, failed to see the importance of education as a field of study in its own right; that is, building a system of scholarly knowledge and contributing to the development of professional consciousness.

Teacher educators have attempted to counter the critics' charges and, in turn, offer new programs and innovations. These include fifth-year programs, programs for culturally different learners, competency-based teacher education, microteaching, new forms of internship, and others. Still, the debate continues.

ALAN H. JONES INTERESTING TIMES

Alan H. Jones is Publisher, Caddo Gap Press, and former Executive Editor of The Education Digest.

"May you live in interesting times." Could it be that the prophet responsible for that cliché had the 1980s—and teacher education—in mind when the admonition was first offered? Indeed, the times are interesting for our field—interesting, exciting, challenging, and often downright frightening, frustrating, and draining.

Such times began, I would suggest, as all of education was indicted by *A Nation at Risk*, followed shortly by a stream of similar reports, nearly all as harsh on the field as had been the National Commission on Excellence in Education. A few of the commentaries of this decade have been more constructive, such as the work of John Goodlad, Ernest Boyer, and Theodore Sizer. But, in general, a specific mindset has seemed to overtake the public view of the field—a mindset that education and educators have failed, that the rush for reform must begin.

As a result, the policymakers controlling American education have rushed to raise academic standards, without due consideration of the impact of such directions on the non-academic curriculum, the marginal student, or the overarching ability of our schools to continue to serve the total public. They have rushed to extend the school day and school year, without consideration for the span of time that either students or teachers can effectively deal with academic work, the preparation time required by dedicated professionals, or the stress and strain which our school facilities can tolerate. They have rushed to test everything and everyone in sight, without attention to the limitations of testing or the other forms of evaluation and measurement available to the educational community.

Surely the most ironic aspect of this binge of reform has been the expectation that such things can be accomplished without additional cost, without the carrot from the federal level or the private sector which has traditionally been a part of efforts to improve or change the schools. Instead, this time around, the expectations from those making national recommendations has been that state and local governments—read that as state and local taxpayers—will foot the bill.

If anything good has come of all of this, it has escaped my observation, with perhaps the single exception of a vastly stronger and sharper public attention to the field of education. Such attention is, I believe, a mixed blessing. The public usually does not understand, and thus does not support, the more arcane aspects of the educational effort. For that reason, an attentive public is likely to be at cross-purposes with reforms that are educator driven. At the same time, there is some evidence that with the public push for reform has come a willingness to at least modestly increase state and local funding for education,

From Alan H. Jones, "Interesting Times," *Teacher Education Quarterly* 14 (Fall 1987):47–56. Reprinted with permission.

with some long overdue improvements in teacher salaries.

There has more recently been a similar turn of the guns of public attention and reform to the field of teacher education. In the last year we have received heavy scrutiny in two major national reports—the work of the Holmes Group and the Task Force on Teaching as a Profession of the Carnegie Forum on Education and the Economy, the latter entitled *A Nation Prepared: Teachers for the 21st Century*. These documents are similar, yet dissimilar. They focus on the need for quality in teacher preparation, although they differ in their definitions and recommendations.

The Holmes report is the work of leaders in education at many of our elite universities—research institutions, both public and private. It is not surprising that its primary conclusions speak for a centering of advanced teacher education at major research universities, leaving the preparation of second- and third-level professionals to other schools and colleges. While recommendations toward deepening the ultimate preparation of the profession are appealing, the abandonment of undergraduate teacher education, the establishment of second- and third-class professionals, and the obvious elitism of the preparers of the Holmes report are distasteful, at least to me.

The Carnegie report has a broader base, with its major motivation coming from an acceptance of the *A Nation at Risk* conclusions that the United States is losing the battle of international economic competition and that we need better teachers in order to turn around such events. While extended teacher preparation as a recommendation is shared with the Holmes folks, most of the other Carnegie recommendations suggest a stronger regulatory role, including the establishment of a national examination and certification board—more academic study, more testing, and more conformity. In these areas, obviously, there is little similarity between Holmes and Carnegie, since the elite Holmes Group universities would not appreciate a stronger national regulatory role which would infringe upon their institutional freedom. In that feeling, I am on the side of the Holmes Group.

ASSUMPTION ONE

In this overall context of reform, there are some interesting assumptions making the rounds: I would like to examine a few of them.

Reform Assumption Number One: *that teacher education should become a graduate-level professional study*. Yes, I agree that there is plenty of important content as well as desired clinical activity to make teacher education a five- or six-year program of study. But I am not ready to see such activity pulled entirely from the undergraduate curriculum. I see instead a critical need to keep teacher preparation in the four-year baccalaureate program, both in order to work early with those students who have chosen teaching as a career and to spread out their professional study and field experiences over a multiple-year period. There is plenty of evidence to suggest that interweaving academic courses in content areas, educational foundations and theory, curriculum and instructional strategies, and field experience from the junior year, or even earlier, through a fifth or sixth year of study is the ideal way to prepare a teaching professional.

In addition, based upon my own experience and observation, I have personal reasons for wishing to maintain a solid role for the small private colleges in the training of teachers. While those institutions, by virtue of their size and varying missions, may educate a relatively small portion of our overall teaching force, I know from my own years as a teacher-education faculty member and department chair in such settings, as well as from my observation of programs in three different states, that in many cases some of the very best teacher education occurs in the small private colleges in this nation. As an aside, I cannot help but note that some of the least impressive teacher-education programs with which I have been associated and have observed have been located at a few of those elite institutions which are now founding members of the Holmes Group. I offer this only as a personal observation, with no blanket indictment intended.

ASSUMPTION TWO

Reform Assumption Number Two: *that teacher education should be relevant.* Many of the cries that we hear in this tempest of reform suggest that the preparation—or, better stated, the training—of teachers must become more relevant or, indeed, must be *only* relevant. The meaning of such statements, if implemented, would cause the abandonment of the traditional academic preparation in pedagogy in favor of a totally field-based program. Such a direction is, in fact, contrary to the pleading for higher academic standards which is also part of this 1980s movement for educational reform, although few of the critics appear to comprehend this irony. They appear not to recognize that, if what we seek is an enhanced profession, the members of that profession must acquire and share a mutual understanding of where the profession has come from, what it stands for, where it is attempting to go, and the common ethical base which it possesses. The role of the historical, philosophical, social, and psychological foundation of education must be expanded, not abandoned, if we want a more professional field.

The other key point that most of the critics fail to comprehend is that the sole purpose of teacher education is not to train teachers for the schools as those institutions are today but rather to provide such new teachers with understandings and abilities which will enable them to play a role in improving our schools. It is especially ironic that many of the same critics who argue that today's American schools are inadequate to our national needs would rush to have teachers in training spend all of their preparation time serving as apprentices in those same apparently inadequate classrooms. They would have the new teachers learn by example from the current teachers whom they, the critics, have already indicted as inadequate. Personally, I am not willing to accept the view that today's schools and today's teachers are wholly inadequate, but neither am I willing to accept the notion that they are en masse sterling enough that we should turn over to them lock, stock, and barrel the preparation of their future colleagues.

The point is, we must recognize that we are training teachers for the twenty-first century, for a time and place that is difficult for any of us to even imagine effectively. Thus, rather than an apprenticeship approach that crystallizes the past and present, we must assemble the most varied and challenging professional preparation possible—a preparation that will provide individuals with a deep background, a broad professional foundation, and a flexible and imaginative repertoire which will enable them to make effective choices in an uncertain future.

To that end, I applauded, as did several others in the audience, last March in Sacramento, when Henrietta Schwartz stressed to the Symposium on School Leadership that the education of school administrators was not supposed to be relevant, that instead it should focus on foundational studies, on the development of professional ethics, and on the formulation of leadership understandings and abilities well above and beyond those which are now viewed as relevant in the schools of this or any other state in the nation. Dean Schwartz was decrying an apprenticeship approach previously described at the symposium by practitioners working with the state department of education and the Association of California School Administrators, both of which —as you know—operate short-term academies and workshops for school administrators, which they had argued were more relevant than the university-based certification programs. There were many other offerings to the temple of relevance at that symposium, as there always are when the professional preparation of educators is discussed, and I think we must all be ready to decry the notion that professional preparation is supposed to be relevant—and suggest that we are all better served if it is, instead, professional.

I am willing to grant that we need improved field experiences, longer field experiences, and more realistic field experiences—all of which can be called more relevant if you have a particular fondness for that term. But we need such things mixed in with and following a generous helping of content preparation, foundational study in the many aspects of our profession, a firm setting of the ethical dimensions of our work, and theoretical exploration of curricular, instructional, and evaluation issues and methodologies. Only then will the field experience be truly relevant—relevant to the profession itself.

It is important to remember that some of the most irrelevant education that takes place in any university setting is the extensive professional preparation offered to doctors and lawyers in our medical and law schools. While I don't suggest these institutions as models which fit my personal definition of good pedagogy, I do admire them for their ability to cast off criticisms of irrelevance and to forge ahead with a professional program based upon their accumulated understandings of the fields they serve. Teacher education should have that same determination, that same freedom to define relevance—or ignore relevance —on its own terms.

ASSUMPTION THREE

Reform Assumption Number Three: *that higher admissions standards and increased testing are good things.* It is often delightful to lull ourselves with the feeling of security which seems to come with the adoption of higher standards, increased grade point averages, entry and exit examinations, cutoff scores, and the notion of a national standards board for teachers. All of this suggests clearly to a worried public that we are taking seriously the mission of securing a better prepared teaching force for our schools.

But consider some other aspects of this assumption. Are all of the potential candidates for the teaching force effectively screened and examined in these ways? To what extent are grade point averages and test scores a good indication of teaching ability and excellence? Of the actual ability to communicate and work with kids? Are we testing the right things? Is this rush for higher standards and high test scores counterproductive to our social and affirmative action commitments to provide a multicultural and multiracial teaching force? Is it realistic to expect that we can recruit in adequate numbers the high-quality students that will meet these new standards and thereby be ready to fill the classrooms of the 1990s and the twenty-first century? Are there enough top-notch students —top-notch according to grade point and test scores—who will choose the teaching profession?

Personally, I doubt that these directions will help us find the best teachers and certainly not enough of them to fill the classroom needs now and in the future. If we deal with only the top 10 percent of our academic population, with the top fifth or so of our university students, we are going to fall well short of adequately serving the needs of our public schools. Yet this is what I see happening far too often this decade—indeed, at my own alma mater, the University of Michigan. I am perplexed by the newly streamlined (read that, "smaller but better") School of Education which is now bragging that its juniors and seniors are, as a cadre, the possessors of the highest average grade point average of any undergraduate group on campus. The reason for this, of course, is that they are now admitting so few students to the teacher education program that they have some ten applicants for every slot at the junior level and can thus be incredibly selective. The tragedy of this, I submit, is that, as they slave this way to the lords of academic excellence, they are turning away the other nine of each ten students who wish to be teachers, each of whom has already shown some rather clear academic ability by getting admitted to one of the most selective universities in the United States and by successfully completing the first two years of study on that campus. Yet students of that caliber are being passed over as future teachers—the public schools of Michigan and the rest of the nation are being denied these prospective teachers—simply because the central administration of one of our elite universities wants to reduce its emphasis on education in favor of other areas of study it views as more significant. This is, as I am sure you know, a pattern that is being repeated all across the nation—and there are many who think of it as reform in the field of teacher education. I think it is criminal.

ASSUMPTION FOUR

Reform Assumption Number Four: *that these higher standards will buy us better teacher salaries*. It is an attractive thought, but I maintain they have it backwards. I see no evidence in the field of education, or for that matter any other field, to suggest that graduates with higher qualifications will receive more money, unless there are other market forces at work. Nor is there reason to believe

that higher-caliber students will be attracted to education simply because the field raises entry standards. Is not the real way to attract higher-caliber people, defined in whatever way one may wish, to offer the better salaries first? Is this not more reasonable than to assume that if we graduate more highly qualified teachers, the local school districts will immediately offer more money to employ them?

Actually the market forces which control salaries are out of the hands of those of us who prepare teachers. Given the great number of teachers which will be needed in the next several years to replace all of those who entered the field in the boom years following World War II—a group that is scheduled to retire en masse in the years between now and 2000—it is far more likely that salaries may have to go up simply to attract an adequate number of recruits. The focus then, however, will be on obtaining adequate numbers of warm bodies, with little attention to high qualifications. If the goal is actually to increase the caliber of the teacher force, to get the field of education into competition with other professional fields for the best college students, then the thrust must be on offering teacher salaries which compare favorably in real dollars, in benefits, and in working conditions with those other university-trained professional fields. Then, and only then, will we see significant numbers of high-caliber recruits choosing to enter the doors of teacher education.

LACK OF MOVEMENT

Given these four uncertain assumptions I have discussed—indeed, in my mind, mistaken assumptions—which form the basis of the reforms of the 1980s, one should not be surprised that such reforms are not rapidly taking hold. I see no significant movement towards the stated goals of the Holmes Group and the

Carnegie Task Force. Much has been written in the public and professional literature about those reports, both pro and con, including the series of articles which comprise the thematic portion of the Winter 1987 issue of *Teacher Education Quarterly*. Much more will be written on such issues, but the specific reforms now discussed and future variations on those themes which might constitute an actual implementation of either Holmes or Carnegie will not come quickly, if at all.

There are good reasons for that lack of movement. The largest is that there is simply too little money available to make such things happen. Expanded or extended programs of teacher education are expensive, as they should be, and the colleges and universities are not oriented to spend money in a field which has traditionally been a money-maker for them. The new orientation toward increased professional study and expanded field work has a high price tag, and it is well known that heavily clinical situations are more costly than on-campus classes. The rush of internships in education back in the 1950s and 1960s did not die out because they constituted a poor way to train teachers, but because when the support from the Ford Foundation dried up, so did the programs. It was not a professional field that the colleges and universities wished to support to that level, and thus we returned to traditional and less expensive student teaching.

The current reform movement has problems other than a lack of money. It is too focused on paper credentialing rather than real programmatic change. We see new tests, new statements of competencies, new certification and employment standards, new accreditation guidelines, and new course descriptions on campus, but there is scant evidence to date of genuine professional reorientation, little change in what is being taught, little improvement in the professional/instructional/ethical program on campus, and little

real involvement of the professional and collegial parties that are needed to create a genuinely effective bridge to the public schools. Here again, the motivation required from top-level administrators at both the colleges and universities and the public schools, the indication that such reforms are really desired, is not forthcoming. Teacher education, to them, is not really that important.

What could make it important? Personally, I don't expect to see real possibilities for reform in teacher education unless or until there is a real influx of funding to the field—unless or until many more states dedicate significantly more money to teacher preparation, far more than the token and minimal salary increases which have been enacted in some states; unless or until we see a new, wholesale federal teacher corps or internship program on a far broader scale than ever before, obviously something which will not materialize during the present national administration or the administration of anyone I have yet to hear discuss his or her candidacy for the highest office of the land.

THE DEMISE OF A GOOD IDEA

Indeed, in all of this national discussion I have to date seen nothing that suggests to me that we are on the road to significant professional change. For that matter, I have come across no real reform ideas which I view as better than, or even nearly as good as, some of the plans which several of us across the state of California were discussing some seven years ago under the rubric of the California Consortium on the Beginning Years of Teaching. We were then talking about extended preparation of teachers—preparation bridging from the undergraduate years through a fifth-year internship, a sixth-year residency, and continuing with professional study during the early years of regular employment. All of this was to be handled through genuine cooperation among university faculty, school district administrators, peer model teachers, professional associations, and the state certification agency. The purpose was to provide a broad professional background; to ease the teacher into the classroom in the context of a strong collegial framework; to stress both the foundational and the practical aspects of education through classroom study, action research, and observation and practice; and to work with that new teacher through the difficult early years of employment. What we were proposing was, we thought, a good answer to the question posed in the title of an earlier article in the *Journal of Teacher Education*, by Bob Bush, also one of the authors of our consortium plan—that earlier article posed the question: "We Know How to Train Teachers Well, So Why Don't We Do So?"

Perhaps the fate of that consortium is a large part of the answer to Bob's question. In another article in the *Journal of Teacher Education* a few years ago, Carol Barnes and I reported on the demise of the consortium's efforts. The consortium had attempted to instill reform without seeking outside funding, based on the assumption that if such changes were brought about only because of a short-term grant, they would fade away once the funds ran out. Instead, we had sought to bring about such changes through cooperation of all of the relevant parties, asking each to assume some of the necessary instructional and supervisory load. It was apparently too much to ask, since the only programs successfully implemented in the model of the original consortium proposal were some abbreviated efforts between several Los Angeles-area institutions of higher education and the Los Angeles Unified School District, aimed at filling teacher vacancies in that huge district and relying on cooperative structures already in place. No new involvements in teacher education came of our efforts.

SOMEONE ELSE'S AGENDA

I would suggest that the problems encountered then remain with us today. At that time, all of the potential parties to meaningful reform of teacher education had their attention turned in other directions. Today their attention is focused on analyzing Holmes and Carnegie. In neither era is there a broadbased, genuine, or collegially oriented discussion of the changes that the real practitioners of teacher education—groups such as yourselves in each of the states across the nation—would wish to make. Instead you are caught up in reacting to someone else's agenda.

So why not ignore those national voices from afar? Why not proceed with the improvements you know will produce the best possible teachers? The answers are the same as they have been for decades. We lack either the funds or the institutional support necessary to achieve academic reform in the campus-based portions of our teacher education programs, and, in most cases, we also lack the potential for extended cooperation of school districts and professional associations, groups which are themselves too strapped by their own financial and professional difficulties to give greater attention to teacher education.

In sum, it is difficult to expect genuine and effective improvement of teacher education in a social, political, and economic milieu which is essentially hostile and cheap—yet that is the reality in which we operate. It has been our reality for decades, and there is little reason to expect it to improve, despite the national clamor for reform. All I can suggest is that we recognize the reality for what it is and make the best of our own internal resources.

There are good people in the field of teacher education all across the country. There is an ever-increasing pool of essential professional knowledge to be combined with the foundational treasures which are the heritage of free public education in this unusual nation of ours. There is the small blessing of increased attention from the public this decade—and from educational policymakers—which accompanies the ill-fated cry for reform. My advice is to make the best of such small blessings.

Argue loudly for the few pieces of the reform recommendations which do make sense in the context of your own institutional program and your school settings. Take advantage of what public support can be obtained for such enhancements. Argue equally loudly against those reform directions which are ill-suited to our needs, which will only make it harder to do your job right. And throughout it all, proceed with doing the best possible job with your current program, making those changes that are necessary and appropriate and striving for the resources and the cooperative arrangements which will allow for the ideal.

The history of our field suggests that you will have to do such things for yourself—despite the clarion calls of Holmes and Carnegie, despite the increased attention of the public and the policymakers, I see no white knights on their way to help you now or in the future. Indeed, it is my expectation that you will have to spend a good bit of time cleaning up after the steeds of this current group of would-be knights have left their droppings and galloped away. Such is the reality of the interesting times in which you live.

CAROLYN M. EVERTSON,
WILLIS D. HAWLEY,
AND MARILYN ZLOTNIK

MAKING A DIFFERENCE IN EDUCATIONAL QUALITY THROUGH TEACHER EDUCATION

Carolyn M. Evertson is Professor, Department of Teaching and Learning; Willis D. Hawley is Dean, Peabody College of Vanderbilt University; and Marilyn Zlotnik is Research Associate, Vanderbilt University.

Teacher education probably has never received as much attention from the public policy makers as it has over the past few years. Teacher educators have long felt neglected and unappreciated, but the recent scrutiny they have experienced may make many wish to return to their backseat status. Schools of education, and perhaps the state agencies and professional organizations that sustain them, are charged with lacking the necessary standards, competence, substance, and academic rigor to do a quality job of educating America's teachers.

The response to the infamy now widely bestowed upon teacher education has been loud and not always coherent. State-level policymakers generally perceive the solution to the problem in regulations that would restrict access to both teacher education and to teaching and that would prescribe specific courses of study and ways to teach. These regulatory actions are sometimes matched with incentives aimed at increasing the quality and quantity of aspirants to teaching. A number of states created loan forgiveness programs to induce students to enter fields such as math and science where teacher shortages exist. A handful of states have increased significantly beginning teacher salaries. And, there is currently pressure to provide "alternative routes" to the teaching profession that presumably make teaching more attractive by allowing individuals with certain academic credentials to bypass formal teacher-preparation programs.

These actions, and more, have occurred largely without much involvement from teacher educators. Those who prepare teachers, however, are beginning to make their moves. The initiatives fall into two broad categories. The first initiative is to join the call for higher standards. In particular, teacher educators—at least those who speak out on the standards issue—are calling for higher grade point averages for admission to teacher education programs, minimum course requirements and faculty qualifications, and preservice tests of teacher knowledge.

A second reform strategy is to require more extensive preentry course work coupled with better supervised practica and internships. This strategy assumes that beginning teachers are less effective than they could be because they do not know as much as they need to know. An additional assumption un-

From Carolyn M. Evertson, Willis D. Hawley, and Marilyn Zlotnik, "Making a Difference in Educational Quality through Teacher Education," *Journal of Teacher Education* 36 (May–June 1985):2–12. Reprinted by permission.

derlying this position is that teaching is not as attractive to talented people as are other professions because requiring only a conventional undergraduate education for entry contributes to the low status attributed to a career in teaching. Advocates for this reform strategy are calling for five and, increasingly, six years of higher education prior to full entry to teaching. Perhaps because so-called extended or postbaccalaureate teacher preparation programs are likely to result in major shifts in student enrollment from private and small public institutions to large public universities, teacher educators are divided on this strategy. But there is little doubt that its advocates are growing in number and influence.

Most proposals for teacher reform are unburdened by evidence that the suggested changes will make a difference in the quality of students preparing to teach in elementary and secondary schools. They avoid questions such as: Can existing research provide guidance for how teacher education might be improved in a cost-effective way? Before addressing this question, we acknowledge at the outset that although the number of studies related to teacher education is large, the research is often of dubious scientific merit and frequently fails to address the types of issues about which policymakers are most concerned. These types of limitations, however, apply to any number of policy questions, and our view is that it is better to be guided by what is known and to be concerned about what is not known than it is to rest public policy decisions on intuition, commitment, and personal experience. We look first at the evidence related to whether formal teacher preparation can and does make a difference in the quality of teaching and learning in schools. Because the answer to that question appears to be affirmative, we will then turn to an exploration of strategies by which this difference can be enhanced. In particular we will examine three sets of reform proposals aimed

at (a) improving the quality of students who get into and out of teacher programs, (b) extending and/or upgrading the curriculum of teacher preparation, and (c) almost independent of the content, teaching would-be teachers differently.

We do not deal with all of the types of research presently being conducted on teacher education and teaching that might be used to infer new directions. We have chosen to limit our review to studies that provide evidence that directly links teacher preparation programs to improvements in teaching or to student achievement. This constraint rules out dozens of studies based on teachers' own evaluations of their preparation as well as studies of how teacher education influences teacher attitudes or their academic achievement. It also excludes a growing body of interesting and useful research on how and why teachers make decisions that theoretically should influence their effectiveness. Our interest, in short, is more in how teacher education might enhance student learning than in how it might affect teachers.

DOES TEACHER EDUCATION MAKE A DIFFERENCE?

At the heart of the move to change the participants and the programs that prepare teachers is the assumption that teacher preparation is basically a waste of time. Though such an assessment is based to some extent on the frailties of teacher preparation programs, much of it seems to come from the view that teaching is an art rather than a science and can best be learned, as most college professors say they learned it, on the job.

There are two types of studies that address the question: Do preservice preparation programs teach teachers to teach effectively? The first of these involves comparisons on the effectiveness of teachers who participate in teacher education programs with the effective-

characterize as being excessive in its emphasis on teaching methods, short on depth in the subjects teachers will teach, and insufficiently rigorous. Many teacher educators are critical of teacher education curricula on the grounds that so much more is known about teaching now than was the case a few short years ago, yet teacher candidates spend little time learning this new knowledge. The inadequate time given to professional studies is attributed both to the limited time available for course work and to the fact that many faculty members are not familiar with recent research. Proposals for change in teacher education curricula are of three general types:

1. More emphasis should be placed on developing subject matter expertise.
2. More courses should be taken in the liberal arts.
3. More time should be given to the development of knowledge about teaching and the capacity to teach.

As we noted above, other more radical proposals are on the agenda that assume that not much is to be learned about teaching that cannot be learned on the job, perhaps in an apprenticeship to a "master teacher." The research cited earlier concerning the relative differences in the performance or in the effectiveness of teachers who have been certified in conventional ways as compared to teachers who did not complete a teacher education program suggests that improving rather than abandoning preservice teacher education would be more efficacious for student learning.[2]

Greater Subject Matter Expertise

It seems sensible to assert that one must know what one is teaching to be effective. But, how well must one know it? Most secondary teachers take the substantial number of courses in the field for which they are certified. Must a person major in the field he or she plans to

teach? Must elementary teachers know calculus to teach arithmetic? Unfortunately, the available research is not very helpful in answering these important questions.

The most extensive assessment of the effects of subject matter knowledge on teaching effectiveness is a recent metaanalysis of sixty-five studies of science education (Druva and Anderson, 1983). Three conclusions from this study seem most relevant to our concerns with teacher education programs.

1. There is a relationship between teacher preparation programs and what their graduates do as teachers. Science courses, education courses, and overall academic performance are positively associated with successful teaching.
2. The relationship between teacher training in science and cognitive student outcome is progressively higher in higher-level science courses.
3. The most striking overall characteristic of the results . . . is the pattern of low correlations across a large number of variables involved. (p. 478)

With respect to the teaching of other subjects, the relationship between teacher expertise and teacher performance is not clear from the research. Massey and Vineyard (1958) found positive but small relationships as did Begle (1972), who characterized the association he found as "educationally insignificant." Maguire (1966), Siegel (1969), and Eisenberg (1977) found no or negative relationships between teacher knowledge (as measured by grade point averages and standardized tests) and student achievement. The General Accounting Office (1984) cites a 1983 synthesis of research by Colin Byrne that it characterizes as finding "no consistent relationship between the knowledge of teachers and the achievement of their students" (p. 33).

We emphasize, again, that this does not mean that good teaching can occur when teachers do not know their subject. The idea that the knowledge now typically required for certification in a given field contributes to teacher effectiveness finds support in the study by Hawk, Coble, and Swanson that is reported in this issue of the *Journal*, which concludes that students of mathematics teachers who were certified "infield" showed higher achievement gain than the students of teachers who were certified to teach but did not hold mathematics certification.

In summary, the research suggests that knowing the subject matter does not necessarily make a person a good teacher of that subject. Furthermore, it seems reasonable to conclude that teachers with good instructional capabilities would be more effective if they had in-depth knowledge of the subjects they teach. This is, logically enough, more true of teachers of advanced courses. The research, however, provides little reason to believe that increasing teachers' knowledge of their subjects beyond that typically required for certification will significantly increase teacher effectiveness.

More Course Work in the Liberal Arts

Who can disagree with the idea that teachers should be well educated? For many people, being well educated means having a broad liberal arts education. Thus, it is not surprising to see the argument being made that professional teacher education plays too great a part in a prospective teacher's undergraduate education. We could not find any evidence in research on teacher education specifically or undergraduate education more generally that would provide support for the idea that a broad liberal arts education promotes the development of the values, analytical skills, love of learning, or other personal and intellectual characteristics one might reasonably attribute to teachers who care about their students and understand what it takes to facilitate learning.

The absence of evidence that greater emphasis on the liberal arts in the education of prospective teachers would result in greater teacher effectiveness does not, of course, prove that such changes are undesirable. Neither the empirical nor the theoretical case has been made. Moreover, recent research on the courses liberal arts students actually take raises doubts about the breadth and rigor of the typical undergraduate curriculum (Galumbos, Cornett, and Spitler, 1985). We hasten to add that we personally endorse, for reasons of our own, the idea that teachers should have to satisfy broad distribution requirements typically required of liberal arts students who major in an academic discipline. Furthermore, we see no reason why courses classified as "professional" could not be as intellectually rigorous and theoretically rich as courses described as "liberal arts."

Increasing the Pedagogical Components of Teacher Preparation

Much has been learned about teaching in recent years. Comprehensive reviews of the research include Brophy and Good (in press), Hawley and Rosenholtz (1984), MacKenzie (1983), and Rosenshine (1983). The research has emboldened many teacher educators (and others) to call for a more extensive pedagogical component to preservice teacher education.

Space limitations do not permit an adequate discussion of the knowledge base that might be covered in the preparation of teachers. There are several recent efforts to identify the types of instructional strategies and the theory necessary to implement them effectively that should be covered, and there appears to be substantial agreement on the topics that should be addressed (Smith, 1983; Egbert and Kluender, 1984; Berliner, 1985). Several researchers advocate that in addition to knowledge and competence in instructional strategies, teacher preparation programs should focus upon teacher decision making, attitude formation, and analytical skills (see, for example, Fenstermacher, in press; Feiman-Nemser and Buchmann, 1983; Tabachnick, et al., 1983; Joyce and Cliff, 1984; Lanier, in press).

The many studies we noted above, demonstrating the efficacy of explicit efforts to train teacher candidates to believe in and to implement specific practices and habits of mind, provide good reason to believe that preservice teacher preparation programs, if structured appropriately and if staffed by qualified faculty, can teach teachers the things being advocated as essential for beginning teachers to know and do. But no program of which we are aware has attempted to incorporate even a significant segment of the knowledge base many teacher educators argue that students should learn before they teach on their own.

Problems in Making Big Changes in What Preservice Teachers Learn

As we suggested earlier, little research exists to support the notion that making significant changes in what teachers learn before they begin their careers will significantly improve the quality of teaching experienced by most students in elementary and secondary schools. What if we did not let this deter us and we decided that significant changes should be required?

Few teacher educators or state agencies acknowledge that what is now taught teacher candidates should be eliminated (though this seems a worthy crusade). Furthermore, many proposals for improving the education of teachers urge at least two and often three of the types of curricular change previously discussed. The results, of course, are proposals to extend preservice teacher training to five and even six years.

Increasing the preservice period of required education naturally increases the cost of becoming a teacher. Because of earnings

foregone, as well as tuition and other costs, requiring an additional year of college could double the cost of becoming a teacher. Unless salaries and other benefits are increased accordingly, requiring extended teacher preparation programs will likely result in a drop in both the quality and quantity of those entering the profession. Student stipends or other rewards could reduce those declines but could also result in a reallocation of funds from current priorities to teacher preparation. Billions of dollars are involved, and a debate about the alternative uses of these funds vis-à-vis their potential impact on student learning seems to be in order.

The idea that significant additions to what teacher candidates should know and be able to do before embarking on a career in education not only has large economic costs, but there is reason to question whether students can learn and effectively transfer to practice all or even much of the pedagogical knowledge and skills that would be taught in extended programs. Considerable evidence exists that experienced teachers think differently about their work than do novices (see, for example, Koehler, 1985; Leinhardt, 1983; Erickson, 1984; Sprinthall and Thies-Sprinthall, 1983). Teachers may learn some things best, such as cooperative learning strategies, once they have an experiential base upon which to build.

TEACHING TEACHERS DIFFERENTLY

Whatever the content of teacher preparation programs, assuming it has some reasonable link to teacher performance, the fact remains that some ways of facilitating the learning of teacher candidates are more effective than others.

It seems safe to say that as teacher educators we frequently do not practice what we preach. That is, one seldom sees teacher educators modeling interactive teaching strategies, cooperative learning techniques, or problem-solving skills. Efforts to strengthen preparation programs must incorporate a strong modeling component, and that modeling should reflect the body of research findings with respect to mastery learning, individualized instruction, cooperative grouping, competency-based education, microteaching, and other approaches documented as effective in strengthening prospective teachers' knowledge and skills. We draw attention from a research perspective to two of these approaches: competency-based teacher education and microteaching. Other excellent reviews are available that support and provide greater documentation for the points we describe (see Gage, 1978). We then turn to the important problem of helping student teachers transfer what they learn during teacher education courses to their classroom behavior.

Competency-Based Teacher Education

Generally, competency-based teacher education (CBTE) refers to specific efforts to train prospective teachers to acquire competencies believed to be associated with effective teaching. The logic of this approach is similar to the pedagogy involved in teaching basic skills in elementary schools: be clear about what is to be learned, design lessons that fit that objective, teach the lesson, test for learning, provide feedback, redesign the lesson, and teach again. By the early 1970s, CBTE and its equivalents were seen by many teacher educators as the one best way to professionalize teacher preparation. But, CBTE came under attack for being too technical and for leading to the increasing specification and proliferation of skills that had no compelling link to student learning (cf. Sarason, 1978–79; Hamilton, 1973, as cited in Bush and Enemark, 1975). The idea that CBTE lacked a validated knowledge base has considerably less credibility now than it did six or seven years ago when attacks on CBTE were in full swing. This fact, plus

the increasing propensity of states and school systems to develop performance-based teacher evaluation programs that spell out specific teaching behaviors, suggests that CBTE (no doubt in various disguises) is likely to be born again.

Research on the effects of CBTE on teacher attitudes and behavior seems to show positive results (Adams, 1982; Joyce, Wald, and Weil, 1981; Piper and O'Sullivan, 1981; Borg, 1972).

Microteaching

Microteaching can take many forms but it essentially involves a prospective teacher's organizing and delivering a short lesson. Often, specific competencies are to be demonstrated in the lesson, such as planning, interactive questioning, and so forth, and the lesson is evaluated accordingly. Microteaching is, in short, a simulation technique that focuses on particular learning objectives for the teacher candidate through which evaluation and feedback are provided.

In general, it appears that microteaching—some versions of which are called minicourses—is an effective pedagogical device (Copeland, 1975; Boeck, 1972; Borg, 1972; Blankenship, 1970; Emmer and Millett, 1968; Kocylowski, 1970), although the acquisition of teaching competence does *not* always occur (Kallenbach and Gall, 1969).

One of the virtues of microteaching appears to be its facilitation of immediate feedback about an analysis of performance. As Gage and Winne (1975) conclude: "Evidence for the efficacy of feedback about teaching performance is fairly consistent. When the information is explicit, clear, and keyed to specific aspects of teaching behavior, feedback results in improvement in the trainees' ability to perform according to a model of teaching" (pp. 160–161). The usefulness of frequent and precise feedback as an instrument for promoting the improvement of teaching effectiveness is not limited, of course, to microteaching (cf. Flanders, 1970).

Student Teaching

Student teaching is usually identified by new teachers as the most rewarding and useful aspect of their preservice professional preparation (Griffin et al., 1983; Nemser, 1983). These claims by teachers, plus widespread skepticism about the rigor and scientific basis of many formal courses in teacher preparation, probably contributed to a rash of contemporary proposals that would place apprenticeship at the core of teacher preparation. The existing research, however, provides little reason to believe that supervised practical experience, in itself and as it is encountered in most student teaching situations, is a very effective way to educate teachers.

A decade ago, Peck and Tucker (1973) reviewed research on teacher education and concluded that "by the end of student teaching, there are some almost universally reported decrements in attitude and in teaching behavior, as compared with the starting position of students prior to their field experience" (p. 967). This conclusion still seems generally accurate. For example, in what may be the most intensive study of practice teaching yet conducted, Griffin and his colleagues (1983) found that little change occurred in the student teachers as a result of their field involvement.

Neither Griffin's research nor any other study we could find linked specific characteristics of the student teaching experience to teacher performance. The research suggests, further, that the role of practice teaching in the preparation of teachers may be overrated.

Theoretically, student teaching, if structured properly, could engender teacher effectiveness. But it may also seem that the problems and costs of successfully implementing practice teaching programs are so great that other processes for achieving teacher education objectives should be explored more fully.

Induction

Some of the contributions that teacher preparation programs make to teacher effectiveness may be undermined by the experience first-year teachers have when they are inducted into the profession. As with practice teaching, the induction phase of a teacher's career more often narrows than expands the range of instructional strategies teachers perceive they can employ. The induction period of teaching is so chaotic and absent of support that teachers often focus on instructional strategies that stress controlling student behavior rather than facilitating student learning (Hawley and Rosenholtz, 1984, chap. 2). Induction is becoming a focus of attention as teacher educators come to think about teacher education along a professional continuum from preservice to inservice (Hall, 1982; Tisher, Fyfield, and Taylor, 1979). At the very least, knowledge about the problems that beginning teachers face as they start their teaching careers can provide important information for the design and evaluations of preservice teacher preparation programs.

Growing evidence indicates that unless teacher educators can mediate the experience teachers have in their first one or two years of teaching, much of what is taught in preservice courses will be seen by teachers as irrelevant (or will be undone). What implications does this conclusion have for teacher education? First, curriculum design can take into account the types of concerns teachers are likely to have by warning them about these realities and providing them with some analytical and problem-solving skills they can use to deal with the conditions that might undermine their effectiveness (cf. Stallings, 1984). Second, students should be introduced to the research on teaching in ways that provide them with an understanding of the variety of options they have, the contingencies that mediate the use of specific practices, and the theory that explains the efficacy of the practices. Efforts to increase the conceptual understanding of teaching by increasing awareness of proven models and practices (Joyce and Showers, 1981; Joyce and Showers, 1982) and by training that includes theory, demonstration, practice, feedback, and classroom application (Showers, 1983) seem likely to be productive. More fundamentally, however, we need to find ways to support the professional growth of teachers once they are surrounded by students of their own.

CONCLUSION

Despite the fact that teacher preparation programs have come under seemingly unprecedented criticism in recent months, the available research suggests that among students who become teachers, those enrolled in formal preservice preparation programs are more likely to be effective than those who do not have such training. Moreover, almost all well planned and executed efforts within teacher preparation programs to teach students specific knowledge or skills seem to succeed, at least in the short run.

The research we reviewed raises questions about the efficacy of a number of popular proposals for reforming teacher education, but it does *not* add up to a defense of teacher preparation as it exists in most institutions. Even the most aggressive apologists for teacher education acknowledge that improvements can and should be made in virtually all programs. Nonetheless, the research suggests, at least, that preservice teacher education programs can make contributions to effective teaching.

Based on our understanding of the research reviewed here and on other evidence

relating the transfer of training to practice and adult learning, the model we find most intriguing is one that involves the following components:

1. A strong liberal arts undergraduate education
2. The development of competence in the subjects to be taught, which would include the equivalent of a major in the primary field for high school teachers
3. Professional education of eight to ten courses, many with a related practicum, to be taken either as an undergraduate or after the baccalaureate is received
4. A year-long internship in a "teaching school" that would be similar in function and culture to a teaching hospital for physicians
5. A one- or two-year induction period, with special support from the employing school system and a school of education
6. Continuing professional development related to the learning needs of individuals that is distributed and organized in accord with their specific present and future instructional functions and with leadership roles of the individual

Such a model, which obviously needs more specificity, would allow teacher educators to rethink what is needed to be taught to teachers at different stages of their development as professionals. We suspect, for example, that educational philosophy is a course best taught to teachers with two or three years of experience.

Hundreds of studies related to teacher education are available, but the lessons they teach do not add up to a particular model for improvement around which teacher educators should rally. Rather, this seems to be an opportune time for experimentation—and evaluation. If some models or elements prove to facilitate student learning more cost effectively than others, we will be in a strong position to prescribe particular structures for implementing those strategies.

Endnotes

1. Popham (1971a) developed a set of *experiments* to examine whether pedagogical training adds to teaching effectiveness of persons with subject matter expertise. This research has been the subject of considerable debate (Glass, 1974; Turner, 1973; and Bausell and Moody, 1973). We are content to treat the work of Popham and his replicators as heuristic rather than determinative primarily because of its narrow focus and the artificial settings in which most of it was conducted.
2. For a research-based defense of teacher education, see Haberman, 1984.
3. The groundwork for the developmental model has been laid—see for example, Fuller and Brown (1975), Gehrke (1981), Sprinthall and Thies-Sprinthall (1983).

References

Adams, R. D. (1982). *Teacher development: A look at changes in teacher perception across time.* Paper presented at the annual meeting of the American Educational Research Association, New York.

Andrews, J. W., Blackmon, C. R., and Mackey, J. A. (1980). Preservice performance and the NTE. *Phi Delta Kappan, 61* (5), 358–359.

Armor, D., Conry-Oseguera, P., Cox, M., King, N., McDonnell, L., Pascal, A., Pauley, E., and Zellman, G. (1976). *Analysis of the school preferred reading program in selected Los Angeles minority schools.* Santa Monica, CA: Rand Corporation.

Ayers, J. B., and Qualls, G. S. (1979). Concurrent and predictive validity of the National Teacher Examinations. *Journal of Educational Research, 73* (2), 86–92.

Baker, L. W. (1970). *An analysis of some assumed predictors of success in teaching.* Doctoral thesis, United States International University.

Bausell, R., and Moody, W. (1973). Are teacher preparatory institutions necessary? *Phi Delta Kappan, 54* (5), 298.

Beery, J. R. (1960). *Professional preparation and effectiveness of beginning teachers.* Coral Cables, FL: University of Miami.

Begle, E. G. (1972). *Teacher knowledge and student achievement in algebra* (School Mathematics Study Group Reports No. 9). Stanford University.

Berliner, D. (1985). *Reform in teacher education: The case for pedagogy.* Tucson: University of Arizona.

Blankenship, M. L. D. (1970). *The use of microteaching with interaction analysis as a feedback system for improving questioning skills.* Doctoral thesis, Pennsylvania State University.

Bledsoe, J. C., Cox, J. V., and Burnham, R. (1967). *Comparison between selected characteristics and performance of provisionally and professionally certified beginning teachers in Georgia.* Athens, GA.: University of Georgia. (ERIC Document Reproduction Service No. ED 015 553)

Boeck, M. A. (1972). *Stability of behavioral change: One year after precision micro-teaching.* Minneapolis: Minnesota University College of Education.

Borg, W. R. (1972). The minicourse as a vehicle for changing teacher behavior: A three-year follow-up. *Journal of Educational Psychology, 63,* 572–579.

Brophy, J., and Good, T. (in press). Teacher behavior and student achievement. In M. Wittrock (Ed.), *Handbook of research on teaching* (3rd ed.). New York: MacMillan.

Bruno, J. E., and Doscher, M. L. (1981). Contributing to the harms of racial isolation: Analysis of requests for teacher transfer in a large urban school district. *Education Administration Quarterly, 17* (2), 93–108.

Bush, R. N., and Enemark, P. (1975). Control and responsibility in teacher education. In K. Ryan (Ed.), *Teacher education: The Seventy-fourth yearbook of the National Society for the Study of Education.* Chicago: University of Chicago Press.

Byrne, C. (1983). *Teacher knowledge and teacher effectiveness: A literature review, theoretical analysis and discussion of research strategy.* Paper presented at the annual meeting of the Northeastern Educational Research Association, Ellenville, NY.

Coleman, J. S., Campbell, E. Q., Hobson,

C. J., McPartland, J., Mood, A. M., Weinfeld, F. D., and York, R. L. (1966). *Equality of educational opportunity.* Washington, D.C.: U.S. Government Printing Office.

Collins, M. L. (1976). *The effects of training for enthusiasm displayed by preservice elementary teachers.* (ERIC Document Reproduction Service No. ED 129 773)

Copeland, W. D. (1975). The relationship between microteaching and student teacher classroom performance. *Journal of Educational Research, 68,* 289–293.

Copley, P. O. (1974). *A study of the effect of professional education courses in beginning teachers.* Springfield, MO: Southwest Missouri State University. (ERIC Document Reproduction Service No. ED 098 147)

Cornett, L. M. (1984). *A comparison of teacher certification test scores and performance evaluations for graduates in teacher education and in arts and sciences in three southern states.* Atlanta: Southern Regional Education Board.

Darling-Hammond, L. (1984). *Beyond the commissioner reports: The coming crisis in teaching.* Santa Monica, CA: Rand.

Denton, J. J. and Lacina, L. J. (1984). Quantity of professional education coursework linked with process measures of student teaching. *Teacher Education and Practice,* 39–64.

Denton, J. J., and Smith, N. L. (1984). *Alternative teacher preparation programs: A cost-effective comparison.* Paper presented at the annual meeting of the American Educational Research Association, New Orleans.

Druva, C. A., and Anderson, R. D. (1983). Science teacher characteristics by teacher behavior and by student outcome: A metaanalysis of research. *Journal of Research in Science Teaching, 20* (5), 467–479.

Ducharme, R. J. (1970). *Selected preservice factors related to success of the beginning teacher.* Doctoral dissertation, Louisiana State and Agricultural and Mechanical College.

Egbert, R. L., and Kluender, M. M. (Eds.). (1984). *Using research to improve teacher education* (The Nebraska Consortium). Washington, D.C.: Eric Clearinghouse on Teacher Education.

Eisenberg, T. A. (1977). Begle revisited: Teacher knowledge and student achievement in algebra. *Journal of Research in Mathematics Education,* 216–222.

Ekstrom, R. B., and Goertz, M. E. (1985). *The teacher supply pipeline: The view from four states.* Paper presented at the annual meeting of the American Educational Research Association, Chicago.

Emmer, E., and Millett, G. B. (1968). *An assessment of terminal performance in a teaching laboratory: A pilot study.* Austin: University of Texas, Research and Development Center.

Erickson, F. (1984). *Teachers' practical ways of seeing.* East Lansing: Michigan State University, College of Education.

Feiman-Nemser, S., and Buchmann, M. (1983). *Pitfalls of experience in teacher preparation* (Occasional Paper No. 65). East Lansing: Michigan State University, Institute for Research on Teaching.

Fenstermacher, G. (in press). Philosophy of research on teaching: Three aspects. In M. Wittrock (Ed.), *Handbook of research on teaching.* (3rd ed.). New York: Macmillan.

Flanders, N. A. (1970). *Analyzing teaching behavior.* Reading, MA: Addison-Wesley Publishing Co.

Francke, E. L. (1971). *Pupil achievement and teacher behaviors: A formative evaluation of an undergraduate program in teacher preparation.* Doctoral thesis, University of Nebraska.

Fullan, M. (1982). *The meaning of educational change.* New York: Columbia University, Teachers College Press.

Fuller, F., and Brown, O. (1975). Becoming a teacher. In K. Ryan (Ed.), *Teacher education: The seventy-fourth yearbook of the National Society for the Study of Education.* Chicago: University of Chicago Press.

Gabrys, R. E. (1978). *The influence of a training intervention for business-like behavior on the business-like behavior and level of warmth of preservice elementary teachers.* Paper presented at the annual meeting of the Association of Teacher Educators, Las Vegas, January.

Gage, N. L. (1978). *The scientific basis for the art of teaching.* New York: Teachers College Press.

Gage, N. L., and Winne, P. H. (1975). Performance-based teacher education. In K. Ryan (Ed.), *Teacher education: The seventy-fourth yearbook of the National Society for the Study of Education.* Chicago: University of Chicago Press.

Galumbos, E., Cornett, L. M., and Spitler, H. D. (1985). *An analysis of transcripts of teachers and arts and sciences graduates.* Atlanta: Southern Regional Education Board.

Gehrke, N. (1981). A grounded theory of beginning teachers' role personalization through reference group relationships. *Journal of Teacher Education, 32,* 34–38.

General Accounting Office. (1984). *New directions for federal programs to aid mathematics and science teaching.* (GAO/PEMD—84–5) Washington, D.C.: GAO.

Gerlock, D. E. (1964). *An analysis of administrators' evaluations of selected professionally and provisionally certified secondary school teachers.* Doctoral dissertation, Florida State University.

Getzels, J. W., and Jackson, P. W. (1963). The teacher's personality and characteristics. In N. Gage (Ed.), *Handbook of research on teaching,* (1st ed.). Chicago, IL: Rand-McNally.

Glass, G. (1974). Teacher effectiveness. In H. Walberg (Ed.), *Evaluating educational performance.* Berkeley, CA: McCutchan.

Gray, H. B. (1962). *A study of the outcomes of preservice education associated with three levels of teacher certification.* Doctoral dissertation, Florida State University.

Griffin, G. A., Barnes, S., Hughes, R., Jr., O'Neal, S., Defino, M., Edwards, S., and Hukill, H. (1985). *Clinical preservice teacher education: Final report of a descriptive study.* Austin: University of Texas, Research and Development Center for Teacher Education.

Haberman, M. (1984). *An evaluation of the rationale for required teacher education: Beginning teachers with and without teacher preparation.* Paper presented for the National Commission on Excellence in Teacher Education.

Hall, G. (1982). Induction: The missing link. *Journal of Teacher Education, 23* (3), 53–55.

Hall, H. O. (1962). *Effectiveness of fully certified and provisionally certified first-year teachers in teaching certain fundamental skills.* Doctoral dissertation, University of Florida.

Hamilton, P. D. (1973). *Competency-based teacher education.* Menlo Park, CA: Standard Research Institute.

Hanushek, E. (1977). The production of education, teacher quality, and efficiency. In D. A.

Erickson (Ed.), *Educational organization and administration.* Berkeley, CA: McCutchan.

Hawley, W. D., and Rosenholtz, S. J. (1984). Good schools: What research says about improving student achievement. *Peabody Journal of Education, 61* (4), 1–178.

Hord, S., and Hall, G. (Eds.). (1978). *Teacher education program evaluation and follow-up studies: A collection of current efforts.* Austin: University of Texas, Research and Development Center for Teacher Education.

Howard, J. L. (1965). *An analysis of change in teacher and pupil behavior: A study of the fifth-year program in teacher education at the University of North Carolina, 1963–64.* Doctoral dissertation, University of North Carolina at Chapel Hill.

Joyce, B., and Cliff, R. (1984). The Phoenix agenda: Essential reform in teacher education. *Educational Researcher, 13* (4), 5–18.

Joyce, B., and Showers, B. (1982). The coaching of teaching. *Educational Leadership, 40,* 4–10.

Joyce, B., and Weil, M. (1972). *Models of teaching.* Englewood Cliffs, NJ: Prentice Hall.

Joyce, B. R., and Showers, B. (1981). *Teacher training research: Working hypotheses for program design and directions for further study.* Paper presented at the annual meeting of the American Educational Research Association, Los Angeles.

Joyce, B. R., Wald, R., and Weil, M. (1981). Can teachers learn repertoires of models of teaching? In B. R. Joyce, C. Brown, and L. Peck (Eds.), *Flexibility in teaching: An excursion into the nature of teaching and training.* New York: Longman.

Kallenbach, W. W., and Gall, M. D. (1969). Microteaching versus conventional methods in training elementary intern teachers. *Journal of Educational Research, 63,* 136–141.

Kocylowski, M. M. (1970). *A comparison of microteaching and conventional systems of preservice teacher education on teaching effectiveness.* Doctoral thesis, Wayne State University.

Koehler, V. (1985). Research on preservice teacher education. *Journal of Teacher Education, 36,* (1), 23–30.

Lanier, J. (in press). Research on teacher education. In M. Wittrock (Ed.), *Handbook of research on teaching* (3rd ed.). New York: Macmillan.

Leinhardt, G. (1983). Novice and expert knowledge of individual student's achievement. *Educational Psychologist, 18*, 165–179.

Lins, L. J. (1946). The prediction of teaching efficiency. *Journal of Experimental Education, 15*, 2–60.

Locke, L. F. (1984). Research on teaching teachers: Where we are now. *Journal of Teaching in Physical Education, 2* (2), 1–86.

LuPone, L. J. (1961). A comparison of provisionally certified and permanently certified elementary school teachers in selected school districts in New York State. *Journal of Educational Research, 55*, 53–63.

MacKenzie, D. E. (1983). School effectiveness research: A synthesis and assessment. In R. Duttweiler (Ed.), *Educational productivity and school effectiveness*. Austin: The Southwest Educational Development Laboratory.

Maguire, J. W. (1966). *Factors in undergraduate teacher education related to success in teaching*. Doctoral dissertation, Florida State University.

Manski, C. (1985). *Academic ability, earnings, and the decision to become a teacher: Evidence from the National Longitudinal Study of the High School Class of 1972* (Working Paper No. 1539). Cambridge, MA: National Bureau of Economic Research.

Massey, H. W., and Vineyard, E. E. (1958). Relationship between scholarship and first-year teaching success. *Journal of Teacher Education, 9*, 297–301.

McLaughlin, M. W., and Marsh, D. D. (1978). Staff development and school change. *Teachers College Record, 80* (1), 69–94.

Millett, G. B. (1969). *Comparison of teaching procedures for promoting teacher behavior and learner translation behavior*. Stanford, CA: Stanford University, School of Education.

Murnane, R. J. (1975). *The impact of school resources on the learning of inner-city children*. Cambridge, MA: Ballinger.

Murnane, R. J., and Phillips, B. R. (1978). *Effective teachers of inner-city children: Who they are and what they do*. Princeton, NJ: Mathematica Policy Research.

Murphy, P. D. (1972). *Teaching strategies exhibited by first year teachers*. Fargo, ND: North Dakota State University.

Nemser, S. F. (1983). Learning to teach. In L.

Shulman and G. Sykes (Eds.), *Handbook of teaching and policy*. New York: Longman.

Peck, R. F., and Tucker, J. A. (1973). Research on teacher education. In R. M. W. Travers (Ed.), *Handbook of research on teaching*. (2nd ed.). Chicago: Rand-McNally.

Piper, M. K., and O'Sullivan, P. D. (1981). The National Teacher Examination: Can it predict classroom performance? *Phi Delta Kappan, 62*, 401.

Popham, J. (1971). Performance tests of teaching proficiency: Rationale, development, and validation. *American Educational Research Journal, 8* (1), 105–117.

Pugach, M. C., and Raths, J. E. (1983). Testing teachers: Analysis and recommendations. *Journal of Teacher Education, 34* (1), 37–43.

Rosenshine, B. (1983). Teaching functions in instructional programs. *Elementary School Journal, 83* (4), 335–351.

Sarason, S. B. (1978–79). Again, the preparation of teachers: Competency and job satisfaction. *Interchange, 10* (1), 1–11.

Sheehan, D. S., and Marcus, M. (1978). Teacher performance on the National Teacher Examinations and student mathematics and vocabulary achievement. *The Journal of Educational Research, 71*, 134–136.

Shim, C. P. (1965). A study of four teacher characteristics on the achievement of elementary school pupils. *Journal of Educational Research, 59*, 33–34.

Showers, B. (1983). *The transfer of training*. Paper presented at the annual meeting of the American Educational Research Association, Montreal.

Siegel, W. B. (1969). *A study of the relationship between selected undergraduate academic achievement variables and teaching success*. Doctoral dissertation, Washington State University.

Smith, D. C. (Ed.) (1983). *Essential knowledge for beginning educators*. Washington, D.C.: American Association of Colleges for Teacher Education.

Soar, R. S., Medley, D. M., and Coker, H. (1983). Teacher evaluation: A critique of currently used methods. *Phi Delta Kappan*, 239–246.

Sprinthall, N. A., and Thies-Sprinthall, L. (1983). The teacher as an adult learner: A cognitive-developmental view. In G. A. Griffin (Ed.),

Staff development: Eighty-second Yearbook of the National Society for the Study of Education. Chicago: University of Chicago Press.

Stallings, J. (1984). Implications from the research on teaching for teacher preparation. In R. Egbert and M. Kluender (Eds.), *Using research to improve teacher education* (The Nebraska Consortium). Washington, D.C.: ERIC Clearinghouse on Teacher Education.

Summers, A. A., and Wolfe, B. L. (1977). Do schools make a difference? *American Economic Review, 67,* 639–542.

Sweitzer, G. L. (1982). *A meta-analysis of research on preservice and inservice science teacher education practices designed to produce outcomes associated with inquiry strategy.* Paper presented at the annual meeting of the National Association for Research in Science Teaching, Chicago.

Tabachnick, B. Zeichner, K., Densmore, K., and Hudak, G. (1983). *The development of teacher perspectives.* Paper presented at the annual meeting of the American Educational Research Association, Montreal.

Taylor, T. W. (1957). *A study to determine the relationships between growth in interest and achievement of high school science students and science teacher attitudes, preparation and experience.* Doctoral dissertation, North Texas State College.

Thacker, J. A. (1965). *A study of the relationship between principals' estimates of teaching efficiency and scores on National Teachers Examinations, academic averages, and supervisors' estimates of potential for selected teachers in North Carolina.* Doctoral dissertation, University of North Carolina, Chapel Hill.

Tisher, R., Ryfield, J., and Taylor, S. (1979). *Beginning to teach: The induction of beginning teachers in Australia* (Vols. 1 and 2). Canberra Australian Government Publishing Service.

Turner, R. (1973). Are educational researchers necessary? *Phi Delta Kappan, 54* (5), 299.

Winkler, D. (1972). *The production of human capital: A study of minority achievement.* Doctoral dissertation. University of California, Berkeley.

DISCUSSION QUESTIONS AND ACTIVITIES _____

1. What are the weaknesses, according to Alan H. Jones, of the Holmes Group report and the Carnegie report?

2. Why does Jones object to the assumption that teacher education should become more relevant?

3. Are higher admissions standards desirable? Will higher standards likely raise teacher salaries?

4. Evertson, Hawley, and Zlotnik cite two reform strategies currently advocated. What educational consequences are likely to accrue should either of these two be adopted?

5. What research evidence is available to show that teacher education programs make a difference in teacher effectiveness?

6. What likely effect will raising admission standards to teacher education programs and testing teachers' knowledge prior to certification have on the quality of teaching?

7. Will increasing teacher's knowledge of their subject beyond what is typically required for certification significantly increase teacher effectiveness? Why?

8. Why do Evertson, Hawley, and Zlotnik claim that the role of practice teaching in teacher preparation may be overrated?

9. Look at their model (consisting of six components). What components would you accept? Reject? Explain why.

10. Gather data on changes in teacher education nationally, note salient trends, and report them to class.

11. Analyze your own teacher education program as to whether research would actually support each aspect of the program.

SUGGESTED READINGS

Leading Reports and Studies

Bestor, Arthur E. *Educational Wastelands.* Urbana: University of Illinois Press, 1953.

Carnegie Task Force on Teaching as a Profession. *A Nation Prepared: Teachers for the 21st Century.* New York: Carnegie Corporation, 1986.

Conant, James B. *The Education of American Teachers.* New York: McGraw-Hill, 1963.

Goodlad, John I. *Teachers for Our Nation's Schools.* San Francisco: Jossey-Bass, 1990.

Houston, W. Robert, ed. *Exploring Competency Based Education.* Berkeley, Calif.: McCutchan, 1974.

Koerner, James D. *The Miseducation of American Teachers.* Boston: Houghton Mifflin: 1963.

Lanier, Judith E. "Research on Teacher Education." In *Handbook of Research on Teaching*, 3rd ed. Edited by Merlin C. Wittrock. New York: Macmillan, 1986, 527–569.

Silberman, Charles E. *Crisis in the Classroom.* New York: Vintage Books, 1970.

Tomorrow's Teachers: A Report of the Holmes Group. East Lansing, Mich.: Holmes Group, 1986.

Critiques and Evaluations

Hoyt, Kenneth. "An Approach to Readiness for Educational Reforms." *Educational Considerations* 15 (Spring 1988): 2–8.

Johnson, William R. "Empowering Practitioners: Holmes, Carnegie, and the Lessons of History." *History of Education Quarterly* 27 (Summer 1987): 221–240.

Pietig, Jeanne. "On Making the Education of Teachers Intellectually Sound." *Teacher Education Quarterly* 14 (Winter 1987): 32–39.

Popkewitz, Thomas S. "Organization and Power: Teacher Education Reforms." *Social Education* 51 (November–December 1987): 496–500.

Smith, Charles W. and others. "The Carnegie and Holmes Reports: Four Views." *Vocational Education Journal* 62 (May 1987): 28–30.

Teachers College Record 88 (Spring 1987). Special issue on Holmes Group Report.

Wirsing, Marie E. "Holmes and Carnegie: The Myth of Bold New Reform." *Teacher Education Quarterly* 14 (Winter 1987): 40–51.

CHAPTER 13

CAREER LADDERS

A number of national commission reports have expressed concern about teacher performance. *A Nation at Risk* (United States Government Printing Office, 1983) emphasized paying higher teacher salaries based on performance. Some school boards have supported either merit pay or career ladders in order to motivate teachers and provide higher-quality instruction.

Merit pay rewards teachers with higher salaries for doing the same or a similar job better than their colleagues. *Career ladders* pay teachers more for performing duties that are different from those of colleagues. Both plans require systematic, periodic assessment of faculty. In contrast, most school systems today base salary on formal education completed and on the amount of teaching experience.

Career ladders differ from merit plans by designating different teacher categories—such as beginning teachers, senior teachers, and master teachers—while merit plans usually have only one category. Usually a certain percentage of teachers can advance in a given year on a career ladder, with master teachers sometimes used as consultants or trainers of beginning teachers. Beginning teachers may remain for three to five years on the first rung of the ladder, and it may require up to five years before being eligible to apply for the next level of the career ladder. Teachers who reach the two top rungs of the career ladder may be employed ten to twelve months annually, supervise beginning teachers, evaluate other teachers, and develop curricula.

Teachers show less disfavor toward career ladders than merit pay. In a 1986 Louis Harris poll, 71 percent were opposed to merit pay systems. Teachers were split in their views of career ladder programs, with 49 percent in favor and 46 percent opposed.

Thomas Deering's article outlines the rationale, objectives, and strengths of career ladders while observing discontents expressed by teachers in several state-directed programs. Timothy Chandler and his coauthors show how the career ladder works, its weaknesses in terms of job satisfaction, and other problems; consequently, they propose a career lattice.

DEVELOPING A CAREER LADDER: GETTING DOWN TO THE BASICS

THOMAS DEERING

Thomas Deering is a faculty member at Missouri Valley College in Marshall, Missouri.

Education is losing the recruitment battle. Understandably, this concern has prompted considerable debate among professional educators and laymen alike about the quality of the teaching force and the effect it has on education.

To address underlying problems—some perceived, some real—several states have developed or are developing career ladders for teachers. A career ladder is a program which offers more extrinsic forms of compensation for teaching than teachers now receive. This compensation acknowledges increased competence, responsibility, and professional growth. Most career ladders have three to six steps, beginning with a first-year teacher and advancing to master teacher.

At each level a teacher receives additional salary and assumes more responsibilities, or is judged to be doing superior work in his or her position (Cornett, 1984). Additional duties might include

- Creating instructional materials
- Aiding other teachers' improvements
- Administering special programs
- Developing new projects
- Working with small groups of children
- Consulting with parents
- Educational research
- Writing (English, Clark, French, Rauth, and Schlechty, 1985).

The career ladder, in essence, is a giant step toward adequately rewarding those currently in the teaching profession and attracting and retaining more competent teachers.

Recent money crunches have aggravated the problems of teacher motivation and retention, but they are not new problems. The only way for teachers to receive additional pay or responsibility in their profession has been to pursue jobs in administration or counseling. Those who choose to stay in the classroom are tied to the same job description throughout their careers as well as a salary schedule based only on years of experience and educational course work. In effect, not only does the profession fail to reward teachers for professional development, but it fails to take advantage of teachers' growth and experience. Increased compensation and responsibilities to those who have demonstrated the above would be an important and welcome innovation in American education. Career ladders reward teachers as individuals and use their talents in often nontraditional but professional ways. The career ladder addresses teachers' concerns while using their experience and expertise for the improvement of education.

From Thomas Deering, "Developing a Career Ladder: Getting Down to the Basics," *Thrust for Educational Leadership* 15 (May-June 1987): 22–24, 260. Reprinted from *Thrust for Educational Leadership,* published by the Association of California School Administrators.

Not surprisingly, career ladders are only one means being devised for rewarding and using professional growth in education. Merit pay plans are another approach to improving the quality of teachers and teaching. Both career ladders and merit pay plans deal with extrinsic rewards for teachers, but there are some broad differences in them. Generally, a career ladder rewards teachers for nonteaching duties and extended contracts as well as for superior teaching. Merit pay plans, however, deal almost exclusively with additional pay based on the teacher's evaluation as it relates to improved student learning and development.

Although it is too early to predict which system will prove most effective, the emphasis in this article will be on career ladders. They have already been adopted in a number of states and are being considered in a number of others. Educators should understand the nature of the career ladder as well as its potential advantages and disadvantages.

Career ladder programs have a number of common features, but states have moved in a variety of directions in developing their programs. Most states have taken one of the following three approaches (Weeks, 1985):

- A few states have enacted comprehensive legislation detailing the structural elements of the plan. Florida, Tennessee, and Texas are among these states.
- Several legislatures have outlined essential features of a plan and charged task forces of the states' boards of education with developing plans for approval.
- A number of states have given local districts the authority to develop their own plans.

As with all issues of a public nature, each of the three methods has supporters and critics. Support or criticism needs to be founded on how well the program is fulfilling its purposes, so as not to be trivial.

Regardless of the approach taken in its development, the objectives of a career ladder need to be kept in mind. According to Johnson (1985), a career ladder should

- Improve the teaching and learning process
- Improve educational institutions as organizations
- Improve the quality of the teacher work force
- Regain community confidence in the school

A career ladder program is far more comprehensive than simply assigning teachers additional duties and raising their salaries. The heart and soul of a career ladder is to improve learning through improved teaching. It is based on the belief that teachers can improve their classroom performance by continual professional growth and development. The career ladder is designed to adequately compensate teachers and thereby improve the quality of public education.

The benefits to education from career ladders could be easily negated if misconceptions arise about the nature and purposes of the program. So as not to misuse a career ladder, it is important for legislators, boards of education, and teachers to be aware not only of what career ladders are, but also what they are not.

A career ladder is *not* (Robinson, 1984)

- A substitution for an adequate salary schedule
- A cost *saving* program, but one that, if administered properly, can be cost *effective*
- A substitution for effective and adequately performed teacher evaluations

Although Robinson was discussing merit pay, his points are equally valid when applied to career ladder plans. Teachers must believe a program is fair. If it is perceived as unjust, or as a method to justify denying teachers a raise, a career ladder will not help to improve learning for students. Instead, it will probably aggravate a problem it is designed to solve.

Sorting out what a career ladder plan is and is not is only an initial step in developing an effective program. Just as important, as Hawley (1985) points out, in order to stimulate good teaching, the rewards associated with a career ladder must:

- Be great enough to compensate for increased effort.
- Be linked to a verifiable quality of performance.
- Not put teachers in competition with each other.

Keeping these and the aforementioned points in mind when developing a career ladder will increase the likelihood of a successful program. Unfortunately, well-designed plans are still not enough to make career ladders work.

In order to be successful, career ladders require the infusion of a considerable amount of money into public education. A good number of teachers, if not most, believe they are underpaid. So, from the teachers' standpoint, to require them to do more, or to require them to perform their jobs at a higher level, will take a considerable amount of money. In addition to the extra money needed for teacher salaries, there is an administrative cost which the district or state must absorb. A number of states have recognized the financial commitment such programs require. Tennessee, for example, has appropriated more than $250 million for the first three years of its career ladder program (Weeks, 1095).

If there is a major weakness in career ladders, it could be the difference in perception between teachers and administrators and the public as to what constitutes an adequate incentive and reward. So it is imperative that teachers be involved in the development of the career ladder. Any state or local district which

is not committed to substantial incentives will find the teachers frustrated, angry, and demoralized. These feelings will work against the best intentions of legislators and boards of education. These are feelings, in fact, which the career ladder is designed to alleviate.

Any state or local district contemplating a career ladder needs to take time to study the issues involved in creating a productive plan. As mentioned, it is imperative that the nature of the program and teacher compensation be considered. There are a number of related elements which need to be a part of the package. According to Robinson (1984), these include

- Effective evaluation procedure
- Adequate basic salary level
- Well-defined educational objectives
- Board and administrative commitment
- Staff involvement in program development
- Assessment measures which are objectively and consistently applied
- Adequate financing
- Availability to all who qualify
- Continuous review of the plan

If the decision is made to continue with the program, it must be done with vigorous commitment. If it is not, nothing will be gained and much may be lost. There are already waves of discontent within several of the state-directed programs, and even talk of repealing them. In Tennessee, teachers have complained about the excessive paperwork which they must complete in order to participate in the program. Many also believe that disharmony among the teachers is in part a result of a quota system which allows only a given number of teachers to advance up the career ladder each year.

Missouri, which recently began its career ladder program, has had different problems. In Missouri the local district has to contribute financially to the program, so many of the state's 500 plus districts are not participating.

In addition, the financial incentives are seen as inadequate to attract the higher-quality student into teaching or retain the best teachers in the profession.

Hasty decisions to develop or repeal career ladders can have serious negative consequences for education. Careful study of available information and a clear understanding of what a career ladder can and cannot do for schools are essential.

Since career ladder plans are still in the experimental stage, it is impossible to predict what impact they will have on education. What *can* be said of career ladders, though, is that they are not a panacea for all of the problems in education. Much needs to be done in all areas of education in order to better serve society as a whole and the students as individuals, but career ladders are a political reality in many states and are becoming one in many more. Teachers and boards of education need to be aware of what career ladders are and be involved in their development and implementation. Only by working together for a common goal can teachers and board members be successful. And, teachers and board members must keep in mind that their ultimate goal is the same: quality education for the students and the society which they serve.

References

American Federation of Teachers. (1983) *Salary Trends for Teachers*. Washington, D.C.: Author.

Cornett, L. (1984). Career ladder plans: Questions faced by states. *Career ladder clearinghouse report*. Atlanta: Southern Regional Education Board.

English, F., Clark, D., French, R., Rauth, M., and Schlechty, S. (1985) *Incentives for excellence in America's schools*. Alexandria, VA: The Association for Supervision and Curriculum.

Gardner, D. P. (1983). *A nation at risk: The imperative for educational reform*. Washington, D.C.: U.S. Department of Education.

Hawley, W. D. (1985). The limits and potential of performance-based pay as a source of school improvement. In H. C. Johnson, Jr. (Ed.), *Merit, money, and teachers' careers studies on merit pay and career ladders for teachers* (pp. 3–1). New York: University of America Press.

Johnson, H. C., Jr. (1985). Introduction. In H. C. Johnson, Jr. (Ed.), *Merit, money, and teachers' careers studies on merit pay and career ladders for teachers* (pp. v–x). New York: University of America Press.

Robinson, G. E. (1984). *Incentive pay for teachers: An analysis of approaches*. Arlington, VA: Educational Research Services.

Weeks, K. (1985). Planning career ladders: Lessons from the states. *Career ladder clearinghouse report*. Atlanta: Southern Regional Education Board.

TIMOTHY J. L. CHANDLER,
STACEY L. LANE,
JANICE M. BIBIK,
AND BERNARD OLIVER

THE CAREER LADDER AND LATTICE: A NEW LOOK AT THE TEACHING CAREER

Timothy J. L. Chandler, Stacey L. Lane, Janice M. Bibik, and Bernard Oliver are in the Department of Health and Physical Education, Syracuse University, Syracuse, New York.

Recent concern over the quality of teachers staffing the nation's schools has prompted widespread development of educational reform packages designed to improve the teaching profession. Stemming from this effort has been the notion that a teaching career must be structured as a career ladder, progressing from informal elementary instructional tasks to full-time responsibilities in the gymnasium. In this paper we discuss some of the assumptions underlying career ladders in order to highlight their strengths and, more particularly, their weaknesses. We suggest that career ladders address not the true needs of teachers but rather the evaluation needs of administrators. As such, career ladders are not a good means of promoting teacher development. We offer the notion of the career lattice as an alternative means of meeting the motivational needs of teachers.*

Educational reformers have highlighted a number of factors as being of concern in the drive to improve public education. One factor has been quality of teachers staffing the nation's schools. It is widely believed that we can improve the quality of education by improving the quality of teachers. The issue has been to find ways of recruiting and then retaining capable teachers. Such concerns have prompted two major questions: What can be done to change the teaching profession so that more bright graduates will be attracted to it? What can be done to motivate talented teachers to remain in teaching? The concept of the career ladder has been widely acclaimed as a means to improve teaching by motivating teachers through a clearly delineated set of career steps. The notion of the career ladder has gained support at both local and state levels across the country during the past five years. At present, at least twenty-seven states are pursuing some type of teacher-related reform that involves a career ladder (Program Planners, Inc., 1985).

WHAT IS A CAREER LADDER?

Teacher-related reform programs are known by a variety of names, such as differentiated staffing and performance-based compensation. Typically, career ladder programs are characterized by some form of differential

From "The Career Ladder and Lattice: A New Look at the Teaching Career," by T. J. L. Chandler, S. L. Lane, J. M. Bibik, and B. Oliver, 1988, *Journal of Teaching in Physical Education*, 7, pp. 132–141. Copyright 1988 by Human Kinetics Publishers. Reprinted by permission. Request reprints from Timothy J. L. Chandler, Department of Health and Physical Education, Syracuse University, Syracuse, New York 13244.

*This is a revised version of a paper prepared for the Annual Meeting of the American Alliance for Health, Physical Education, Recreation and Dance, Las Vegas, April 13–17, 1987.

staffing, for example, by ranking teachers as apprentice, associate, or master teachers. These rankings depend on experience, education and, most significantly, performance evaluation. Although there are variations from locale to locale, the typical career ladder has four rungs (stages, steps, or levels), depending on the terminology employed (Association of Teacher Educators, 1985). (See Figure 13.1).

The entry-level position is that of *teacher*. At this level the novice educator typically only instructs students and has no additional pro-

fessional responsibilities. To ease the process of induction into teaching, Level I, or entry-level, teachers are assisted in various ways by teachers at Levels II, III, and IV.

The Level II teacher is sometimes referred to as an associate teacher. In addition to full instructional demands, associates are assigned other professional responsibilities such as supervising student teachers or serving as mentors to novice teacher colleagues.

Level III, or senior teachers, although responsible for instruction, spend less time with students and more time on in-service educa-

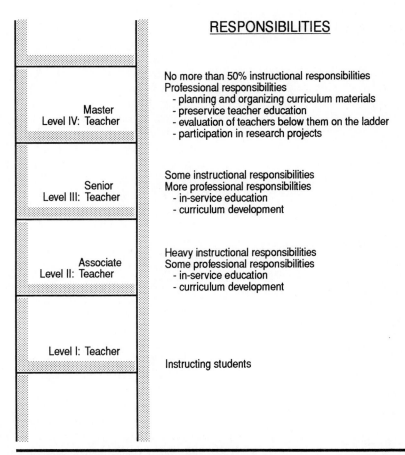

FIGURE 13.1 Career ladder concept.

tion, curriculum development, and similar professional duties. Level IV, or master teachers, spend no more than 50 percent of their time instructing students. They are responsible for planning and organizing activities ranging from developing curriculum materials and preservice teacher education to evaluating teachers below them on the ladder to participating in research projects. Many career ladder systems mandate transition years between levels so that teachers have time to learn new skills and roles before being evaluated for advancement.

What are the real strengths of career ladders, in terms of the teaching profession in general and physical educators in particular? The greatest benefit of a career ladder is that it gives some degree of "career-staging" to a formerly careerless career (Lortie, 1975). It offers a succession of hierarchically related jobs, with increasing prestige, recognition, and material benefits. Some of the assumptions underlying the notion of career ladder relative to teacher development include these (Association of Teacher Educators, 1985):

1. Rewarding outstanding teachers improves schools and teacher morale.
2. A career ladder helps identify levels of competence in teaching and enables a school to use its staff most effectively.
3. A career ladder provides incentives throughout a teaching career. From a teacher preparation viewpoint, there are two additional assumptions:
4. A career ladder encourages a better pattern of initial teacher preparation and improves the process of induction into teaching, while giving focus to ongoing staff development.
5. A career ladder sharpens the role of teacher education institutions in both initial preparation and continuing professional development.

Career ladders have several aims with regard to teacher retention. They offer motiva-

tion for teachers to improve their skills in order to advance to higher levels and reward them for doing so. They also facilitate the identification of exemplary teachers for the purpose of acting as mentors to student interns, student teachers, and probationary-year teachers. (A related benefit of career ladders is their potential to improve the transition from student to teacher, as well as to bridge the gulf that often separates these two roles.)

Career ladders can provide regular "cooling-out" points for disillusioned, burned-out, or dissatisfied teachers, thus making room for new recruits. Finally, career ladders should increase teacher accountability and encourage more adequate and equitable methods of teacher evaluation.

The issue of evaluation is an important one. Although the rationale behind career ladders has been one of fostering teacher development, the major drive for such ladders has come not from teachers but from governors such as Lamar Alexander of Tennessee and state legislatures like Florida's. This leads us to ask in whose interests career ladders are being implemented and begs the question, *Cui bono*: Who benefits?

Representatives of both the National Education Association (Gary Watts) and the American Federation of Teachers (Albert Shanker) have been lukewarm at best about many career ladder proposals (Pipho, 1984). We believe that such responses are best understood in terms of Herzberg's (1959, 1966, 1976) motivation-hygiene theory of management (see Figure 13.2).

Herzberg noted that job satisfaction and dissatisfaction are not polar opposites but instead are different concepts. What makes a person happy about a job is the work itself, achievement, and responsibility—all factors that lead to psychological growth. These are the equivalent of the very important psychic rewards in teaching. Promoting such growth requires a human relations approach by management. Herzberg related job dissatisfaction

Motivation Needs
The work itself
Achievement
Responsibility

Hygiene Needs
Working conditions
Salary
How workers are treated

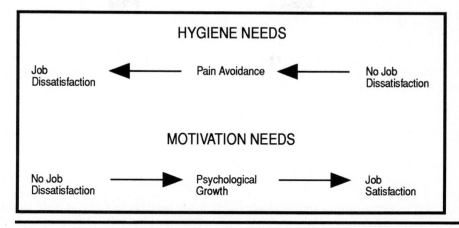

FIGURE 13.2   Motivation-Hygiene Theory.

Note: From "Motivation-Hygiene Theory and Sport Participation—Finding Room for the 'I' in 'Team' " by C. Roger Rees and W. F. Straub (Ed.), *Sport Psychology: An Analysis of Athlete Behavior* (1980), Ithaca, NY: Mouvement. (Originally adapted from: *The Managerial Choice*)

to working conditions, salary, and how workers (in this case teachers) are treated. These problems could be improved through scientific management techniques (Callahan, 1962). In Herzberg's terms, the former are motivation needs, the latter are hygiene factors. Meeting hygiene needs only averts dissatisfaction; it does not institute motivation.

Based on this theory, career ladders address the needs of the system but not the true development of teachers. In effect, only the hygiene needs of teachers are being met, but not their motivation needs. In other words, administrators are fostering a scientific management approach, similar to that outlined by F. W. Taylor at the turn of the century, by stressing incentives and rewards (which, in Herzberg's terms, counter job dissatisfaction) rather than a human relations approach. By stressing human relations, motivation comes

from psychic rewards, psychological growth, and professional autonomy. These are the motivation needs that, according to Herzberg, bring job satisfaction.

Another criticism of career ladders is that they will be nothing more than job ladders, thereby further undermining the status of teaching as a profession. The career ladder may become an evaluation-driven mechanism, peopled mainly by administrators, because of the political pressure for states to implement career ladders to increase teacher accountability. We believe this is a likely though perhaps unintended outcome of a career ladder system. For in implementing what F. W. Taylor would refer to as "quality control" (Callahan, 1962), the tendency is to encourage competence through standardization rather than excellence through motivation. This, we believe, would be disastrous.

EVALUATION AND A "ONE BEST SYSTEM" OF PEDAGOGY

We fear that career ladders may encourage a "one best system" of pedagogical practice in which teachers learn only those skills necessary to "pass the test" and move from one rung on the job ladder to the next. A physical educator who truly wanted to move from a Level I instructor to a Level II physical educator may be tempted to adopt the "party line." Because of this pressure, we might discourage and lose rather than retain innovative, creative physical educators. An unintended consequence of the career ladder program could be as damaging as its intended outcome is strengthening.

Although a career ladder system of evaluation may lead to identification of competence levels in teaching to improve classroom practice, the question is, identification by whom? We worry that in a push for teachers to focus on more easily evaluated, objective, measurable, behavioral outcomes, the art or craft of teaching physical education may become subservient to rather than an equal partner with the "science" of teaching. This issue is being faced and even overcome, as evidenced by the efforts of Phillip Schlechty and his colleagues in the Charlotte-Mecklenburg schools of North Carolina (Schlechty, 1985). To resolve the issues of evaluation satisfactorily, however, teachers must have as much input as administrators and legislators in devising evaluation instruments and processes. Teachers must have a say in the standards demanded of their own profession. Furthermore, there should be no quotas for the numbers of people eligible for each rank/rung/level. If this happens, then the career ladder becomes a puppet of the budget rather than a tool of teacher development.

In stressing the danger of evaluation driving the system, we have implied that administrators and legislators will wield more power

in the gymnasium then they already do. In fact, the majority of career ladder plans call for a system of evaluation in which a broad range of interested parties participate. Although this may be perceived as making the evaluation system fairer, we believe it will also make it very unwieldy. There may be a temptation to focus primarily on student learning measures such as mastering learning, with their accompanying limitations as objective measures, rather than trying to find new systems that don't merely settle for the efficient competence of the quality control mentality but actually promote excellence. We hope the evaluation unit does not become a self-serving enterprise, rewarding those who were mentored through one system at the expense of those who didn't go to the "right" school. (This type of networking exists to a limited degree in the state of New York with the selection of question writers for the Regent's exams [Fleury, 1985]. A dangerous precedent would be set if this is allowed to happen.)

AN EMPHASIS ON INSTRUCTION

As if the problems of evaluation did not provide enough concern, we foresee a far more damaging potential consequence in instruction resulting from a career ladder system. One of the attractions of teaching has traditionally been the high degree of autonomy and responsibility afforded the teacher from the first day he or she enters the classroom or gymnasium. This is one of the most appealing aspects of teaching's "subjective warrant" (Lortie, 1975). A state-mandated, evaluation-driven ladder system can only limit a teacher's autonomy. This will negatively affect the subjective warrant of teaching in general, and thus of teaching physical education in particular.

Furthermore, because of the emphasis on instruction at the lower levels of the career ladder, teachers at the entry level, and to a lesser degree at Level II, will be responsible only for the execution of skills and not for their conception. We will be encouraging the isolated execution of someone else's plans— the ultimate in scientific management! To use Apple's notion (1982), we will be "deskilling" our teachers in the interests of efficiency and productivity rather than reskilling them in the interests of their own development and thus their job satisfaction and motivation. We may therefore have the unintended consequence of cooling out, in the very early stages of their careers, talented inductees who want more from being educators than becoming instructional technicians. For a beginning physical educator to be told what to teach, when, to whom, and how to teach it in order to best satisfy the evaluation unit seems to be a worse scenario than that already faced by beginning teachers.

We do believe that good things can come from career ladders for teachers and students, however, but only if they are used primarily as a tool for teacher development and not for summative evaluation.

CAREER LADDERS AND TEACHER EDUCATION

Career ladders, effectively designed and implemented, can have positive consequences in terms of teacher preparation.

1. The student teaching experience will become less haphazard. Exemplary teachers will be identified by a district or state system, and cooperating teachers will be properly remunerated for their efforts with students, because their involvement would be counted as part of their teaching load.

2. The end of student teaching will not be a point of closure. Career ladders promote the fact that learning to teach well is a lifelong process; teacher preparation institutions can persuade their students, and themselves, that

the production of seasoned professionals is not their goal. If properly articulated, the transition from student teaching in physical education to teaching students physical education should become much smoother and aid in the retention of first-year teachers.

3. Ladders will further encourage in-service and continuing education of teachers at all levels. Learning to teach requires practice and reflection. Teacher preparation institutions could offer summer workshops or seminar series for graduates as an ongoing program once they are initially certified at Level I. These institutions need to help insure that graduates have both feet securely planted on the first rung of the career ladder.

All of the above are based on the assumption that the relationship between public schools and teacher preparation institutions is well articulated. Where this is not the case, we in teacher preparation institutions should be striving toward it. What are the possible outcomes if this articulation is poor or if a performance-based career ladder system starts to drive the teacher preparation system?

If articulation is poor, it seems likely that little will change in terms of teacher preparation. First-year teachers will have to rely on the safety net of the career ladder's Level I to help them through the induction process. This may be preferable to the present system, which offers little organized help for beginning teachers, but it would be best if the teacher preparation institution offered its graduates ongoing support.

If a performance-based career ladder system begins to drive the teacher preparation system, we foresee serious problems. Perhaps the most serious is that teacher preparation institutions might narrow their focus to preparing students for success in gaining permanent Level I status. That is, their aim would be solely to produce good instructors with the skills to move from Level I to Level II, rather than concentrating on preparing flexible, reflective, well-rounded, informed educators. This would be particularly serious if institutional accreditation were to be evaluated in any way on the basis of graduates' success as Level I instructors. Teacher preparation institutions would then become party to "deskilling" teaching; and in a performance-based evaluation-driven system in which quality control and scientific management techniques were king, this would surely be a possibility.

Concerning physical education, such deskilling would be particularly serious, because we are already accused by some of knowing only the how-to with little understanding of the why of teaching. Physical educators as well as art and music teachers need more than ever to be able to justify their presence in schools at a time when teaching problem-solving skills, higher-order thinking skills, and computer literacy is the order of the day. We must be able to persuade our colleagues and our clientele that being physically "literate" is also of primary importance for tomorrow's citizens.

We have suggested that career ladders focus primarily on the hygiene elements in Herzberg's motivation-hygiene theory. Although the rewards and incentives of career ladders may limit the potential job dissatisfaction of teachers, they do little to alter the career possibilities for teachers; thus they do not promote greater job satisfaction in Herzberg's terms.

As presently conceived, career ladders limit autonomy at the lower levels and thus may negatively affect both the retention levels of young physical education teachers and the subjective warrant for teaching physical education. Physical education already attracts recruits with low GPAs and low scores on national aptitude tests (Templin, Woodford, and Mulling, 1982). If the physical education profession already attracts people with the specific disposition of, and interest in being, physical activity *instructors*, we may do further damage in terms of our subjective warrant by deskilling our future physical educators and further jeopardizing the quality of the teaching/learning process in physical education.

ALTERNATIVE CAREER PERSPECTIVES

The underlying assumption of those who stress career ladders as a means of promoting teacher development and career advancement is that teachers see, or want to see, their lives in objective, even materialistic, terms. We do not believe that teachers necessarily see themselves as individual agents competing for personal advancement and promotion. One problem with structuring teaching careers as ladders is that we are further bureaucratizing the existing system—a system in which any movement is either up, down, or off the ladder. Our career analysis then is seen only in materialistic terms wherein individuals compete for personal advancement. We dehumanize teaching if we view it in this way. Evaluation becomes the equivalent of quality control and is in the hands of the evaluation unit or its business equivalent, the senior management team. Before we know it, teacher preparation institutions will have to offer warranties on their products!

Certainly there is a need to offer hope for improved instruction to parents and for a structured sequence of posts to teachers who see their career in those objective terms. There also is a need to stress the subjective aspect so that teachers can define their careers in their own terms. Hughes (1937) described this approach as " 'the moving perspective' in which people see their lives 'as a whole' and through which they interpret the meaning of their various attributes, actions, and the things which happen to them" (p. 27). Although a career ladder can aid and abet the process of improving the quality of instruction in physical education, it needs to be embedded within a broader framework that improves the educational experience for teachers as well as for students.

It is in identifying this need to benefit teachers and their development that the notion of a career lattice has been broached as a means of increasing the options available to teachers in career paths and patterns. The lattice offers teachers the opportunity to extend themselves, do the things they are best at, and to concentrate on tasks in which they can contribute most. A career lattice would benefit students by promoting greater motivation and job satisfaction for teachers and would bring greater efficiency for school systems through the improved utilization of their human resources.

The career lattice would combine the career ladder idea of growing into progressively more responsible positions with the notion of variety in terms of roles adopted and activities performed. In effect, the lattice is an attempt to offer lateral movement within education as well as the traditional up-and-down options available with the ladder concept. The lattice implies a network of relationships (California Round Table on Educational Opportunity, 1984). It more fully reflects the subjective career experiences desired by many teachers (Ball and Goodson, 1985) and thus, we believe, would both improve the subjective warrant of teaching and increase the motivation to remain in the profession.

Physical educators have been employing a nascent form of the career lattice for many years by taking on the major roles of both teacher and coach. However, the present teaching structure has only brought role conflict to this effort. Many physical educators are specifically employed to perform both roles in their school. Conflict between the two roles arises because schools and their reward systems, remuneration and consideration, are

not structured accordingly. Kneer (1987) has suggested that the two major causes of teacher/coach conflict are time (in terms of teaching load) and values. She offers a number of viable solutions to the problem, two of which involve separating teaching from coaching.

Yet if interscholastic competition is to maintain its scholastic base and educational value, then the solution to the problem of role conflict is not to be found by separating those roles. Rather, the solution would be better conceived as being contained within the lattice concept. Reducing the teaching load of physical educators who have coaching responsibilities would decrease the level of job satisfaction (hygiene) caused by the role conflict. It would increase job satisfaction (motivation) in that qualified physical educators could use their talents in both areas fully and could gain recognition and achievement for their efforts without suffering the dissatisfaction and guilt associated with role conflict.

If the lattice concept were extended beyond the simple teacher/coach roles, then physical educators at all levels could be more involved in such activities as performance measurement, discipline, tutoring, counseling, administration, curriculum development, program evaluation, and research. The advantages of the lattice, which incorporates the ladder, over the ladder alone include the following:

1. Career diversity for educators
2. Differentiated roles
3. Opportunities for advancement without leaving the gymnasium
4. An increased sense of profession
5. A cadre or community of educators, rather than subject matter specialists, administrators, and so forth
6. Opportunities for staff to utilize their skills and interests to maximum effect
7. Reskilling of physical educators by combining the elements of conception and ex-

ecution in the educational process (California Round Table, 1984).

The lattice concept would force institutions involved in teacher preparation to rethink and restructure their programs. Questions of subject matter knowledge, professional education, and pedagogical skills must all be addressed so as to clarify the focus (although not necessarily unify the vision) in teacher preparation for the future. If the education of our children and the professional lives of teachers are to be improved and enriched, then we must restructure teaching in terms of a lattice. We should not go on trying to improve a system that can only meet the hygiene needs and not the far more important motivation needs of teachers. This is not teacher development. Only a new structure such as that suggested by the lattice concept can truly address the issue of teacher development.

Talk is cheap, and talk of lattices is no exception. States and local districts have found that adopting ladder programs can be extremely expensive. Lattice programs will undoubtedly be even more so. But career development is a vital issue in recruiting and retaining talented teachers. If we are to reform education, merely strengthening the rungs of a ladder that already exists will not suffice. A reshaping of the structure is necessary. We believe the career lattice has the potential to achieve this and would more fully reflect the subjective career experiences desired by many teachers.

At present the lattice is little more than a dream. Further conceptualization and research can determine whether it is a dream worth pursuing, but we believe it bears promise. Improvement of the quality of life for teachers, and thus improved education, would be better broached through truly stressing teacher development. This would involve addressing the problems of (a) recruitment of teachers, including physical education teachers, by improving teaching's subjective warrant; (b) retaining more talented teachers through better career staging and the use of the lattice system; and (c) seeing teaching in human relations terms—as a problem of motivating teachers rather than trying to improve schools by addressing only hygiene needs (thereby further imposing on teachers the techniques of scientific management drawn from business and the technical rationality that that implies).

References

Apple, M. W. (1982). *Education and power*. London: Routledge & Kegan Paul.

Association of Teacher Educators. (1985). *Developing career ladders in teaching*. Reston, VA: Author.

Ball, S. J., and Goodson, I. F. (Eds.). (1985). *Teachers' lives and careers*. London: Falmer.

California Round Table on Educational Opportunity. (1984). *A new design for the K–12 teaching profession and recommended next steps*. Sacramento, CA: Author.

Callahan, R. E. (1962). *Education and the cult of efficiency*. Chicago: University of Chicago Press.

Fleury, S. C. (1985). *State examinations as social policy: A study of factors influencing curriculum policy-making*. Unpublished doctoral dissertation, Syracuse University.

Herzberg, F., Mausner, B., and Snyderman, B. B. (1959). *The motivation to work*. New York: John Wiley.

Herzberg, F. (1966). *Work and the nature of man*. New York: Thomas Crowell.

Herzberg, F. (1976). *The managerial choice*. Homewood, IL: Dow Jones-Irwin.

Hughes, E. C. (1958). *Men and their work*. Glencoe, IL: Free Press.

Kneer, M. (1987). Solutions to teacher/coach problems in secondary schools. *Journal of Physical Education, Recreation, and Dance*. **58**(2), 28–29.

Lortie, D. C. (1975). *Schoolteacher*. Chicago: University of Chicago Press.

Pipho, C. (1984, October). The momentum of education reform. *Phi Delta Kappan*, pp. 85–86.

Program Planners, Inc. (1985). *Metropolitan Life survey of state actions to upgrade teacher education*. New York: Metropolitan Life Insurance Co.

Schlechty, P. C. (1985). Evaluation procedures in the Charlotte-Mecklenburg career ladder program. *Educational Leadership*, **43**(3), 44–47.

Templin, T. J., Woodford, R., and Mulling, C. (1982). On becoming a physical educator: Occupational choice and the anticipatory socialization process. *Quest*, **34**, 119–133.

DISCUSSION QUESTIONS AND ACTIVITIES

1. What is the underlying rationale of career ladders?

2. Explain its objectives.

3. Deering notes that despite positive features of career ladders, teachers have expressed discontent within several state-directed programs. What is the basis of this discontent?

4. According to the article by Chandler and his coauthors, what are the stages of the career ladder and the responsibilities of each stage?

5. Explain Herzberg's theory of job satisfaction, and use it to evaluate career ladders.

6. Chandler and his coauthors fear that career ladders may encourage a "one best system" of pedagogical practice. What do they mean by this, and are their fears well founded?

7. What is the career lattice? Would incorporating the career ladder in the career lattice be superior to using the career ladder alone?

8. Gather information about three states that utilize career ladders. Compare the provisions in each state system, select the one most likely to be effective, and give grounds for your selection.

9. Invite to class teachers who have taught within career ladder systems, and ask them to express their views about the system's effectiveness in achieving its objectives.

10. Organize a debate: "Most Public Schools Should Adopt Career Ladders."

SUGGESTED READINGS

Bobbitt, Sharon A. *Teacher Incentive Programs in the Public Schools: Survey Report*. Washington, D.C.: National Center for Education Statistics, 1989.

Burke, Peter, and Kathryn G. Lind. "Performance Assessment Techniques for Teacher Career Ladder Advancement." *NASSP Bulletin* 71 (September 1987): 27–35.

Capps, Emerson, and others. "Teacher Evaluation and the Career Ladder." *Teacher Education and Practice* 4 (Spring–Summer 1987): 19–24.

Freiberg, H. Jerome. "Career Ladders: Messages from Experience." *Journal of Teacher Education* 38 (July–August 1987): 49–56.

Furtwengler, Carol B. "Lessons from Tennessee's Career Ladder Program." *Educational Leadership* 44 (April 1987): 66–69.

Futrell, Mary. "Career Ladders: An NEA Perspective." *Teacher Education Quarterly* 13 (August 1986): 60–64.

Hart, Ann Weaver. "A Career Ladder's Effect on Teaching Career and Work Attitudes." *American Educational Research Journal* 24 (Winter 1987): 479–503.

Hawley, Willis D. "Designing and Implementing Performance-Based Career Ladder Plans." *Educational leadership* 43 (November 1985): 57–61.

Johns, Horace E. "Faculty Perceptions of a Teacher Career Ladder Program." *Contemporary Education* 59 (Summer 1988): 198–203.

Johnson, Susan Moore. "Incentives for Teachers: What Motivates, What Matters." *Educational Administration Quarterly* 22 (Summer 1986): 54–79.

Malen, Betty, and Ann Weaver Hart. "Career Ladder Reform: A Multi-Level Analysis of Initial Efforts." *Educational Evaluation and Policy Analysis* 9 (Spring 1987): 9–23.

Murphy, Michael J., and Ann Weaver Hart. "Career Ladder Reforms." *Teacher Educational Quarterly* 13 (Autumn 1986): 51–59.

Oliver, Bernard, and Timothy Chandler. "Quality Programs through Quality Instruction." *Journal of Physical Education, Recreation, and Dance* 58 (August 1987): 55–58.

CHAPTER 14

BILINGUAL EDUCATION

Bilingual education has become an important part of American and Canadian education, marked by the testing of a number of approaches during the 1960s and the growth and spread of bilingual education during the 1970s. Historically, the United States has tended to assimilate foreign-speaking people from European backgrounds, but American Indians, Puerto Ricans, and Mexican-Americans have been less linguistically assimilated. In Canada, even before the Bilingualism and Biculturalism Commission's report (1968), educators urged the introduction of French (or English in French-speaking schools) in elementary grades at as early an age as possible.

Bilingual children traditionally tended to find that neither language served them well in coping with academic work. Educators, however, have generally underestimated the influence of the home language and culture. Those who survive academically are frequently asked to choose between their heritage and the dominant culture, a choice that may result in isolating themselves from their culture and their family.

Bilingual education seeks to overcome these problems. Bilingual education is designed to provide schooling fully or partly in a second language for the purpose of enabling students to acquire proficiency in the second language while simultaneously maintaining their proficiency in the first language and fully promoting their overall educational development. English is learned not as an end in itself but as one of many tools—the home language is another—for the development of skills, attitudes, and basic concepts.

At one time school officials, in those cases where there were few bilingual children, did nothing about the problem or perceived it as a problem of low IQ. Some early programs focused on vocabulary items without building a syntactic framework for using words. This was followed by an approach in the 1950s and early 1960s of teaching English as a second language by using drill exercises; however, this approach found little role for the mother tongue. As late as 1967 in the United States, the Bilingual Education Act developed curricula and Spanish language instruction but gave little attention to the development of bilingual teachers.

EQUITY, QUALITY, AND EFFECTIVENESS IN BILINGUAL EDUCATION

GEORGE M. BLANCO

George M. Blanco (b. 1937) has taught at the elementary, high school, and university levels. His main interests have been in the areas of second language teaching and learning and bilingual education. He held the position of Director of Foreign Languages at the Texas Education Agency and, later, that of Director of the Office of Bilingual Education at the University of Texas at Austin. He has served as a consultant to state and federal agencies, as well as to American schools in various Latin American countries. He currently teaches full-time in the area of bilingual education at the University of Texas at Austin.

Federal and state attention to bilingual education in the United States during the past eighteen years has been characterized by controversy and debate concerning its effectiveness, its cost to the taxpayer, its philosophy, and its lack of a conceptual framework with the necessary research underpinnings. Bilingual education during this period has also been characterized as compensatory in nature, i.e., designed primarily for lower socioeconomic students of limited English-language proficiency. It has also been implemented as a transitional program whereby the students' first language is eventually replaced altogether by English for instructional purposes.

Essentially, the goal of bilingual education in the United States has been to insure that non-English-speaking (NES) or limited-English-speaking (LES) students acquire a good command of the English language and succeed academically in the subjects that comprise the school curriculum.

This paper addresses the issue of equity of instruction for a segment of the student population referred to by Hawley (1982:207) as "children at risk." In his words:

Children at risk are assumed to have special needs that set them apart, at least to some extent, from other children and, therefore, disadvantages . . . What children at risk have in common is a set of circumstances which, while different, are likely to reduce the effectiveness or, in come cases, make inappropriate conventional educational practices. Business as usual for children at risk is risky business.

NES/LES children fall into the category of children at risk by virtue of the linguistic and cultural circumstances which make them different from the monolingual English speaker of the majority culture in the United States. The issue that NES/LES children are linguistically and culturally different has always worked to their disadvantage—the fact that they spoke a language other than English was *their* problem, not the school's, and it was *their* duty to conform to the school's all-English model from the outset. This was usually the case, despite the much touted maxim heard by several generations of future teachers: "Begin where the child is."

The United States Supreme Court case *Lau v. Nichols*, decreed that English-only educa-

This essay was written especially for this book.

tional programs did not provide equal educational opportunity to Chinese-speaking students in San Francisco. In the educational arena, the terms *equal* and *equitable* have often been used synonymously. According to Salomone (1982:11) equality "refers specifically to division, partition, and redistribution . . . it refers to numerical equality and to equal treatment or inputs. Equity, on the other hand, is a broader concept encompassing justice, equality, humanity, morality, and right."

Following this line of thinking, children at risk need not only educational opportunities that are equal but also opportunities that are equitable. Educational equity for NES/LES students, as it is implemented in the schools, refers to special programs, strategies, and materials which go beyond those regularly in place for monolingual English-speaking students. The mounting of special programs for children at risk, then, is seen as a necessary step toward assuring that equity be present before true equality can exist. Given the fact, however, that programs for children at risk, such as bilingual education, are compensatory in nature, the question of quality, effectiveness, and excellence surfaces.

EDUCATIONAL QUALITY AND EFFECTIVENESS

While there is a considerable body of literature regarding bilingual education outside the United States (Paulston, 1978), research in this country has been supported in a concerted manner by the federal government since 1979 through funding under Part C Research Agenda of ESEA Title VII. Prior to this effort, most of the research conducted fell into the area of program evaluation using a quantitative paradigm. Comparative studies using a quantitative paradigm required large student samples to provide reliable statistics. According to Goodrich (1980), the only language groups that have large enough numbers of students to warrant use of quantitative comparisons are the Spanish, French, and Navajo. Vázquez (1981) feels that this observation is important because cultural and linguistic differences affect such elements as educational practices, student achievement, motivation, and so forth, thus rendering interlanguage group comparisons less reliable. Research to show bilingual education effectiveness, or lack thereof, has been difficult to conduct. The evaluation of Title VII Spanish/English bilingual education programs conducted by the American Institutes for Research (AIR) (Danoff, 1978) has been criticized for its inadequacies (Gray, 1977 and 1978; O'Malley, 1978). Yet, Troike (1978) states that not all of the negative findings can be dismissed and that program weaknesses should be corrected. Both Saravia-Shore (1979) and Vázquez (1981) feel that effectiveness is a relative term concerning several critical questions: What is to be measured? In relation to what? Using what criteria? Selected by whom?

Troike (1978 and 1981) in his reviews of bilingual education program evaluations in the United States concludes that quality programs can be effective in providing equal educational opportunities for NES/LES children. He feels strongly that if a program does not provide equal educational opportunities, there is something wrong with the program. It is interesting to note that in the programs examined by Troike, the students in the bilingual education programs generally performed as well as, and in some cases better than, students in monolingual programs at the district or national levels in a variety of subjects. It is particularly noteworthy that the standardized tests used in these programs were in English. One of the main criticisms about bilingual education has been the notion either that children are not exposed sufficiently to the English language or that time spent on instruc-

research

tion in the native language takes valuable time away from exposure to English.

There has been considerable research, both at the applied and the theoretical levels, to show that learning through two languages not only helps children learn the required subject matter, but that it also promotes their mastering the English language better than an all-English setting. Saravia-Shore and Arvizu (in press) compiled a descriptive summary of a series of research projects which also support the general use of the students' native language for a portion of the instructional program.

We return to the issue of effectiveness, since its definition or definitions are of prime importance to the concept of bilingual education. The major part of the literature on effective instruction deals with monolingual settings. Even in such settings, it is highly improbable that there exist universal conditions of teaching, given the complex nature of the classroom teaching and learning (Tikunoff and Vázquez-Faría, 1982).

Barnes (1981:2) provides an operational definition of the "effective teacher": "The 'effective teacher' is the teacher whose classes regularly score higher on standardized achievement tests than do classes of other teachers of similar students after entering differences among classes are statistically removed."

Barnes (1981:10) goes on to state that "teachers who establish both a task or work-oriented atmosphere in the classroom and a warm, supportive environment for their students are providing those students with a successful learning environment." *The Significant Bilingual Instructional Features Study* (SBIF) (Tikunoff, et al., 1981) was based on the premise that effective instructional strategies are probably generic and are similar in monolingual and bilingual settings. The SBIF Study did not use traditional achievement test performance as a measure of effectiveness.

Actual observation was used, based on an adaptation of the observation system used by Good and Grouws (1979). Two types of student outcomes were used for 232 students in fifty-eight classrooms: Academic Learning Time (ALT) and establishing the students' competent participation in instructional work activity. ALT is the amount of time a student spends in a content area engaged in learning tasks with a high degree of accuracy. These students achieved a success rate of 80 percent, which averages to eighty-four minutes per student per day of ALT. The second student outcome, participation in instructional work activity, is particularly important for NES/LES students. Participation requires "that a student understand what is going on, what the task requirements are, what the completed product must look like, what the steps are for completing the task, what the teacher's expectations are with regard to task completion, and so forth." (Tikunoff and Vázquez-Faría, 1982:249–50). It is obvious, then, that if students do not understand the language of instruction, they will not perform satisfactorily and will fall behind academically.

The SBIF Study speculates that the teacher sample used was effective, as judged by their use of active teaching behaviors and by their producing desired student performance in terms of ALT and student participation in instruction. Further, three skills or behaviors distinguish successful teachers in the sample from effective teachers in monolingual settings.

1. *Teachers in the sample used both L1 and L2 [first language and second language] for instruction . . . Particularly for NES/LES who have no English or little English proficiency, this allows access to instruction.*

2. *Teachers focused some instructional time on English language development, using variations of the bilingual instructional strategies . . . designed to develop English language proficiency while concurrently insur-*

ing that NES/LES will have access to regular instruction in the content areas so that they don't fall behind while learning English.

3. *Preliminary analysis of the descriptions of instruction for teachers in the sample reveal frequent use of behavior which appears to be culturally relevant and specific for the ethnolinguistic group of NES/LES in a given classroom.*

For children to participate successfully in the instructional process, they must understand what is going on and what is expected of them. Equitable instructional programs, therefore, require that a school go above and beyond the regular school curriculum for children at risk who do not understand or speak the school language. Equally important, however, is the finding that effective teachers exhibit similar behaviors whether the setting being evaluated is monolingual or bilingual.

There are, of course, studies to support an antibilingual education stance. The AIR Study (Danoff, 1978) cited earlier, is perhaps, the best known example. Paulston (1978:188) states that "A study can be found to support virtually every possible opinion." The issue, then, is not so much whether bilingual education, ESL, or any other educational treatment "works" for the NES/LES children but whether students can participate actively in the instructional activities of the curriculum. Of the present options available, bilingual education seems to be the only approach that promotes understanding and thus encourages active participation by NES/LES students in the instructional activities, as far as the content areas are concerned.

Critics of dual-language instruction, however, are quick to point out that time learning subject matter in L1 is time taken away from the learning of English. As was shown by some of the studies reviewed by Troike (1978), participation in a sound bilingual education program does not retard student academic progress nor the learning of English. There is

abundant anecdotal information regarding the academic success experienced by foreigners, such as Mexicans, who come to the United States and who often surpass their Spanish-speaking classmates born in this country (Lazos, 1981). The fact that foreign-born students often surpass their United States-born classmates in English (and consequently in the content areas) is, perhaps, best explained by the work of Cummins (1979) and the research conducted in Scandinavia by Skutnabb-Kangas and Toukomaa (1976) and Skutnabb-Kangas (1980).

Cummins has come forth with two hypotheses which may help to explain the anomalous situation of foreign-born students' achieving a higher level of academic success than United States-born NES/LES students. The first is the threshold hypothesis which proposes that certain levels of L1 development must be attained by children to avoid cognitive deficits and to obtain cognitive benefits of bilingualism. If children's L1 is interrupted and discontinued before reaching the "threshold," around the age of ten or eleven, their cognitive development will be retarded. Cummins (1979) and Skutnabb-Kangas and Toukomaa (1976) have advanced the hypothesis that the cognitive aspects of L1 and L2 are interdependent and that proficiency in L2 is partially a function of the L1 proficiency level at the time the child was intensively exposed to L2. Since L1 and L2 cognitive/academic language proficiency are manifestations of the same underlying linguistic proficiency, literacy in L1 will have a direct bearing on literacy in L2. These hypotheses appear to be supported by the work of Skutnabb-Kangas and Toukomaa (1976), who indicate that, in general, the better students preserve their native language, the better are their prerequisites for learning a second language. These researchers report that the ability to do abstract thinking in the mother tongue is a prerequisite for learning mathematical concepts.

From the standpoint of cognitive development for NES/LES students, then, the research strongly supports the idea of insuring L1 development until they have reached the "threshold" level and have attained the necessary literacy skills. From the point of view of English language development, the research also suggests a strong L1 base, since proficiency in L2 is directly related to proficiency in L1. This relationship has also been supported by some of the research reported by Saravia-Shore and Arvizu (in press). An equitable solution to the dilemma would be to insure a quantitative and qualitative *continuation* of the children's L1 for a longer period of time than is now commonly done. The issue does not revolve solely around the question of whether children can exit from a bilingual program to participate in an all-English learning environment. Rather, it deals with the notion of insuring the most efficient type of instruction for NES/LES students. By exiting students from the bilingual education program before L1 is firmly established, we may be truncating their cognitive/academic skills and their English language development.

LANGUAGE ATTITUDES

Sociolinguists maintain that the importance and prestige of a language are essentially based on the persons who use it, the audience, the purpose, and place where it is used (d'Angelan and Tucker, 1973; Fishman, 1972; Labov, 1966). If students perceive their native language to be unimportant by virtue of its minimal use or its use in a begrudging fashion, the result can only be negative. Tikunoff and Vázquez-Faría (1981:252–53) agree, stating that:

> A strong argument for bilingual instruction for NES/LES rests with the assumption that when instruction is provided only in English, a hierarchy of language use is constructed. At the top of that hierarchy is English, and those who can use it competently thereafter are perceived to be somehow "better" than those who cannot. If the NES/LES never hears his/her home language used in the classroom for instruction, or hears it only in a negative context for reprimands, attitudes might develop which place English in a positive frame and the child's home language in a negative frame.

Hansen and Johnson (1981), in their extensive review of the literature on language attitudes, found that language learning is related to self-esteem. "This literature clearly demonstrates that some language varieties are generally held to be inferior to others and that children quickly adopt the dominant evaluations, perhaps to the detriment of their own self-esteem or cultural identity" (Hansen and Johnson, 1981:4). Positive self-esteem is seen as promoting positive attitudes toward learning and participating and succeeding in school work (Tikunoff and Vázquez-Faría, 1981).

The question of language attitudes in general and toward minority languages and minority groups in particular is an extremely complex one. Whatever the source of language attitudes or attitudes toward ethnolinguistic groups may be, it is quite evident that children adopt "dominant evaluations," to reiterate Hansen and Johnson's term. Children very often exhibit negative attitudes toward their native language, even in a bilingual education program. The pressure to abandon the native language in favor of English, exclusively, is significant, and it is pervasive throughout the educational system, the students' homes, and society at large.

The learning of English is one, if not the primary, goal of bilingual education programs in the United States, and it is vital that NES/LES students learn English and learn it well. The work of Cummins (1979) and the Scandinavian research cited earlier (Skutnabb-Kangas and Toukomaa, 1976), have a direct bearing on the ability of bilingual education students to learn English well. If children are tacitly or openly encouraged to abandon their native language in favor of English before reaching the threshold level, bilingual education will not go beyond a compensatory program with all of the negative opinions that accompany such programs. It is my contention that effective teaching in bilingual or monolingual programs is directly related to and, indeed, shaped by forces outside the school itself. The school, as one of the main purveyors of the mainstream culture, necessarily reflects the attitudes and values of that society. This perspective is not new, and it is supported in the literature on language attitudes and on social educational change.

FACTORS BEYOND THE CLASSROOM

Paulston (1978) contends that questions regarding bilingual education have shifted with more attention focused on factors outside the programs themselves as causal variables. Bilingual education has usually been looked on as the independent variable and the children's behavior as the dependent variable. Paulston (1978:191) goes on to state that:

> We can begin to understand these questions only when we see bilingual education as the result *of certain societal factors, rather than the* cause *of certain behaviors in children. Unless we attempt in some way to account for the sociohistorical, cultural, economic, and political factors which lead to certain forms of bilingual education, we will not be able to understand or to assess the consequences of that education.*

The issue of research which focuses on the classroom, as opposed to research which looks at the larger context within which the classroom exists, is examined by Akinnasso (1981). This researcher states that the sociolinguistic studies of educational inequality have been criticized by such writers as Ogbu

(1974) Karabel and Halsey (1977) for emphasizing micro rather than macrocosmic processes. These studies result in explanations that tell *how*, but not *why*. Gumperz (1980) feels that one cannot dismiss the classroom altogether. Since students spend a significant part of their formative years in school, he says that what happens there can either change or reinforce values and attitudes brought from outside the classroom.

Hansen and Johnson (1981:2) synthesize this whole issue:

> *Classroom learning is seen as more than a simple acquisition of knowledge and skills such as reading, writing, and arithmetic; it is seen as a process of active effort to understand and cope with the demands, opportunities, and restrictions of the social environment of the classroom and school—demands, opportunities, and restrictions that are themselves changing, and often are symbolically created not only by teachers, administrators, and policymakers, but also by the child's community and family, and by new technologies of teaching, learning, and living.*

It is my opinion that the negative attitudes about minority ethnolinguistic groups and their languages have a direct effect on the nature of the instructional program and on the learning processes of the students themselves. We have evidence that bilingual education can be effective, that it can promote academic quality, that students can learn the required subject mater, and that they can learn the English language . . . provided that the right educational and societal circumstances are present.

CONCLUDING REMARKS

The school and societal contexts in which programs for children at risk operate are as important, if not more so, than the actual instructional strategies used by the teacher. Programs, such as those using a dual-language approach, often operate as an append-age, as something to be tolerated, rather than as an integral part of the instructional and curricular program. The result is circular: the programs are appendages because of negative attitudes, and the fact that the programs are appendages further reinforces these attitudes. The opinion held about such programs on the part of all teachers, administrators, parents, the community, and society at large determines what the teacher can or cannot do. Negative attitudes about programs for children at risk and about their native language and cultural group breed equally negative attitudes, on the part of the students, about the special instructional efforts and about themselves.

Educational quality, achievement, effectiveness, and equity are not mutually exclusive concepts. Quite the contrary, these concepts should be mutually supportive to produce the desired educational results.

References

Akinnaso, F. N. "Research on Minority Languages and Educational Achievement: A Synthesis and an Interpretation." 1981. ERIC Document ED 216 517.

Barnes, S. *Synthesis of Selected Research of Teaching Findings*. Austin, TX: The University of Texas at Austin, Research and Development Center for Teacher Education, 1981.

Cummins, J. "Cognitive/Academic Language Proficiency, Linguistic Interdependence, the Optimum Age Question and Some Other Matters." in *Working Papers on Bilingualism*, No. 19. Toronto: Ontario Institute for Studies in Education, 1979.

d'Anglejan, A. and Tucker, G. R. "Sociolinguistic Correlates of Speech Style in Quebec." In R. W. Shuy and R. W. Fasold, eds., *Language Attitudes: Current Trends and Prospects*. Washington, D. C.: Georgetown University Press, 1973.

Danoff, M. N. *Evaluation of the Impact of ESEA Title VII Spanish/English Bilingual Education Programs: Overview of Study and Findings*. Palo Alto, CA: American Institutes for Research, 1978.

Fishman, J. A. *Sociolinguistics: A Brief Introduction*. Rowley, MA: Newbury House Publishers, 1972.

Good, T. L. and Grouws, D. "The Missouri Mathematics Effectiveness Project: An Experimental Study in Fourth-Grade Classrooms" *Journal of Educational Psychology*, 1979, 71, 335–362.

Goodrich, R. L. *Planning Factors for Studies of Bilingual Instructional Features. Bilingual Instructional Features Planning Study*. Vol. 3. Washington, D. C.: National Institute of Education, 1980.

Gray, T. C. "Responses to AIR Study." (Duplicated.) Arlington, VA: Center for Applied Linguistics, 1977.

———. "Challenge to USOE Final Evaluation of the Impact of ESEA Title VII Spanish/English Bilingual Education Program." (Duplicated.) Arlington, VA: Center for Applied Linguistics, 1978.

Gumperz, J. J. "Conversational Inference and Classroom Learning." In J. L. Green and C. Wallat, eds., *Ethnography and Language in Educational Settings*. Norwood, NJ: Ablex, 1980.

Hansen, D. A. and Johnson, V. A. *The Social Contexts of Learning in Bilingual Classrooms: An Interpretive Review of the Literature on Language Attitudes*. Rosslyn, VA: National Clearinghouse for Bilingual Education, 1981.

Hawley, W. D. Preface, "Effective Educational Strategies for Children at Risk." *Peabody Journal of Education*, 1982, 59 (4), 207–208.

Karabel, Jr. and Halsey, A. H. "Educational Research: A Review and an Interpretation." In J. Karabel and A. H. Halsey, eds., *Power and Ideology in Education*. New York: Oxford University Press, 1977.

Labov, W. *The Social Stratification of English in New York City*. Arlington, VA: Center for Applied Linguistics, 1966.

Lazos, Héctor. *A Study of the Relationship of Language Proficiency in the Motor Tongue and Acquisition of Second Language Reading Skills in Bilingual Children at Age Twelve*. Unpublished Doctoral Dissertation. The University of Texas at Austin, August 1981.

Ogbu, J. U. *The Next Generation: An Ethnography of Education in an Urban Neighborhood*. New York: Academic Press, 1974.

O'Malley, J. M. "Review of the Evaluation of the Impact of ESEA Title VII Spanish/English Bilingual Program." *Bilingual Resources*, 1978, 1 (2), 6–10.

Paulston, C. B. "Bilingual/Bicultural Education." In L. S. Shulman, ed., *Review of Research in Education*, 6. Itaska, IL: R. E. Peacock Publishers, Inc., 1978.

Salomone, R. M. "Public Policy and the Law: Legal Precedence and Prospects for Equity in Education." 1982, in press.

Saravia-Shore, M. "A Ethnographic Evaluation/Research Model for Bilingual Programs." In R. V. Padilla, ed., *Bilingual Education and Public Policy in the United States*. Ypsilanti, MI: Eastern Michigan University, 1979.

Saravia-Shore, M. and Arvizu, S., eds., *Cross-Cultural and Communication Competencies: Ethnographies for Educational Programs for Language Minority Students*. West Cornwall, CT: Horizon Communications (in press).

Skutnabb-Kangas, T. *Language in the Process of Cultural Assimilation and Structural Incorporation of Linguistic Minorities*. Rosslyn, VA: National Clearinghouse for Bilingual Education, 1980.

Skutnabb-Kangas, T. and Toukamaa, P. *Teaching Migrant Children's Mother Tongue and Learning the Language of the Host Country in the Context of the Sociocultural Situation of the Migrant Family*. Helsinki: Finnish National Commission for UNESCO, 1976.

Tikunoff, W. J. and Vázquez-Faría, J. A. "Successful Instruction for Bilingual Schooling." *Peabody Journal of Education*, 1982, 59 (4), 234–271.

Tikunoff, W. J. et al. *Preliminary Analysis of the Data for Part I of the Significant Bilingual Instructional Features Study*. San Francisco: Far West Laboratory for Educational Research and Development, 1981.

Troike, R. C. "Research Evidence for the Effectiveness of Bilingual Education." *NABE Journal*, 1978, 3 (1), 13–24.

Troike, R. C. "Synthesis of Research on Bilingual Education." *Educational Leadership*, March 1981, 498–504.

Vázquez, J. A. "The Social, Political, and Instructional Contexts of the Bilingual Public Education Movement in the U. S.: A Brief Overview." In W. J. Tikunoff, et al., *Preliminary Analysis of the Data for Part I of the Significant Bilingual Instructional Features Study*. San Francisco: Far West Laboratory for Educational Research and Development, 1981.

MURIEL PASKIN CARRISON

¡BILINGUAL—NO!

Muriel Paskin Carrison, a former elementary school teacher in New York and California, has extensive experience in multicultural programs at the school and university levels. She is now Professor of Education at California State University, Dominguez Hills, in Carson.

People of Hispanic heritage are the second largest minority group in the United States, comprising about 7 percent of our population. Almost 70 percent of this group are of Mexican ancestry. Of this 70 percent, 35 percent have little or no facility in English, 25 percent earn incomes below the poverty level, and 23 percent have less than five years of education.[1] While such low levels of achievement might not be surprising among recent immigrants, they persist even among a disproportionate number of Mexican-American families *who have lived in the United States for several generations.*[2]

Over the past few decades, educators, community leaders, and legislators became convinced that the academic and socio-economic problems of Mexican-Americans were caused by the failure of public education to meet their distinctive needs. Therefore, they reasoned, school curricula should be changed to emphasize pride in Hispanic traditions and to provide instruction in Spanish as well as in English; these two steps would improve achievement among Mexican-American children and help them take their rightful place in our national life.

Accordingly, in 1965 Congress passed the first federal legislation to help school systems establish programs for students with limited proficiency in English. In the seventeen years since, we have invested more than one billion dollars for specific Spanish language and heritage curricula.[3]

How were bilingual education programs designed and implemented? What do they tell us about educating the children of the immigrants we can expect in coming decades? Perhaps most important, how productive has our billion-dollar investment in bilingual education been?

PROGRAM DESIGN

The Bilingual Education Act required the schools to teach (1) some degree of each child's native language, (2) some degree of English, (3) some degree of each child's native heritage, and (4) some degree of the cultures of all children in the United States, and to maintain some degree of class integration.[4] "Bi" lingual was defined as teaching in two languages—the child's native tongue and English.

Apart from these broad requirements, the act left all specific decisions about course methods, grade-level content, and student admission and exit criteria to individual school districts. The type of program selected seems to have been determined by the availability of teaching personnel and by political pressures within the community.[5]

Although the act specified no single minority group, 70 percent of English-language de-

From Muriel Paskin Carrison, "¡Bilingual—No!" *Principal* 62 (January 1983): 9, 42–44. Reprinted with permission.

ficient students are of Hispanic heritage, and three-quarters of this group are of Mexican ancestry.[6] The legislation was primarily spearheaded by leaders of this ethnic community, the major portion of funding is allocated to this group, and the federal, state, and school district directors of these programs have been, for the most part, of Hispanic and Mexican ancestry.[7] Hence an analysis of programs for Mexican-American children offers a good overall view of the assumptions, practices, and results of our national experiment with bilingual education.

In general, school districts responded to the Bilingual Education Act with four types of linguistic programs and one cultural heritage model. Those developed for Mexican-American youngsters ranged from total English immersion with little native language and culture, to almost total Spanish instruction and Mexican heritage studies.

1. English Immersion/ESL

Several school districts, such as Fairfax County, Virginia, and Buena Park, California, have a shortage of qualified language teachers and children from many different language communities—sometimes as many as eighty native languages including such exotic tongues as Lao-Hmong and Swahili.[8] Since adequate "bi" lingual programs were obviously impossible, these districts provided intensive English immersion or ESL (English as a Second Language) techniques as needed by each child.

Children are placed in separate classes for special training in English until they are acceptably proficient and are then placed in regular grade-level classrooms for instruction in all subjects in English. These districts have reported success in academic achievement and no perceived psychological trauma to the minority learner.[9] Critics state that immersion was a failure in the past, and that its use

represents an essential denial of Spanish being as equally viable a language as English.[10]

2. Mixed Language Proficiency

Some school districts initially place all children, regardless of their English-speaking ability, in regular grade-level classrooms, but then provide additional instruction for them in various combinations of English and their native tongue. This separate instruction is provided by special teachers, assigned to one or more schools, who take the children from their regular classes for subject-matter and language instruction for a few hours each week. Where qualified teachers are unavailable, some schools have hired native-language speaking community aides.

Schools using these types of "pullout" programs also report success.[11] Critics claim these procedures frequently result in children's being labeled as "inferior" by their classmates and teachers, that language is taught in artificial settings, and that the child's studies are fragmented.[12] Although the aides are an important link with the community, they often have less than a grade school education themselves and no valid educational training but are given total responsibility for the child's instruction.

3. Segregated Language Proficiency

A third type of remedial language program has been developed by school districts with substantial populations speaking the same minority language. Children are tested and separated into classes of proficient English speakers, limited English speakers (LES) and non-English speakers (NES)—often called "LES/NES" programs. In some school districts, such as Los Angeles and San Antonio, special schools and special classrooms have been created for these children.

Since there is a shortage of bilingual personnel, children are usually crowded into LES/NES classrooms, taught for the most part in Spanish, and have very little opportunity for interacting with English-speaking peers. In cities such as Los Angeles, where the majority of low-achieving Hispanics live in neighborhoods isolated from the English-speaking parts of the city, this "tracking" model of bilingual education tends to intensify existing social and linguistic segregation.

4. Native Language Immersion

In this type of program, Spanish seems to be the only language of instruction and there are no clear-cut criteria for the degree of proficiency a student must attain before moving into regular classes. It appears that political pressures for dual-language parity and the latent prejudices of school personnel have supported this type of program. One study of thirty-eight federally funded projects found that only one-third of the students had any deficiency in English, and that 85 percent of the students were kept in "Spanish-only" classrooms long after they were proficient in English.[13] Although its research techniques have been criticized, the study supports claims that this type of bilingual education fails to produce students who are proficient in English. In other words, instruction in Spanish does not teach the students English.

5. The Cultural Heritage Model

In the seventeen pages and almost one thousand lines of the Bilingual Education Act Amendment of 1978, only ten lines—one-tenth of one percent of the total wording—make any reference to "culture."[14] Further, the wording of these cultural components of the act is confusing. For example, it mandates schools to teach appreciation of a child's own native culture and "that of other children in American society." This would indicate a "multi" rather than a "bi" cultural approach,

although the terminology used in the act is "bicultural."

This contradictory wording and fuzzy legislative emphasis produced superficial cross-cultural components. For example, some funds were used to translate a few Hispanic folk tales into English ditto handouts, and others provided only very narrow native heritage experiences.[15] Carlos Cortes, professor of history at the University of California, Riverside, has called these experiences "The Three F's: Foods, Festivals and Famous Men . . . Children are treated to tortillas, piñatas, and golf."[16]

RESEARCH FINDINGS

An old adage says that one can always find research evidence to support any opinion one would like to hold. Inasmuch as language is probably the most emotional component of culture,[17] research studies measuring the effectiveness of bilingual education are hampered not only by bias but by the confusion of goals, program types, and population variables.

While the legislated goal of bilingual education was to improve academic achievement by instruction in both the native language and English until the student was proficient in English, some bilingual proponents now seem to advocate native language instruction even *after* students become proficient in English.[18] Other bilingual advocates argue that a major purpose of bilingual education is to compensate for our nation's negligence of foreign languages at the secondary and university levels.[19]

However, this argument blurs the issues: the purpose of foreign language instruction is to help Americans understand and relate to other cultures; the purpose of bilingual education is to help new immigrants succeed in American society. Basing support of bilingual education on the foreign-language needs of American student is as pointless as arguing that since an elephant and a piano both weigh 2,000 pounds, they may both be used as musical instruments.

This confusion of program goals makes reliable research evaluation quite difficult. Furthermore, since program types vary on a continuum from total English immersion to total instruction in Spanish, measurements of success or failure are often quoted without clearly defining the type of bilingual program being studied and evaluated.

Several large research studies conclude that bilingual education programs have produced no perceptible change in academic achievement or drop-out rates of Hispanics.[20] Other studies demonstrate improvement in achievement and conclude that bilingual education is the *only* viable instructional approach for non-English speaking students.[21]

Faced with such conflicting findings, what are we to conclude?

Sifting the wheat of these research reports from the chaff, it is clear that many bilingual programs can, indeed, lay claim to modest success of *some* sort. But if we look at the *intended goal* of the legislation—improvement in the academic and social mobility of Mexican-American youngsters—we find no significant difference: after fifteen years and a billion dollars, these programs have produced no improvement in drop-out rates, in overall academic achievement, in college entrance rates, or in college graduation rates.[22]

Fundamental reasons for this failure may be that the remedies themselves are unsound and difficult to implement or that the causal factors on which these remedies were based are incomplete and invalid.

Let us consider some possibilities.

THE REASONS WHY

First, as to implementation: remedial programs funded to provide native-language teachers for each English-deficient child ig- nored the realities of public school settings. It is not possible to locate or train qualified teachers for school districts with student populations speaking dozens of different native languages. Even school districts where most adults and students were of Hispanic heritage encountered shortages: after more than a decade of successful university training of Spanish bilingual personnel, Los Angeles County alone still has 8,000 unfilled bilingual teaching positions.[23]

Further, linguistically tracked classrooms and schools intensified existing segregation and prevented needed student contact with English-speaking peers. In fact, the Bilingual Act inadvertently gave school officials who were already prejudiced against Mexican-Americans further opportunities to separate children of Mexican heritage from their Anglo classmates.

Second, as to causes: proponents of bilingual legislation assumed that the roots of low achievement among Hispanics were poor self-image and lack of English proficiency. But self-concept and language deficiencies are symptoms—not causes. Segregation with Spanish-speakers may make a limited-English-speaking student more comfortable for a while and increase his self-esteem. But it does not help that student function more effectively in American society. Though pride in native traditions is probably related to an individual's concept of himself, high self-esteem also derives from personal achievement and a feeling of successful participation in the major culture.

Many other immigrant groups also came from poorly educated, rural backgrounds to industrial metropolitan areas in this country with little, if any, knowledge of English. Schools made very few special provisions for these groups. Their children received instruction in English with little provision for any special language instruction. After one or two generations, these people managed to maintain valued parts of their cultural traditions, while at the same time comfortably joining the American mainstream.[24]

Why have Mexican immigrants been less successful than other nationals?

While nonachieving Mexican immigrants share some characteristics with these other groups, there are substantial differences. The rural *campesino* culture from which a majority of our Mexican immigrants come is just beginning to emerge from the medieval serfdom imposed on it by the Spanish conquistadores.[25] For generations, this caste type of feudal agrarianism—much like that of our southern blacks—produced individuals who both wished for change and yet feared it. Because experience has taught them that the future holds little hope and that they have virtually no control over their own destiny, they place little value on institutional education—which is future-oriented.

Instead, their enduring values, priorities, and security rest in maintaining close family relationships. Many adults from nonliterate peasant cultures correctly fear that if their children learn to read—especially in a foreign language—that accomplishment will create a dividing line between adults and children. As a fifty-one-year-old Mexican woman living in the east Los Angeles barrio reported, "my mother was afraid that if we learned a lot we might leave her. She didn't want us to learn English . . . maybe she think we'd look down on her."

Another large and previously unevaluated difference between Mexican immigrants and others is that geographic proximity has always made it possible for them to return home often. This propinquity, combined with Anglo prejudice and irrational immigration laws, appears to have created a mental set of "temporary visitor." Many Mexicans refer to the United States as *al norte*. In other words, they are just going north for a while and then will return *al sur*.[26] Considering themselves "between cultures" in a visiting status, many Mex-

ican immigrants see no reason to make a full emotional commitment to life in the United States and feel no pressure to learn a new language.

Bilingual funds alone will not increase English proficiency or academic achievement in American schools for these Mexicans who really never left home and who prefer to function only within their own native language and culture.

SUMMARY STATEMENT

The concept of bilingual education was probably based on myths generated by political rhetoric and well-meaning emotionalism, rather than on any real research evidence or logical considerations. The realities of bilingual education are that (1) given the linguistic diversity of America's schoolchildren—more than ninety-five different native languages and a currently unprecedented wave of immigration greater than that of the 1900s—it will probably never be possible to adequately staff bilingual programs,[27] (2) bilingual programs have not produced the desired academic, economic, or social changes in Hispanic populations; and (3) bilingual education, in segregating children by linguistic ability, inadvertently worsened societal prejudices and may have prevented children from becoming proficient in English.

In the absence of evidence to the contrary, this writer postulates that the lack of success of some children of Hispanic heritage in our public schools was due to the debilitating prejudice of their teachers and the static, agrarian, child-rearing values of their families. If there is even minimal validity to these postulates, then merely teaching Mexican-American children in Spanish, in rigidly segregated environments, is an expensive exercise in futility; it will only intensify latent prejudices and insure that they will never develop the English language skills necessary for success in higher education and the upwardly mobile professions.

The purported goal of bilingual education legislation was to change the social and economic achievement levels of Hispanic students. To date, there is no evidence that this goal has been achieved. Drop-out rates, underemployment, and college-entrance rates remain unchanged.

In the light of this evidence, logic points to the need for new solutions to the problem. Perhaps one billion dollars should now be allocated to the very difficult problem of attitude change—to modify American prejudice toward Hispanics and to engender the hope of upward mobility within the Hispanic community.

One of the greatest losses any nation can sustain is inadequate utilization of its human potential. We have in our Mexican population a vast reservoir of inadequately employed human potential. Monies spent to *effectively* assist and integrate this population into the mainstream of America will be returned many times over and will greatly enrich the culture of our nation and all its diverse peoples.

Notes

1. U.S. Department of Commerce, *Statistical Abstract of the United States* (Washington, D.C.: Bureau of the Census, 1980). pp. 32, 36–8.

2. Thomas P. Carter, *Mexican Americans in School: A History of Educational Neglect* (New York: College Entrance Examination Board, 1970); Education Commission of the States, *National Assessment of Educational Progress—Hispanic Student Achievement in 5 Learning Areas*, 1971–75 (Report No. BR–2, Washington, D.C.: Government Printing Office, 1977); Alan Pifer, *Bilingual Education and the Hispanic Challenge: President's Annual Report* (New York: Carnegie Corporation of New York, 1980).

3. W. Vance Grant and Leo J. Eiden, *Digest of Educational Statistics* (Washington, D.C.: U.S. Government Printing Office, 1981), p. 184; José

Cardenas, "Budgeting for Bilingual Education," in *Bilingual Education: Current Perspectives*, Center for Applied Linguistics, June 1977; George Neill, "Public Hostility, Budget Cuts Confront Bilingual Education," *Education Week*, March 1982, p. 1.

4. National Clearinghouse for Bilingual Education, *The Bilingual Education Act*, Public Law 95 –561, Education Amendments of 1978, Title VII (Washington, D.C., 1979), p. 3.

5. Elaine Yaffe, "Ambiguous Laws Fuel Debate on Bilingual Education," *Phi Delta Kappan*, June 1981, p. 740.

6. Marquis Academic Media, *Standard Education Almanac* (Chicago: Marquis Who's Who, Inc., 1980) p. 455; G. H. Brown et al., *The Condition of Education for Hispanic Americans* (Washington, D.C.: U.S. Government Printing Office, 1980).

7. Jack K. Campbell, "Senator Yarborough and the Texan 'RWY' Brand on Bilingual Education and Federal Aid," *Educational Studies*, Winter 1980–81, pp. 403–15; "Language: Politics and Survival," *Los Angeles Times*, February 5, 1981.

8. Kenneth Nickel, "Bilingual Education in the Eighties," *Phi Delta Kappan*, May 1982, p. 638; Gerald F. Seib, "English and the Melting Pot," *Wall Street Journal*, October 10, 1980.

9. "English as a Second Language and a First Concern," *Nation's Schools Report*, July 19, 1982, pp. 4–6.

10. Kal Gezi, "Issues in Multicultural Education," *Educational Research Quarterly*, Fall 1981, p. 7; Tomas A. Arciniega. "Bilingual Education in the Eighties: One Hispanic's Perspective." *Educational Research Quarterly*, Fall 1981, p. 26; Charles E. Foster, "Defusing the Issues in Bilingualism and Bilingual Education," *Phi Delta Kappan*, January 1981, p. 342.

11. H. Dulay and H. Burt, *Learning and Teaching Research in Bilingual Education* (San Francisco: National Institute of Education Task Force on Learning and Teaching, 1977).

12. Ricardo Garcia, *Learning in Two Languages* (Bloomington, Ind.: PDK No. 84, 1976), p. 11; Thomas M. Iiams, "The Gathering Storm over Bilingual Education," *Kappan*, December 1977, pp. 226–230.

13. American Institute for Research, *Evaluation of the Impact of 38 ESEA Title VII Spanish/English Bilingual Education Programs* (Washington, D.C.:

U.S. Office of Education, 1978); K. N. Nickel, "Experimentation, Extrapolation, Exaggeration: Thy Name Is Research," *Phi Delta Kappan*, December 1979, pp. 260–61.

14. National Clearinghouse for Bilingual Education, *op cit.*

15. Arenas Soledad, "Innovation in Bilingual/Multicultural Curriculum Development," *Children Today*, May-June 1980, p. 19.

16. Carlos Cortes, "Multicultural Education," an address given to the Conference for Multicultural Education, San Francisco, California, April 1980.

17. Joan Hertzler, *Sociology of Language* (New York: Random House, Inc., 1967).

18. Jose Cardenas and Blandena Cardenas, *The Theory of Incompatibles*, (San Antonio, Texas; Intercultural Center, Research Associates, 1972); Kal Gezi, *op cit.*

19. Elaine Rand, "Elementary Secondary Language Programs: How Bilingual Education Can Help," *National Clearinghouse for Bilingual Education Forum*, November/December 1981, pp. 3–6; Charles R. Foster, *op cit.*

20. American Institutes for Research, *op cit.*: Comptroller General of the United States, *Bilingual Education: An Unmet Need* (Washington, D.C.: General Accounting Office, 1976), Development Associates, *Evaluation of California's Educational Services to Limited and Non-English Speaking Students, vol. II: Executive Summary, Final Report* (Sacramento: Development Associates, December 1980); Catherine Camp, *School Dropouts*, a discussion paper, California Legislature Assembly Office of Research, May 1980; "Characteristics of Children and Young Adults by Race and Spanish Origin," *Education Week*, March 17, 1982, p. 16.

21. Kal Gezi, "Bilingual-Bicultural Education: A Review of Relevant Research," *California Journal of Educational Research*, 1974, pp. 223–239; H. Dulay and H. Burt, *op. cit.*

22. U.S. Department of Labor, *Youth Knowledge Development Report*: Special Needs Groups—A Profile of Hispanic Youth, Washington, D.C., 1980.

23. William Trombley, "Bilingual Education: Even the Experts Are Confused," *Los Angeles Times*, September 5, 1980.

24. Thomas Sowell, *American Ethnic Groups* (The Urban Institute, 1978).

25. J. E. Mosseley, ed., *The Spanish-Speaking People of the Southwest* (Indianapolis: Council on Spanish American Work, 1966); Ralph Roeder, *Juarez and His Mexico* (New York: Atheneum Press, 1968); J. B. Trend, *The Civilization of Spain* (Oxford University Press, 1952) Sanford A. Mosk, *Industrial Revolution in Mexico* (New York: Van Nostrand, 1950).

26. Reynolds Baca and Dexter Bryan, "The Mexican Dream: Al Norte and Home Again," *Los Angeles Times*, April 12, 1981.

27. California Task Force for Integrated Education, *Integrator*, "Desegregation Programs Face Bilingual Needs," February-March 1981, p. 1–4; Frank A. Fratoe, "The Education of Nonmetro Hispanics," *The Education Digest*, December 1980, pp. 43–45; Soriano, *op cit.*

DISCUSSION QUESTIONS AND ACTIVITIES

1. Who are the "children at risk"?

2. What is the difference between *equality* and *equity*? Is it a valid distinction?

3. Why is research to demonstrate bilingual education effectiveness difficult to conduct?

4. Does time spent on native language take away valuable time from the study of English?

5. The issue, according to Blanco, is not whether bilingual education works but "whether students can participate actively in the instructional activities of the curriculum." What does he mean by this statement?

6. Should the focus in bilingual education be on the classroom? Forces beyond the classroom? Both?

7. Carrison distinguishes five types of programs. What are their characteristics?

8. How do the goals of foreign-language instruction and bilingual education differ?

9. What are the reasons, according to Carrison, that bilingual education has not produced a significant difference in drop-out rates and student achievement?

10. Observe bilingual programs in operation, and report to the class on your observations.

11. Invite a bilingual educator to relate his or her teaching experience in the program.

12. Ask students who grew up in bilingual homes about their early school experiences.

SUGGESTED READINGS

Behuniak, Peter, and others. "Bilingual Education: Evaluation Politics and Practices." *Evaluation Review* 12 (October 1988): 483 –509.

Chamot, Anna Uhl. "Bilingualism in Education and Bilingual Education: The State of the Art in the United States." *Journal of Multilingual and Multicultural Development* 9, nos. 1–2 (1988): 11–35.

Garcia, Eugene E. "Attributes of Effective Schools for Language Minority Students." *Education and Urban Society* 2 (August 1988): 387–398.

Hakuta, Kenji, and Eugene E. Garcia, "Bilingualism and Education." *American Psychologist* 44 (February 1989): 374–379.

Hakuta, Kenji, and Laurie J. Gould, "Synthesis of Research on Bilingual Education." *Educational Leadership* 44 (March 1987): 38–45

McFadden, Bernard J. "Bilingual Education and the Law." *Journal of Law and Education* 12 (January 1983): 1–27.

Ochoa, Alberto M., and Yvonne Caballero-Allen, "Beyond the Rhetoric of Federal Reports: Examining the Conditions Necessary for Effective Bilingual Programs." *Equity and Excellence* 23 (Summer 1988): 20–24.

Rosenbaum, David. "Bilingual Education: A Guide to the Literature." *Education Libraries* 12 (Winter 1987): 5–23.

Rossell, Christine M. "The Problem of Bilingual Research: A Critique of the Walsh and Carbello Study of Bilingual Education Projects." *Equity and Excellence* 23 (Summer 1988): 25–29.

Rotberg, Iris C. "Bilingual Education Policy in the United States." *Prospects: Quarterly Review of Education* 14, no. 1 (1984): 133–147.

Zakariya, Sally Banks. "How to Keep Your Balance When It Comes to Bilingual Education." *American School Board Journal* 174 (June 1987): 21, 24–26, 40.

CHAPTER 15

MULTICULTURAL EDUCATION

When waves of immigrants were coming to American shores, the melting pot ideology held sway over the thinking of educators. This ideology viewed the role of the school as that of assimilating the immigrant into the life of the culture by teaching the dominant values and beliefs. Many youth were assimilated, and some rose in the socioeconomic scale but frequently at the cost of turning their backs on their own culture. Ethnic minorities today generally find public schools alien to their values and belief systems. Multicultural education has been proposed as a remedy. Multicultural education may emphasize ethnic literacy so that the different groups, including the white majority, will gain an understanding of cultural differences. Pluralists (proponents of multicultural education) believe that when assimilationists talk of promoting the common culture they often mean Anglo-American culture rather than a culture that reflects ethnic and cultural diversity. Through multicultural education, minority students not only acquire social and economic skills but skills to promote significant social change. Thus it will teach them how to bargain from a position of strength in order to gain full participation in society.

But critics note that such programs may exaggerate differences among groups and thereby be as harmful as the older practice of ignoring real differences. Additionally, should a situation arise where each group demands its own autonomy, it could cause fragmentation, cultural separation, and divisiveness. Usually it is assumed that racial bias is centered on the white middle class; however, ethnic minorities have prejudices that might be exacerbated by a narrow conceptualization of their grievances. Ethnic programs, critics add, assume monolithic groups and ignore variations in age, sex, occupations, social class, and the racially mixed background of many Americans. Though complaints may be sound about teaching a common culture founded on majoritarian values and greater emphasis upon interdependence rather than competition may be more appropriate for a complex, interdependent society, some basic democratic values—liberty, justice, and equality—need to be taught.

In his essay, James A. Banks reviews different conceptions of multiethnic education and contrasts four leading hypotheses. M. Donald Thomas argues vigorously against certain pluralistic forms of multicultural education.

MULTIETHNIC EDUCATION AND THE QUEST FOR EQUALITY

JAMES A. BANKS

James A. Banks (b. 1941) studied at Chicago City College, Chicago State University, and Michigan State University; has held an NDEA Fellowship for three years; and was a Spencer Fellow. He has taught in elementary schools and is presently Professor and Chairman, Department of Curriculum and Instruction at the University of Washington in Seattle. In addition to serving as a consultant on ethnic studies, he is the author of Multiethnic Education: Theory and Practice (Allyn and Bacon), Teaching Strategies for Ethnic Studies, 4th edition (Allyn and Bacon), and other works.

Multiethnic education requires that the total school environment be changed so that students from diverse ethnic and racial groups will experience educational equality. Many educators mistakenly assume that they can produce multiethnic education by simply infusing bits and pieces of ethnic content into the curriculum. Not so. Multiethnic education requires reform of the total school.

This reform must encompass staff attitudes and perceptions, the formal curriculum, teaching strategies, tests and testing procedures, and school-sanctioned languages and dialects.[1] Only when the total environment of a school promotes educational equality for all students can multiethnic education be said to exist.

Proponents of multiethnic education assume that schools have the power to substantially increase the academic achievement and life chances of minority students. This assumption contrasts sharply with the arguments set forth by theorists such as Christopher Jencks and by revisionists such as Samuel Bowles and Herbert Gintis, who contend that schools are severely limited in their ability to increase the educational equality that would seem to be a prerequisite of enhanced academic achievement and life chances.[2]

EQUALITY AND EQUITY

From the "separate but equal" Supreme Court ruling in *Plessy v. Ferguson* in 1896 until the mid-fifties, black schools in the South had been unequal to white schools in terms of such input variables as teachers' salaries, facilities, instructional materials and supplies, and per-pupil expenditures. After the Supreme Court ruling in *Brown v. Board of Education* in 1954, however, southern and border states made major efforts to change all of that. During the sixties and seventies, many schools in economically depressed areas used funds authorized by the Elementary and Secondary Education Act of 1965 to make their input variables more equal to those of schools in economically advantaged areas. By the end of 1979 the federal government had granted

From James A. Banks, "Multiethnic Education and the Quest for Equality," *Phi Delta Kappan* (April 1983):582–585. Reprinted with the permission of James A. Banks and Phi Delta Kappa.

$23.2 billion under this act to local school districts.[3]

But the massive and controversial Coleman Report, released in 1966, indicated that such input variables as school facilities and curricula are not the most important correlates of academic achievement.[4] James Coleman concluded that such variables as the teachers' verbal ability, the children's sense of control of their environment, and the children's educational backgrounds play the most important role in academic achievement.

The gains made in equalizing such school input variables as teachers' salaries and school facilities during the 1960s and 1970s and the findings of the Coleman Report—coupled with the continuing failure of many minority students to attain educational parity with middle-class white youths—made the notion of measuring educational equality by inputs increasingly unpopular during the 1970s.[5] Instead, educators and social scientists began to define educational equality in terms of the results or effects of schooling. From this perspective, such groups as blacks, Chicanos, and Native Americans are thought to have equal educational opportunity only when their scores on standardized tests and other leading indicators of educational achievement are roughly equal to those of their white counterparts.

The output conception of educational equality, like other notions of equality, is both helpful and problematic. This conception does not explicitly recognize the clear relationship between school input variables and pupil achievement. But the school alone cannot bring about educational equality as measured by output; such other institutions as the family, the church, and the mass media also play powerful educational roles. Despite the problems inherent in the output conception of educational equality, this notion can help educators to set specific goals and to measure their progress toward closing the achievement gap

between ethnic minorities and middle-class white students.

Clearly, educators must focus on educational equality, but this is not sufficient. They should also focus on the educational process, through which they can help children to experience educational *equity*. According to Patricia Graham,

> *Equity differentiates itself from equal educational opportunity by attention to the internal process of education, to the circumstances in which teaching and learning are embedded. The focus is not only the "input" (such as access) or "output" (such as result) but on the educational process in between.*[6]

In other words, input variables, output variables, and the process of education are integrally interrelated; each must receive attention if education is to help minority youths attain the literacy and other skills essential for survival in our technological society.

I agree with Graham that the process of education should receive the greatest emphasis, since educational outcomes rest to a considerable degree on the quality of this process. Moreover, I believe that multiethnic education offers the best hope of educational equity for minority students, because it focuses on reforming those variables of the school environment that now prevent minority students from having effective, enriching, and stimulating learning experiences.

During the 1960s and the 1970s educators increasingly realized that children whose family and community cultures differed markedly from the culture of the school were likely to find academic success more elusive than children whose home and community cultures were congruent with that of the school. For example, many Hispanic children are socialized in the barrio. If they are to achieve on the same academic level as middle-class white youths, the school culture—whose norms, goals, and expectations are primarily white and middle class[7]—must be changed substantially. Merely treating such Hispanic children "equally" (i.e., the same as middle-class white children) will not help many of them to attain the knowledge, skills, and attitudes they need to function effectively in this highly technological society. Because of differing motivational styles, languages, and values, Hispanic and Anglo students may often have to be taught differently if we expect them to learn the same skills and knowledge.[8] In other words, children from some ethnic groups may have different educational entitlements and needs. To reflect cultural democracy and to promote educational equality, the school may be required to provide specialized services, programs, and instruction for these students.

It is true that Jewish and Japanese-American students have been very successful academically; yet they have had no federally mandated bilingual programs in the public schools. (Both groups have established private, after-school language classes). But the academic success of these groups does not necessarily imply that Hispanic children do not need bilingual education in order to attain educational parity with other students. *Some* Hispanic students may need bilingual programs; others may not.

EDUCATION AND SCHOOLING

The public school must play an important but limited role in bringing about educational equality. The family, the mass media, the community, the church, and the youth culture also play important roles in educating the young.[9] To the extent that these other institutions promote norms, behaviors, and values that contradict those that the school promotes, the school is hindered in achieving its goals. Thus policymakers must recognize both the possibilities and the limitations of the school in bringing about equal educational opportunity.

Within the last decade, the school has been handicapped in helping children to attain basic skills because it has received little help or support from the family, the community, and other important social institutions. The efforts of the school to teach children such values as justice and equality have often been undercut by practices in the larger society that contradict those teachings. Admittedly, the public school has not distinguished itself by its efforts to promote those values we think of as the American creed. Nevertheless, it rarely gets much community support when it tries to do so. Although I will focus solely on the role of the school in bringing about educational equality, readers should keep in mind the severe limitations under which the school operates and the extent to which this institution is simply a reflection of the larger society. Our high expectations for the school should be tempered by these realities.

Minority youths are not likely to achieve full educational equality until other institutions within the society implement reforms that support those that I will propose here for the school. Educators should also realize that the notion of equal educational opportunity is an ideal toward which we should work. Working toward this ideal is a continuing process.

To help minority youths attain educational equality during the 1980s, educational programs should reflect the enormous diversity *within* ethnic groups. Too often, social scientists and educators describe ethnic minorities as monolithic groups, rather than as groups that display enormous socioeconomic, regional, cultural, and linguistic diversity. We have all heard or read such oversimplified and misleading statements as: "Blacks made continuous progress during the 1960s and 1970s," or "Indian children have low self-concepts." Such statements generally conceal more than they reveal and reinforce harmful educational practices.

Like educational programs, educational

policy related to ethnic minorities should reflect the tremendous differences *within* ethnic groups. Most Puerto Ricans, blacks, Chicanos, and Native Americans are on the lower rungs of the socioeconomic ladder. But each of these groups also has a sizable middle class—with values, interests, behaviors, and education needs that differ to some extent from those of the rest of the group.

Although these middle-class individuals usually identify to some extent with their ethnic groups, they also have strong social-class interests that bind them in many ways to other middle-class groups in the society. Middle-class members of ethnic groups often find that their class interests conflict with their ethnic allegiances, and their class interests are often more important to them than their ethnic attachments. Thus middle-class blacks and Chicanos often move to suburban communities and send their children to private schools—not to enhance their ethnic identities, but to live in a manner consistent with their social class. Many middle-class black and Chicano parents are more interested in having their children attain the requisite skills for admission to prestigious universities than they are in having their children enroll in schools sympathetic to black English or barrio Spanish. Many middle-class black and Chicano parents, like their white counterparts, are deserting the public schools.[10] Ethnicity remains a cogent factor in United States society, but it is often mediated by class interests.

Shaping and implementing educational policy for minorities in the eighties will become increasingly complex as more members of lower-status ethnic groups join the middle class.[11] Most middle-class blacks, Chicanos, and Puerto Ricans wish to retain their ethnic identities without sacrificing the full benefits and opportunities afforded other members of their social class. They may encourage their children to apply to prestigious universities, but they also expect them to relate well to their

cousins in the inner city and to take active roles in ethnic activities. During the 1960s and 1970s educators focused on helping lower-class minority children to achieve educational parity. Middle-class minority children were often overlooked—or the school assumed that they, too, were poor and "culturally deprived." Educators should be keenly sensitive to the class diversity within minority communities. This diversity is likely to increase throughout the 1980s.

Of course, ethnic minorities include other important subgroups besides the very poor and the middle class. Blue-collar laborers and their families make up one substantial and important segment of ethnic communities, and their educational needs must also be considered when educational policy is shaped for the 1980s. In many working-class ethnic families, both parents work. The children of such parents do not qualify for special programs that benefit children from poorer families. Yet these working-class parents often cannot afford the educational experiences, enrichment activities, and expensive colleges that are within the means of middle-class parents. Consequently, children from working-class ethnic families are often at a disadvantage; their parents simply do not make enough money to provide them with the educational opportunities they need and deserve.

The problems of educating minority and poor youths first attracted serious attention from educators and educational researchers in the 1960s. Yet our understanding of the reasons for the higher rate of academic failure among these youngsters than among other youths remains sparse and uncertain. We can make few conclusive statements about why minority youths often perform poorly in school and about what can be done to increase their academic achievement and emotional growth. Hypotheses abound, but most of the research is inconclusive and contradictory. As is true in other areas of social science, both the research and the hypotheses reflect the ideologies, assumptions, and values of the researchers and theorists.[12]

I do not intend to suggest that we should ignore the hypotheses and research that relate to the education of ethnic groups. Rather, as consumers of these hypotheses and of this research, we should be sensitive to the ideologies, assumptions, and values that underlie them. And we should be aware of our own goals and values as well. Only in this way can we use the hypotheses and the research appropriately, in ways that will enable us to help minority youths reach their full potential.

Hypotheses regarding the education of minority youths are diverse and conflicting. In the 1960s Arthur Jensen and William Shockley revived the genetic explanation for the low academic achievement of minority youths.[13] Richard Herrnstein, by contrast, hypothesized that intelligence is related to social class.[14] The geneticists argue that minority groups do not perform as well academically as nonminorities because of their genetic characteristics; consequently, the capability of the school to bring about educational equality is severely limited. When assessing the genetic hypothesis, educators should remember its history in the United States. In earlier times, other theorists "explained" the intellectual inferiority of such groups as the Irish and the Jews as a matter of genes. Moreover, in studies of intelligence in a nation such as the United States, it is difficult to control for race. Racial purity is the exception, not the rule.

The cultural-deprivation hypothesis, which also emerged during the 1960s, maintains that poor youths do not achieve well in school because of the poverty-stricken environment in which they have been reared.[15] In these environments, the argument goes, they are unable to experience the kind of cognitive stimulation that develops intellectual skills. Unlike the geneticists, those who believe in cultural deprivation are confirmed environmentalists;

they think that the school can and should play a significant role in establishing education equality for poor youths. The school can do this, they believe, by intervening in the lives of poor youths at the earliest possible age and providing them with a rich and stimulating educational environment. Those who support the cultural-deprivation hypothesis believe that intensive, behaviorally oriented instruction will enable poor youths to greatly increase their academic achievement and emotional growth.

Another group of educators—the integrationists—emerged in the 1950s. The integrationists began to develop their arguments and research during a period of segregated schooling in the United States. Integrationists contend that the best way to bring about educational equality for minority youths is to place them in racially desegregated, middle-class schools.[16] Like the cultural deprivationists, the integrationists are environmentalists who believe that the school can and should play a significant role in bringing about educational equality. The school, they say, can increase educational equality by creating environments in which students from diverse racial groups and social classes are free to interact and learn in an atmosphere that values and respects each group. School desegregation has become a major target of the neoconservative scholars who emerged during the 1970s.[17] Urban demographic trends have greatly diminished the likelihood of successful school desegregation in the 1980s. Yet the integrationists remain strongly committed to their dream of a racially integrated America.

A fourth group of scholars and researchers, who support the cultural-difference (or multicultural) hypothesis, emerged during the 1960s and the early 1970s. They reject the views of both the geneticists and the cultural deprivationists. They do not necessarily reject the ideas of the integrationists, but they have different priorities. Led by such researchers as

William Labov, Geneva Smitherman, Joan Baratz, Manuel Ramirez, and Alfredo Castañeda,[18] those who support the cultural-difference hypothesis argue that ethnic minorities have rich and diverse, not deprived, cultures. Minority youths do not achieve well in school, these theorists suggest, because the school culture is alien to them and often in conflict with their home cultures. Moreover, the IQ tests used to assess the academic aptitude of these youths are invalid because they are grounded in the mainstream culture.[19] To help minority youths increase their academic achievement and emotional growth, they say, we must reform the culture of the school to make it more congruent with the cultures of ethnic minority youths.

Because of the thin, contradictory, and inconclusive nature of the hypotheses and research on the education of poor and ethnic minority youths, our policies and programs must be guided primarily by our own value commitments. In his classic work, *An American Dilemma,* Gunnar Myrdal argues that Americans believe deeply in the American creed, which includes such core values as equality, justice, and human dignity.[20] But Americans face a dilemma, Myrdal wrote, because their treatment of blacks contradicts this creed. Myrdal believed, however, that the faith of Americans in the American creed would help them to create a society that would become increasingly more humane and just.

I also believe that the American creed is deeply embedded in the American conscience. It dictates that we choose hypotheses to guide the education of minority youths that are consistent with equality, justice, and human dignity.

Educational programs that spring from the idea of cultural deprivation show disrespect for students' home cultures. Educational programs that spring from the genetic hypothesis violate human dignity and other values set forth in the American creed, because they

deny the possibility of a dignified existence for many minority youths.[21] Views that foster cultural freedom for minority youths, such as the cultural-difference or multicultural hypothesis, provide the greatest possibility for an education that will engender justice and equity and thus improve the human condition.

Endnotes

1. For further discussion of these points, see James A. Banks, *Multiethnic Education: Theory and Practice* (Boston: Allyn and Bacon, 1981).

2. Christopher Jencks et al., *Inequality: A Reassessment of the Effect of Family and Schooling in America* (New York: Basic Books, 1972); and Samuel Bowles and Herbert Gintis, *Schooling in Capitalist America* (New York: Basic Books, 1976).

3. Patricia A. Graham, "Whither Equality of Educational Opportunity?" *Daedalus,* Summer 1980, pp. 115–32.

4. James S. Coleman et al., *Equality of Educational Opportunity* (Washington, D.C.: U.S. Government Printing Office, 1966).

5. James S. Coleman, "The Concept of Equality in Educational Opportunity," in *Equal Educational Opportunity* (Cambridge, Mass.: Harvard University Press, 1969).

6. Graham, p. 123.

7. William Greenbaum, "America in Search of a New Ideal: An Essay on the Rise of Pluralism," *Harvard Educational Review,* August 1974, pp. 411–40.

8. Geneva Gay, "Interactions in Culturally Pluralistic Classrooms," in James A. Banks, ed. *Education in the '80s: Multiethnic Education* (Washington, D.C.: National Education Association, 1981).

9. Lawrence Cremin, *Public Education* (New York: Basic Books, 1976).

10. James S. Coleman, Thomas Hoffer, and Sally Kilgore, *Public and Private Schools* (Chicago: National Opinion Research Center, March 1981).

11. William J. Wilson, *The Declining Significance of Race: Blacks and Changing American Institutions* (Chicago: University of Chicago Press, 1978).

12. Philip Green, *The Pursuit of Inequality* (New York: Pantheon, 1981).

13. Arthur R. Jensen, "How Much Can We Boost

I.Q. and Scholastic Achievement?," *Harvard Educational Review,* Winter 1969, pp. 1–123; and William Shockley, "Dysgenics, Geneticity, Raceology: A Challenge to the Intellectual Responsibility of Educators," *Phi Delta Kappan,* January 1972, pp. 297–307.

14. Richard J. Herrnstein, *I.Q. in the Meritocracy* (Boston: Little, Brown, 1971).

15. Carl Bereiter and Siegfried Englemann, *Teaching Disadvantaged Children in the Preschool* (Englewood Cliffs, N.J.: Prentice-Hall, 1966).

16. Thomas Pettigrew and Robert L. Green, "School Desegregation in Large Cities: A Critique of the Coleman 'White Flight' Thesis," *Harvard Educational Review,* February 1976, pp. 1–53.

17. Peter Steinfels, *The Neoconservatives: The Men Who Are Changing America's Politics* (New York: Simon and Schuster, 1979).

18. William Labov, "The Logic of Nonstandard English," in Frederick Williams, Ed., *Language and Poverty: Perspectives on a Theme* (Chicago: Markham Publishing Co., 1970); Geneva Smitherman, *Talkin' and Testifyin': The Language of Black America* (New York: Houghton-Mifflin, 1977); Joan C. Baratz, "Teaching Reading in an Urban Negro School System," in Williams, *Language and Poverty . . .* ; and Manuel Ramirez III and Alfredo Castañeda, *Cultural Democracy, Bicognitive Development, and Education* (New York: Academic Press, 1974).

19. Jane R. Mercer, "Testing and Assessment Practices in Multiethnic Education," in Banks, *Education in the '80s . . .* , pp. 93–104.

20. Gunnar Myrdal, *An American Dilemma: The Negro Problem and Modern Democracy,* Vols. 1 and 2 (New York: Harper and Row, 1944).

21. Hannah Arendt, *The Human Condition* (Chicago: University of Chicago Press, 1958).

M. DONALD THOMAS   THE LIMITS OF PLURALISM

M. Donald Thomas (b. 1926) studied at the University of Dubuque and the University of Illinois. He has been a high school teacher, counselor, principal and is currently Superintendent of Salt Lake City School District. He is the author of monographs, workbooks, and teacher guides and is the recipient of a number of awards.

My topic is not a popular one. And I must tread carefully, because my position may be so easily misconstrued. I am arguing against the accepted principle that pluralism is good for our schools. Here are my reasons for doing so:

• Pluralism in schools, at some point, destroys any sense of common traditions, values, purposes, and obligations. Without such commonly supported positions, the schools lack unity and direction.

• Pluralism in schools, at some point, makes it impossible for them to teach a common body of knowledge. Pluralism diverts the schools' attention from their basic purpose— to educate for civic, economic, and personal effectiveness.

• Pluralism in schools, at some point, tends to create moral anarchy. It lends support to no-fault morality, which claims that all values are of equal worth and that the ends justify the means. When no moral criteria exist, no obligations to adhere to those criteria are held.

I have arrived at these conclusions slowly over the past ten years. They are the result of careful examination of what has happened to our schools under the influence of pluralism.

What began as a fresh breath of reform has grown stale and become another way by which schools have lost credibility and public support.

I am not arguing the need to preserve and to value the achievements of the diverse ethnic and racial groups of this country. There is certainly nothing wrong with racial and ethnic pride and the desire to give maximum freedom to each individual. What is unacceptable is the position that everything is of equal value, that the schools have a responsibility for teaching every possible belief and every perceived value, and that behavior is moral if it is believed to be so by any person or any group. There *are* limits to pluralism, and such limits must be articulated by schools and school leaders.

Nor am I a critic of United States public education. On the contrary, I believe that our public schools have served our nation well. I also believe that they are doing a good job at the present time. Public schools are and will continue to be the protectors of our freedoms and one of the bases for personal growth. I abhor critics who attack our schools without knowing and appreciating the contributions of schools to economic growth and social mobility. My point is simple: Pluralism, at some point, can diminish the effectiveness of public

From M. Donald Thomas, "The Limits of Pluralism," *Phi Delta Kappan* (April 1981). © 1981, Phi Delta Kappan, Inc. Reprinted by permission.

schools, and we should not permit that to happen.

A society cannot exist without a common ethos—a common set of beliefs, traditions, and values that glues it together. Without such unity, there is no common bond that acts to motivate and to inspire. Without accepted obligations that are universally known, there is no purpose or direction in most schools.

In particular, schools need a common set of assumptions to guide their work and measure their success. Schools were established to educate for the democratic ethos. That purpose is still a good one. If everyone is permitted to do anything he or she wishes, the work of the school may be left undone.

Schools should not be expected to deal with every social issue that arises, nor should they be torn apart by vested interests that wish to use the schools for private purposes. The historical purposes of our schools are clear: (1) to teach basic skills required for verbal and mathematical literacy, (2) to teach an understanding of political democracy and the ability to function within that system, (3) to prepare students for higher education or employment, (4) to develop personal discipline in students that will make it possible for them to live satisfying and productive lives.

Today, however, we have gone far beyond these purposes. In doing so we have gone far beyond our ability to establish purpose, meaning, and direction in our schools. We are trying to educate our students to satisfy the demands of a fragmented society, and we are failing. John C. Sawhill stated it well: "In thrusting the schools to the forefront of social change, we have diverted them from their basic purpose—education."

Pluralism in our expectations, in the services schools render, in the duties they perform, has deprived schools of a coherent set of principles—a common ethos. Schools can no longer teach basic historical beliefs about our country. They have no time to teach the basic tools of literacy, no curriculum to prepare students for higher education, and no funds for adequate vocational education. Cast adrift in a sea of pluralistic demands and conflicting interests, they have abandoned their traditional role of being the "glue" that keeps society's attention fixed on the national ethos, the *common destiny* of a varied people. Attention to dozens of ethnic and personal needs paralyzes the schools' ability to unite students for common purposes.

Pluralism in the curriculum has created weakness in teaching the basics. Demands to serve the needs of everyone have made it almost impossible to serve well the needs of anyone. With the present levels of funding, how can schools serve well the varying interests and values of all ethnic groups, all handicapped students, all gifted students, all undermotivated children, and all parents? It is an impossible task, and attempting it reduces our effectiveness in a primary responsibility—teaching a common body of basic knowledge to all children. Providing students with the skills to become effective citizens, able workers, and disciplined individuals is enough for schools to do.

However, we are asked to meet the various social, economic, and personal needs of minorities; we are asked to assist students with various language difficulties; and we are asked to participate in the "politics" of using the schools to solve all of our social and political problems. Pluralism has indeed gone mad. The efforts of schools have been atomized at the request of a thousand "me-first" groups. The schools simply do not have the personnel, the energy, or the skills to serve well all the needs of all the children, all the parents, and all the politicians who come into contact with them.

Among those things that schools can and have done well are

- Teaching most students basic linguistic and mathematical literacy skills
- Teaching most students the basic structure and purposes of a democratic nation
- Teaching most students skills necessary to succeed in higher education
- Teaching most students skills sufficient to obtain employment after high school graduation
- Teaching most students skills required to continue learning on their own

Among those things that schools have not done well are

- Teaching students how to be effective parents and family members
- Teaching students to be wise consumers and effective conservationists
- Teaching all handicapped students
- Teaching all students the culture of all the various ethnic groups that attend our schools
- Teaching a second language to a large number of students.

The truth of the matter is that we are not now and perhaps never will be able to do these things successfully without massive new resources. My hope is that such tasks will be taken from the schools and given back to the home or to other agencies and institutions.

Requiring the schools to perform pluralistic jobs has spread out personnel so thinly that the basic responsibilities have been neglected. Pluralism has put an unbearable strain on the resources of the schools of this nation. It is time to put limits on pluralism and design the work of schools within those limits. If we continue the current trend toward greater pluralism, the end of public education may indeed occur within our lifetime. Schools simply cannot teach everything that every person or group wishes them to teach. We have already gone too far, and it is time to call a halt.

Perhaps the most devastating effect of plu-

ralism in our schools is the moral anarchy it breeds. Recent trysts with moral relativism have led to a "no-fault" morality and a do-it-yourself system of justice. Alastaire MacIntyre has written: "It is no wonder that the confusions of pluralism are articulated at the level of moral argument in the form of a mishmash of conceptual fragments."

The trend toward ethical pluralism has produced too many people all too willing to put success ahead of personal standards and cleverness ahead of character. Pluralism leads at its worst to no ethics and at its best to a school society with ambivalent ethics of conflict and confrontation. Without an emphasis on individual ethical responsibility, a common core of values that will unite our schools, we shall continue to sink deeper into the quagmire of the so-called new morality—which is not moral at all. It is a philosophy that favors ends over means, a philosophy that will, in the end, destroy all moral precepts.

Today there is too much credence given to slogans such as "morality is what I say it is." The belief is widespread that each individual defines moral action for himself or herself and that there exist no more universals to which the entire society is committed. However, the need remains for certain moral criteria: respect for individuals, respect for law, respect for property, common civility, honesty in our relationships, protection of personal liberties, freedom to learn without interference and conflict, and freedom from fear.

What is wrong with the values of pluralism is that they acknowledge no commonly accepted moral standards. Unrestrained pluralism results in a school society based on personal license and undisciplined personal behavior. Unfortunately, such behavior is common among students and adults in many schools. Each individual believes that moral behavior derives solely from personal judgment and that conscience alone arbitrates moral decisions. The problem is that conscience allows so many of us to cheat, disobey the law, interfere with the rights of others, harm others, use destructive means for personal ends, and do whatever conscience defines as right. The result is moral chaos and a fractured and fearful school society.

United States education has been and will continue to be the bedrock on which our political democracy is built. It will continue to provide the foundation for social stability and common purpose. It is still the best hope for free men and women all over the globe. We cannot, however, allow creeping pluralism to fragment our national unity, to divert us from our purpose, and to destroy that core of values that has made this country great. The future of this nation depends on our ability to confront pluralism and to bring it under control. The sooner we do so, the better our schools and our nation will be.

DISCUSSION QUESTIONS AND ACTIVITIES

1. What is the purpose of multiethnic education?

2. Explain the differences in the concepts of outputs, inputs, and equity.

3. What are the roles of institutions, other than educational ones, for bringing about greater equality?

4. What influence does social class have on ethnic groups?

5. Compare and contrast the following four hypotheses: geneticism, cultural deprivation, integrationism, and cultural difference. Which of the hypotheses do you consider more valid? Why?

6. Should schools teach a common body of knowledge? According to Thomas, why does pluralism threaten such knowledge?

7. Does pluralism actually undermine educating for civic, economic, and personal effectiveness?

8. Can pluralism create moral anarchy? Does pluralism fail to acknowledge any commonly accepted moral standards?

9. Ask those class members of racial and ethnic minorities to comment on their own schooling in light of the essays.

10. Invite a teacher or administrator of a multiethnic program to speak to the class.

11. Survey what your local community is doing in multicultural education, and make recommendations for needed programs.

SUGGESTED READINGS

Appleton, Nicholas. *Cultural Pluralism in Education.* New York: Longman, 1983.

Banks, James A. *Multiethnic Education: Theory and Practice,* 2nd. ed. Boston: Allyn and Bacon, 1988.

Banks, James A., and Cherry A. Banks, eds. *Multicultural Education: Issues and Perspectives.* Boston: Allyn and Bacon, 1989.

Broudy, Harry S. "Cultural Pluralism: New Wine in Old Bottles." *Educational Leadership* 33 (December 1975): 173–175. A critique.

Capaldi, Nicholas. *Out of Order; Affirmative Action and the Crisis of Doctrinaire Liberalism*. Buffalo, N.Y.: Prometheus Books, 1985. A critique.

Glazer, Nathan. *Affirmative Discrimination*. New York: Basic Books, 1975. A critique.

Gollnick, Donna M., and Philip C. Chinn. *Multicultural Education in a Pluralistic Society*, 2nd ed. Columbus, Ohio: Merrill, 1986.

Lindsey, Alfred J. "Consensus or Diversity? A Grave Dilemma in Schooling." *Journal of Teacher Education* 36 (July–August 1985): 31–39. A critique.

Mitchell, Bruce M. "Multicultural Education: A Second Glance at the Present American Effort.: *Educational Research Quarterly* 11, No. 4 (1987): 8–12. A national survey.

Ogbu, John U. *Minority Education and Caste*. New York: Academic Press, 1978.

Pai, Young. *Cultural Foundations of Education*. Columbus, Ohio. Merrill, 1990.

Pratte, Richard. *Pluralism in Education*. Springfield, Ill.: Charles C. Thomas, 1979.

Schaefer, Richard T. *Racial and Ethnic Groups*, 4th ed. Glenview, Ill.: Scott, Foresman, 1990.

Sleeter, Christine E., and Carl A. Grant. "An Analysis of Multicultural Education in the United States." *Harvard Educational Review* 57 (November 1987): 421–444.

Sleeter, Christine E., and Carl A. Grant. *Making Choices for Multicultural Education*. Columbus, Ohio: Merrill, 1988.

CHAPTER 16

MAINSTREAMING

An increasingly widespread concern over the education of handicapped children and doubts about whether their special education is adequate to their needs have led to the development of mainstreaming. The movement was promoted by Public Law 94–142 and reinforced by the education of the handicapped acts enacted by individual state legislatures. Mainstreaming involves moving handicapped children from their segregated status in special classrooms and integrating them into regular classrooms. Under mainstreaming, the handicapped child would be in a regular classroom for all or part of a day and receive the necessary support services of both special and general education. Mainstreaming for some students might only entail integrating with other students for nonacademic work such as physical education, but for others it might involve assignment to a regular classroom and provision therein for special education as appropriate. The theory of mainstreaming holds that children have a right to, and would benefit from, participation in the least restrictive educational program they can manage.

The United States courts have so far decided that handicapped children have a right to participate in public education, regardless of the classification or the severity of the handicap, and that an education should be furnished consistent with individual learning needs, including treatment and therapy appropriate to the disability.

One problem of labeling children with disabilities is that they may be misclassified, which might mean being almost indefinitely trapped in the wrong program and segregated from peers. Minority groups seem especially likely to be misclassified. At times children have been singled out for some behavior quirk or learning habit, labeled, and placed in a special classroom; this practice has led to emphasizing their differences rather than similarities with students in regular classes.

Even those in favor of mainstreaming recognize a number of difficult problems: regular classroom teachers need special preparation and assistance in working with handicapped children; these children may not be accepted by their classmates and may not receive special help needed from them in performing routine school activities; modification of the physical plant may be necessary; changes in curriculum and class size will be needed; and additional funding exclusively for such programs is essential. Moreover, research suggests that while the handicapped in regular classes learn more, those in special classes are better adjusted.

THE CASE FOR KEEPING MENTALLY RETARDED CHILDREN IN YOUR REGULAR CLASSROOMS

MARTIN TONN

Martin H. Tonn (b. 1921) studied at the University of Iowa and held a USOE special education fellowship. He has been a speech therapist in the public schools, a consultant on speech and hearing to government agencies, and has held office in speech and hearing associations. In addition to articles in professional journals, he has written humorous articles and articles on child care for mass-circulation magazines. Tonn is Director of Special Education at Moorhead State College, Moorhead, Minnesota.

Before the turn of the century, mentally handicapped children faced one of two rather bleak prospects: an isolated existence at home or institutionalization. In the early 1900s a third choice was opened for these children: special, segregated school (mentally handicapped children were placed in self-contained, special classrooms and taught by special education teachers). Only in the last decade or so has another option been offered: integration of handicapped children into the regular classroom program. It's something you should know more about.

The idea of placing mentally handicapped children in the mainstream of the school program gained impetus from a November 1968 magazine article published in *Exceptional Children*. The article's author, I. M. Dunn, spoke out against the exclusive use of self-contained classes for the educable mentally handicapped. Dunn did not call for abolishing all special classes, but he offered evidence to support the use of alternate programs. His article sparked further research and debate that, in turn, have changed some of the traditional recommendations for teaching moderately retarded children.

Support for integrating educable mentally handicapped children into regular classes rests on these seven points:

1. Dunn and others say research shows that, with one exception, mentally handicapped children do better in regular classes than in special classes—the exception: peer acceptance.

2. Labeling and stigmatizing children by sending them to "retarded" classes may prove detrimental to them.

3. Special classes isolate children, preventing meaningful contact that could be helpful both to mentally handicapped and other students.

4. Many special classes do not meet—in a real way—the educational and social needs of children.

5. Special classes have an unrealistically high proportion of minority children and children from low socioeconomic backgrounds. This lack of balance, researchers claim, is the result of a middle-class oriented test bias and of

From Martin Tonn, "The Case for Keeping Mentally Retarded Children in Your Regular Classrooms," *American School Board Journal* 161 (August 1974):45. Reprinted with permission.

environmental deprivation rather than of actual intellectual inferiority inherent in the child.

6. Isolating students in special classes is not in keeping with our democratic philosophy of education.

7. Results from standardized IQ tests are not sufficient evidence for placing children in special classes.

More about the final point: Psychologists and educators know that standardized IQ tests are subject to fluctuations caused by factors such as emotional problems, environmental deprivation, sensory defects, and special learning disabilities. At the educable level, children with IQs of 50 to 75 generally are placed in special classes. Studies have shown, however, that some students with moderate mental handicaps perform better (on a battery of various cognitive tests) than do children who have IQs above 75 and who attend regular classes.

Several alternative programs have been devised by school officials who are convinced that a number of mentally handicapped children can profit from experience in the regular classroom. In some districts, handicapped children are placed in ordinary classes when they reach a certain level of achievement in their special classes and when their special class teachers recommend the transfer. A mentally handicapped child who moves into the traditional classroom setting receives help each day from a special education resource teacher. This additional assistance is flexible—increased when the child is experiencing problems and decreased as he progresses with his school work. Resource teachers also can help classroom teachers plan curriculum programs for handicapped children.

A program called Individually Prescribed Instruction continually assesses and monitors the abilities and progress of a mentally handicapped child who attends a regular class. Special instructional materials are produced for the child as he reaches each new or different level of learning. This method allows a handicapped child to work at his own pace.

The Harrison Resource Learning Center in one of Minneapolis' inner-city schools provides prescriptive instruction to those moderately mentally handicapped youngsters who attend regular classes. The amount of time each child spends in the Resource Learning Center is flexible and based on individual needs. With the help of this program, a number of mentally handicapped children have been enrolled full-time in regular classes.

No one is suggesting the elimination of all special classes for retarded children, some of whom may suffer from severe handicaps or a combination of emotional and physical problems. These children may be served best in special classes.

But this question *is* being asked: Do all special children necessarily need special classes? Donald MacMillan, writing in *Focus on Exceptional Children,* poses the question this way: "To what extent, and under what circumstances, can a wider range of individual differences be accommodated in the regular class than is presently the case?"

School board members and superintendents should be aware of the districtwide implications of this trend to integrate certain handicapped children into the traditional classrooms:

1. More resource teachers and teacher aides will be needed.
2. Smaller classes will be beneficial, if not necessary.
3. Regular classroom teachers who work with mentally handicapped children will need more specialized inservice training.
4. Top school officials should insure that administrators, teachers, parents, and the general community are aware of the goals and objectives of new programs for handicapped children within their districts.

MAINSTREAMING: A FORMATIVE CONSIDERATION

HARRY N. CHANDLER

Harry N. Chandler is Associate Editor of the Journal of Learning Disabilities.

I do not think that it is as simple as a pendulum swing. In this case professional opinion seems to be changing before we see any theory to suggest a change. We rushed into deinstitutionalization with faith but little foresight, we stampeded into mainstreaming with panic and no preparation. Now things are getting sorted out, now are finding a center of gravity. Someday we might even witness a nearly unprecedented event: educators and social scientists attempting to plan instead of react.

There is little evidence that mainstreaming LD students results in better academic achievement. The mainstreaming argument was originally a civil rights move toward social equality and came most strongly from parents of retarded children. The limited research used to argue that special students did better in "regular" classrooms was dated and flawed.

Much of our present mainstreaming data has been on the social and emotional adjustment of retarded students. We have some studies of how teachers and peers view LD students and of how LD students feel about themselves. This conflicting evidence hints that mainstreaming has had some benefit to special students, their peers, and their teachers. Many of these are not real studies but articles of the "see how kind the third graders are to this Downs child" which, while heartwarming, is little more than a public relations performance.

Mainstreaming, especially at the secondary level, should be done to increase a child's academic, vocational, or artistic skills. Mainstreaming for social reasons too often means that some authority has decided to stop trying to teach the child, that the only way to show growth is in a well advertised social placement. I am biased: I know that any good special education teacher can teach an LD, EMR or TMR child more basics than a regular class teacher. We can also better teach the basic concepts in content areas. Unless we have made a special study of a content area, we might not have as complete a knowledge of the subject as the content teacher, but some content-area teachers can only teach advanced concepts to equally advanced students.

At this point my liberalism bumps into my pedagogy, or, as my wife puts it, my dogma overcomes my karma. By teaching an LD child a content-area subject, am I not also deciding that the child cannot learn as much as an "average" child? Yes, I am deciding, but I'm deciding with the consent of the parent and the child. No, I am not giving up; any time the child wants to return to the regular classes he can with parental assent. Anytime I

From Harry N. Chandler, "Mainstreaming: A Formative Consideration," *Journal of Learning Disabilities* 19 (February 1986):125–26. Reprinted by permission of the publisher, Pro-Ed, Inc.

know the child is ready for more than I can teach, I will pass him on.

Given time and necessary resources, it is possible to teach almost anyone almost anything—the catch: "time" and "resources." LD kids begin falling behind in kindergarten and keep on getting further and further behind. In some districts, decisions about "tracking" begin as early as the fifth or sixth grade: will academics or a more vocational curriculum be given the child? In our democratic and, at times, egalitarian society we would like to leave options open as long as possible, but another decision point comes in high school: What next? More schooling, work, the military, welfare . . . ?

One of our greatest problems is that our institutions are constantly forcing us into decisions: time moves on, children get older, resources dwindle or change. We find ourselves confronted with either mainstreaming or a self-contained classroom; either academics or vocational or prevocational training. No matter how we try to tailor a program for a child as implied in PL 94–142, opinions, prejudices, schedules, finances, theorists, anxious parents, and impatient children force us into "cobbling up" poorly designed programs with few options.

Like euthanasia, medical triage, or voting Republican, questioning mainstreaming is something a liberal educator does not like to do. Several recent happenings have forced me to look more closely than comfortable at mainstreaming: I reread PL 94–142 so I could explain it to a student teacher; I reviewed the book, *Perspectives in Special Education: Personal Orientations;* and I interviewed Pat Ellis, associate superintendent of public instruction for the state of Oregon and director of the Division of Special Education and Student Services.

PL 94–142 reminded me that we should junk the term *mainstreaming* and use the more accurate but less picturesque "least re-

strictive environment." According to PL 94–142, we are supposed to place children to the maximum extent possible with nonhandicapped peers and they should be in a special class only when the nature or severity of their handicap prevents them from successfully being educated in regular classes with the use of supplementary aids and services. That phrase, "supplementary aids and services" was inserted when the framers of PL 94–142 thought the law would be fully funded. Few schools can afford those "aids and services" so, while the phrase is on the books, it is honored only by being ignored. Even state and federal audit teams do not look to see if a child could be successful in a regular class if given "aids and services." The "nature and severity" of the handicap is hard to determine since one has to take into account the handicaps of the school system and its teachers as well as the handicap of the child. The variables here are the teacher, the administration, the budget, the design of the school, and the nature of the student body. It is primarily the skill or incompetence of the regular class teacher which makes or breaks special students in the "mainstream."

The book, *Perspectives in Special Education: Personal Orientations,* by Burton Blatt and Richard J. Morris is the most thought provoking I have found in the area of special education (even better than Mann's *On the Trail of Process* or Ball's *Itard, Seguin, and Kephart*). It is the autobiographies of ten of special education's outstanding modern personalities (see the review in last month's *JLD*). I used the term *personalities* advisedly, since all those represented are not only "experts" but have very personal ideas about the special-education field—ideas which do not always square with conventional wisdom. Not all take up the topic of mainstreaming, but all who do see that it has flaws. The greatest concern is that it was an attractive and humane theory which was rushed into law with no planning, no training of those responsible for making it work, and little funding to teach how to do it, to support it, or to monitor it. But, as I did in the book review, let the authors speak for themselves.

Seymour B. Sarason, professor of psychology at Yale and director of Yale's graduate program in clinical psychology and of the Yale Psycho-Educational Clinic:

> *"I had very mixed feelings about 94–142. Of course, I was heartily in favor of it. At the same time, however, I was certain that neither the proponents of that legislation nor school officials understood the resource problem. The problem and its amelioration were being defined in a way that was unrealistic and was setting the stage for backlash. Also the fact that the word or concept of* mainstreaming *did not appear in the legislation said to me that the special class was in no way threatened—indeed it was implicitly receiving further legitimization. Finally and very important, in my travels around the country I learned that the bulk of school officials had no idea what PL 94–142 really said."*

Samuel A. Kirk, professor of special education at the University of Arizona (and, of course, the man who coined the term "learning disabilities"):

> *I recommended to an advocate of mainstreaming many years ago that he teach a second- or third-grade of thirty children, accept into that class three or four mentally retarded, learning disabled, and emotionally disturbed children, and study exactly how mainstreaming could be accomplished adequately. He did not accept my suggestion. As everyone knows, it is easy to tell someone else what to do but it is more difficult to accomplish the task adequately and to describe exactly how it is done. We, as yet, have no detailed description of how mainstreaming is accomplished nor an exact distribution of responsibilities of both regular and resource teachers.*

Herbert Goldstein, professor emeritus in educational psychology and special education, New York University:

> *In fact, recent data suggest that moving children about and occupying committees and teachers' time to cobble up IEP's are reducing students' and teachers' effectiveness . . . The Individual Education Plans (IEPs) have generated a decade of professional deception—at least when it comes to disturbed youngsters [no, to all youngsters, my comment H.N.C..]. We seldom have the resources or are willing to make the investment necessary to make the significant difference. Our superficial appreciation of our business is its most depressing condition. I do not blame the teachers; their leadership has misled them.*

James J. Gallagher, director of the Frank Porter Graham Child Development Center and Kenan Professor of Education at the University of North Carolina at Chapel Hill:

> *The special education teacher and the regular education teacher are peers. If there is a disagreement, then how does it get settled? If the special educator wants to make a suggestion about how to change a student's program, how can it be done without offense? Who takes the lead in discussions or planning for the student? There is a range of role uncertainties cluttering the landscape on such issues, and they make a difficult situation even more difficult.*

Burton Blatt, the late dean of the School of Education at Syracuse University:

> *Is mainstreaming a valid educational issue? I conclude that it is not! The program, the curriculum, the label, the organization—the most obvious components of education—are strangely irrelevant to the relationships we seek to understand. Those educational components which do matter—largely ignored in our research—are the teacher as a human being who teaches and learns, children as learners with potentials and rights, and the environment—rich, flexible, and thoughtfully created.*

Pat Ellis' remarks ranged over the field of special education, but she kept coming back to special-child programs. What follows are just a few of her remarks. Direct quotes are set off in quotation marks, the rest is a paraphrase which is, I hope, accurate and not colored by my biases:

How do we know what we are doing is correct for any special child? Are we being pressured into a position by parents who have been sold a bill of goods by theorists who have never tested their theory against the reality of everyday life? Mainstreaming special children makes them and their parents think that they will be mainstreamed in life after school, but life isn't like that. "Why strive for an appropriate education if they have nothing when they leave the education system?" Have we wasted our time and their money in special education when society will not treat them specially after they leave us?

We have not fulfilled the hope of PL 94–142 in testing or planning. We rely too much on tests and not enough on clinical data or on direct observation. We have to look at functional abilities and promote them in children. There are seldom enough people in the planning stages, too often just a teacher, quite often not even a parent. When we are planning for IEPs, we should make it clear that a standard diploma is not realistic for most special children. We need a "meaningful completion document," and not just for students on IEPs. "Currently most diplomas are of very little value; they have no objective meaning as a certificate of high-quality education."

There should be a close linkage between vocational education and special education. Vocational education is in trouble; if it is phased out, then special education is in equal trouble. We need to train students for jobs. We have to try to bring in social services, to look at housing and vocations of and for the students we serve. All of these things: education, homes, jobs, friends, and family make a whole person. Now each is treated separately by separate agencies with little communication among them. We need more alternative educational settings for all students. Schools cannot afford to keep students until they are twenty-one, although they might have to as other social services close down.

As I wrote at the beginning of this article, this is not a pendulum swing yet. Some very respected people in the special education field are beginning to take a careful look at how we deliver educational services. Perhaps someday we might even get around to some long range planning. Stranger things have happened!

DISCUSSION QUESTIONS AND ACTIVITIES

1. What are the seven points that support the integration of educable mentally handicapped children into regular classes?

2. What alternative programs are provided for those mentally handicapped children who are mainstreamed?

3. Can those school systems that use mainstreaming dispense with all special education classes?

4. Gather evidence on school systems where mainstreaming has generally proven successful and those where the results have been unfavorable.

5. According to Chandler, why is mainstreaming for social reasons undesirable?

6. On what basis does Samuel Kirk (in the Chandler selection) claim that as yet we have "no detailed description of how mainstreaming is accomplished nor an exact distribution of responsibilities of both regular and resource teachers."

7. Will handicapped students be disillusioned because they will not be mainstreamed in life after school? Is this a reason for not mainstreaming them in school?

SUGGESTED READINGS

Conway, Robert F., and Lyn Gow. "Mainstreaming Special Class Students with Mild Handicaps through Group Instruction." *Remedial and Special Education* 9 (September–October 1988): 34–40, 49.

Danby, Joy and Chris Cullen. "Integration and Mainstreaming: A Review of the Efficacy of Mainstreaming and Integration for Mentally Handicapped Pupils." *Educational Psychology* vol. 8, no. 3 (1988): 177–195.

Garrar-Pinhas, Adrienne, and Liora Pedhazur Schmelkin. "Administrators' and Teachers' Attitudes toward Mainstreaming." *Remedial and Special Education* 10 (July–August 1989): 38–43.

Johnson, Robert C. "Mainstreaming? It All Depends . . ." *Perspectives for Teachers of the Hearing Impaired* 7 (January–February 1989): 12–15.

Kearly, Patt. "Historical and Philosophical Issues in Normalization of Handicapped Students." *Child and Youth Services* vol. 10, no. 2 (1988): 3–33.

Lanier, Nancy J. "Attitudes toward the Mainstreaming of Moderately to Severely Handicapped Students." *Reading Improvement* 25 (Fall 1988): 242–244.

Messersmith, James L., and Gloria A. Piantek. "Changing the 'I' to 'We': Effective Mainstreaming through Cooperative Teaching." *NASSP Bulletin* 72 (October 1988): 66–71.

Schechtman, Zipora. "A Program to Enhance Teachers' Motivation in Integrating Handicapped Students into Regular Classes." *Reading Improvement* 26 (Spring 1989): 79–87.

Stone, Wendy L., and Anette M. LaGreca. "The Social Status of Children with Learning Disabilities: A Reexamination." *Journal of Learning Disabilities* 23 (January 1990): 32–37.

Westling, David L. "Leadership for Education of the Mentally Handicapped." *Educational Leadership* 46 (March 1989): 19–23.

CHAPTER 17

EDUCATING THE GIFTED

The gifted and talented are once more the object of attention after a period of relative neglect. When the Soviet Union launched Sputnik in 1957, alarm swept through the land that the United States had fallen behind in the space race and therefore more scientists, engineers, and mathematicians would be urgently needed. The National Defense Education Act of 1958 provided funds to promote the intellectually talented in those fields. But by 1965 with the Elementary and Secondary Education Act, interest in culturally different learners and compensatory education became a dominant concern; this trend was followed by provisions for handicapped children. Until recently many administrators assumed the gifted could make it alone. Now interest has again returned to the gifted and talented, and some important changes are evident since the earlier years.

An important development is that giftedness is no longer restricted to intellectual talent. In 1972, the United States Office of Education's (USOE's) Office of Gifted and Talented defined these two terms as referring to children capable of high performance in any one or more of these areas: general intellectual ability, specific academic aptitude, creative and productive thinking, leadership ability, visual and performing arts aptitudes, or psychomotor ability. By this definition, 3 to 5 percent of the school-age population could be considered gifted. An elementary teacher with a class of thirty-five students would likely have one or two gifted children each year. Or, to use another example, out of a hypothetical roomful of 100 children who represent all children in the fifth grade, 68 of them are likely to be average learners, 13 above average, 13 below average, 3 retarded, and 3 gifted.

The two educational approaches to the gifted are acceleration and enrichment. Acceleration may involve early enrollment in kindergarten, skipping grades, advanced placement, and early high school and college entrance. Acceleration, however, removes the child from age mates and may cause social isolation. Enrichment programs, which are now part of many elementary schools, enable the child to spend most of the time in the regular classroom but meet several hours each week with other gifted children.

REFLECTIONS ON THREE DECADES OF EDUCATION OF THE GIFTED

A. HARRY PASSOW

A. Harry Passow is the Jacob H. Schiff Professor of Education at Teachers College, Columbia University. He is past president of the World Council for Gifted and Talented Children. He founded the Talented Youth Project in 1954 and has been active in gifted education ever since.

In August 1985, approximately 1,000 persons from forty-seven different countries participated in the Sixth World Conference on Gifted and Talented Children and Youth in Hamburg, West Germany. A total of 529 different kinds of presentations were made—plenary lectures, papers, workshops, poster displays, symposia, and conversations. The world conferences have been held every other year since the first such conference assembled in London in 1975. In November 1985, more than twice that number attended the Thirty-second Annual Convention of the National Association for Gifted Children in Denver. Surveys, such as those of the Council of State Directors of Programs for the Gifted, indicate a growing number of states which have mandates for gifted/talented programming are providing state funding for such programs, are providing state directors for supervising gifted/talented programs, and are giving increased attention to such programs.

In February 1954, when I initiated the Talented Youth Project at Teachers College's Horace Mann-Lincoln Institute of School Experimentation, I was advised that one of our first activities should involve consciousness-raising concerning gifted education among administrators, teachers, state departments of education, parents, and other groups. My colleague, Will French, and I spoke to dozens of state and national professional groups across the country. One of my first articles on this topic, "Are We Short-Changing the Gifted?" appeared in the prestigious *School Executive* and was widely reprinted elsewhere. In May 1955, my colleagues and I published *Planning for Talented Youth: Considerations for Public Schools.* The purpose of this publication was described as follows:

> *In this pamphlet an attempt is made to provide a framework within which schools can consider the total problem of educating the talented as they begin to develop their own programs for these children. Research findings and generalizations are sketched briefly; pertinent issues and problems are raised; and areas in which research is needed are pointed out. (Passow, Goldberg, Tannenbaum, and French, 1955, p. 7)*

Quite naturally, in thinking about how to respond to the challenge and opportunity the editor provided in inviting me to prepare this

From A. Harry Passow, "Reflections on Three Decades of Education of the Gifted," *Roeper Review*, Vol. 8, No. 4 (May 1986): 223–226. Copyright © 1986 by Roeper City & Country School, Inc., Bloomfield Hills, Michigan 48013. Reprinted with permission.

statement, I reread what we had written in *Planning for Talented Youth* and looked again at the Fifty-seventh Yearbook of the National Society for the Study of Education titled, *Education for the Gifted*, for which I had served on the Society's Committee on Education for the Gifted and contributed a chapter on "Enrichment of Education for the Gifted" (Passow, 1958). Rereading these two publications and reflecting on more than thirty years of involvement with gifted education result in a paradox regarding the education of the gifted: so much has remained unchanged in three decades and yet so much has changed. The issues and considerations listed in *Planning for Talented Youth* are still timely, on target, and useful. With an updating of the bibliography and some editing, this 1955 publication could be reissued and used as "a basis for intensive study and planning" in schools. Much of the content of the Fifty-seventh NSSE yearbook is still informative. Yet, the state of gifted education thirty years later is not unchanged. In many aspects we have built on what we knew and what we were doing and have extended our knowledge and insights while in others we seem not to have progressed very much as reflected in current practice. Space constraints make it impossible to deal with all that is implied by this observation, but I will comment briefly on some aspects.

In several places, most recently in *Gifted Children: Psychological and Educational Perspectives*, Tannenbaum (1983) has described the cyclical history of gifted education. When the Talented Youth Project was started in 1954, we were in a trough which the launching of Sputnik in October 1957 changed dramatically. Despite the broadening of the concept of giftedness in the 1960s, schools gave higher priority and focused their efforts on other areas and programs for the gifted withered and declined so that the U.S. Office of Education's Marland Report issued in 1971 could assert that gifted students were not being adequately served. The Marland Report certainly dates the beginning of a renaissance for education of the gifted, although there were numerous other factors that made this possible. In reflecting on what has and is happening to gifted education in the United States and in nations around the world—the World Council for Gifted and Talented Children, Inc., has certainly stimulated and facilitated the exchange of information about developments in other countries—one can begin to hope that the cyclical nature of gifted education will become history. On good days, I would like to believe that our efforts to reconceptualize gifted education, create mandates for identifying and educating gifted, educate teachers concerning the nature of teaching gifted students, develop and implement differentiated curriculum for gifted students, provide necessary funding, conduct research which contributes to theory development, build advocacy groups, extend the resource base and other activities will pay off and we will make gifted education an integral part of education for all, rather than an add-on fad or frill which can be dropped when educators and policymakers are diverted by other demands. I should add that I do not think we will ever reach the point where we will not have to justify the need for special programs for the gifted nor will we ever have to stop explaining why such programs are not elitist.

THE NEED FOR TOTAL PLANNING FOR THE GIFTED

I have long been concerned with approaches to planning for the gifted which I consider too narrow, limited, and constricting. We provide a pullout program, an accelerated course, an honors class, a special class or some other program with a clever acronym and consider that we have provided adequately for the gifted. Tannenbaum (1983) distinguishes between what he calls "programs" and "provisions" for the gifted. The latter he sees as "ad hoc provisions . . . as fragmentary learning experiences, lacking in complex form, long-range purpose, or clear directionality" (p. 423). Programs, on the other hand, are "designed by a curriculum committee and codified in the school records as a comprehensive, sequential plan that commands attention by the lay board and professional staff and is supported solidly by a school budget" (p. 423). In making this distinction, Tannenbaum is arguing for gifted education programs which are not dependent on a single teacher, have some permanence and stability, and contribute to the articulation and integration of gifted students' experiences.

While I agree completely with Tannenbaum's conceptual difference between programs and provisions, there is another dimension which I think needs constant restatement: *What is needed is total planning for the total experience of the gifted student.* All students, including gifted students, really experience four curricula—a general education curriculum, a specialized curriculum, a covert/subliminal curriculum, and a nonschool educative-settings curriculum. Some writers include a fifth curriculum—the extracurricular or co-curricula program—but these sets of learning opportunities contribute to the other four, usually on a more informal or unstructured basis.

The general education curriculum is aimed at providing the knowledge, skills, insights, and understanding required of all individuals to participate effectively in society. It is the general education curriculum which provides the opportunities to engage in appropriate learning experiences and subject areas which contribute to an understanding and appreciation of our cultural heritage but also nurtures the individual as a creative participant and productive contributor to that heritage. It is the general education curriculum in which the

basic skills and processes and the learning-how-to-learn skills are developed. It is this curriculum which, as Phenix (1966) puts it, engenders essential meanings.

The specialized curriculum is aimed at nurturing the special talent areas of the individual by developing the knowledge, skills, insights, and understandings which will enable the gifted individual to grow towards becoming a gifted adult, a producer of knowledge and of creative products and performance. It is in the specialized curriculum that there is the match between the learner's unique potential for outstanding performance and learning opportunities. If the general education curriculum is the common, core, or required curriculum, the specialized curriculum is more focused on individual talent potential.

The covert/subliminal curriculum consists of those learnings which are an outcome or a consequence of the climate and environment of the classroom, the school, and the community. Self-concepts, attitudes, task commitment and perseverance, values—these are some of the things students learn from each other and from adults through the covert curriculum. The interpersonal relationships, the norms and values, the motivations and attitudes are all affected by the structured and unstructured, formal and informal transactions which occur, and these are all very powerful mediators of cognitive and affective growth. This curriculum impacts strongly on the more formal curricular experiences of students through the general and specialized curricula.

The fourth curriculum consists of those curricula found in a variety of nonschool agencies and institutions which educate and socialize—the family, the media, libraries, museums, business, industry, youth groups, and so forth. These institutions, agencies, and groups instruct children and youth directly, systematically, and deliberately. They provide learning opportunities and educative resources which complement and supplement those provided in and by the school. There are personnel and material resources available in these nonschool settings which can be used to enrich, challenge, and extend school learnings.

These four curricula are not discrete, especially the general education, specialized education and covert/subliminal curricula. Many learning engagements which contribute to the development of the specialized talents of gifted students are provided in the general education or common core curriculum by differentiation of those experiences. Many general education learning opportunities are provided concomitantly with opportunities for specialized talent development. The covert/subliminal curriculum, providing a climate or environment or context within which other learnings take place, clearly affects and is affected by other curricula. Community-centered, experience-based learning opportunities extend the opportunities for study in both general and specialized education.

My basic argument is that adequate and appropriate education for the gifted student does not take place only in those programs we label "gifted education" or "program for the gifted" but rather in the total learning environment which individuals experience. We will differentiate curricula differently as we plan for learning opportunities in these four curricula areas, but we must plan for the total learning experience, not just a part of it. There are those who argue that such total planning is only possible in special schools for the gifted such as the Bronx High School of Science or the North Carolina School for Mathematics and Science where the whole faculty is involved in planning a total learning environment and community for nurturing talent.

I am arguing that such planning is essential and possible in any setting if the faculty believes that the development of special talents is a schoolwide and communitywide responsibility and that it cannot be accomplished if left to one or a few teachers who provide unarticulated learning experiences. I am not arguing that we should not pay special attention to that piece of the total program which we provide to nurture specialized talents and abilities—what we call the "program for the gifted"—but that we must also attend to the general education and the opportunities for nurturing individual talents through the total learning experiences students have in school and outside of the classroom. Gifted individuals are learning in many different settings and are experiencing many different curricula; it is this range and variety of learning experiences which constitute the total learning environment to which we must be sensitive and for which we must plan.

RETHINKING THE CONCEPT OF DIFFERENTIATED CURRICULUM

In *Planning for Talented Youth's* chapter on instruction, we wrote:

> *An enriched curriculum may help talented students become familiar with a greater variety of subject matter or sample new creative areas. Or, it may provide opportunities for more concentrated study, deeper probing of a particular area. It may enable talented students to follow through on original ideas and delve into problems that confront them. Thus, an enriched curriculum may provide greater breadth or greater depth of experience, or both. (p. 51)*

Interestingly, our discussion of acceleration which was defined as "progress through an educational program at rates faster or ages younger than conventional" (Pressey, 1949, p. 2), was contained in our chapter on "Administrative Adaptations."

Discussions of curriculum usually dealt with analyses of the virtues of acceleration and/or enrichment in general or as they related to specific subject areas. The National Education Association Project on the Academically Talented Student, for example, produced a dozen publications in 1960–61, each in association with a professional association concerned with that subject or function (e.g., administration or guidance). Seven of these "green books" as they came to be known, dealt with curriculum and instruction in a specific subject area, and an eighth dealt with elementary education. Each of these green books discussed identification of the academically talented in that subject or discipline, what to teach them, how to enrich or accelerate instruction in that area, and what other kinds of provisions need to be made for students talented in that area. A 1961 publication titled, *Curriculum Planning for the Gifted* (Fliegler, 1961) deals with subject areas (e.g., social studies, arithmetic, science, foreign languages, and so forth) and processes (e.g., creative writing, reading) on a chapter-by-chapter basis. In a summary chapter Fliegler discussed philosophical issues, aims and objectives, curriculum considerations, and the need for research-in-action. He observed: "The quintessence for educating the gifted is curriculum differentiation—a differentiation based upon the needs of the child" (p. 380). The pattern of thinking about differentiating curriculum at that time might be described as one of enriching or accelerating content in the subject areas, facilitating independent study leading to acceleration or enrichment, or, beginning in the 1960s, developing creativity activities.

Note should be made of Ward's (1961) effort to develop "a systematic theory of differential experience for the gifted," a theory based on "the behavioral characteristics of the group as a whole and upon their anticipated roles" (p. 9). Ward proposed a set of general principles or axioms which he hoped would contribute to a coherent theory of gifted education and help gear "school practice along more defensible lines." Ward's reflections elsewhere in this issue should be interesting in terms of how he views his efforts in retrospect.

When the Marland Report (1971) asserted in its definition of gifted and talented children that "these are children who require differentiated educational programs and services beyond those normally provided by the regular school program," the phrase *differentiated curriculum* became the rallying call for gifted educators (p. 2). What emerged has been a number of "models" or "paradigms," which are viewed as guides to program design and curriculum differentiation. In some instances, these were developed quite specifically for gifted students, while in others they have been adapted or adopted for the gifted. Bloom's taxonomy of educational objectives with its six categories of objectives in the cognitive domain, together with its companion volume describing five categories in the affective domain, was aimed at providing a "classification of the goals of our educational system" and was "expected to be of general help to all teachers, administrators, professional specialists, and research workers who deal with curricular and evaluation problems" (Bloom et al., 1956, p. 1). Educators of the gifted have made the Bloom taxonomy their own as they aim at helping students engage in what are perceived as the higher-level processes, although Bloom and his associates saw the need for students to achieve objectives in all six classes of objectives in the hierarchy.

Other models which seem to have become quite popular include, in no particular order: Meeker's (1969) structure of the intellect; Gordon's (1971) synectics; Phenix's (1964) realms of meaning; Parnes, Boller, and Biondi's (1977) creative problem solving; Williams's (1972) total creativity program; Taylor's (1968) multiple talent approach; Taba (1966) cognitive functioning in elementary school children; Kohlberg's (1971) moral development; Ward's (1980) DEG or differentiated education for the gifted; and, of course, Renzulli's (1977) enrichment triad. In addition, curriculum planners now have other matrixes to assist in their curriculum planning such as Tannenbaum's (1983) enrichment matrix and Tennant's (1980) gifted extension model.

In my view, these models are best described as process models in that they are not related to specific content or disciplines. They generally represent processes to be applied to various content areas or disciplines or considered as processes, skills, or behaviors which have merit and contribute to the development of higher-order cognitive development, for example. These curriculum models differ from the Advanced Placement Program, for instance, which now has syllabi and examinations in twenty-four specific subject areas offering college-level studies in the high school as an approach to differentiating curriculum for gifted students, or the International Baccalaureate which aims at offering "a comprehensive curriculum of general education that responds to the need for greater challenge on the upper secondary level and for new opportunities to achieve excellence in education," aims which correspond with those for gifted programs.

Two contrasting content-specific curriculum models can also be found in the Johns Hopkins Studies of Mathematically Precocious Youth, which advocates fast-paced mathematics classes leading to advanced mathematics courses and Mathematics Education for Gifted Secondary School Students (MEGSSS) (Kaufman, Fitzgerald, and Harpel, 1981) which is an integrated, articulated grades-seven-to-twelve mathematics program for students with excellent reading and reasoning ability aimed at exploring the upper content limits of mathematics which gifted students can understand and appreciate. While MEGSSS does accelerate content, it aims at providing a breadth of mathematics knowledge through dealing with mathematical problems, ideas, and theories. Some of the curricula developed following Sputnik such as

the Biological Sciences Curriculum Study included special programs for students gifted in those areas.

Clearly, in the post-Marland period, differentiated curriculum has taken on even more significance in gifted education than in earlier periods, but I am not sure that we have more than a veneer or overlay as a result. I have argued elsewhere that all components of the curriculum are susceptible to differentiation—the goals and objectives, the content, the instructional strategies, the resources, time, space, organization, and evaluation—and that these elements must be considered in an integrated, articulated whole. Moreover, if the notion I have suggested earlier concerning students being involved in four curricula and the need for total planning [obtains], then curriculum differentiation takes on a more inclusive meaning.

SOME CONCLUDING REFLECTIONS

Looking back on gifted education in the early 1950s from a perspective of the late 1980s, it seems to me that we are giving more attention to the notion of differentiated curriculum in terms of teaching and learning than we did in the past when organizational or administrative provisions (e.g., enrichment in the regular classroom, ability grouping, and administrative means of acceleration) were viewed as the major approaches to curriculum differentiation. We have accumulated a body of literature concerning all aspects of gifted education, including the nature of giftedness, identification, curriculum and instruction, guidance and affective development, extended resources, and evaluation—a body of literature which consists of a mix of research, exhortation, and promising practices. We still do not have a comprehensive theory of giftedness and of gifted education, but, then, we do not have such comprehensive theories about most of the rest of education either.

I began by citing a few items which suggest

that we may have long since passed the consciousness-raising stages and that we, along with educators in many different parts of the world, are actively engaged in planning and implementing educational opportunities for nurturing giftedness and talents in a variety of populations and settings. I began also by asserting that many, if not most, of the issues and questions raised in our 1955 publication, *Planning for Talented Youth*, are still current and applicable. I am not sure that that should be disheartening, as it seems to be to some gifted educators. Rather, I think that the considerations are perennial ones that gifted educators *must always* attend to and that we now have much better knowledge, understandings, and insights with which to deal with these issues and problems.

I am often asked how I feel about the field of gifted education after more than thirty years of involvement. My immediate response is always that I am bullish! It would be nice if we still did not have to push for legislation, funding, mandates, and so forth, but then there would be no challenge and no excitement!

References

Bloom, B. S., ed. (1956), *Taxonomy of educational objectives: Cognitive domain.* New York: David McKay Co.

Fifty-seventh Yearbook, Part II, National Society for the Study of Education. Chicago: University of Chicago Press.

Fliegler, L. A., ed. (1961), *Curriculum planning for the gifted.* Englewood Cliffs, NJ: Prentice-Hall, Inc.

Gordon, W. J. J. (1971), *Synectics.* New York: Collier Books.

Kaufman, B., Fitzgerald, J., and Harpel, J. (1981), *MEGSSS in Action.* St. Louis, MO: CEMREL, Inc.

Kohlberg, L. (1971), "Stages of moral development as the basis for moral education." In C. M. Beck, B. S. Crittenden and E. V. Sullivans, eds. *Moral education: Interdisciplinary approaches.* New York: Newman Press.

Kratwohl, D. R. et al., eds. (1964), *Taxonomy of educational objectives: Affective domain.* New York: David McKay Co.

Marland, S. J. (1971), *Education of the gifted and talented.* Washington, D.C.: Government Printing Office.

Meeker, M. (1969), *The structure of intellect: Its interpretation and uses.* Columbus, OH: Charles E. Merrill Publishing Co.

Parnes, S. J., Noller, R. B., and Biondi, A. M. (1967), *Guide to Creative Action.* New York: Scribner's Sons.

Passow, A. H. (1958), "Enrichment of education for the gifted." In N. Henry, ed. *Education for the gifted.*

Passow, A. H., Goldberg, M. L., Tannenbaum, A. J., and French, W. (1955), *Planning for talented youth: Considerations for public schools.* New York: Teachers College Press.

Phenix, P. H. (1964), *Realms of meaning.* New York: McGraw-Hill Book Co.

Renzulli, J. S. (1977), *The enrichment triad model.* Weathersfield, CT: Creative Learning Press.

Taba, H. (1964), *Teaching strategies and cognitive functioning in elementary school children.* (U.S.O.E. Cooperative Research Project No. 1574). San Francisco: San Francisco State College.

Tannenbaum, A. J. (1983), *Gifted children: Psychological and educational perspectives.* New York: Macmillan Publishing Co.

Taylor, C. W. (1968), "The multiple talent approach." *Instructor 77, 27:* 142, 144, 146.

Tennant, C. G. and Morgan, H. J. (1980), "Elementary level programs for the gifted and talented." In H. J. Morgan, C. G. Tennant and M. J. Gold, *Elementary and secondary level programs for the gifted and talented.* New York: Teachers College Press.

Ward, V. S. (1961), *Educating the gifted: An axiomatic approach.* Columbus, OH: Charles E. Merrill Publishing Co.

Williams, F. E. (1972), *A total creativity program kit.* Englewood Cliffs, NJ: Prentice-Hall, Inc.

EQUITY VS. EXCELLENCE: AN EDUCATIONAL DRAMA

JAMES J. GALLAGHER

James J. Gallagher is Director of the Frank Porter Graham Child Development Center and Kenan Professor of Education at the University of North Carolina at Chapel Hill. He was President of the World Council for Gifted and Talented Children and was President of the Association for the Gifted. He is the author of Teaching the Gifted Child *and other works.*

For many years educational programs for elementary- and secondary-level gifted children have had to struggle with a conflict in American societal values that have inhibited their establishment or their wholehearted support, once established. This reluctance has had little to do with the quality of the programs, since the available program evaluation evidence suggests positive results for most of the program adaptations (Gallagher, Weiss, Oglesby, and Thomas, 1983). The reluctant support of programs for gifted students has more to do with a conflict in values in the society—a conflict that continues to this day. John Gardner (1961) posed the central question for us when he wrote the book, *Can We Be Equal and Excellent Too?* In that book he tried to come to grips with the two dominant political sets of beliefs abroad today: a deep and abiding desire to have equality of opportunity and treatment for all citizens while, at the same time, preserving the American tradition of high achievement and production as a national characteristic.

The drive for equity in this country, which reached a policy peak in the 1960s and 1970s, can best be reflected by programs such as Head Start and PL 94-142, the Education for All Handicapped Children Act. These and many similar programs had as their goals the improvement of performance of youngsters who had early problems in school performance because of physical or social conditions. The underlying value undergirding such policies is probably best expressed by the term *vertical equity*, which is defined as "the unequal treatment of unequals in order to make them more equal" (Haskins and Gallagher, 1981).

In a rather peculiar way this equity movement indirectly improved educational opportunities of some gifted children. In about half of the fifty states, the laws supporting programs for exceptional children also included gifted as a part of that definition. So when resources were increased for handicapped children, this automatically meant an increase for programs for gifted children as well in those states (Mitchell, 1981). The full meaning of this can be seen in a review of state spending on gifted education (Gallagher, Weiss, Oglesby, and Thomas, 1983), which revealed that of the five states who have spent more than ten million dollars a year on gifted education, four of them had their programs administered under the general heading of exceptional children in those states.

From James J. Gallagher, "Equity vs. Excellence: An Educational Drama," *Roeper Review,* Vol. 8, No. 4 (May 1986): 233–235. Copyright © 1986 by Roeper City and County School, Inc., Bloomfield Hills, Michigan 48013. Reprinted with permission.

Another indicator of the relative pulling power of the need of the handicapped child versus the gifted child may be seen in the budget within the United States Office of Education in which over a billion dollars has been provided for handicapped children, while no money at all has been allocated for gifted children. It must be noted, however, that gifted children have profited to some extent from the current interest in mathematics and science education (Coleman and Selby, 1983).

THE DRIVE TO EXCELLENCE

This concern for equity does not imply that there has not been a societal interest expressed in the United States in *excellence in education* as well. Too often such an interest has had its most effective expression at the higher educational level. Our commitment to graduates and professional education in the United States is enormous and provides many different vehicles for the development of the superior intellectual gifts of these gifted children, once they reach that educational level. The concern is that we may have lost many youngsters of high talent to a boring and inappropriate education during the elementary and secondary years (Whitmore, 1980).

Another associated factor working to the disadvantage of programs for gifted children in the public schools is the tendency for our governmental institutions to respond to manifest crises rather than to long-term goals. When children are clearly failing in school or where they are major disruptive forces to the normal education process, the pressure to do "something" about them immediately is very great. The behavior of state legislatures and the Congress can reveal a similar tendency to focus on the open wounds in the educational system, in preference to attending to the potential for excellence that may be going unused. It seems similar to a situation in which we can tolerate a car operating on four cylinders instead of six of which it is capable, while we pay serious attention only if the car refuses to run at all.

One answer to this problem is to make these contradictions visible to the public for their further review, but another is clearly program advocacy. There has been a recent increase in the organized efforts specifically designed to advocate for programs for gifted education, in a similar fashion to those strategies used by advocates for other programs in education (Gallagher, Kaplan, and Sato, 1983; Mitchell, 1981). It is in this arena that parent organizations have had significant effect. They have successfully sponsored legislation, kept local programs from being gutted, and provided a place for the exchange of ideas between parents with similar problems.

To be an effective advocate, one has to sincerely believe in the cause. One belief that advocates of gifted education would share would be that investment in the educational stimulation of these children is one of the most constructive acts we could take on behalf of our society. Gallagher (1985) has pointed out that the money that would go toward installing an MX missile could also support a four-year scholarship for 10,000 of our brightest college students. He raises the point that since the MX will be used only to place a period to our current civilization, we should question which expenditure is truly in the best interests of the defense of our country.

EQUITY VS. EXCELLENCE ABROAD

The educational tug-of-war between equity and excellence is not by any means limited to the United States. Gallagher (1984) reviewed reports from many other countries and concluded that this issue was a central one in practically all countries. For example, the Soviet Union, even after the October Revolution, carried on special education of specially gifted and talented children for ten or fifteen years (Berezine and Foteyeva, 1972).

In 1936, such programs were denounced as anti-Marxist, and a policy of heterogeneous grouping was adopted. Since then there has been a continuous debate in Soviet journals and magazines about the virtues of special schools for the gifted in mathematics and such enrichment programs, as are emphasized in the Pioneer Houses, an after-school enrichment opportunity (Brickman, 1979). The arguments in the Soviet society take on a curiously similar ring to those in our own country, with the opponents arguing that the programs are elitist and not in the Communist spirit, while the supporters claim that the programs for high-ability students are in the national interest, creating a stronger and more effective country (Dunstan, 1983).

Countries who perceive themselves under threat seem even more inclined to swing to the excellence side of the argument. Countries such as Taiwan (Wu, 1983), South Africa, and Israel (Schmueli, 1983; Landau, 1979; Butler-Por, 1983) have committed themselves to a more thorough talent-development program based upon a national-interest argument. In other countries where a socialist philosophy dominates the political scene, the country leans toward the "equity" side of the argument. France and Sweden, for example, are not active in promoting programs for gifted students (Terrassier, 1981 and Husén, 1974).

STRATEGIES FOR POLICY SUPPORT

Of course, recognizing the problem that we face in overcoming these value conflicts and doing something constructive about it are two different things. First, though, we do have to identify the true nature of the resistance and not go tilting at windmills. Then, the question is how to overcome that resistance.

We could invoke basic American values and say that every child is entitled to the education that each needs, and that means that different children will receive different types of education. We have clearly recognized that position for children with mental retardation or special learning disabilities, but gifted children do not readily get accepted into a policy that has been used to help those who may need special assistance merely to perform at a minimum level in the society.

We can intone that famous line that "the equal treatment of unequals is very unequal." Good logic perhaps, but not very good politics, and it is politics or public opinion that we are dealing with here. Such arguments and one dollar can get you a cup of coffee, but not much else.

The best arguments that I can suggest are some analogies to athletes and space, two popular topics in our society. The space argument is that, "we are all in this human species together traveling on Spaceship Earth, with declining resources and a rapidly growing passenger list. The gifted students can, with their creativity, increase our dwindling resources through agricultural research and our problem-solving capabilities through development of computers, and so forth.

The athletic analogy is that all humanity is on the same team, and we have some formidable opponents: war, hunger, disease, ignorance. We will need the strongest performance of the best of our team members to prevail against such opposition. There is, in fact, no built-in guarantee that mankind will prevail against its enemies, and so we must make optimal the opportunities for our most talented team members—even if we sometimes don't like them personally—to do their best for all of us.

We can remind our publics that we, as a society, have adopted that idea enthusiastically at the higher education level where we have built the largest collection of "schools for gifted children" the world has ever seen. After all, what is the Harvard Law School or the Stanford Medical School or any of our major universities if they are not special schools for gifted students, and we know why we have created them. It is to make a strong nation and, incidentally, provide us individually with competent physicians, lawyers, and psychiatrists when, and if, we need them. If it is good policy at the higher education level, does it not follow that it would be desirable to do some analogous activities for gifted students at the elementary and secondary school levels as well?

The more the business, political, and intellectual leaders in our society think about the future and what will be necessary to survive and prosper in that future, the better should be the status of gifted children. Over the past few years, we have stopped apologizing for demanding the best from our students. We need to redouble our efforts at demonstrating what can be done if the students with high aptitude are given a full opportunity for intellectual and artistic growth. Such illustrations of program excellence can then become the benchmarks, the guidelines, for what we can and should do in educating all children.

References

Berezina, G. and Foteyeva, A. (1972). Educational work and extracurricular educational establishments. In N. Kugin et al., *Education in the U.S.S.R.*, Moscow Progress Publishers.

Brickman, W. (1979). Educational provisions for the gifted and talented in other countries. In A. Passow (Ed.), *The gifted and the talented* (78th Yearbook of the National Society for the Study of Education, pp. 308–330). Chicago: University of Chicago Press.

Butler-Por, N. (1983). Giftedness across cultures. In B. Shore, F. Gagne, S. Larivee, R. Tali, and R. Tremblay (Eds.), *Face to face with giftedness* (pp. 250–270). New York: Trillium Press.

Coleman, W., Jr., and Selby, C. (1983). *Educating Americans for the 21st Century*. Washington, D.C.: National Science Board Commission on Precollege Education in Mathematics, Science, and Technology.

Dunstan, J. (1983). Attitudes to provision for gifted children: The case of the U.S.S.R. In B. Shore, F. Gagne, S. Larivee, R. Tali, and R. Tremblay (Eds.), *Face to face with giftedness* (pp. 290–327). New York: Trillium Press.

Gallagher, J. J. (1985). The evolution of education for the gifted in differing cultures. In J. Freeman (Ed.), *The psychology of gifted children* (pp. 335–350). Chichester, West Sussex, England: John Wiley & Sons, Ltd.

Gallagher, J. J. (1984). Excellence and equity— A worldwide conflict. *Gifted International*, 2(2), 1–11.

Gallagher, J., Kaplan, S., and Sato, I. (Eds.), (1983). *Promoting the education of the gifted and talented: Strategies for advocacy*. Los Angeles, CA: National/State Leadership Training Institute on the Gifted and the Talented.

Gallagher, J., Weiss, P., Oglesby, K, and Thomas, T. (1983). *The status of gifted/talented education: United States survey of needs, practices, and policies*. Los Angeles, CA: National/State Leadership Training Institute on the Gifted and the Talented.

Gardner, J. W. (1961). *Excellence: Can we be equal and excellent too?* New York: Harper & Row.

Haskins, R., and Gallagher, J. J. (Eds.). (1981). *Models for analysis of social policy: An introduction*. Norwood, NJ: Ablex.

Husén, T. (1974). *Talent, equality and meritocracy: Availability and utilization of talent*. The Hague: Nyhoff.

Landau, E. (1979). The young persons institute for the promotion of science. In J. Gallagher (Ed.), *Gifted children: Reaching their potential* (pp. 105–109). Jerusalem, Israel: Kollek & Sons.

Mitchell, P. (Ed.). (1981). *An advocate's guide to building support for gifted and talented education*. Washington, D.C.: National Association of State Boards of Education.

Shmueli, E. (1983, August). *The gifted disadvantaged of Israel*. Paper presented at the Fifth World Conference on Gifted and Talented Children. Manila, Philippines.

Terrassier, J. (1981). The negative Pygmalion effect. In A. Kramer (Ed.). *Gifted children: Chal-*

lenging their potential. (pp. 82–84). New York: Trillium Press.

Whitmore, J. (1980). *Giftedness, conflict, and underachievement.* Boston: Allyn and Bacon.

Wu, W. T. (1983, November). *Evaluation on educational programs for intellectually gifted students in junior high schools in the Republic of China.* Paper presented at National Association for Gifted Children Meetings in Philadelphia, PA.

DISCUSSION QUESTIONS AND ACTIVITIES

1. Why has the history of gifted education followed a cyclical pattern?

2. Passow identified four curricula for the gifted. What are the distinguishing characteristics of each curriculum?

3. What are the functions of process models and content-specific curriculum models in educating the gifted?

4. According to Gallagher, how has the equity movement improved educational opportunities for some gifted students and how has it clashed with gifted education?

5. What evidence can be adduced that the conflict between equity and excellence is not only a problem in American education but in many other countries as well?

6. What cogent arguments can be used to overcome this value conflict?

7. Investigate what provisions have been made in your home community for educating the gifted, and determine the adequacy and success of these programs.

8. Invite a teacher experienced in working with the gifted to your class to speak.

9. In his *Excellence: Can We Be Equal and Excellent Too?* (New York: Harper & Row, 1961), John Gardner sought to find a place in a democratic society for both equality and talent. Read his book to determine whether he was able to do so convincingly.

10. In John Rawls' *A Theory of Justice* (Cambridge, Mass.: Harvard University Press, 1971), two fundamental principles are articulated: (1) each person is to have an equal right to the most basic liberties compatible with a similar system of liberty for all; and (2) social and economic inequalities are to be arranged so that they are both (a) to the greatest benefit of the least advantaged, and (b) attached to offices and positions open to all under conditions of fair equality of opportunity. Although the first principle has priority over the second one, would we still assume that the gifted would receive less resources if these two principles were adopted? In other words, would the second principle allocate extra resources to the handicapped, mentally retarded, and culturally disadvantaged? Thus what would be just and fair in the use of scarce societal resources for educating the gifted?

SUGGESTED READINGS

Barron, Frank. *Creativity and Psychological Health.* Princeton, N.J.: Van Nostrand, 1963.

Feldhusen, John F. "Synthesis of Research on Gifted Youth." *Educational Leadership* 46 (March 1989): 6–11.

Mitchell, Bruce M. "The Latest National Assessment of Gifted Education." *Roeper Review* 10 (May 1988): 239–242.

Passow, A. Harry. "Needed Research and Development in Educating High-Ability Children: An Editorial." *Roeper Review* 11 (May 1989): 223–229.

Reis, Sally M. "Reflections on Policy Affecting the Education of Gifted and Talented Students: Past and Future Perspectives." *American Psychologist* 4 (February 1989): 39–48.

Rogers, Karen B. "A Content Analysis of Literature on Giftedness." *Journal for the Education of the Gifted* 13 (Fall 1989): 78–88.

Sellin, Donald, and Mary Peterson, eds. "What Others Say about the Gifted." *Journal for the Education of the Gifted* 13 (Fall 1989): 105–108.

Sisk, Dorothy A. "The State of Gifted Education: Toward a Bright Future." *Music Educators Journal* 76 (March 1990): 35–39.

Terman, Lewis M., and others. *Genetic Studies of Genius.* Stanford, Calif.: Stanford University Press, 1925.

Terman, Lewis M. *The Gifted Group at Mid-Life.* Stanford, Calif.: Stanford University Press, 1967.

Torrance, E. Paul. "Teaching Creative and Gifted Learners." In *Handbook of Research on Teaching*, 3rd ed. Edited by Merlin C. Wittrock. New York: Macmillan, 1986.

FURTHER THOUGHTS ON INNOVATIONS AND ALTERNATIVES

Those who develop an innovation may use various thought processes and procedures. Participants in school settings may have a sense of uneasiness, a feeling of frustration, or a disequilibrium that signals something is amiss. They may then formulate the problem, set up hypotheses, test the hypotheses, and then either accept or reject them. But if the innovative process is examined from the point of view of the school system, the following changes are likely: (1) establishing goals and priorities; (2) determining where changes need to be made; (3) developing a model for an innovative program or practice; (4) testing the model in a pilot program; (5) modifying the innovation in the light of testing; (6) introducing the innovation in appropriate settings and continuing to determine what further changes may be needed; and (7) once the innovation has proven successful, disseminating it to other interested parties and educational systems.

Take the case of merit raises. Dissatisfied school board members, abetted by the complaints of influential citizens, explore the reasons for low student achievement test scores. They then define the problem more precisely as how to bring about improved achievement, and they form two hypotheses: (1) if greater incentives and rewards are given to teachers, improved teaching will result and will lead to greater student achievement; and (2) a merit pay plan is likely to be the best way to bring about such changes. The next step is to state the goals and priorities more precisely. A pilot program may be initiated that involves selected schools or grade levels within the school district and, in light of the findings, a decision is made whether the innovation should be continued in its present form, altered significantly, or discontinued altogether.

TYPES OF INNOVATIONS

The innovations presented in part II fall into different categories. Both career ladders and merit pay require systematic, periodic assessment of faculty. However, whereas career ladders provide higher salaries and increased responsibilities for teachers performing duties different from their colleagues, merit pay rewards teachers with higher salaries for doing the same or a similar job than their colleagues. Career ladders represent a differential staffing plan, which assumes that various tasks of increasing complexity need to be performed and that qualified, experienced teachers can be identified for such tasks. Both plans use a measurement model that presupposes that performance can be observed and accurately evaluated.

With merit plans, material incentives are used to induce teachers to perform at a higher level; career ladders, however, not only utilize material incentives but also attempt to motivate by providing positions of greater responsibility and prestige. Both systems are thought to be cost-effective to the extent that incompetents are eliminated, and rewards are distributed based on observable standards.

Bilingual education and mainstreaming stress individual differences and a compensatory model. Certain groups of students, it is believed, have previously been neglected, or the education provided them has been inadequate; therefore, new provisions should be offered them in a more integrated setting.

Decision making in education has traditionally been from the top down, through state departments of education and large bureaucracies in centralized school districts. In contrast, school-based management breaks with this pattern by placing governance in the hands of the professional staff, thereby empowering teachers as decision makers in affairs that directly affect their schools. It reduces centralized control and engages the principal, teachers, and parents in shared decision making; thus it provides an alternative model for school governance.

Wherever educational equity is to be gained through financial reform, the underlying principle is that the quality of public education should not be a function of wealth other than the total wealth of the individual state. This places the principal burden to provide financial equity at the state level. An underlying assumption is that equity is measured by inputs in the form of per-pupil expenditures in contrast to outputs, which are measured on standardized achievement tests. The outputs approach is less concerned with inputs (whether they be per-pupil expenditures, teacher salaries, or other inputs) than with outputs on standardized test scores, irrespective of how they are obtained.

ASSESSING INNOVATIONS

It is important to determine the significance of an innovation, its appropriate use, and its likelihood of success. Several factors should be considered in making a full assessment of an innovation.

1. Initiator of the innovation. Was the innovation introduced by an organization, a group, or an individual? For instance, is a national, regional, or local organization sponsoring the innovation, and how influential is the organization within the school systems in which the innovation will be introduced? As for groups, are the groups involved central or marginal to the educational system, and how open and effective are their lines of communications? If introduced by an individual, is the person part of the establishment or outside of it? For instance, look at the reformers in part I. How would you classify them in relation to the establishment? Would it be more difficult to get their reform proposals accepted if they were not part of the establishment? But whether one is within or outside the establishment is only one factor; some of the others include the incisiveness of one's argument in favor of the innovation or alternative, one's speaking ability, access to and effectiveness in using the media, and backing by powerful public and private organizations.

2. Scope of the innovation. How many people are directly affected by the innovation? Does it affect part or all of an educational system? Does the innovation affect only local schools or schools throughout the nation?

3. Necessity of retraining. The greater amount of retraining needed before an innovation can be used effectively, the less likelihood the innovation will be successful (other things being equal). Some may resist an innovation from fear of change or lack of confidence in their ability to acquire the newly demanded skills or from serious doubts about whether the innovation will actually mark an improvement over present practice. Innovations that demand little or no retraining and are easy to understand, use, and evaluate are more likely to prove successful. This is true not only for teaching but also for business and industry.

4. Testing of the innovation. The innovation needs first to be tried out to determine its likelihood of success when adapted to a wider educational setting. Some innovations may not prove viable and will have to be discontinued or modified considerably before they can be broadly accepted. A Rand Corporation study of federal education programs found that a school district's acceptance of funding for a project did not mean that the project would be implemented the way the federal government intended. Many projects were not implemented, and the few that were did not continue the innovations after the funding ended. Moreover, innovations were not usually disseminated to other school districts. Obviously greater supervision by the Department of Education and cooperation with local districts are needed to ameliorate these conditions.

5. Support. Both adequate financial support and support from influential organizations and key individuals are needed for innovations to have the greatest likelihood of success. Some earlier innovations, such as computer-assisted instruction in the early 1970s, were quite costly; other innovations, such as programmed materials, were much less expensive. Large-scale funding alone, however, cannot assure the success of innovations, as was found in the case of certain compensatory education programs of the 1960s and the curriculum reform movement that led to the new science and mathematics. Thus, adequate funding is a necessary condition but not a necessary and sufficient condition.

Organizational support may be needed before an innovation may be widely accepted. In the United States, for instance, the backing of the National Education Association may mean the difference between success and failure for an innovation. Also, to have an innovation supported by an influential educator provides a boost for the innovation's chances of acceptance. A boost was given to such innovations as programmed materials (from B. F. Skinner), the discovery method (from Jerome S. Bruner), innovations in teacher-education programs (from James B. Conant), and career education (from Sidney Marland).

6. Likelihood of long-term success. Education leaders are reluctant to invest funds, time, and energy in an innovation without considerable probability of success. There is no surefire way to ascertain the chances of long-term success; however, the factors enumerated above may prove helpful in doing so. Thus, before adopting an innovation, the following factors should be considered: the initiator of the innovation, the scope of the innovation, the need for retraining, the testing of the innovation, and the support available.

APPENDIX

SOURCES FOR RESEARCH PAPERS

Encyclopedias and Research Summaries

American Educators' Enclycopedia. Edited by Edward L. Dejnozka and David E. Kapel. Westport, Conn.: Greenwood Press, 1982. Features nearly 2,000 entries pertaining to all levels of education; each entry averages 100–200 words, followed by a short list of references. An appendix lists federal legislation, award winners, education association presidents, and other data.

Educational Research, Methodology, and Measurement. Edited by John P. Keeves. Oxford: Pergamon Press, 1988. Offers separate chapters on a wide range of statistical techniques and research methodologies.

The Encyclopedia of Comparative Education and National Systems of Education. Edited by T. Neville Postlewaithe. Oxford: Pergamon Press, 1988. The first part presents articles about comparative education; the second part offers descriptions of 159 different systems of education.

Encyclopedia of Educational Research. 5th ed., 4 vols. New York: Macmillan, 1982. This considerably expanded edition features 256 signed entries and 317 contributors. Intended for professional educators and interested nonprofessionals, the entries are classified under eighteen broad headings beginning with Agencies and Institutions and ending with Teachers and Teaching. Each article is followed by extensive research references.

Handbook of Research on Teaching. 3rd ed. Edited by Merlin C. Wittrock. Chicago: Rand McNally, 1986. Includes thirty-five chapters on such areas as theories and methods of research on teaching, research on teachers and teaching, social and institutional context, differences among learners, and teaching of subjects and grade levels.

The International Encyclopedia of Education. 6 vols. T. Husen and T. N. Postelthwaite, editors-in-chief. New York: Pergamon, 1983. International in scope, representing many different perspectives on education.

The International Encyclopedia of Higher Education. 10 vols. San Francisco: Jossey-Bass, 1977. Includes individual articles on educational systems in 198 countries and territories, 282 articles on contemporary topics in higher education, entries about 142 fields of study, information about education associations, acronyms, and a glossary.

The International Encyclopedia of Teaching and Teacher Education. Edited by Michael J. Dunkin. Oxford: Pergamon Press, 1987. Divided into sections dealing with concepts and models, paradigms for research, teaching methods, classroom processes, contextual factors, and teacher education.

International Higher Education: An Encyclopedia. 2 vols. Edited by Philip G. Altbach. New York: Garland Publishing, 1991. Provides fifteen essays on higher education followed by descriptions and interpretations of postsecondary education in fifty-two countries.

World Education Encyclopedia. 3 vols. Edited by George Thomas Kurian. New York: Facts on File Publications, 1988. A descriptive survey of national educational systems of the world.

Dictionaries

The Concise Dictionary of Education. Gene R. Hawes and Lynne Salop Hawes. New York: Van Nostrand Reinhold, 1982. In one continuous alphabetical listing, this source not only provides concise definitions for such pedagogical terms as *behavioral objectives* and *individual differences*, but it also gives biographical sketches of educational pioneers (e.g., Clark Kerr, Abraham Maslow) and identifies key programs and issues throughout the history of education (e.g., Outward Bound, *Bakke* decision).

A Dictionary of Education. P. J. Hills. London: Routledge & Kegan Paul, 1982. This is actually two books in one: an introductory text to the different areas of education and an alphabetical arrangement of terms. Part One provides an excellent overview of the various fields of education with short bibliographies for additional reading. Part Two, the dictionary portion, gives considerable detail, where necessary, and also frequently suggests further readings. Note that this is a British reference source, and the selection of terms has a definite British bias.

Dictionary of Educational Acronyms, Abbreviations, and Initialisms. 2nd ed. James C. Palmes. Phoenix, Ariz.: Oryx Press, 1985. This book, prepared by Palmes under the aegis of the ERIC Clearinghouse for Junior Colleges, identifies over 4,000 acronyms that have appeared in ERIC's *Resources in Education* and 150 professional journals in education and related fields of study. The dictionary is divided into two sections: Part I, the acronyms, abbreviations, and initialisms; Part II, a reverse list, with the full name of the term or educational agency arranged alphabetically and their corresponding acronyms.

International Dictionary of Education. Compiled by G. Terry Page and J. B. Thomas. London: Kogan Page, 1977. International in scope, the 10,000-plus entries range from the fine points of curriculum development and educational research to the colloquialisms of the classroom.

Abstracts and Indexes

British Education Index. Edited by Philip Sheffield. Leeds, England: Leeds University Press, vol. 1–, 1954/58–. Covers United Kingdom and selected international journals.

Current Index to Journals in Education (CIJE). New York: Macmillan, vol. 1–, 1969–. A publication in the ERIC system to cover periodical literature. It selectively indexes over 700 journals and provides separate subject and author indexes that refer readers to the annotated main entry section.

Educational Administration Abstracts. Newbury Park, Calif.: Sage Publications, vol. 1–, 1966–. Summarizes latest information and research findings on educational administration from various sources.

Education Index. New York: Wilson, vol. 1–, 1929–. A monthly subject/author index in the English language that indexes over 200 journals, as well as yearbooks, proceedings, bulletins, and government documents. Its uneven coverage lists no author index from 1961–1969.

Higher Education Abstracts. Claremont, Calif.: Claremont Graduate School, vol. 1–, 1984–. Abstracts of publications about students, faculty, administration, and higher-education problems.

Human Resources Abstracts. Newbury Park, Calif.: Sage Publications, vol. 1–, 1975–. Section titled "Education, Training, and Career Development" offers abstracts about school counseling, educational administration, and educational sociology.

Multicultural Education Abstracts. Oxfordshire, England: Carfax Publishing Co., vol. 1–, 1982–. Mostly Anglo-American coverage.

Psychological Abstracts. Arlington, Va.: American Psychological Association Inc., vol. 1–, 1927–. Features abstracts in educational psychology. Also available on compact disk.

Resources in Education (RIE). Washington, D.C.: Educational Resources Information Center, vol. 1–, 1966–. *RIE*, which is part of the ERIC system and a companion volume to CIJE, covers unpublished or limited distribution literature. It includes books, documents, reports, proceedings, papers, and curriculum material by subject, author and sponsoring institution, and it includes abstracts of all articles listed. Many of the articles are available on microfiche.

Sociology of Education Abstracts. Oxfordshire, England: Carfax Publishing Co., vol. 1–, 1965/66–. Provides international coverage.

Historical Sources

Biographical Dictionary of American Educators. 3 vols. Edited by John F. Ohles. Westport, Conn.: Greenwood Press, 1978. Provides biographical information about those who have shaped American education from colonial times to 1976. Included are over 680 biographical sketches of eminent educators who had reached the age of sixty, retired, or died by January 1, 1975.

Education in the United States: A Documentary History. 5 vols. Edited by Sol Cohen. New York: Random House, 1974. Brings together significant documents extending from the sixteenth and seventeenth century European background to the earliest colonial beginnings to the present. Each volume is prefaced with an historical overview.

Statistical Sources

Digest of Educational Statistics. Washington, D.C.: U.S. Government Printing Office, 1962–. A compendium of statistics on all levels of education. It has a subject index and lists successive years of data to give historical perspective.

Standard Education Almanac. Chicago: Marquis Academic Media, 1968–. An annual almanac that provides statistical data and essays on all levels of education. It features personnel, geographic, and subject indexes and is arranged topically.

U.S. National Center for Educational Statistics. The Condition of Education: A Statistical Report on the Condition of Education in the United States. Washington, D.C.: U.S. Government Printing Office, 1975–. An annual compilation of text and statistics on education in relation to political, social, and demographic factors in the United States.

World Survey of Education Policy, Legislation, and Administration. Paris: UNESCO, 1971. Provides basic information about the educational systems of most UNESCO member countries in terms of aims and policies, administration, and the legal basis of the educational system.

Book Reviews

Book Review Index. Gale Research Co., 1965–. Indexes 422 periodicals in quarterly and annual cumulative editions. Periodicals indexed are primarily in social sciences and the humanities, with some in education.

Education Index. New York: Wilson, vol. 1–, 1929–. Book reviews drawn from over 200 journals are listed alphabetically by author in the back of each volume.

INDEX

A bbot v. Burke, 121
Abstraction in instruction, 2
Academic Learning Time (ALT), 244
Academic Preparation for College: What Students Need To Know and Be Able To Do, 30
Academic press, 171, 172
Academic teaching, 31
Acceleration, 279, 283–284
Accountability, 112–113, 114, 154
   of schools, 72
   substituting participation for authority, 159
Achievement, related to societal inequalities, 50
Achievement test scores, 176–178
Activity curriculum, 97–98
Adams, R. D., 210, 216, 219
Adams Avenue Middle School, 184–185
Adler, Michael, 76, 79
Adler, Mortimer, 2, 22–23, 30, 33, 37–47, 92
Advanced Placement Program, 285
Akinasso, F. N., 247, 248
Alexander, Lamar, 232
Alternative schools, 99–102
Alternatives, in education, 94–116, 293–295
Alum Rock (voucher plan) program, 111
Alvarado, Anthony, 192, 193, 195, 196
American College Testing (ACT examinations), 211
An American Dilemma, 264
American Federation of Teachers, 229, 232
American Institutes for Research (AIR) study, 243, 245, 255n–256n
Anderson, R. D., 211, 213, 220
Andrews, J. W., 211, 219
Annual school performance report, 154
Anthroposophy, 101
Apple, Michael W., 86n, 235, 238
Apprentice teachers, 6, 201–202, 230–231
Arciniega, Tomas A., 255n

Arendt, Hannah, 265n
Arkansas, limited statewide open enrollment plan, 193
Armor, D., 209, 219
Aronowitz, Stanley, 83n, 89
Arvizu, S., 244, 246, 249
Assimilation, 258
Associate teachers, 230–231
Association of Teacher Educators, 231, 232, 238
Athletes, 28, 34
Atlanta, magnet schools, 180
Australia
   school decentralization, 159
   site-based management, 162
Ayers, J. B., 211, 219

B aca, Reynolds, 256n
Back-to-basics movement, 11, 86, 95, 114
Bacon, Francis, 3
Baker, L. W., 211, 219
Ball, S. J., 237, 238
Banks, James A., 258, 259–264
Baratz, Joan C., 263–264, 265n
Barnes, Carol, 205
Barnes, S., 221, 244, 248
Barzun, Jacques, 45, 46
Basic educational requirements of a citizen, 29–30
Basic schooling
   content of, 42–43
   continued at higher level in college, 44
   objectives, 39, 40
Bausell, R., 219
Beck, C. M., 286
Becker, Gary S., 129n
Beery, J. R., 209, 219
Begle, E. G., 213, 219
Behavioral objectives, 102, 103–104
Behaviorism, 113–114
Behavior modification, 114
Bell, T. H., 22
Benson, Charles S., 128n
Bereiter, Carl, 265n
Berezina, G., 288–289, 290
Berliner, D., 214, 219
Berman, P., 158, 159, 160
Berry, B., 161
Bestor, Arthur, 198

B.E.T.A. School. *See* Better Education Through Alternatives School
Better Education Through Alternatives (B.E.T.A.) School, 192
Bibik, Janice M., 230–238
Bilingual education, 241–248, 294
   cognitive aspects of both languages interdependent, 245–246
   educational and societal circumstances, 247, 248
   effectiveness seen in research studies, 252–253
   funding, 254
   language attitudes, 246–247, 248
   program goals confusion, 253
   self-esteem of students, 253
   Spanish language and heritage curricula funding, 250
   threshold level, 245, 247
   types of linguistic programs and cultural heritage model, 251–252
Bilingual Education Act, 241, 250, 251, 253
   Amendment of 1978, 252
Bilingualism and Biculturalism Commission's report (1968), 241
Bill of Rights, 34
Biological Sciences Curriculum Study, 285
Biondi, A. M., 284, 286
Bird, Otto, 45
Blackmon, C. R., 211, 219
Blacks, 260, 262
   treatment contradictory to American creed, 264
Blanco, George M., 242–248
Blankenship, M. L. D., 216, 219
Blatt, Burton, 275, 276
Bledsoe, J. C., 209, 219
Bloom, Benjamin S., 103, 284, 286
Bloom taxonomy, 284
Boeck, M.A., 216, 219
Boorstin, Daniel J., 46
Borg, W. R., 216, 219
Boston, schools of choice, 195
Botstein, Leon, 45

Bowles, Samuel, 259, 264n
Boyd, W. L., 159, 160
Boydston, Jo Ann, 84n
Boyer, Ernest L., 12–21, 23, 45,
  46, 92, 199
Boyer Report, 12–23
Bradbury, Katharine L., 133n
Brameld, Theodore, 8, 9
Branching, 103
Brickman, W., 289, 290
Brigham, Frederick H., Jr., 79
Bronx High School of Science, 283
Brophy, J., 214, 219
Brown, C., 221
Brown, G. H., 255n
Brown, O., 219n, 220
Brown University, 35
Brown v. Board of Education
  (1954), 259
Bruner, Jerome S., 104, 295
Bruno, J. E., 212, 219
Bryan, Dexter, 256n
Buchmann, M., 215, 220
Bulletin, 27
Bureaucracies, 77
Burnham, R., 209, 219
Burt, H., 255n, 256n
Bush, Bob, 205
Bush, George, support of
  vouchers, 193
Bush, R. N., 216, 219
Busing, compulsory, 141, 180
Butler-Por, N., 289, 290
Byrne, Colin, 213, 219

California
  effectiveness in schools, 171,
    173
  English Immersion/ESL program
    in Buena Park, 251
  financial reform, 117, 120, 121,
    142
  Los Angeles Unified School
    District, 205
  Segregated Language Proficiency
    program in Los Angeles, 251,
    252
  site-based management, 162
  unfilled bilingual teaching
    positions, 253
California Consortium on the
  Beginning Years of Teaching,
  204–205
California education code, 13

California Round Table on
  Educational Opportunity,
  237–238
California School Administrators,
  Association of, 202
California Task Force for
  Integrated Education, 256n
Callahan, R. E., 233, 238
Cambridge, Massachusetts, 79n
Camp, Catherine, 256n
Campbell, E. Q., 219
Campbell, Jack K., 255n
*Can We Be Equal and Excellent
  Too?,* 287
Caputi, Nicholas, 45
Cardenas, Blandena, 256n
Cardénas, Jose, 255n, 256n
Career ladders, 225–238, 293
  aims, 232
  approaches used by states to
    develop programs, 227
  career-staging, 232
  deskilling, 235, 236
  effect on teacher education, 235
  elements needing to be part of
    the package, 228
  financial incentives, 228–229
  objectives, 228
  rewards associated, 228
  teacher/coach conflict, 237
  vs. career lattice, 237–238
Career lattice, 225, 230–238
  advantages over career ladder
    alone, 237–238
Career-staging, 232
Carnegie Foundation, 12, 18
Carnegie Task Force report, 200,
  203–206
Carnegie units, 14
Carnoy, Martin, 129n
Carrison, Muriel Paskin, 250–255
Carroll, J. B., 103
Carter, Thomas P., 255n
Casner-Lotto, J., 157, 158, 159,
  160
Castañeda, Alfredo, 263–264, 265n
Cater, Douglass, 45
Centralized direction of schools, 28
Certification, teacher, 72
Chandler, Harry N., 274–277
Chandler, Timothy J. L., 225,
  230–238
Chapman, J., 159, 160
Charles, Joyce, 196

Checklist for Teachers, 61
Chicago, schools of choice, 195
Chicanos, 260, 262
Child-centered education, 5
Child labor, 128
"Children at risk," 242, 243, 245,
  247–248
Children's rights, 11, 143
Children's School (Margaret
  Naumberg's), 8
"Choice office," 69, 71, 72
Choice of public school system,
  75–77
Christopherson, Claire, 133n
Chubb, John E., 69–79, 93
Citizenship education in the high
  school, 18, 40
Civil rights movement, 18, 58, 115
Clark, D., 229
Class domination theory, 89
*Classrooms and Corridors: The
  Crisis of Authority in
  Desegregated Secondary
  Schools,* 184, 191
Class size, 15, 20
  changes needed for
    mainstreaming special
    education students, 271, 273
  Montessori school, 100
Cliff, P., 215
Cliff, R., 221
Cliffs, N. J., 221
Climate, 176
Closing the Gap, 58
Clune, William H., 117, 154, 155,
  156, 158, 160
Coaching, 30, 48
  of teachers in the arts of
    teaching, 43
Coaching method of instruction,
  41, 42
Coble, 213–214
Cognitive skills, 33, 106, 139, 148
  emphasis on, 65, 66
Cohen, David K., 27, 79
Cohen, M., 154, 161
Cohn, Elchanan, 129n
Coker, H., 209, 222
Coleman, James S., 74–75, 79,
  123, 125n, 137–149, 212, 219
  on multicultural education, 260,
  264n
Coleman, W., Jr., 288, 290
Coleman Report (1966), 61, 260

Collective bargaining, 69, 72
College Board, 30
Collins, M. L., 210, 220
Colorado, financial reform, 122
Comenius, John Amos, 3
Commission on Educational Issues, 27
Common-school ideal, 140–144, 148, 149
Community-control movement, 11
Compartmentalization, 26, 29, 98–99
Compensatory education, 106–107
Competency-based teacher education (CBTE), 216
Competency education, 116
Competency testing, 10, 114
Comprehensive high school, 18
Compulsory education, 6, 10, 26, 29, 128
standards, 33, 34
Computer-assisted instruction (CAI), 102–103, 114
Conant, James B., 18, 19, 23, 198, 295
Conant Report, 18–19
Connecticut, financial reform, 117
Conry-Oseguera, P., 219
Conservatism, 59
Control of school program, 31
Contracts, instructional, 96
Conventional critic, 10
Conventional establishment educator, 10
Cook County Normal School, 99
Cooley, W., 171, 174
Coons, John, 117
Cooperative living, 100
Copeland, W. D., 216, 220
Copley, P. O., 209, 220
Corcoran, T. B., 153, 159, 161
Core curriculum, 12, 14–16, 19–22, 28, 65
learning engagements provided for gifted students, 283
as Paideia group's proposal, 47–49
Cornett, L. M., 209, 211, 214, 220, 221, 229
Corporal punishment, 11
Cortes, Carlos, 252, 256n
Council of State Directors of Programs for the Gifted, 280
Councils, composition of, 164

Counseling students, 2
Counts, George S., 8, 9
Cowan, Donald, 45
Cox, J. U., 209, 219
Cox, M., 219
Cremin, Lawrence, 264n
Crim, Alonzo, 45, 46
Crisis of authority, 145–146, 149
Criterion for learning
age grading, 29, 30
"inspiring" students to do the learning, 29, 30
reconstructing knowledge versus compartmentalization, 29
"time spent," 29, 30
Critical triangle, 27
Crittenden, B. S., 286
Cross, K. Patricia, 83n
Crowder, Norman, 102–103
Cuban, Larry, 157, 161, 170, 175–178
Cubberly, Elwood P., 127n
Cultural bias, 60
Cultural capital, 90
Cultural-deprivation hypothesis, 263, 264
Cultural-difference (multicultural) hypothesis, 263–264
Cultural Heritage Model, 252
Cultural literacy, 33, 52–66, 92
Cultural Literacy Foundation, 60
Cultural Literacy: What Every American Needs to Know, 63, 64
Culture, 90
"Culture cracking," 64
Cummins, J., 245, 246–247, 248
Curriculum, 92
changes needed for mainstreaming special education students, 271
content of secondary education, 33, 37
course content regulated by state board of education, 121
for gifted and talented students, 282–285
high school, 28
reform, 47, 48, 59
required, 40, 42
school-based management, 156
skill-oriented in a magnet school, 185

standardization recommended, 187–188, 190
Curriculum development goals, 12
Curriculum Master Plan Council, 156
Curriculum Planning for the Gifted, 284, 286

Dalton Plan, 96, 97
D'Angelan, A., 246, 248
Danoff, M. N., 243, 245, 248
Darling-Hammond, L., 161, 212, 220
David, Jane L., 153–160, 161
Deal, Terrence E., 83n
Decency, promoted as a virtue, 30
Decentralization, 153
Decision making reform rationale, 10, 11
Deductive approach, 2
Deering, Thomas, 225, 226–229
Defino, M., 221
Deification, of child, 99
Democratic values, 8–9
Densmore, K., 223
Denton, J. J., 209, 211, 220
Deschooler, 10
Desegregation
effect on parental choice of magnet schools, 196
grants to schools involved in, 180, 186
inducement of magnet schools, 189
magnet school enrollment racial quotas, 182
social effects, 183, 185, 190
success diminished by urban demographic trends, 263
Designs for Change, 195
Development Associates, 256n
De Vitis, Joseph L., 18
Dewey, John, 5–6, 9, 66–67, 84–85, 93, 98–100, 104
Dewey Laboratory School, 99–100
Didactic method of instruction, 41, 42
Different by Design: The Content and Character of Three Magnet Schools, 184, 191
Differential staffing, 293
Differentiated curriculum, 284, 285
Differentiated staffing, 108–109, 230–231

Diploma award criteria, 30
Discipline, 19, 21
  breakdown of, 142–143
  control problems, 184
Discovery learning, 104–105
Discretionary School Improvement
  Fund, 16
Docility as an adolescent trait in
  high school, 34
Domanico, Raymond, 79
"Dominant evaluations," 246
Doscher, M. L., 212, 219
Dress codes, 11
Dropouts
  High School Graduation
    Incentives plan, 194
  and magnet schools, 183, 193
  rates, 103
  research studies of bilingual
    education programs, 253
Druva, C. A., 211, 213, 220
Ducharme, R. J., 211, 220
Dulay, H., 255n, 256n
Dunn, I. M., 272
Dunstan, J., 289, 290
Duttweiler, R., 222

"The Early History of School
  Financing," 127
Edelman, Murray, 49, 188–189
Edgewood Independent School
  District (Texas), 119
Edgewood v. Kirby, 121
Edmond, Ron, 122
Education, definition of, 37
Education Commission of the
  States, 193, 255n
Educational liberalism, 59
Educational philosophy, 37
Educational reform, 93
  teachers having central role,
    83–84
Educational success, 187
Educational Testing Service, 64
Educationese, 32
Education for All Handicapped
  Children Act, 287
Education for the Gifted, 281, 286
Education Voucher Agency (EVA),
  111, 112
Edwards, S., 222
Effectiveness, 176
Effective schools, 67, 73, 170–178
  characteristics, 170

curricular and climate variables,
  171–174
Effective schools formula
  (Edmond's), 122
Egalitarianism, 115–116
Egbert, R. L., 214, 220, 223
Eiden, Leo J., 255n
Eisenberg, T. A., 213, 220
Ekstrom, R. B., 212, 220
Elective courses, 42
  elimination of, 40
Elementary and Secondary
  Education Act (ESEA) of
  1965, 115, 259, 279
  Title I, 106
Elitism, 56–57, 59
  fostered by magnet schools, 180,
    186, 189, 194, 195
Elizario Independent School
  District, 118–119
Ellis, Pat, 275, 277
Elmore, R. F., 154, 161
Emergency School Aid Act
  (ESAA), 1976 amendment,
  180
Emmer, E., 216, 220
Enemark, P., 216, 219
Englemann, Siegfried, 265n
English, F., 229
English Immersion/ESL (English
  as a Second Language), 245,
  251
Enrichment, 279, 283–284, 285
Enrollment Options plan, 194
Environmentalists, 263
Equal educational opportunity
  principle, 38, 39
*Equality of Educational
  Opportunity Report,* 123
Equalization guarantee formula
  (New Mexico, 1974), 120
Equal-protection clause,
  California, 120
Equal-protection clause, federal,
  119
Equity, educational, through
  financial reform, 117–135
Equity reform rationale, 10, 11
Equity vs. excellence, 287–290
Erickson, D. A., 221
Erickson, F., 215, 220
Essentialism, 4–5, 19, 92, 113, 114
Essential Schools, 31
Estes, Thomas H., 52, 63–66

Esty, John, 27
Ethos, democratic, 267
EVA. *See* Education Voucher
  Agency
Evertson, Carolyn M., 207–219
Exceptional children, 287
Expenditure per pupil, 130, 131
Experience curriculum, 97–98
External discipline, 5
Extracurricular activities, 34, 42

Fadiman, Clifton, 45, 46
Falco, John, 192, 194
Farrar, Eleanor, 27, 79
Feiman, Nemser, S., 215, 220
Fenstermacher, G., 215, 220
Field trips, 99
Financial reform, 27, 117–135
Finn, Chester E., Jr., 26, 32–35,
  78, 79
Fishman, J. A., 246, 248
Fitzgerald, J., 285, 286
Flanders, N. A., 217, 220
Fleury, S. C., 234, 238
Flexible scheduling, 110
Fliegel, Sy, 79
Fliegler, L. A., 284, 286
Florida
  career ladder program legislation
    enacted, 227
  major drive for career ladders,
    232
  school-based management, 152,
    153
  site-based management, 162
Focus on Exceptional Children,
  273
Follow-Through, 106–107
Ford Foundation, 204
Formalism, and early European
  educational philosophy, 2
Foster, Charles R., 255n, 256n
Foteyeva, A., 288–289, 290
Fox, Thomas G., 117, 126–135
France, no programs for gifted
  students, 289
Francis W. Parker School, 99
Francke, E. L., 210, 220
Frankfurt School, 82
Frank Porter Graham Child
  Development Center, 276
Fratoe, Frank A., 256n
Free activity, 5
Freeman, J., 290

Free schools, 2, 6, 95, 110, 113, 115–116
Freire, Paulo, 2, 82
French, R., 229
French, Will, 280, 286
Freud, Sigmund, 7–8
Friday, William, 46
Friedman, Milton, 133n
Fullan, M., 154, 159, 161, 210, 220
Fuller, F., 219n, 220
Functional literacy, 53, 54, 60–61
Funding, 71, 111–112
   disparities, 117–125
   due to Elementary and Secondary Education Act of 1965, 259–260
   for bilingual education, 254
   for improved teacher salaries, 199–200
   gifted children programs, 287, 288
   lacking in mainstreaming law's monitoring, 275–276
   nonpublic school chartering as a public school, 93
   outside, 149
   statewide taxation, 142
Fund raising, to support reform programs, 2
Fyfield, J., 217, 223

Gabrys, R. E., 210, 220
Gage, N. L., 216, 220
Gall, M. D., 216, 221
Gallagher, James J., 276, 287–290
Galumbos, E., 214, 221
Garcia, Ricardo, 255n
Gardner, D. P., 229
Gardner, John W., 287, 290
Garms, W. I., 154, 158, 161
Gary Plan, 98–99
Gay, Geneva, 264n
Gehrke, N., 219n, 221
Gendler, Tamar, 117, 118–125
General Accounting Office, 213
Genes, relation to intelligence, 263
Georgia
   financial reform, 122
   professional knowledge common tests, 211–212
   school-based management, 152
Gerlock, D. E., 209, 221
Getzels, J. W., 212, 221

Gezi, Kal, 255n, 256n
Gifted and talented, 18, 116
   curriculum, 282–285
   definition of terms, 279
   discriminated against in achievement tests, 178
   education of, 279–286
   entrance requirements for magnet schools, 186
   magnet school curriculum, 185, 186
   need for total planning, 281–283
   programs, 281–282, 283
   provisions, 281–282
   strategies for policy report for educational programs, 289–290
Gifted Children: Psychological and Educational Perspectives, 281, 286
Gintis, Herbert, 259, 264n
Giroux, Henry A., 82–90, 93
Gjelten, T., 158, 159, 160
Glass, G., 219n, 221
Glenn, Charles, 79, 80n, 193, 195, 196
Goals of schooling, 37
Goertz, M. E., 212, 220
Gold, M. J., 286
Goldberg, M. L., 280, 286
Goldstein, Herbert, 276
Good, T., 214, 219
Good, T. L., 244, 248
Goodlad, John I., 153, 161, 199
Goodman, Jesse, 85, 86n
Goodman, Paul, 6
Goodrich, R. L., 243, 248
Goodson, I. F., 237, 238
Gordon, W. J. J., 284, 286
Government control, 27
Graham, Patricia Albjerg, 14–15, 260, 264n
Grant, W. Vance, 255n
Gray, H. B., 209, 221
Gray, T. C., 243, 248
Great Books of the Western World, 37
Great Depression, 8
Great Hall, City College of New York, 55
Green, Philip, 264n
Green, Robert L., 265n
Greenbaum, William, 264n
"Green books," 284
Griffin, G. A., 217, 221

Grouws, D., 244, 248
Gumperz, J. J., 247, 248
Guthrie, James W., 125n, 156, 159, 160, 161
Gutman, Carol J., 52, 63–66
Gutmann, Amy, 75, 79

Haberman, M., 221
Hall, G., 210, 217, 221
Hall, H. O., 209, 221
Hallinger, Philip, 170, 171–174
Halsey, A. H., 247, 248
Hamilton, P. D., 216, 221
Hampel, Robert, 27
Handicapped children, education of, 271–277
Hansen, D. A., 246, 247, 248
Hansen, W. Lee, 129n
Hanushek, E., 212, 221
Harpel, J., 285, 286
Harrison, Elise K., 52, 63–66
Harrison Resource Learning Center, 273
Hartman, William T., 125n
Haskins, R., 287, 290
Hawaii, limited statewide open enrollment plan, 193
Hawk, 213–214
Hawley, Willis D., 46–50, 207–219, 221, 228–229, 242, 248
Head Start, 106–107, 287
Heath, Shirley Brice, 183
Helena v. Montana, 121
Henry, N., 286
Herrnstein, Richard, 263, 265n
Hertzler, Joan, 256n
Herzberg, F., 232–233, 236, 238
High School and Beyond, 69
High School Graduation Incentives plan, 194
Hirsch, E. D., Jr., 33, 52–61, 63–67, 92
Hirschman, Albert, 75, 79
Hispanics. See Mexican-Americans; Minorities; Puerto Ricans
Hobson, C. J., 219, 220
Hoffer, Thomas, 74, 75, 79, 147n, 264n
Holmes Group report, 200, 201, 203–204, 205, 206
Holt, John, 2, 6
Home instruction plans, 95
Homogeneous groupings, 114
Honors track, 28

Horace's Compromise: The Dilemma of the American High School Today, 22, 27, 32–35
Hord, S., 210, 221
Howard, J. L., 210, 221
Hudak, G., 223
Hughes, E. C., 236, 238
Hughes, R. Jr., 221
Hukill, H., 221
Humanistic education, 7
Hunt, Richard, 45
Husén, T., 289, 290
Hutchins, Robert Maynard, 39
Hygiene needs, 233, 236, 237, 238

Idaho, financial reform, 122
Ideology, Culture and the Process of Schooling, 89
Iiams, Thomas M., 255n
Illich, Ivan, 6
Illinois
  school-based management, 152
  schools of choice plan for Chicago, 193
Income group differences among schools, 28
Individual education programs (IEPs), 276, 277
Individualized instructional plans, 115
Individually Prescribed Instruction, 273
Inductive methods, 99
Inductive process of learning, 3
Informal learning, 6
In loco parentis principle, 142–144, 148, 149
Innovations, in education, 2, 94–116, 293–295
  assessment of, 294–295
  curriculum, 95, 96–98, 99, 105–107
  instruction, 95, 96–97, 102–105
  organization, 95, 96, 99, 107–110
  rationale, 95
Innovative critic, 10
Innovative establishment educator, 10
Institutional choice in education, 75–77
Instruction, different kinds of, 41
Instructional contracts, 96
Instructional objectives, 102

Integrationists, 263
Intellectual quotient (IQ) tests, 264
  results not sufficient for special placement, 273
  Intellectual skills of learning, 40, 41
  calculating skills, 40
  language skills, 40
  technological skills, 40
Interest groups, 77
International Baccalaureate, 285
Intern teacher, 108
Iowa, limited statewide open enrollment plan, 193
Irish, 263
Isaac Newton School for Science and Mathematics, 192, 194
Israel, education of the gifted, 289
Issacs, Susan, 110
Itard, Seguin, and Kephart, 275

Jackson, P. W., 2, 212, 221
Japanese-Americans, academic success, 261
Jencks, Christopher, 111, 259, 264n
Jensen, Arthur R., 263, 264n–265n
Jesse Owens Middle School, 184–185, 186
Jewish Americans, academic success, 261, 263
Job satisfaction, 232–233
Johns, Roe L., 127, 128n
Johns Hopkins Studies of Mathematically Precocious Youth, 285
Johnson, H. C., Jr., 227, 229
Johnson, S. M., 160, 161
Johnson, V. A., 246, 247, 248
Jones, Alan H., 199–206
Jose Feliciano Performing Arts School (formerly East Harlem Performing Arts School), 192
Joyce, B. R., 210, 215, 216, 218, 221

Kallenbach, W. W., 216, 221
Kandel, I. L., 127n, 128n
Kanter, R. M., 154, 159, 161
Kaplan, S., 288, 290
Karabel, Jr., 247, 248
Kaufman, B., 285, 286
Kelty, Mary G., 67
Kentucky, financial reform, 117

Kilgore, Sally, 74, 75, 79, 147n, 264n
Kilpatrick, William Heard, 4, 98
King, N., 219
King, Richard A., 125n
Kirk, Samuel A., 276
Kliebard, Herbert, 85n
Kluender, M. M., 214, 220, 223
Kneer, M., 237, 238
Knott, Jack, 77, 79
Knowledge
  acquisition in specific subject areas, 40
  role in educational development, 66
Kocylowski, M. M., 216, 221
Koehler, V., 215, 221
Koerner, James, 198
Kohl, Herbert, 6
Kohlberg, L., 284, 286
Kolderie, T., 159, 161
Kostakis, Manny, 194
Kozol, Jonathan, 6
Kramer, A., 290–291
Kranz, Jennifer, 162–168
Kratwohl, D. R., 286
Kraushaar, Otto F., 79

Labelization of students, 7
Labov, William, 246, 248, 263–264, 265n
Lacey, Colin, 82, 89–90
La Chalotais, 127n
Lacina, L. J., 209, 220
Ladd, Helen F., 133n
Landau, E., 289, 290
Lane, Stacey L., 230–238
Lanier, J., 221
Lau v. Nichols, 242–243
Lazos, Héctor, 245, 248
Leadership, 176
Learning
  by discovery, 43
  capacity, 39
  different kinds of, 41
  experiments, 2
  quality of, 43
  style, 48
"Learning disabilities," 276
Learning disabled students, mainstreaming of, 274–277
"Least restrictive environment," 275
Leinhardt, G., 171, 174, 215, 221

Levine, D., 171, 174
Limited-English-speaking (LES) students, 242–246, 251–252
Lins, L. J., 211, 222
"List knowing," 65
Literacy skills, adults, 2
Literate culture, 54–57, 59, 60, 64
  connections with statehood, 57
Local control, 141–144, 148, 149
Local financing, 142–144, 148, 149
Locke, L. F., 210, 222
Lortie, D. C., 232, 234, 238
Louisiana, school-based management, 153
Love, Ruth B., 45, 46
Lovelace, 211
Lu Pone, L. J., 209, 222

McCarty, D., 85n
McDonnell, L., 219
MacIntyre, Alastaire, 268
MacKenzie, D. E., 214, 222
Mackey, J. A., 211
McLaughlin, M. W., 212, 222
MacMillan, Donald, 273
McPartland, J., 220
Magnet schools, 180–196
  bibliography for further reading, 191
  financial support, 189
  as form of segregation, 195–196
  numerical racial balance effect, 196
  obligation to innovate in education beneficial, 186
  potential, 184–185, 190
  purpose, 182–183
  social effects, 183, 185, 190
  specialties and number of, 180, 192
Maguire, J. W., 211, 213, 222
Maieutic method of instruction, 42
Mainstreaming, 271–277, 294
  districtwide implications of trend on staff and facilities, 273
  vocational education's linkage with special education, 277
Malen, Betty, 162–168
Malthus, Thomas, 127
Management pedagogies, 86
Mann, Horace, 128–129
Manski, C., 212, 222
Manual skill development, 42
March, James, 77, 80n

Marcus, M., 211, 222
Marenbach, Dieter, 129n
Market controls, 73–79
Marland, Sidney J., 286, 295
Marland Report (1971) (U.S. Office of Education), 281, 284
Marquis Academic Media, 255n
Marsh, D. D., 212, 222
Maryland
  financial reform, 122
  George's County magnet school system, 196
  Largo High School, 196
  school-based management, 152, 153
Massachusetts, Cambridge controlled choice plan, 195
Massey, H. W., 209, 211, 212, 213, 222
Master teachers, 108, 225, 226, 230–232
Mastery learning, 103–104
Mathematics Education for Gifted Secondary School Students (MEGSSS), 285
Mays, Benjamin, 46
Mean wage differentials, 58
Medina, Carlos, 192
Medley, D. M., 209, 222
Meeker, M., 284, 286
Meier, D., 153, 159, 161
Memorization, 63–64, 66
Mentally retarded students, education of, 272–273
Mercer, Jane R., 265n
Meritocracy, 115–116
Merit (pay) plans, 108, 109, 225, 227, 230, 293
Metz, Mary Haywood, 181, 182–191
Mexican-Americans, 241, 245, 250–255
  barrio socialization, 260–261
  "temporary visitor" mental set, 254
Michigan, University of, School of Education selectivity of candidates, 203
Microteaching, 216–217
Middle schools, 107
Miles, M., 159, 161
Militancy on campus, 18
Miller, Gary, 77, 79
Miller Analogies Test (MAT), 211

Millett, G. B., 210, 216, 220, 222
Minnesota, 79n
  mandatory statewide open enrollment plan, 193, 194–195
  Minneapolis limitations in choice of schools, 196
  site-based management, 162
Minorities, 241–255, 258–270, 294
  higher percentage in special classes, 271, 272–273
Mirabeau, Rolland, 127n
Mississippi, compulsory attendance, 128
Missouri, career ladder program, 228
Mitchell, P., 287, 288, 290
Mitman, A., 174
Mixed Language Proficiency, 251
Moe, Terry, 69, 70, 73–79
Montana, financial reform, 117, 121, 122, 123–124
Montessori, Maria, 100
Montessori School, 100–101
Mood, A. M., 220
Moody, W., 219
Moore, Donald R., 195–196
Morgan, H. J., 286
Morris, Richard J., 275
Morrison, Henry C., 103
Mosk, Sanford A., 256n
Mosseley, J. E., 256n
Motivation, of teachers, 226
Motivation-hygiene theory of management, 232–233, 236
Motivation needs, 232–233
Mulling, C., 236, 239
Multicultural education, 258–270
  class interests, 262
  different educational entitlements and needs, 261
  diversity displayed within ethnic groups, 261–262
  equality and equity, 259
  genetic explanation for low academic achievement of minority youths, 263
  norms, behaviors and values promoted by other institutions, 261
Multiculturalism, 55, 59
Multiethnic education. *See* Multicultural education
Murname, Richard, 79, 80n
Murnane, R. J., 209, 212, 222

Murphy, Joseph, 170, 171–174
Murphy, P. D., 210, 222
Myrdal, Gunnar, 264, 265n

NASSP, 27
Nathan, Joe, 79
"National Assessment of
    Educational Progress" (1986),
    64, 67, 176
National Association of
    Independent Schools, 27
National Catholic Education
    Association, 80n
National Center for Education
    Statistics, 80n, 131
National Center on Effective
    Secondary Schools, University
    of Wisconsin, 185–186
National Clearinghouse for
    Bilingual Education, 255n,
    256n
National Commission on
    Excellence in Education, 35,
    199
National Defense Education Act of
    1958, 18, 279
National Educational Finance
    Project (1972), 127
National Education Association
    (NEA), 53, 54, 232, 295
National Education Association
    Project on the Academically
    Talented Student, 284
National Endowment for the
    Humanities, 64
National Governors' Association,
    153
National Teacher Examination
    (NTE), 211
A Nation at Risk, 22, 199, 200,
    225
A Nation Prepared: Teachers for
    the 21st Century, 200, 203–204
Native Americans, 241, 260, 262
Native Language Immersion
    program, 252
Nault, Richard, 79, 80n
Naumberg, Margaret, 8
Neill, A. S., 2, 8, 34
Neill, George, 255n
Nelson, James, 45
Nemser, S. F., 217, 222
Neoprogressivism, 34
New institutionalism, 77

New Jersey
    financial reform, 117, 119–124
    school choice pilot plan, 193
New Jersey Constitution's
    Education Clause (1875), 119
New Mexico
    financial reform, 120–121
    school-based management, 153
New York
    financial reform, 122
    founding of teacher college, 198
    school-based management, 152
    schools of choice, 195
    site-based management, 162
Nickel, Kenneth, 255n
Noller, R. B., 284, 286
Non-English-speaking (NES)
    students, 242–246, 251–252
Nongraded schools, 107–108, 115
Normal schools, 198
Norms, ingrained, 164, 165
North Carolina
    career ladder system of
        evaluation, 234
    teacher performance study
        (provisionally certified vs.
        regular certified), 209
North Carolina School for
    Mathematics and Science, 283
Nuclear annihilation, 8

Occupational introduction, 42
OEO. See Office of Economic
    Opportunity
Office of Economic Opportunity
    (OEO), 111, 112–113
Office of Educational Equity
    (Massachusetts education
    department), 193, 195
Ogawa, Rodney T., 162–168
Ogbu, John U., 183, 247, 248
Oglesby, K., 287, 290
Ohio
    financial reform, 122
    Hudson High School, 147, 148
Oliver, Bernard, 230–238
Olsen, Johan, 77, 80n
O'Malley, J. M., 243, 248–249
O'Neal, S., 221
One-track system of schooling, 39
On the Trail of Process, 275
Open classrooms, 6, 10, 19, 110,
    115
    in a magnet school, 185

Open-space schools, 110
Options reformer, 10
Oral communications, 15
Oregon, financial reform, 122
Organized knowledge acquisition,
    41
Organized subject matter, 7
Orr, Daniel, 133n
Ortiz, F. I., 153, 156, 159, 160,
    161
O'Sullivan, P. D., 211, 216, 222
O'Toole, James, 45

Paideia, definition, 45
Paideia group members, 45
The Paideia Proposal, 22, 30, 33,
    37–50, 92
Parent information center, 71, 72
Parker, Francis W., 4, 99
Parkhurst, Helen, 96
Parnes, S. J., 284, 286
Part C. Research Agenda of ESEA
    Title VII, 243
Pascal, A., 219
Passow, A. Harry, 280–286
Pauley, E., 219
Paulston, C. B., 243, 245, 247, 249
Peck, L., 221
Peck, R. F., 217, 222
Pedagogy, the act of teaching, 33
Peer acceptance, of educable
    mentally retarded students,
    272
Pennsylvania
    financial reform, 123
    Philadelphia schools of choice,
        195
Perennialism, philosophy of, 37,
    92, 93
Performance-based compensation,
    108, 109, 225, 227, 230, 293
Performance contracting, 112–113
Performance habits, development
    of, 41
Performing arts, schools for, 95
Perpich, Rudy, 194
Personal development, opportunity
    as moral obligation, 40
Personalization, 31
Personalized teaching and learning,
    30
Perspectives in Special Education:
    Personal Orientations, 275
Pestalozzi, Johann Heinrich, 3

Petch, Alison, 76, 79
Peters, R. S., 93
Peterson, S. M., 154, 158, 159, 161
Pettigrew, Thomas, 265n
Phenix, P. H., 282, 284, 286
Phillips, B. R., 212, 222
Phillips Academy, 34
Piaget, Jean, 110, 113
Pifer, Alan, 255n
Pioneer Houses, 289
Piper, M. K., 211, 216, 222
Pipho, C., 232, 239
Placement tests, 18
Planning for Talented Youth: Considerations for Public Schools, 280–281, 283, 286
Platoon System, 98–99
Plessy v. Ferguson (1896), 259
Pluralism, 258
  limits of, 266–269
  moral anarchy bred in schools, 268–269
Policy-making power, 141
Politics, Markets, and America's Schools, 69
Popham, J., 219n, 222
Postman, Neil, 6
Post-Secondary Options program, 194
Powell, Arthur G., 27
Power equalizing formula, 117
Practical problems of education, 37
Pragmatism, 5–6
Preschool education, 39, 49
Pressey, Sidney L., 102
Primary pedagogy of high school, 30
Principal's autonomy, 77, 78
Private schools, 32
  advantages, 69
  effect of partial privatization of public school finance, 133
  market and political systems of control in education, 74
  vs. public schools, 74–77, 93, 147–149
  vs. public schools in educational quality, 138–147
Probationary teacher, 108
Problem solving, 5
  Dewey's, 104
Process of enlightenment, 41

Professional staff quality, 28
Programmatic reform, 2
Programmed instruction, 102–103, 114
Program Planners, Inc., 239
Progressivism, 4–6, 8, 92, 96–97, 99, 113, 115
  child-centered, 4–5
  methods and content to engage students outside the mainstream in school learning, 183
  similar to open education, 110
  vs. romantic naturalism, 6, 7
Project Method, 98
Proletarianization of teacher work, 84–85
Proposition 13, in California, 173
Prospective teachers, 2
Psychoanalytic theory, 8
Psychoneurosis, theory of, 7–8
Psychotherapy, 8
Public and Private Schools, 138, 147–148
Public Law 94–142 (PL 94–142), 271, 275, 276, 277, 287
Public schools, origins of, 127–128
Public support for public schools, 142
Puck, Theodore, 45
Puerto Ricans, 241, 262
Pugach, M. C., 211, 222
Pupil-teacher planning, 97
Pupil-teacher ratios, 137
Purkey, Stewart C., 80n, 154, 159, 161
Pygmalion, 55, 59

Quality control, 233, 234, 236
Quality of basic schooling, 44
Quality reform rationale, 10
Qualls, G. S., 211, 219
Quantity reform rationale, 10
"Quincy System," 99

Racial steering by real estate agents, 188
Ramirez, Manuel, III, 263–264, 265n
Rand, Elaine, 256n
Rand Corporation, study of federal education programs, 295
Raths, J. E., 211, 222

Ratich, Wolfgang, 2–3
Rauth, M., 229
Raywid, Mary Anne, 79, 80n, 154, 158, 161, 193, 195–196
Reagan, Ronald, support of voucher plan, 193
Reconstructionism, 8–9
Rees, C. Roger, 233
Reflective thinking process, 5
"Reforming School Finance in Illinois," 120
Reform rationales, 10–11
Renzulli, J. S., 284–285, 286
Research papers, sources for, 296–298
Restoration reform rationale, 10, 11
Retention, of teachers, 226
Rich, John Martin, 12, 18–23
Rickover, Admiral Hyman, 198
Riew, John, 117, 126–135
Rights reform rationale, 10, 11
Robinson, G. E., 228, 229
Robinson v. Cahill, 119, 121
Rodriguez v. San Antonio (1973), 117, 119, 121
Roeder, Ralph, 256n
Rogers, Carl, 217
Rogers, Joseph, 147–149
Romanticism, 3
  vs. essentialism, 5
Romantic naturalists, 6–7
Rosenholtz, S. J., 214, 217
Rosenshine, B., 214, 222
Rossell, Christine, 79, 80n
Rossmiller, Richard A., 125n
Rote learning, 2, 3
Rousseau, Jean Jacques, 3–4, 6–7, 99, 127n
Rugg, Harold, 8
Ryan, K., 220

Salaries for teachers, based on performance, 225
Salomone, R. M., 243, 249
San Antonio v. Rodriguez (1973), 117, 119, 121
Sarason, Seymour B., 216, 222, 276
Saravia-Shore, M., 243, 244, 246, 249
Sato, I., 288, 290
Sawhill, John C., 267
Scheffler, Israel, 84n, 87n

Schlechty, Phillip C., 234, 239
Schlechty, S., 229
Schmidt, Adolph, 45
Schmueli, E., 289, 290
Scholarships, 71, 93
Scholastic Aptitude Test (SAT),
    211, 212
  achievement scores, 130–131
  1984 report of College Board, 64
School administrators, relevancy of
    education, 201
School-based management, 152
  budget, 154–155, 158, 160
  curriculum, 156, 158
  decentralization, 157, 159–160
  findings from studies, 158–160
  future developments, 160
  school autonomy, 154–157
  school-site budgeting, 157, 158
  "second-order" changes, 156–157,
    159
  shared decision making, 154,
    157–158, 159
  staffing, 155–156, 158
  waiver process, 157, 160
School-Based Management/Shared
    Decision-Making Program,
    153
School day and school year,
    extension proposed, 199
School improvement priorities, 21
  core curriculum of common
    knowledge, 14, 15–16, 17, 19,
    20, 21
  school leadership, 14, 16–17, 19
  thinking skills, 14–15, 17, 19
  writing skill, 14–15, 17, 19
School reform, 33
Schools
  historical purposes, 267
  objectives not well realized, 268
  successful objectives, 267–268
Schools of choice, 192–196
School-site budgeting, 153
Schwartz, Henrietta, 201–202
Scientific competency, 33
Scientific method of education, 5,
    104
Scotland, parental rights of choice
    within public school system,
    75–76, 79
Secondary school design (1890's),
    29, 31
Sedlak, Michael, 183

Segregated Language Proficiency,
    251–252
Segregation, by use of schools of
    choice, 195–196
Seib, Gerald F., 255n
Selby, C., 288, 290
Senior Independent Project, 16, 21
Senior teachers, 231–232
Sense realism, 2–3
Serrano v. Priest, 117, 120, 121,
    142
Sexuality, role in human
    development, 7–8
Shanker, Albert, 46, 232
Shannon, Patrick, 86n
Shapiro, Svi, 83n
Shaw, George Bernard, 55, 56
Sheehan, D. S., 211, 222
Shelley, Percy Bysshe, 55
Shim, C. P., 209, 211, 222
Shockley, William, 263, 264n–265n
Shore, B., 290
Showers, B., 218, 221, 222
Shulman, L., 222
Sickler, J. L., 156, 159, 160, 161
Siegel, W. B., 211, 213, 222, 223
*The Significant Bilingual
    Instructional Features Study
    (SBIF),* 244
Silberman, Charles E., 18–19, 22,
    23, 28, 198
Simmons, Adele, 45
Single-track core curriculum, 46,
    47
Site-based management, 152, 162,
    294
  definition, 162–163
  general approach, 163
  guidelines, 165
  reasons for ineffectiveness and
    unfulfilled promises, 163–168
Sizer, Theodore R., 22, 23, 26–35,
    45–46, 92, 199
Skills curriculum, 58
Skinner, B. F., 2, 102, 295
Skutnabb-Kangas, T., 245,
    246–247, 249
Smith, Adam, 127
Smith, D. C., 214, 222
Smith, James, 58
Smith, Marshall S., 80n, 154, 159,
    161
Smith, N. L., 211, 220
Smith, Rogers, 77

Smitherman, Geneva, 263–264,
    265n
Soar, R. S., 209, 222
Social class, 55, 188, 190, 262
  intelligence related to, 263
Social education, 96
Social life, schools introducing and
    legitimating forms of, 87–88
Social occupations, 100
Socratic method of instruction, 42
Sokolowski, Carl J., 128n
Soledad, Arenas, 256n
Soriano, 256n
Sources for research papers,
    296–298
South Africa, education of the
    gifted, 289
Soviet Union, education of gifted
    students, 288–289
Sowell, Thomas, 256n
Space race, 10, 18
Special education group, 28
Special education students,
    education of, 271–277
Specialization, 40
  barbarism of, 44
Specialized job training, 42
Spencer, Herbert, 93
Spitler, H. D., 214, 221
Sprinthall, N. A., 215, 219n, 222
Sputnik, 10, 15, 18, 22
Staff teacher, 108
Stallings, J., 217, 223
Standardization, 177
Standardized achievement tests,
    211
Standard literate culture, 57
Standard literate language, 57
State transfers, 132
Statistical data as basis for judging
    schools, 29
Steiner, Rudolf, 101–102
Steinfels, Peter, 265n
Steinhilber, August W., 128n
Straub, W. F., 233
Structure of the disciplines
    approach, 105–106
Student behavior, docility in
    classroom, 28
Student-teacher ratio, 31
Student teaching, 217
Study of High Schools, 27
"Subjective warrant" of teaching,
    234, 236, 237, 238

Sublimination, 8
Sugarman, Stephen, 117
Sullivans, E. V., 286
Summerhill, 8, 10, 34, 113
Summers, A. A., 211, 212, 223
"Supplementary aids and services,"
 275
Supply of schools, 70, 75
Swanson, 213–214
Sweden, no programs for gifted
 students, 289
Sweitzer, G. L., 210, 223
Sykes, G., 222
Sylvester, Kathleen, 181, 192–196
Symposium on School Leadership
 (Sacramento), 201
Systemic reform, 2
System reformer, 10

Taba, H., 284, 286
Tabachnich, B., 215, 223
Taiwan, education of the gifted,
 289
Talented Youth Project (Teachers
 College), 280, 281
Tallyrand, 127
Tannenbaum, A. J., 280–282, 285,
 286
Taylor, C. W., 284, 286
Taylor, F. W., 233
Taylor, Gus, 46n
Taylor, S., 223
Taylor, T. W., 209, 217, 223
Teacher autonomy, 86
Teacher education, 27, 43, 84–85,
 198–219
 admissions standards, 202,
  207–208, 212
 apprenticeship (student
  teaching), 217
 cooperative learning strategies,
  215–216
 effectiveness of teachers,
  213–214, 217
 efficacy of programs, 200–201
 entry and exit examinations,
  202
 feedback efficacy, 216
 field experiences, 202
 funding needed, 204, 205
 "induction period" continuing
  support, 210, 217–218
 internships, 204
 liberal arts emphasis, 214

mathematics certified teachers,
 214
preparation program staying
 power, 210
proposals for curricula change,
 213, 215, 217
provisionally certified teacher
 performance, 209
purpose, 201
regularly certified teacher
 performance, 209
salaries related to teacher
 standards, 203
science education studies'
 conclusions, 213
screening for potential teaching
 effectiveness, 211–212
specific practices and habits of
 mind, 215
subject knowledge related to
 teacher effectiveness, 214
teacher college founded, 198
teacher evaluations, 209–210
teacher preparation overall
 effects, 209–210
verbal ability of teacher related
 to student verbal test scores,
 212
"Teacher-proof" curriculum
 packages, 86
Teacher-pupil planning, 5
Teacher salaries, 148
"Teachers as transformative
 intellectuals," 83–88
Teacher's authority, 2, 5
Teacher specialist, 108–109
Teachers' unions, 77
Teacher working conditions, 12
Teaching, quality of, 2, 43
Teaching machines, 114
Team leader, 109, 110
Team member, 110
Team teaching, 109–110
Technological literacy, 33
Television instruction, 105
Templin, T. J., 236, 239
Tennant, C. G., 285, 286
Tennessee
 career ladder program legislation
  enacted, 227
 funding for career ladder
  program, 228
 major drive for career ladders,
  232

Tenure laws, statewide, 69, 72
Terrassier, J., 289, 290–291
Tesconi, Charles A., Jr., 83n
Texas
 career ladder program legislation
  enacted, 227
 financial reform, 117–119,
  121–124
 Houston, magnet schools, 180
 Segregated Language Proficiency
  program in San Antonio, 251
Texas Education Agency, 122
Textbook selection, 122
Thacker, J. A., 211, 223
Theoretical problems of education,
 37
Theosophy, 101
Thies-Sprinthall, L., 215, 219n,
 222
Thinking skills, 30, 31
Thomas, M. Donald, 258, 266–269
Thomas, T., 287, 290
Thomson, Scott, 27
Thorndike, Edward Lee, 114
Tikunoff, W. J., 244, 246, 249
Tisher, R., 217, 223
Title VII Spanish/English bilingual
 education programs, 243
Tone of the high school, 30
Tonn, Martin, 272–273
Toukomas, P., 245, 246–247, 249
Tracking, 20, 31, 39–40, 114, 194
 beginning as early as fifth or
  sixth grade, 275
 control problems, 184
 lack of, 46
 Segregated Language Proficiency
  program, 252
Traditional schools, 3
Transition school, 20
Travers, R. M. W., 222
Trend, J. B., 256n
Troike, R. C., 243, 245, 249
Trombley, William, 256n
Tucker, G. R., 246, 248
Tucker, J. A., 217, 222
Tuition fees, 71, 133–134, 144, 148
Tuition remission grants, 134
Tuition tax-credit legislation, 138
Tuition tax credits, 193; *see also*
 Voucher plans
Turner, R., 219n, 223
Tweedie, Jack, 69, 73–79, 80n
Tyack, David, 48

Tyler, Gus, 46

Uchitelle, Susan, 79, 80n
Understanding of ideas and values,
    40, 41
Unions, teachers, 72
U.S. Bureau of the Census, 80n
U.S. Department of Commerce,
    255n
U.S. Department of Labor, 256n
United States Office of Education's
    (USOE's) Office of Gifted and
    Talented, 279
Universal program of study, 30
Universal secondary education, 28
University of Glasgow Department
    of Education, 79n, 80n
Utah, site-based management, 162

Values education, 7
Van Doren, Charles, 45
Van Doren, Geraldine, 45
Van Doren, John, 45
Vazquez, J. A., 243, 249
Vazquez-Faría, J. A., 244, 246, 249
Vertical equity, 287
Vietnam War, 18
Vineyard, E. E., 209, 211, 212,
    213, 222
Virginia
    English Immersion/ESL program
        in Fairfax County, 251

school-based management, 152
Vocational education, 18, 20, 34,
    40, 277
Voucher plans, 79n, 95, 111–112,
    116, 193

Wald, R., 216, 221
Waldorf education, 101–102
Waldrop, 210
Walker, L. J., 161
Ward, James Gordon, 120, 125n
Ward, V. S., 284, 286
Warranted assertibility, 5
Washburne, Carleton, 96, 97
Washington (state)
    financial reform, 117
    schools of choice plan
        specifically for dropouts, 193
Watson, John B., 113
Watts, Gary, 232
Weeks, K., 229
Weil, M., 174, 210, 216, 221
Weinfeld, F. D., 220
Weingartner, Charles, 6
Weiss, P., 287, 290
Welch, Finis, 58
West Virginia, financial reform,
    117
White, J. L., 161
White, P. A., 154, 155, 156, 158,
    160
Whitehead, 26

Whitmore, J., 288, 291
Whole child education, 7
Williams, F. E., 284, 286
Williams, Frederick, 265n
Willms, J. Doug, 76, 80n
Wilson, William J., 264n
Winkler, D., 212, 223
Winne, P. H., 216, 220
Winnetka Plan, 96–97
Wirt, William, 98–99
Wise, Arthur E., 117–125, 156,
    161
Wissler, D. F., 153, 156, 159, 160,
    161
Wittrock, M., 220, 221
Wolfe, B. L., 211, 212, 223
Woodford, R., 236, 239
World Council for Gifted and
    Talented Children, Inc., 281
Written word, reliance on, 2
Wu, W. T., 289, 291

Yaffe, Elaine, 255n
Yale Psycho-Educational Clinic,
    276
York, R. L., 220
Young, 211

Zeichner, Kenneth M., 85, 223
Zellman, G., 219
Zlotnik, Marilyn, 207–219
Zohn, Barbara, 194–195, 196